HISTORY OF INDIA

FROM THE EARLIEST TIMES TO THE PRESENT DAY FOR THE USE OF STUDENTS AND COLLEGES

HISTORY OF INDIA

FROM THE EARLIEST TIMES TO THE PRESENT DAY FOR THE USE OF STUDENTS AND COLLEGES

BY

H. G. KEENE, CIE

HON MA OXON

Author of "The Fall of the Mughal Empire" "The Turks in India" &c

Vol. II

GYAN

Published by

GYAN

Gyan Publishing House
5, Ansari Road
Daryaganj, New Delhi-110002
Phone: 011-47034999, 9811692060
E-mail: books@gyanbooks.com

Distribution Network
gyanbooks.com
India, USA, Canada, UK, Australia, France

ISBN : 978-81-212-2178-8 (Set)
ISBN : 978-81-212-2180-1 (HB)
First Published, 1893

2nd Impression 2021

Printed at: Gyan Press, Delhi.

History of India Vol. II
Author: H. G. Keene

HISTORY OF INDIA

FROM THE EARLIEST TIMES TO THE PRESENT DAY

FOR THE USE OF STUDENTS AND COLLEGES

BY

H G KEENE CIE

HON MA OXON

Author of "The Fall of the Mughal Empire" "The Turks in India" &c

VOL II

LONDON

W H ALLEN & CO LIMITED

Publishers to the India Office

13 WATERLOO PLACE SW

1893

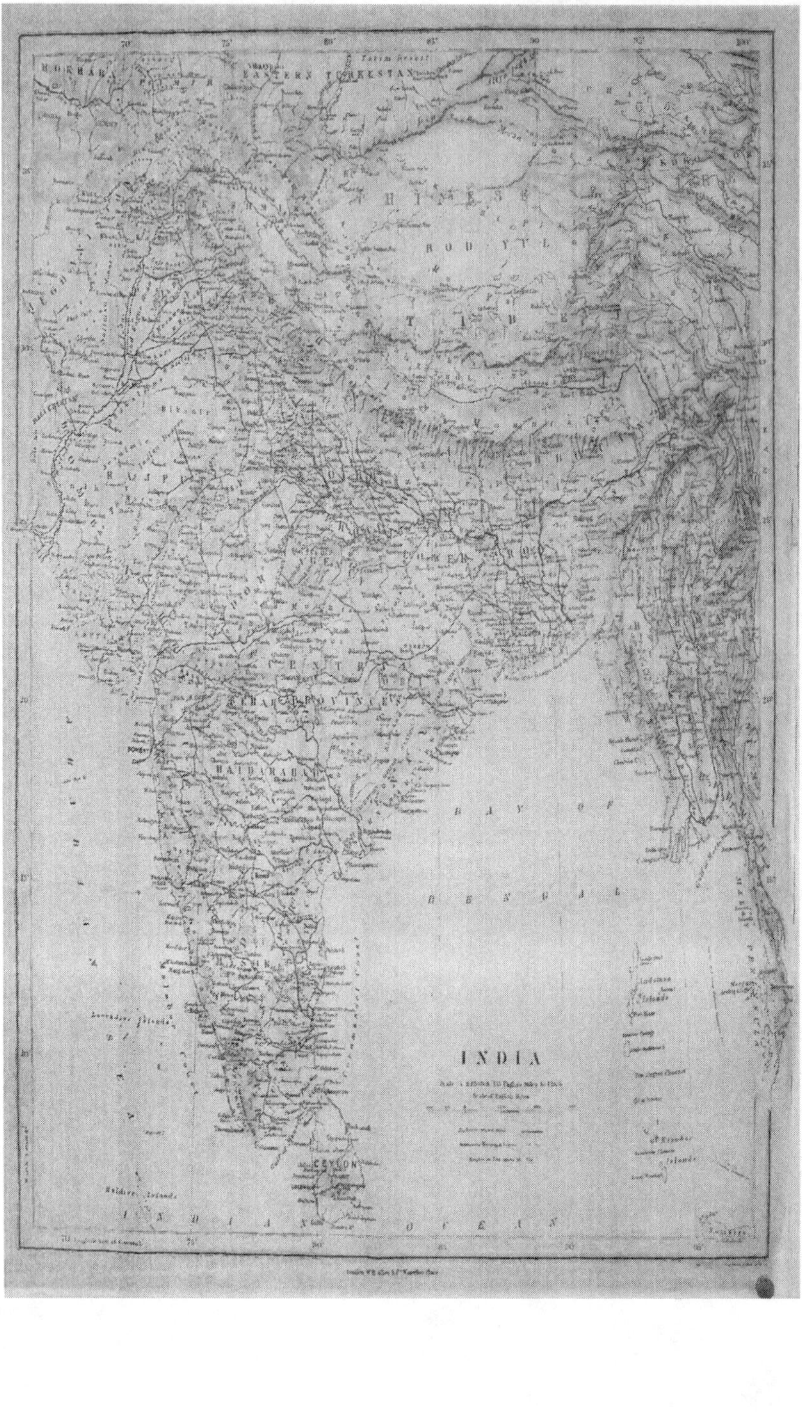

EASTERN TURKESTAN
TIBET
CENTRAL PROVINCES
HAIDARABAD
BAY OF
BENGAL
INDIA
CEYLON
Laccadive Islands
Maldive Islands
Andaman Islands
Nicobar Islands
INDIAN
OCEAN

CONTENTS OF VOL. II.

LIST OF MAPS—VOL. II.

HISTORY OF INDIA

CHAPTER XIII.

THE DAWN OF EMPIRE.

Section 1: Change in the Company's position—Section 2: The Nepalese war and minor disturbances—Section 3: The Pindari war.

SECTION 1.—The new Governor-General, Lord Moira, was of that excellent Anglo-Irish stock, which, from the days of Sir Eyre Coote to those of Lord Roberts, has supplied British India with so many fine officers.* As Colonel Rawdon, he had been distinguished—so far as distinction was to be had there—in the American war, where he attained the post of Adjutant-General, and learned the art of strategy. After his return to Europe he was created Baron Rawdon; and about 1793 succeeded his father who had been raised to the peerage as Earl of Moira. Two years later he took part in the attack of the French royalists on Quiberon, which was so signally defeated by Hoche. A favourite of the Prince of Wales, he followed the Whigs, and in 1806 obtained the post of Master-general of the Ordnance. After a few years of London life, and the political activity of which we have already had a glimpse, he was imposed on India by the will of his master—now become Regent. Moira had by this time attained his 59th year, an age at which modern Indian

* Such were also the Wellesleys, Gillespie, C. Napier, Gough, the Lawrences, and Mayo.

officials are usually superannuated : he had no better record but that of a fair soldier and a zealous courtier; and he was undertaking the Herculean task of governing an unknown country with the additional duties of Commander-in-Chief, and under entirely new conditions.

Before relating the events of the epoch so singularly opened, it will be well to give some conception of these changes, and of the causes by which they were produced. The authority of the Company, which had chafed Wellesley and shackled Barlow and Minto, was no longer to impede the spread of the Empire; and the manner of this emancipation must now be briefly reviewed.

The Company had obtained a renewal of the Charter in 1793, as we have already noticed; on which occasion attempts were unsuccessfully made by Glasgow, Liverpool, and Bristol, to secure a share in the Eastern trade.* But, indeed, the existing state of things was not without its recommendations, and the acts of so remote a period ought not to be altogether judged from the point of view that offers itself a hundred years later. In 1793 a great deal remained to be done before the public mind became convinced that the Eastern trade could be safely thrown open. In China there was but one port, Canton; but it was watched and regulated by a strong and jealous Government. In India difficulties of the opposite nature existed. There could not well be treaty-ports, for want of a valid native government, with which to make treaties. There were strong reasons why the King of Great Britain should not conquer the various States of India by means of his own armies, or rule them through his own administrators. So a compromise was adopted, for which the Declaratory Act of 1788 had, in some degree, prepared the way; provision being made for a small allotment of tonnage to private trade, the monopoly of the Company had been in general renewed for another twenty

* v. Vol. I p. 290.

years; the presence of Europeans not connected with the Company continued to be forbidden; and the interdict was made expressly to include persons undertaking to go to India as missionaries or instructors of the people. Whether consciously or not, the men of those days were avoiding the errors of the Portuguese, who had lost the trade that they had tried to carry on with no chartered company and no territorial empire, but with ardent efforts for religious proselytism.

But in 1813 times were a good deal changed; and such rules might well be considered open to discussion, even among those who might have thought the matter plain twenty years earlier. Questions of deep import had arisen; as for instance in the Persian business when the Governor-General (Lord Minto), had claimed a right to send an ambassador to Teheran on the express ground that the Company's Government was vested with sovereign power within its own borders; and in that character had, as he said, been acknowledged by the Sháh. "This acknowledged character," Minto added, "as it constituted the basis so it must form the cement of our external relations." This was plain speaking, and conveyed a challenge almost bound to be taken up by Parliament and the King's Cabinet. The matter of Sovereignty was seen to involve two questions; If the Company was a Sovereign ought Sovereigns to trade? If it were engaged in trade ought it to be a Sovereign? These questions soon began to engage the attention of politicians when once they had been perceived; but there still remained minor points hardly less interesting to Parliament and the public at large. One was the point of patronage: if the Company were abolished would not the nomination to Indian administrative posts and military commissions, falling into the hands of Ministers, add a mass of influence which would enable the party in power to corrupt the Commons and the constituencies, so that it might become immovable and autocratic? That was one important point: another being as to missions and missionaries. If the Company were to be maintained what precautions would have to be taken against the dangers indicated by the mutiny at Vellore, on one hand, and by Minto's recent action, on the other?

The subject of the widest national interest was, and perhaps is still, the Eastern trade. In those days, certainly, when the British Isles still grew their own food, it was natural that an ideal should exist that the best relations between India and England was this: that the former should take the manufactures of the latter, paying for them in raw material, at the lowest possible rates. In early days it had not been so; if, indeed, any ideal had at all been formed; but it may rather be said that the existence of the East India Company had been required and maintained by the impossibility of obtaining an adequate supply of nutmegs and tea, pepper and piece-goods through any instrumentality equally convenient and trusty. An important modification, however, occurred about the beginning of the 19th century. The Company's agency might still be useful in regard to tea, but spices were easier to come by, now; while, as to piece-goods, the enormous improvements in machinery for twisting and spinning, and the introduction of steam-power, had made it possible to produce fabrics, at home, whose cheapness almost forbade importation. In 1808 the value of imported Indian textiles had fallen from three millions sterling to little over four hundred thousand pounds: and the trade of the Company was so disorganised that the Court of Directors had to call home their cash-balances. In September of that year Mr. Dundas, the President of the Board of Control, sent a letter to the "Chairs," in which he informed them that the propriety of renewing the Charter was about to be considered by the Government, and invited them to submit to the early decision of Parliament any arguments that they might desire to urge against the abolition of the Company. To this the Chairs made answer that they could and would presently show that the maintenance of their commercial monopoly and of their political power was alike desirable in the interests of both themselves and the public, i.e., of "England and India alike," as we should now phrase it.

A Select Committee of the Commons was appointed, which during the next four years examined many witnesses of conspicuous knowledge and importance; all the arguments for and against the commercial and political claims of the Company, were discussed in the press and debated in both chambers of the legislature; in November, 1811, a statutory notice was sent to the Court of Directors by the Speaker, signifying that the Company's commercial privileges would cease on the 10th April, 1814. That notice, indeed, was only formal, and did not, by itself, preclude the possibility of renewal; nevertheless, the tenor of all that Mr. Dundas wrote was decidedly in the direction of non-renewal. He even intimated a design of amalgamating the Company's troops with the Royal Army. Early in 1812, the President, who, on the death of his father, had become Lord Melville, explicitly apprised the Directors that he remained entirely unconvinced by any of the arguments urged in favour of their commercial monopoly, excepting so far as the Canton trade was concerned. On this the Directors took earnest action; and, after duly consulting their constituents, the "proprietors" (as the shareholders of the Company were called), preferred their petition for renewal on 7th April, 1812. The attention of the mercantile community was now fully aroused; and petitions on the other side poured into the Lower House, alike from London, which desired to inherit the Company's monopoly, and from the merchants of the "outports" of Liverpool, etc., who wished that all monopoly should be swept away.

In May the Prime Minister was assasinated, and the unsuccessful attempt at Cabinet-making by Lord Moira took place which has been already mentioned as the cause of that nobleman's appointment to India. Two politicians acquainted with the affairs of that country were appealed to, the Marquis of Wellesley and Mr. Canning; but they both declined to take office, as also did the Whig peers, Lords Grey and Grenville; nevertheless the views of these four statesmen did not allow of their joining in a complete or formal Opposition. The Earl of Buckinghamshire, who had governed Madras for four years towards the end of the last century, succeeded Melville at the Board of Control. His views, as Indian Minister, were even more opposed to the claims of the Company than had been those of his predecessor. He was in favour of a drastic treatment; and at first proposed that if the Company should be permitted to preserve commercial privileges, it should be on condition of a total abandonment of all political power. He considered that the separation of these two functions was absolutely essential to the future of India, where the administration had been often crippled by the diversion to commercial exigencies of funds required for purposes of State. The Company, on learning this, presented a fresh petition to either House of Parliament, repeating former arguments, insisting that the one function was necessary to the efficiency of the other, and both to the welfare of India and Great Britain.

And now opened the final struggle. On the 22 March, 1813 Lord Castlereagh, who, though nominally only Foreign Secretary, was Leader in the Commons, submitted a series of resolutions to a Committee of the whole House; the general purport being the maintenance of the Company as a political power, with the complete opening of all the Eastern trade excepting that to Canton. A similar measure was introduced by Buckinghamshire in the Lords.

In the debates that followed much ability was shown on both sides. As to the political question, indeed, no general difference of opinion appeared. There was a strong feeling that the distribution of appointments, the "patronage" as it was called, was safer in the hands of the Directors than elsewhere; while most public men, whether in office or only in expectation, were alike satisfied with a system which gave Ministers practical power, yet left most of the responsibility on other shoulders. The struggle, therefore, was really over the Indian trade. On that subject some of the most eminent officials (retired, or at home on furlough), were examined as witnesses, and deposed in favour of the Company. Munro in particular spoke strongly and shrewdly; making much, as did also his old friend Malcolm, of the dangers that might follow on the unrestricted admission of irresponsible Europeans into the country. He pointed out the friction and disputes between these men and the natives that must from time to time arise; and showed that for such friction no real legal remedies were provided by Indian institutions. In these opinions he was supported by the two most distinguished Anglo-Indian civil officers then living, Lord Teignmouth and the venerable Warren Hastings. That they were not altogether wrong is proved by the subsequent indigo difficulties of Bengal, and by the continual troubles and tinkerings in judicial procedure that have since disquieted the country, from the days of Lord W. Bentinck to those of the Marquess of Ripon. But, when these witnesses went on to state that the trade with India was unlikely to increase, they were not only on less firm ground, but the expectation, had it been better based, ought to have afforded a neutralisation of their other objection. Munro alone showed grounds for his views, which were, moreover, much more moderate and reasonable than those of other witnesses on the same side. In stating actual ascertained facts concerning the very small average expenditure of the natives on secondary wants,* he showed reason for anticipating no great immediate expansion of commerce between the two countries. He did

* According to the examination of a large population, Munro estimated this at no more than 25s. yearly per individual, taking an average of rich and poor.

more, indeed; for he went far to account for the fact that the commerce so warmly contended for, was not a source of profit, except in the one article of tea, which it was not intended should be touched.

On the subject of missions for the propagation of the British religious creeds, again, the experts were mostly hostile to change. They concurred in thinking that any interference by the Government in this direction would not only be fraught with grave political dangers, but would be a detriment to the cause of Christianity. Even Lord Teignmouth, himself a leader of the Evangelicals and chairman of the Bible Society, was constrained to join, generally, in this opinion: he would open a door to missionary enterprise, but abstain from all approach to State aid; and he added that it would be advisable to leave the local Government free to determine the amount of control to be exercised over persons so engaged.

The House proceeded to take the evidence into consideration in its bearing on Castlereagh's Resolutions; and a brisk debate occurred in Committee on the 31st May. The members connected with the Company brought up the usual arguments, alleging once more that the territories acquired by the Company belonged to the Company by right of conquest, and claiming to have proved that a mercantile monopoly was essential to the maintenance of sovereignty. The new scheme, by striking at the Company's commercial privileges, would lead to its political decay, and so deprive the British Islands of advantages "much too valuable to be sacrificed for a trifling reduction in the freight of Indian goods." They once more brought up the danger of European immigration, and the somewhat incompatible estimate that no increase was likely to take place in the trade.

These arguments were disposed of by Canning; who, though hostile to Castlereagh personally, and not very friendly to the collective Cabinet, made a wise and moderate speech in support of the Resolutions. In this he showed the foresight—with some of the flippancy—of a great mind dealing with inferiors: pointing out the exaggerated assumptions that had been made, both as to the habits of the natives and the character of European commercial agents. He did not believe in the immutability of Asiatic manners, or anticipate rebellion from immigrants whom he regarded as something of the nature of needy knife-grinders. He could not admit the Company's claims of absolute sovereignty, but was not unwilling that the servants of the Company should retain the control of India as a temporary concession from Parliament. No other speech in the Commons was quite up to Canning's intellectual level; yet, as soon as the missionary question was approached, the earnestness of Mr. Wilberforce gave to the expression of his arguments in favour of the thirteenth Resolution a weight and dignity wholly wanting on the other side. The policy of that Resolution was—after all—not of a very wide or alarming character: all that was contemplated being that the Government should not be debarred, by Statute, from licensing a certain number of Christian teachers to set sail for, and dwell in the territories subject to the East India Company. Wilberforce made two fine speeches in support of this resolution; exaggerating—as was perhaps almost inevitable—the moral defects and evil results of the Hindu and Muhamadan religions; and so affording an opening to the opponents of the plan; but giving interesting instances of cruel practices arising out of Hinduism, and of the ease with which some of them had been put down by European officials. This, at least, was a solid basis of argument and one that has even now been only partially explored. There are two kinds of practice, alike abhorrent to modern civilisation, yet by no means equal in their capacity of reform. Practices that are of little moral bearing, and merely affairs of taste and traditional custom, are hardly to be changed by a foreign ruler: hence such difficulties as imposing a new style of head-dress on the sepoys, or making high-caste boys sit on the same school-bench as low-caste boys. But, as soon as the reformer touches on morals, it is commonly seen that the human heart is alike in all parts of the world, and in almost every stage of civilisation. When Albuquerque prohibited widow-burning in Portuguese India, when Wellesley forbade the exposure of infants on Saugor island, they proposed changes which at once recommended themselves to the public conscience, and they were acclaimed as public benefactors.

The upshot was that a large majority of the Commons accepted the principle that the same fair field should be left to the faith of the ruling nation as was open to the creeds of the Muslims, Hindus, and other followers of other faiths. So far, at least, there was nothing in the project that could offend the most scientific ideas of the State's duties. The rest was perhaps more questionable; only ten thousand pounds a year was set aside for the education of the people from whose humble contributions the Government was already deriving an annual revenue of seventeen millions. At the same time provision was made for the establishment of dignitaries of the Anglican denomination. On the Resolutions a bill was framed which passed the Commons and went to the hereditary Chamber on 17th June. In the meanwhile their lordships had held an interesting debate of their own in the course of which several unexpected things took place. Lord Wellesley, who had formerly incurred the displeasure of the Directors for the encouragement which, as Governor-General, he had given to unlicensed trade (and who had even laid down in a despatch the principle that such ought to be the established practice), this same Wellesley now appeared as the champion of privilege and the apologist of monopoly. Nor was this the only surprise which the debate (9th April, 1813) produced in the Lords. The plans of the Government, were to a certain extent, espoused by Lord Grenville whom we lately saw rejecting the combination proposed by Lord Moira after the death of Mr. Perceval.

Although ostensibly in opposition Grenville on the whole spoke for the Government: nay, more, he supported the measure with foresight and eloquence, not exceeded by Canning, and without that element of somewhat acrid pleasantry seldom absent from the speeches of the brilliant commoner. Remembering that he had been a kinsman and colleague of Pitt, in Pitt's best days, he put the case upon a higher plane than that of party, uttering truths never recognised before, which have since been approved by the experience of succeeding generations. Going far beyond the plans of Government he thought that any renewal at all ought to be made subject to occasional revision; twenty years being a period far too long for farming out the sovereignty of sixty millions of souls, especially at that moment when twenty months might determine the fate of the whole British empire. If indeed British India were declared to be a portion of that Empire it might share its fortunes: but what respect could they expect foreign powers to show to a commercial association professing to exercise authority delegated by the extinct dominion of the "Great Mogul?"*

Passing on to the mercantile aspect, Grenville crushed the arguments of the Company's champions by a clear exposition of economic principles. The attempt to bolster-up trade with India by the exercise of dominion had been an economic failure. The Company had lost money by their trade with India in proportion to the growth of their political sway; the only part of their trade that was now profitable was China, where they had never had any power, and where intercourse was

* This point was settled by Moira in the following year when he passed by Delhi without paying a visit to Akbar Sháh, whom he refused to recognise as—even nominally—Emperor of Hindustan, which had been done by some of his predecessors.

restricted to one port. Free the Indian trade, and the self-interest of buyers and sellers would soon surmount all existing obstacles; commerce must always increase by commerce, and industry by industry: that was a universal law enforced by the necessity of things and proved by all experience. It was impossible that India could escape its action: the extension of trade must promote industry and excite secondary wants.

As for the patronage difficulty, Grenville acknowledged its existence, but could not admit that the retention of Indian patronage by the Directors was the only alternative to its being made an engine of political corruption. It seemed to him that civil appointments might well be given to candidates chosen by competition; he would not send them to a special college, but would give them an education at the Universities in common with the youths of their time and position.*

Such were some of the leading ideas of this address, alike memorable for its originality and for the hold which its principles have taken on all subsequent arrangements. Grenville here resembles Warren Hastings; though in a minority of one, each laid down rules, or established principles, which have been found of durable application by succeeding statesmen. And, indeed,—even at the time—one can readily believe that some of Grenville's words fell like a presage upon the more intelligent members of the Company; for they speedily accepted the compromise offered by Ministers as better than total annihilation. The history of the next twenty years shows that the arrangement finally arrived at in 1813 was not without elements of working utility. Undeniable as was the abstract truth of the views expressed by Buckinghamshire and Gren-

* The East Indian College had been opened in Hertford Castle after the partial abrogation of Wellesley's College of Fort William. It was removed to the still more isolated situation of Haileybury about 1809. This was much questioned at the time; and Grenville's plan is essentially that which has since taken its place.

ville, it must be admitted that the conditions then existing in India were unfavourable for the immediate introduction of drastic political change. The Southern Peninsula, indeed, was fairly quiet; in the Telugu and Támil countries the patient labour of Munro and his colleagues was extending the arts of peace and calming the minds of men. But in Central India the Pindari desolation was extending; Rajputana, wasting away under the oppressions of Sindia and the depredations of Amir Khán, was piteously invoking British protection; while Hindustan was in the state of France after the hundred years' war. Audh was a scene of misgovernment and insecurity; Rohilkhand and the Duáb were full of turbulent barons, each with his castle garrisoned by disbanded soldiers—the dregs of the late wars—often unable to draw their pay, and dependent for subsistence on the plunder of the adjacent villages.*

Such, then, was the state of affairs when Moira relieved Minto in October 1813; becoming the first Governor-General under the new system. From his private journals we obtain a clear view of the principles on which he proposed to exercise his office. Without ever expressing the contempt of the Directors openly professed by his predecessor Lord Wellesley, he considered that India was, ultimately, under the Government of the Crown and Parliament of Great Britain; and he conceived that "our object ought to be to render the British Government paramount, in effect, if not declaredly" (February 6th, 1814). The difficulties in the way he did not ignore. In spite of Minto's able financial policy, the surplus had disappeared under the drain caused by the orders of the Court of Directors. Hostile clouds were gathering, from the Himalaya to the Vindya mountains; and he recorded at the time that he saw

* A respectable agriculturist in Audh asked a British officer, in 1814, the same question that Elphinstone had been asked by the hermit, in 1802, as he marched through Cuttack—"When are you going to take this wretched country?" ("Hastings's Journals," Vol. I., p. 236.)

around him "the elements of a war more general than any that we have hitherto encountered" (Journal I., 47). But he seems to have contemplated the situation with the "cheery stoicism" so common among British chiefs of that day; he prepared boldly to make the best use of his imperfect resources; and in the beginning of the hot season—when modern viceroys are comfortably installed in an Alpine châlet—he set out for a journey by boat to the Upper Provinces. For the next two years, the dauntless veteran remained for the most part under canvas, defying heat and pestilence at an age when most men crave repose; and carrying a vigilant eye and cheerful courage to every quarter in which his presence seemed most required, from the banks of the Tapti to the foot of the Himalaya range.

[The debates are well summarised in Marshman's second volume; and, still more fully, in Wilson, Vol. VII. Lord Grenville's speech—revised by himself—was published as a pamphlet in the same year.]

SECTION 2.—In the note recorded by Moira, for his own use, on the 1st February, 1814, there is a sketch of the tasks to which he had to address himself on assuming the reins of power. We shall refer to this interesting paper again; for the present it is only interesting as showing that he did not include in the list any dispute with the State of Nepal. "The differences," so he writes, "with the Nepaulese Government have been amicably settled." Moira's high and humane temper made him a lover of peace; and here, as in other cases, he hoped that the dispute had arisen out of a misunderstanding which candid negotiation had removed. In so judging, however, he had not allowed for the character of the people with whom he had to deal; or with the spirit in which they regarded their situation. The proper territories of Nepal may be taken to be very much what they are now, occupying nearly 500 miles of the sub-Himalaya; bounded on the north by the valley of the Sanpu, on the east by the small chiefdom of Sikhim, on the

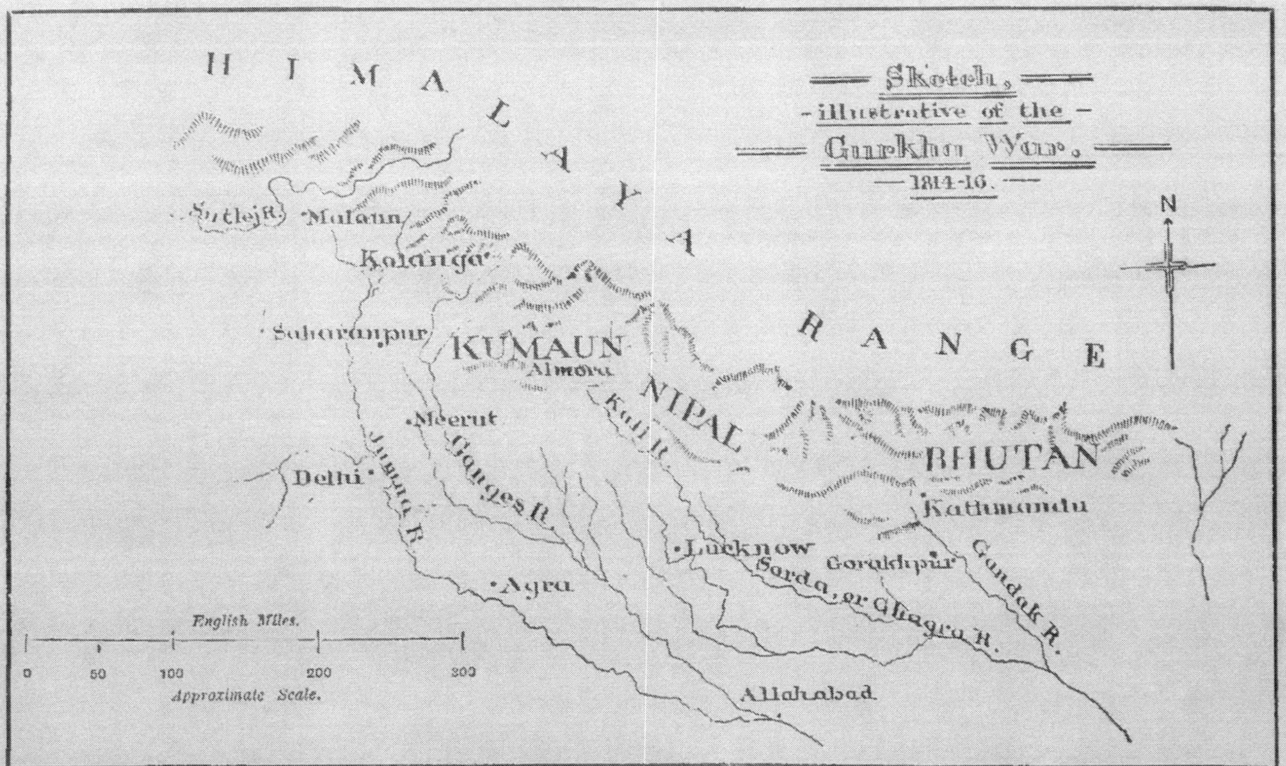
Sketch,
illustrative of the
Gurkha War.
1814-16.
N
HIMALAYA RANGE
Sutlej R.
Malaun
Kalanga
Saharanpur
KUMAUN
Almora
NIPAL
Kali R.
BHUTAN
Kathmandu
Meerut
Delhi
Jumna R.
Ganges R.
Lucknow
Gorakhpur
Gandak R.
Sarda, or Ghagra R.
Agra
Allahabad
English Miles.
0 50 100 200 300
Approximate Scale.

west by the river Sarda—called "Káli" on its upper course—and looking south upon the plains of Gorakhpore and Audh. Originally occupied by Mongolian tribes, who adopted the creed of Sakyá Muni (Buddhism), it was entered, probably from the Gangetic valley, by a set of Hindu immigrants—claiming to be Brahmans and Rajputs—in the 12th century A.D. It has been sometimes thought that the invaders came from the west, through the Kamaun hills; but the better opinion seems that which traces them to Gorakhpore, and thus accounts for the eye of desire which they continued to cast in that direction. The name, in both cases, is connected with Gorakh-Nath (the "Lord of Cowherds") a title of the God Shiva. These people intermarried with the Mongolian women; and as they made their first capital at a place called Gurkha—on the western side of the country—they got to be known as *Gurkháli*, or Gurkha, by which name they are still called. A mixed race, they exhibit some of the Tartar characteristics grafted on an Aryan base. Good-humoured and easily amused, they are of great pugnacity, with a love of punctilio not found incompatible with reckless falsehood. They usually obey the commands of their rulers; but instances have occurred where a Nepalese ministerial crisis has been solved by such crude expedients as pitching the members of the Cabinet out of the Palace windows. To understand such a national character one has to invest statesmen and warriors with some of the attributes of ill-brought-up boys; and for this, neither Moira nor his Council were at first prepared. The Gurkhas had expanded east and west; they had conquered Kamaun, overrun the Doons of Dehra and Sirmur, and even built forts on the Upper Sutlej. Unable to spread farther westward, owing to the strong opposition of Ranjit, the Rája of Lahore, and repressed on the northward by the Chinese, to whose empire they were feudatory, they resolved to claim the Ganges as their southern boundary. They commenced proceedings by laying claim to two small districts beyond the forests at the foot of their hills above Gorakhpore. The British—who had obtained these tracts as grants from the Nawáb of Audh—opposed this, and an enquiry was agreed to before a mixed commission. The enquiry resulted in the claims of the Gurkhas being found baseless; and it was to this result that the anxious Governor-General—his wish being father to his thought—gave the above-noted welcome. But the Gurkhas had no intention of abiding by the award; and, in the course of the summer of 1814, their troops came down into British territory and massacred the parties of police put to watch the frontier.

Hastily calling upon the Nepalese Government for an apology—which was no less promptly refused—Moira prepared for a strong punitive advance as soon as the periodical rains should cease. Small as was the power of the enemy, ruling a mixed population of not much more than two millions, the extent of the frontier was considerable. From Káthmándu to Malaun is rather over than under seven hundred miles; and on that whole line the Governor—who was also Commander-in-Chief—resolved to operate. Four divisions of the army, supplied with guns, mortars, and all the resources of European military science, were sent against this petty Hill-State; it being Moira's abiding principle to apply the whole of his strength at once to any given point and compensate for initial outlay by making war as short as possible. The largest division—comprising the 24th Foot, six battalions of Native Infantry, and a proportion of gunners and pioneers, making altogether a force of 8,000 strong—was to march on Káthmándu, the Gurkha capital, under Major-General Marley; but three other divisions, under Generals Wood, Gillespie, and Ochterlony were to move up along the frontier in the order here mentioned—Ochterlony being on the extreme left, or western extremity. To confront this attack, the audacious Gurkhas were only able to oppose a force of 12,000 regular troops; but they were men seasoned in conquest, of hardy and active habits, and commanded by an able and prudent general, Amar Sinh, of the Thapa, or agricultural, order, to which most of the military leaders belonged. Officers and men were inspired by the patriotism of mountaineers, and thoroughly at home in their wild and difficult country.

The British advance was commenced by Ochterlony and Gillespie, officers who had little in common but a consummate valour. The former was a wise and cautious Scot, distinguished by his heroic defence of Delhi against Jaswant Ráo Holkar, in 1804: the latter a typical Irish light horseman, who had fought for his King and country in various regions, from S. Domingo to Java, everywhere evincing the most ardent and dashing chivalry. The plan of their part of the campaign was that Ochterlony should proceed against the right of the Gurkha defence, where Amar Sinh commanded in person, having his headquarters at Malaun; while Gillespie should occupy the Dehra Doon, and then sweep to the westward and support his colleague. The Doon was only held by a force of Gurkhas, tantamount to a weak battalion, under Colonel Balbhadar Sinh. This officer had taken post in a small fort on a hill above the village of Kalinga—not much less than 1000 feet above the surrounding land—about four miles north-east of the town of Dehra. Gillespie thought that the reduction of this fort was requisite before he could proceed to support Ochterlony; and he estimated that it might be reduced by the same sort of rush by which he had succeeded so brilliantly in Java and elsewhere. Had all his men been actuated by the fire that burned in their Commander, and had all his officers accurately carried out his combinations, his plans might have prospered, and the war have been concluded in a few weeks. As it was, a grave disaster—amounting to disgrace—befel the British arms; many valuable lives were lost, including Gillespie's own; and the war went on for a year and a half. Balbhadar Sinh defended Kalinga against three attacks, during which his men killed the General, and a number of British officers and men far exceeding their own. When at last a complete battering-train was brought up against them and their water-supply was cut off, the gallant mountaineers—as many as survived, about seventy in number—evacuated the no longer tenable position, in November, and effected their escape into the hills of Garhwál.*

This misfortune not only delayed the operations of the western column, it also demoralised the officers and men of the divisions to the eastward. The army under Marley, which was to have marched on the Gurkha capital—a distance of only a hundred miles—was handled with the utmost imbecility. Instead of advancing as he was ordered, Marley hung back, waiting—as he declared—for more artillery. He left his outposts unsupported, so that several of them were cut off with the loss of many men and British officers, in January, 1815. The reinforcements which Marley now received raised his army to 13,000; but with odds of nearly ten to one in his favour he still held back; and at last he was so completely prostrated that, on the 10th February, he mounted his horse by night and fled, alone, to Dánapore, his headquarters. Colonel Dick, who succeeded for the time, by virtue of seniority, gained a momentary success, and opened the road to Káthmándu; but General G. Wood, who eventually arrived, proved little more energetic than Marley; and this division went into summer quarters without having produced any effect upon the war. The other eastern division, under General J.

* It is impossible to describe this place: the description given by Prinsep does not tally with the plan in Gillespie's "Memoirs," or with the account given to the present writer by the late General Hoggan—who was present. The writer himself has examined the spot, but no vestiges of the fort are left—*etiam periere ruinæ*. Two obelisks in a neighbouring field mark the burial-place of the dead. Gillespie was interred at Meerut, where his command was

S. Wood, after sustaining some reverses, similarly retired upon Gorakhpore.

These unfortunate repetitions of bad generalship shook the British prestige throughout most parts of India, exciting equally the courage of pure patriots who resented foreign conquest, and of marauders who deprecated the establishment of peace and order. The crooked-minded Peshwa—Báji Ráo—took heart, and began a scheme of hostility based upon his claim to be President of the old Mahratta Confederacy. Sindia collected his men for a forward movement; and Amir Khán—who, in addition to the resources of his own estates, virtually commanded those of Tulsi Bai, the Lady-Regent of Holkar's dominions—massed an imposing force within a hundred miles of the western frontier. But Moira calmly pursued his projects, calling up the Madras army, and placing a contingent from Bombay on the borders of Holkar. He at the same time augmented the Bengal army, and manfully awaited the fortune that attends the strong of heart and arm.

In truth, the enemy's line of defence was too long for its already diminishing forces; and that line was now to be cut in two by a stroke little contemplated at the beginning of the war. The skill and tenacity of Ochterlony, to whose exploits we shall presently come, were, no doubt, the cause of the defeat of Amar Sinh: but it was a private individual who conceived—and helped to execute—the comparatively bloodless operations which, atoning for the incompetence of the professional leaders, and isolating Amar Sinh from his communications and his sources of supply, contributed, in no small degree, to Ochterlony's success, The man who did this was a retired Mahratta officer—William Linnæus Gardner, who had been living, for the last ten years, at Eta, North-Western Provinces, with a small force of irregular cavalry which he had raised for Lord Lake, and had received an assignment of land for their maintenance at the termination of the war. The nephew of a British peer, he had a cousin under Metcalfe at the Delhi Residency; and, on hearing of the Kalinga disaster, he wrote to this kinsman—the Hon. E. Gardner—in November, 1814, to suggest an attack on Almora. If the Gurkhas, defeated on the western points, should fall back upon Kamaun—of which Almora was the fortified capital—the want of generalship in the eastward might lead to grave misfortunes; and it was accordingly suggested by Gardner that the passes beyond the Ganges ought to be closed. "Your army," he wrote, "when you get it, will score as a false attack if we are otherwise successful . . it will help to divide their force and distract them." The argument prevailed, and on the 8th December Gardner accompanied his cousin into Kamaun; a column under a brave, but imprudent officer, named Hearsey, supporting the advance on a parallel line. A month later a second small column followed under Colonel Nicholls, with some field-pieces.

It was high time that something was done. The past successes of the Gurkhas, though chiefly due to the incompetence and timidity of most of the British generals, had given rise in many minds to an exaggerated estimate of the difficulties of the task undertaken by the British Government. At the end of 1814, Metcalfe, who had come over from Delhi to Moradabad on a visit to the camp of the Governor-General, had recorded a despondent minute. In a further paper written a few days later, he pointed out that Ranjit was beginning to look on with unfriendly anxiety from the Punjab; while the Mahratta chiefs of Gwalior and Nágpore were "menacing our frontier from Agra to Cuttack." With such ill-wishers, to whom were to be added the Pindaris and their patron, Amir Khán, not only precautions of defence were needed, but prompt triumphs against Nepal, followed by immediate peace with that State. It is not until one weighs the burden of such opinions—and those of Ochterlony in the field and of the

Council at Calcutta were not a whit more sanguine—that one is able to appraise the full value of Gardner's project, or of the unostentatious services by which he and his associates were enabled to carry it out. It is true that they had the sympathy of the hill-men, to whom the Gurkhas were foreign conquerors of an oppressive sort; but that feeling was one of the factors in Gardner's plan.

Hearsey—as Gardner had anticipated—got his column into trouble, and was defeated and made prisoner. But the Gurkhas naively assumed that he was a Frenchman, and could procure them foreign help; on which account they kept him in honourable custody at Almora. That fortress fell to Colonel Nicholls on 26th April; and a convention was made with the Gurkha general, under which Hearsey was given up, with all the strong places in the Province, which was to be evacuated by the Gurkha forces on receipt of the necessary means of transport. Gardner and his cousin remained in occupation, and Amar Sinh found himself severed from his base.* Nor was this the worst: a spirit of despondency began to prevail amongst the gallant highlanders of whom British officers had conceived such exalted notions. Cut off from their homes, constantly defeated in minor skirmishes and sieges, distressed for food, and at last blockaded by the manœuvres of Ochterlony, these brave little warriors themselves gave way to despair. After a defence for which he deserves all credit, Amar Sinh found himself driven back in every direction. By the end of April all the forts but Malaun had fallen; and on the 8th May the bulk of the Gurkha soldiery surrendered to Ochterlony, most of them entering the British service. On the 10th, after undergoing a brisk cannonade in Malaun, Amar Sinh himself surrendered with his few re-

* The total British loss in this little campaign was 180 sepoys and one English officer. The Gurkha general was named Bám Sáh; a Kamauni by birth, and somewhat lukewarm in the cause of Nepal.

maining followers ; he also engaged to abandon all the Gurkha conquests west of the Jumna, and to send orders for the evacuation of the domains of the Rája of Tehri, which lay between Malaun and Almora.

This capitulation, according to the accepted usages of civilisation, might have been fairly looked on as ending the war. On a review of the situation, the Durbar of Káthmándu, with apparent sincerity, resolved on negotiation, and sent commissioners to treat with the British Government. But before the negotiations began, the Gurkhas, with the puerile insincerity that was habitual to them, sent a mission to the Chinese Government, to which they professed allegiance, reporting that they had met with their late misfortunes in attempting to defend their frontier of the Celestial Empire against a British invasion, and inviting the help of a Chinese army—which was accordingly sent. Meanwhile, they affected to agree to the terms proposed by Moira, which involved the cession of all lands conquered by the British, and the limitation of Nepal, on the north-west, by the line of the river Káli. A treaty based on these conditions was signed by the Nepalese commissioners, 2nd December, 1815, and duly forwarded to Calcutta, where the Governor-General was for the moment residing. But in the meantime the Durbar—advised by Amar Sinh, who had got back to Káthmándu, and perhaps inspired by the approach of the Chinese—determined to repudiate the action of their own agents, and informed Moira that the war would be continued. Readily accepting the challenge, he sent up a strong force under Ochterlony—who had been made a Baronet for his late services. With a division composed of four brigades, and supported by two reserve columns under Nicholls and J. S. Wood, Sir David Ochterlony entered the hill-country on 12th February, 1816. After threading a gloomy and difficult ravine —where the enemy never thought of expecting him—the General brought the bulk of his force to an open space in front of the fort of Makwánpore, which commanded the Káthmándu road. Here a short action was fought on the 27th, in which the British loss was no more than forty-five killed and a hundred and seventy-five wounded; and the Gurkhas were driven to flee the field by push of bayonet. Here the General was joined by Colonel Nicholls, who had brought his column by another mountain-path; and the fort of Makwánpore would have been stormed if it had not been for the final submission of the Durbar. Peace was restored on 3rd March, 1816, when Mr. E. Gardner was appointed Resident of Káthmándu. At the same time the mendacity of the Gurkha appeal to China was duly made plain to the approaching General of that Empire: who was justly indignant, and only restrained from inflicting punishment on the Durbar for the deception by earnest intercession from the British Government.

The war had caused an amount of anxiety among the more responsible British officials which, to us (judging after the event), may, perhaps, appear excessive. Looking at the small advantage that was taken by the enemy of the British failures on the eastern side, and at the ease with which the small parties of Gurkha troops were conquered when properly taken in hand, one may ask, what was the great danger of attacking 12,000 ill-equipped barbarians, however brave? The answer is suggested by what happened immediately afterwards, showing what extensive combinations were possible elsewhere, and how much the nascent Empire depended upon quick military success. The conclusion of peace with the Gurkha Government—based on demonstrations of British strength and justice—came just in time to free the hands of the Governor-General for an undertaking of the most supreme importance; while in the friendship of the gallant highlanders it furnished him and his successors with a recruiting-ground for the native army, and a convalescent home for the Europeans. On those cool heights, where the bird and the bee sing, and the breeze from the sparkling inaccessibility of the glacier-world scatters the breath of the wild rose about the grassy hill sides, the heat-smitten exile is restored to hope, and the weary statesman recovers strength to labour at his ease. It may be fairly assumed that the possession of such stations as Simla, Dagshai, Chakráta, Landour, Ranikhet, and Náini Tal has done more to strengthen the British possession in Upper India than would have been effected by the addition of a whole army corps to the military establishment.

These benefits had, indeed, been dearly bought, both in blood and money. But of these the former is the eternal price of Empire, the latter one of its most anxious tasks. The money charges of the war had been lightened by loans from Ghazi-ud-din, the new Nawáb of Audh; and—partly out of a kindly sense of obligation, partly as a politic assertion of supremacy—he was allowed by Moira to assume the title of "King," a promotion which, without affecting his actual position or authority, raised him to a social equality with the ex-Emperor, henceforth known as the King of Delhi. Everywhere the British power was growing, as if by natural process; but equally universal were the friction and resistance.

Disturbances occurred in Cutch and Kattiwar, outlying provinces of Gujarát, in 1815, but they were suppressed by Colonel East without bloodshed. The two sons of the Nizám, who had set up an anarchic rule of their own at Haidarabad, were reduced to obedience by their father before serious collision between the troops and the Muslim malcontents could occur. In 1816 a rebellion broke out at Bareilly, in Rohilkhand, where the introduction of the house-tax was opposed with as much resolution as formerly at Benares, and with much more violence. Supported by the fortuitous collection of Afghán adventurers at Rampore, and by the designed absence of the Nawáb by whom those Afgháns ought to have been restrained, the Muhamadans of Bareilly permitted themselves great excesses. Twice they encountered the police and troops; they murdered an unoffending and unarmed Englishman; and they did not give way until (April, 1816) a number, estimated at 1,500, had been killed or wounded. A still more serious affair occurred in the Upper Duáb where the Talukdars of Háthras and Mursan—with strong forts and numerous armed followers—defied the British District Officers. Moira took his accustomed course; seeing that the punishment of their Bargujar neighbours at Kamauna in 1807 had not had a deterrent effect, he determined at once to crush the incorrigible Ját Barons by an irresistible employ of force. Six cavalry regiments, two of British infantry, seven of sepoys, with seventy-one mortars and howitzers, in addition to thirty-four battering guns, formed part of this formidable expedition, which was under Major-General Dyson Marshall. The town was breached and stormed, after which the fort was bombarded; and, being exposed to a ceaseless tempest of shells for fifteen hours, the garrison was fain to surrender, though Daya Ram, the rebel chief—with a few followers in armour—cut his way through the besiegers, and, for the time, effected his escape, This otherwise well-managed affair took place in March, 1817, when the fort was demolished, as should have been done long before.*

At the same moment partial insurrections occurred in Cuttack and the northern Sarkars. The latter were only troubled for a season, owing to the exactions of a contractor of land-revenue, on whose removal opposition ceased. But in Cuttack the evil was of deeper seat and more difficult eradication. The heavy assessment of the land had caused rack-renting; the salt-tax, the tax of the common multitude, was

* Shipp says that the Rája and his men escaped by an ill-guarded gap, but admits—owing to their armour—the British Horse "would have made but little impression on them." Daya Ram was afterwards apprehended and pardoned."

much too heavy; and distress, great and general, had been bred by the discharge of the superfluous militia and policemen at the annexation: these formed a class known locally by the name of "Paiks."

In 1817 the Paiks—whose earlier rebellion has been already mentioned—again broke out under the leading of one Jagbandhu, formerly a high official under the Raja of Khurdha, but now much reduced. Two detachments of regular troops had to be sent against him; one of these parties was even repulsed with the loss of the European leader. The sacred town of Jagannáth was occupied by the insurgents; and the commanding officer retired his men, taking with him the treasure. The whole district of Puri was in arms, but the Rája refused to join; Captain Le Fevre attacked and defeated the insurgents with a battalion of sepoys; and the rebellion was gradually put down in the course of the hot weather, after martial law had been introduced. It is pleasant to add that all this trouble was not altogether vain. Special commissioners were appointed to examine into the grievances of the people; and, on these being redressed, the country resumed its tranquility, which has been ever since maintained. Hundreds of thousands of people from all quarters crowd the town of Puri yearly, but the place is as manageable as any portion of the Queen's dominions.

[See private journals of Marquis of Hastings, edited by his daughter, 2 vols., 1858; article in "Calcutta Review" for 1891, "The Real Major Gahagan;" "Memoirs of John Shipp," 3 vols., 1829 (reprinted 1892); Kaye's "Life of Metcalfe," 2 vols., 1867; "Life of Gillespie," 1816.]

SECTION 3.—Mention has been made of a note recorded by the Governor-General soon after assuming office. This paper, although only recorded in a private journal, gives the substance of much discussion and minute writing, in which the Members of Council—who may be conceived of as a sort of Cabinet inherited from Lord Minto—were not altogether at one with their new chief. As already noted, Moira meant to make the British power "paramount, in effect, if not declaredly so;" at the same time he shrank—with true chivalry—from the attitude of domineering over Native Courts which he saw, or believed that he saw, adopted by the British agents who resided there. He deplored the "captious bickerings" which were going on all round; and considered that "a rational jealousy of our power was not likely to excite half the intrigues against us which must naturally be produced by the wanton provocations which we have been giving on trivial subjects to all the States around." No sooner would the Company's forces engage with a capable enemy, than these hostile elements would begin to combine. So argued the new ruler; and not unreasonably, if the particular anticipations of this period were not all realised. Thus the dispute with Nepal, which Moira believed he had ended, broke into open war; on the other hand, the danger which he indicated as then threatening from a simultaneous attack from Burma and Lahore (which would "ungarnish our prodigiously extended flanks") this came to nothing, fortunately for all concerned.

Yet there were true grounds for anxiety. That the spirit of Native Courts was bad the Governor-General had knowledge from men like Elphinstone at Poona and Jenkins at Nágpore, men not easily alarmed. The finances were exhausted by remittances to London; positive orders forbade action. Nevertheless, action must be taken, were it only against "the Pindarries." These freebooters were becoming a menace to every form of civilisation. They derived their name from *Pandára*, a Maráthi word signifying the foragers of an army; and they are mentioned by contemporary writers as serving against the Emperor Álamgir in the Deccan wars of the 17th century. When a certain amount of peace ensued they put themselves under disbanded officers and lived by pillage, like the old French *routiers* before they were finally dispersed by

Charles VII. They were divided into bands, called by themselves "Darras," each under a chief, called "Sirdár," who might be a Muslim or might be a Hindu; for, among many singularities, this disordered spawn of war had formed a solidarity apart from that of caste or creed or common origin. Nor did they aim at military conquest, having neither infantry nor artillery, knowledge of war, or fixed fortresses or cantonments.* Living like gipsies in the jungles, they mounted their wiry little steeds at the end of the rainy season, armed with long lances, each carrying a brass pot and a blanket, and followed by their women and children, also on horseback. Then, like a swarm of hungry insects, they poured over the plains, cutting the newly-ripened crops, plundering the householders with insult and torture, and carrying off such of the young women as caught their fancy. So long as they paid black-mail to the Rájas, their proceedings were not interfered with by those lords of misrule; Amir Khán—as general for Holkar—kept a body of them in his employ, others were known as the "Sindia Sháhi," or subjects of Sindia. These last had headquarters in Nimár, a wild, wooded country between the Tapti and the Narbada, abutting on Berár to the east, and on Málwa to the west. Their chief Sirdars were two Muslim adventurers named Karim Khán and Dost Muhamad; with a Ját, called Chitu, probably the ablest of all, who had been endowed by Sindia with five districts, and usually resided at Satwás, near the old historic town of Handia, in what is now the district of Hoshangabad.

It has been already mentioned that, in Minto's time, the British district of Mirzapore had been entered, and the chief

* In 1814 the Pindari force was estimated to consist of

			HORSE	FOOT	GUNS
Sindia Sháhi	...	...	18,000	1,300	15
Holkar Sháhi	...	...	3,000	200	3
Making a total of	...	...	21,000	1,500	18

town threatened by a large body of these marauders. Since that time they had continued to harass the frontier, and had also made raids in the territories of the Peshwa and the Nizám. But the authorities in London—the policy of the Ministry being expressed through the mouth-piece of the Secret Committee of the Directors—continued to prohibit all active measures; and the Governor-General, so long as his Council opposed him, was unable, or unwilling, to take steps against the will of his "honourable masters." Luckily, the audacity of the marauders, presuming too far, at last furnished a provocation which overcame the quiescence of the Calcutta Council, and provided the Governor-General with his opportunity.

In October, 1815, Moira had returned to Calcutta, armed with facts and arguments supplied by Metcalfe, the Resident of Delhi, with which he made a determined attempt to alter the views of his Council at Fort William and of his employers in London. The condition of Central India was fully exposed, and the danger of delay ably exhibited. It was shown that the States in whose midst the Pindaris were harboured might be considered in three groups.

The first class consisted of States substantive, having a recognised political character, in alliance with the British, but all really inimical. Such were; the Peshwa, seeking in crooked, subterranean ways to recover his position as head of the Mahratta Confederacy; the Bhonslá of Berár — commonly known as "The Rája of Nágpore," from the name of his capital—not in subsidiary alliance, but enjoying British protection; Sindia, the lord of Gwalior and part of Málwa, smarting under defeat, yet professing friendship; and Holkar, a boy under the tutelage of the Lady-Regent, Tulsi Bai, and overshadowed by the Pathán adventurer, Amir Khán. The second class was formed of what were called the military States, of which the most formidable was that put together by this same Amir Khán; not a very courageous man, as we saw in Lake's time, and now growing old; but an able organiser, who had profited by the friendship of the late Jaswant Ráo to create a principality with a good force of cavalry and infantry and a serviceable artillery. With these chiefs interest and ambition were paramount; and they differed from the "substantive" class in being still less trustworthy, because they had more to gain by the perpetuation of anarchy in Central India. It was Metcalfe's opinion that the first class might be utilised, if not conciliated, while for the second extermination was the appropriate remedy. Wise as he was, it will be presently seen that events did not altogether justify his forecast. In the third class were grouped feebler States—such as the old Rájadoms of Rajputana—whose constant dread of their unscrupulous neighbours led them to desire the protection of which they had been deprived by the policy of Barlow.

The objections of the Court of Directors—or of the Board of Control, under which Barlow had acted—were still in force, and derived fresh strength from the treaties concluded in 1805-6. To restore order in Central India—so it was argued—would be to incur the resentment of Sindia, and perhaps to provoke a general war with the whole Mahratta Confederacy. Metcalfe thought, and Moira agreed with him, that this was not a necessary consequence but that the time had come when safety required that the risk ought to be incurred. The Council, however, still differing, Moira's plans had to go home to the Directors unsupported. It was at this moment that the audacity of the Pindaris precipitated the solution. During the whole cold season they had been darting about the country between Nágpore and the Bay of Bengal like a destructive fire; and although chased out of Cuttack, they had so wasted the land to the southward, that Gantur, Masulipatam, and Cadapa were completely devastated. In the short space of ten days one hundred and eighty-two of the inhabitants had been killed, and over three thousand wounded or tortured:

many of the women had leapt into wells, preferring death to dishonour. According to reports received by the Government the total loss was estimated at a million sterling; and the Pindaries were reckoned at 23,000. Simultaneously with the news of these atrocities, committed on British subjects, the Government received a despatch from home prohibiting "plans of general confederacy or offensive operations"; but the time was gone by when such a policy could, with any regard to prudence or decency, be maintained. During the year Buckinghamshire died, his place as Indian Minister being taken by George Canning: the timid counsels of the Directors were not suddenly cancelled; but a change was evidently hoped for. Writing in his journal, under date 23rd December, 1816, the Governor-General records that the ravages of the Pindaris in British territory had induced his colleagues to declare themselves "ready to record an unanimous opinion that the extirpation of the Pindarries must be undertaken notwithstanding the orders of the Court of Directors." He could not act, he added, in the teeth of a positive prohibition from home, so long as the Council might pen adverse minutes: but now he felt free to begin, and would at once proceed to pin Sindia to one of two lines: either to join the marauders and accept the position of an open enemy, or to take part—passive, if no more—on the side of the British. At the same time Moira left Calcutta, really on a short shooting expedition, but so as to give Sindia reason to expect him on the frontier and to have his choice determined the more quickly. Moira's hopes were further raised by the change of tone beginning to appear in the despatches of the Secret Committee since it came under Canning's inspiration. On the 26th September, 1816, some intelligence of the outrages on British subjects having by that time reached London, Moira was informed by the home authorities that his measures would be approved, even if they extended beyond repelling invasion to the extent of "pursuing and chastising the invaders." And, if Sindia, or any other chief, took the part of the Pindaris, such chief might be treated as an enemy.

It was thought time, when this permissive despatch got to Calcutta, to go somewhat beyond its mild suggestions; and Moira at once prepared to take the field in person, after making alliances with the chief Native powers. Sindia answered the Governor-General's appeal in a manner which was enough to show how vain and uncalled for had been the timid policy of the past. He at once entertained the proposal, practically guaranteeing a benevolent neutrality, and only asked in return that any of his territory from which the marauders might be expelled, should be restored to him. It was a hardy act of Moira, at his age, to set off in July for the Upper Provinces; but his activity at once bore fruit. Little or nothing as the Native chiefs might know of English policy or changed views in Leadenhall Street, they could understand a statesman who proclaimed that misrule and anarchy were to cease, and that universal tranquility was to be at once established "under the guarantee and supremacy of the British Government." Notwithstanding the earlier measures of Wellesley, this was the first formal announcement of Imperial authority; and when it was made by the master of unconquered legions, himself advancing on the scene of disorder, a sense of their own interest was touched, in friend and foe alike. Strange it is, but no less true, that, while Sindia, the great object of anxiety, accepted the new policy almost at once, one of the last powers to act upon that feeling, was one which had never been regarded as hostile, namely, the Kachwáha State of Jaipore.

The past and present condition of that State may be briefly recapitulated. Although other principalities of the Rajputs might boast of more antiquity or social distinction, there was none that had been so conspicuously or so continuously mixed up with the affairs of Hindustan. Though inferior to the exclusive pride of the Sun-descended Sisodias of Marwar,* the House of Jaipore could point to a more than respectable record. Dhundhar, as the country was originally called, was under a ruler of that house in the time of the Mughal conquest, and the Emperor Akbar married his daughter in 1562. He was succeeded by one son after the other, both having served Akbar in many directions with equal fidelity and skill. The great grandson of the second of these rulers was the famous Jai Sinh I., the Mirza Rája, who served Sháh Jahán and Álamgir, and captured Siváji in 1665. Up to this time the Capital of the State had been by the rock-bound tarn of Amer, or Ambér, where the palace built in 1600 by Rája Mán Sinh to this day commands the wonder of travellers. But a second Jai Sinh, in 1728, transferred his residence to Jaipore, on the plain about five miles away; and this, now one of the finest cities of India, has ever since continued to be the capital of the State. Jai Sinh II. was a follower of science, who died a natural death after a reign of forty-three years. His grandson Pratáp Sinh, was leader of the Jaipore forces in the war with Mahádaji that followed the demise of Mirza Najaf Khán. Towards the end of the last century he became involved in troublesome disputes with his neighbours, and died in 1803, just in time to be spared the desertion of Cornwallis and Barlow, and the spoliation of his country by Jaswant Ráo Holkar.

Such was the State, interesting but almost exhausted, which was the immediate object of British anxiety in the approaching crisis. An alliance with Jaipore was considered an indispensable preliminary to the new system, both by way of a declaration to Sindia, Holkar, and Amir Khán that they must henceforward hold back their hands from so accessible a source of plunder, and also as completing the chain by which the Pindaris were

* "Jodhpore" and "Udaipore" in modern parlance. See the descriptions in earlier chapters; also "Imperial Gazetteer," in v.v.

to be hemmed in. But whether from soreness at past desertion, or from still more unworthy motives, there were many about the Rája Jagat Sinh who counselled him to reject the repentance of the Company's agents. Therefore, although the Rája had been "harassing" Moira "with importunate supplications" for protection under a subsidiary treaty, he drew back before the middle of the year; and Metcalfe, who, as Resident at Delhi, had been charged with the negotiation, received orders to press Jaipore with an ultimatum.

With States from which less was expected, better luck befel the Governor-General. Thus, in Berár, the sudden demise of of Rághuji Bhonslá brought forward an ambitious young kinsman who desired to act as Regent, the new Rája being disqualified by physical and mental infirmity. The Bhonslá, it may be called to mind, had held his head high, and declined a subsidiary alliance when offered one by Wellesley. He had now passed away, and had left his dominions in a weak and exposed condition, with Amir Khán on one side, Sindia on another; his blind and imbecile son, sure to die soon or late, without issue. Appa Sahib, the kinsman of the deceased, at once assented to the renewed offer of a subsidiary alliance, for which he was to pay a handsome tribute; and it not only isolated Sindia but furnished a new barrier to the movements of the marauders. "Should he prove treacherous," so wrote Moira shrewdly, "we may have a struggle, but . . . it would only make the ultimate arrangement more beneficial."

At the time when the Governor-General was busy with these preparations, the attitude of the Peshwa Báji Ráo was becoming more and more a source of annoyance and doubt. His favourite henchman, Trimbakji, had been put in confinement on a charge of murdering the envoy of the Gaikwár, an offence of which he was notoriously guilty, but pleaded his master's order. Escaping from captivity, Trimbakji became a fugitive, but kept up communications with the Peshwa, who began levying troops in contravention of his treaty engagements. Being taxed with these practices the Peshwa promised amendment, but urged many frivolous grievances against the Company's servants which only showed his own captious frame of mind. He was much offended at the separate arrangements with Nágpore, also offered to Sindia and Holkar. Although these were virtual corollaries of the treaty of Basain, the Peshwa affected to be still the head of the Mahratta confederacy, and continued to importune Moira and the Resident at Poona for the pardon of the fugitive Trimbakji. The Resident was the Hon. Mountstuart Elphinstone, one of the most distinguished Anglo-Indians of the day; a man of vigilant and unflinching courage, who tracked the Mahratta chief through all his wiles. At last, on the eve of Moira's departure from Calcutta, the Peshwa was informed that he must in future regard himself as a feudatory of the Company, offer a reward for Trimbakji's capture, resign all his rights in Sangor and Bundelkhand abandon the reception of agents from other Mahratta States, and cede territory worth twenty-four lakhs a year, in lieu of maintaining a subsidiary force. This treaty, which virtually deposed the Peshwa from his hereditary supremacy, was most unwelcome to the Peshwa; but Elphinstone's firmness, joined to a secret hope that it might be broken by and by, led him to give it entertainment, and it was finally signed, June 13th, 1817. The Governor-General left Calcutta to take command of "the Grand Army" on July 5th.

The measures of the Governor-General, henceforth to be known by his new title of Marquess of Hastings, were taken with all the intrepid circumspection of the consummate soldier-statesman that he was. Despatching Malcolm, the generous, joyous diplomatist of whom we have already had some glimpses, to visit and sound the various native Courts of the south, he at the same time assembled two powerful armies, with numerous supporting columns, to converge upon the central haunts of the

Pindaris. In so doing, he was combining, with full knowledge and intention, the extirpation of the marauders with the extensive reduction of all India, between the Sutlej and the sea, to political subordination; and he was well aware that nothing short of a general, determined, and imposing effort could possibly effect that purpose. Accordingly while taking personal command of the central, or "Grand" army, he summoned Sir Thomas Hislop, the Commander-in-Chief of Madras, to march up from the Deccan with all the troops that could be collected. The Grand Army was assembled at Agra, Cawnpore, and Kalinjar in September; and it was distributed in three divisions, of which the centre (consisting of eight sepoy battalions, the 87th Foot, some native cavalry, and the 24th Dragoons, with fifty-four guns) was intended to hold Sindia in check, while it barred the escape of the Pindaris into Hindustan: the right under General Donkin, consisted of the 8th regiment of dragoons, some irregular horse, three battalions of native infantry and eighteen guns: while the left, under Dyson Marshall (the captor of Hathras) were all native troops at first. Farther eastward the line was completed by two columns, each containing a regiment of British foot; while Sir D. Ochterlony, commanding a similar column with contingents supplied from Patiala, Sardhana and Alwar, served as a final reserve on the north.

The army of the Deccan was arranged on similar principles, that is, Hislop's central division, with dragoons and European infantry, was supported by General Doveton on one side, and General Lionel Smith on the other, while Malcolm and Munro led bodies chiefly composed of subsidiary and other native forces. Lastly, Sir W. Keir held Gujarát with the flower of the Bombay army, including two European regiments. Early in November a general advance took place; but before we follow the movements of the Deccan army, we must pause to notice the political anxieties that met the Governor-General, and the difficulties that hampered his action. The force which he had

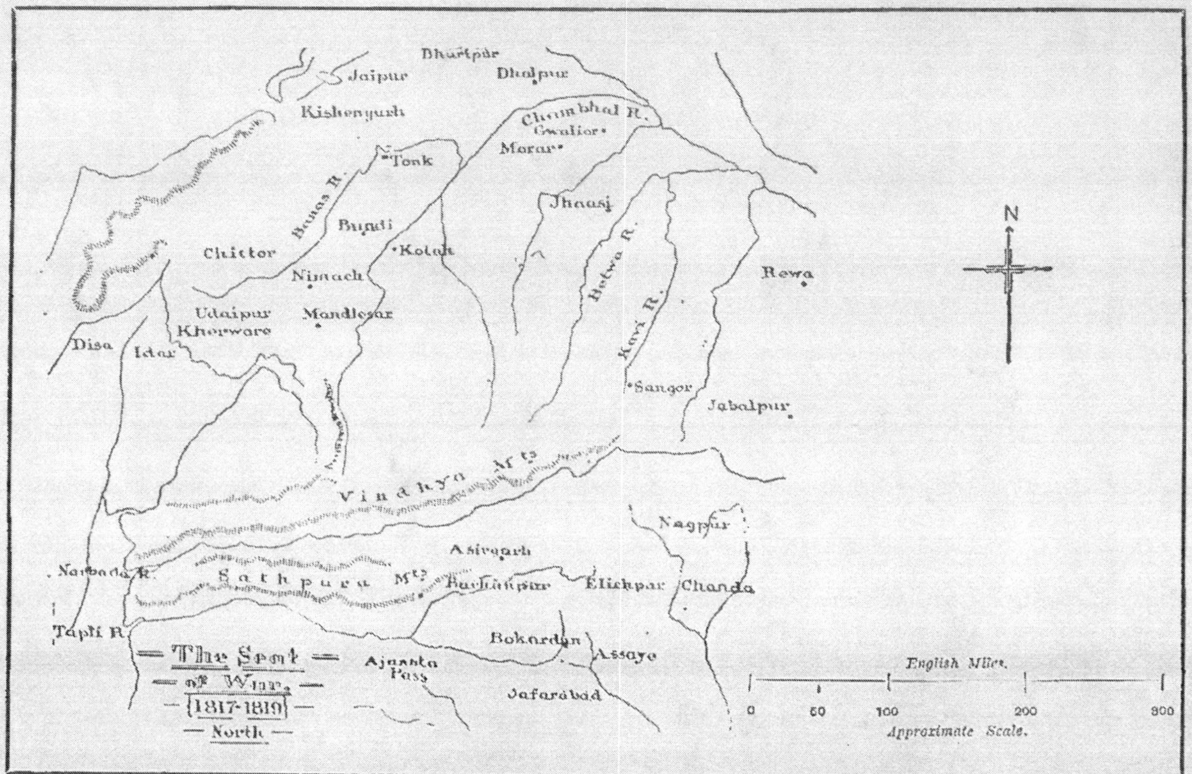
The Seat of War.
1817-1819
North
N
Bhartpur
Jaipur
Dholpur
Kishengurh
Chumbhal R.
Gwalior
Morar
Tonk
Banas R.
Jhansi
Bundi
Kotah
Chittor
Nimach
Betwa R.
Rewa
Udaipur
Kherwara
Mandlesar
Kavi R.
Disa
Idar
Sangor
Jabalpur
Vindhya Mts
Nagpur
Asirgarh
Narbada R.
Sathpura Mts
Burhanpur
Elichpur
Chanda
Tapti R.
Bokardan
Assaye
Ajanta Pass
Jafarabad
English Miles.
0
50
100
200
300
Approximate Scale.

collected on all sides may seem extravagant for the police duty of breaking up a few gangs of dacoits, especially when the vast number of the auxiliaries is taken into consideration. But some of these auxiliaries were, in truth, the main object of all the precautions taken; for if they were not overawed it was greatly to be apprehended that, in place of taking part with the British against the Pindaris, the contingents would take part with the Pindaris against them. The Northern army was 43,687 strong, the Southern 70,487, all told.

The anxiety arising from the contingents did not apply to the Rájputs indeed, but it was an essential part of the present and prospective relation with Berár, and with Amir Khán; while it appeared to Hastings that the cases of Sindia and the Peshwa, were cases of hostility almost beyond the reach of hopeful speculation. Neutrality was the utmost that he thought could be looked for here, and even neutrality was only to be expected where the slippery Mahrattas could be confronted by resistless force. The troops of the Peshwa were estimated at 28,000 horse, 14,000 foot, and thirty-seven guns, and he had a resolute General named Gokala: on the other hand some of his corps were under European officers, and unlikely to act against the Company. The army of Sindia was more homogeneous, and not less numerous, consisting of over 14,000 cavalry, 16,000 infantry, and 140 guns; the infantry tinctured still with the old discipline, great part of them commanded by J. B. Filose, an Italian half-breed who had served under Perron.

Leaving the Peshwa to be dealt with by Malcolm and Elphinstone, the Governor-General addressed himself to the securing of Sindia's quiescence, an object which depended mainly on appealing to the chieftain's fears. He had promised, as may be remembered, a benevolent neutrality, and if he were to keep his promise nothing more would be required of him, But already, in the course of September, the vigilance of Hastings discovered that Sindia was engaged in secret negotiations with the Mahratta States, and even with the lately vanquished Gurkhas of Nepal. The letters were good-humouredly but publicly restored to Sindia, but the fact that they had been intercepted gave oil to the diplomatic wheels. On full consideration, Lord Hastings resolved to embody, in the treaty that was to be offered for Sindia's acceptance, a formal abrogation of the existing agreements by which the Company had been bound to leave the Rájputs to the uncovenanted mercies of the Mahrattas. Thus, and only thus, might Jaipore, Jodhpore, and Udaipore be brought within the subsidiary system. As for Sindia, he was not to be trusted farther than one could see, but then one would keep an eye on him.* The treaty so conceived, was presented to Sindia about the end of the month, at the same time that Hastings advanced with his division, within two marches of Sindia's headquarters, and Donkin moved down to the same neighbourhood from another direction. The great object of so many years of alarm and indecision, was now approached; and it proved to be a mere scarecrow. Daulat Ráo Sindia was wanting in the jovial wisdom of his predecessor, the great Mahádaji, but he was accustomed for years to a life of ease, and, above all, he was a reasonable man. Surrounded as he was by a courteous, but firm pressure, he saw the necessity of abandoning the Peshwa, and desisting from any active attempts to stimulate hostility among more neighbouring malcontents. He signed the required treaty on 5th November. Four days later Amir Khán's agent, on behalf of his employer, signed a treaty with Metcalfe, based on that officer's proposals; all the lands in the Pathán chief's possession were guaranteed to him, and under some friendly pressure from Ochterlony, Amir Khán became an ally whose adherence was never after slackened, and whose successors have ever since continued to rule his State.

* v. Hastings to Metcalfe, 5th October, 1817; Kaye's "Metcalfe," I. 330.

Thus had Metcalfe's general policy been effectually secured, even though some of his detailed previsions had not been made good. Amir Khán, whom he would have selected for extermination, proved a serviceable ally; Sindia, whom he considered inimical, promised at least to give no trouble in present circumstances; Jaipore, the power looked on as most dependent on British help, was the last to hold aloof. The crooked Peshwa, indeed, was not to be trusted; nevertheless, Malcolm hoped to keep him neutral, if not friendly, by dint of friendly argument. Elphinstone, more persistent, hoped against hope for what might be gained by an appearance of "not caring."* Malcolm came to Poona in August, and departed a victim of the Peshwa's wiles, and of his own self-confidence. Elphinstone remained to show how weak is Asiatic firmness, and how purblind Mahratta diplomacy, when opposed by honest resolution and unresting watchfulness.

[See "Life of M. Elphinstone," 2 vols.. by Sir T. E. Colebrooke, London, 1884; "Life of Malcolm," 2 vols., by Sir J. W. Kaye, London, 1856; "Mahratta War," (maps and plans) Colonel V. Blacker, London, 1821.]

* Elphinstone's favourite device (from the story of Hippokleides in Herodotus.)

CHAPTER XIV.

BRITISH SUPREMACY ESTABLISHED.

Section 1: War with the Peshwa, and extirpation of Pindaris—Section 2: End of the Mahratta War, and Pácification of India—Section 3: Founding the Empire.

SECTION 1.—The most cursory observation can hardly fail to be struck by the contrast between the tortuous treachery of the Mahratta chiefs and the manly straightforwardness of their opponents. The only thing that could be urged against the Governor-General and his agents—and it was urged both by the natives and by Munro—was that the British expected from the native courts an impossible degree of rectitude.* The consequence was curious; while professing to pursue the Pindaris as common enemies, the Company's forces were drawn into war against the Company's allies; bombarding and assaulting their forts in the name of their respective owners, and ultimately deposing some of these chiefs, and even putting them in captivity.

The Peshwa—acting in secret understanding, perhaps, with Sindia—was the first to break the meshes of the diplomatic net. After a series of more or less concealed intrigues—

*Munro, writing to Hastings about this time, strongly deprecated a continuance of the Wellesley system, "The observation of Moro Dakshat (Báji Ráo's best Minister) in speaking of the late treaty 'that no native power could, from its habits, conduct itself with such strict fidelity as we seemed to demand,' is perfectly just. . . . I have a *better opinion of the natives of India* than to think this spirit will soon be completely extinguished." Arbuthnot's "Munro": p. 132. Moro was a peaceable man, and for the alliance.

during which the soldier Bapu Gokala urged him to war, while Moro, the civilian, counselled adherence to engagements —the Peshwa received news that the armies of Hastings and Hislop were inactive, and that of Munro employed in the South; while General Smith—who had been expected at Poona —had marched off east, to join Hislop at Elphinstone's express entreaty. On 19th October was the great day of the *dasahra*, the annual festival on which Indian armies were wont to begin for action. Elphinstone was present at the review held on that day, when he and his escort were insulted and almost swept away by charging squadrons. Feeling the approach of a crisis, Elphinstone at once began the concentration of his forces.

The sketch on the opposite page may serve to illustrate his plans. The small force at his disposal was cantoned a little west of the city, in a position where it was exposed not only to attack but to seduction. Having written to General Smith for aid, and sent to hurry up the Company's European regiment from Bombay, Elphinstone proceeded to provide a safe place of meeting; and with this view ordered the force to evacuate the cantonment, and concentrate upon Kirki. On the morning of the 5th November he received an insolent message from Báji Ráo demanding an explanation of these movements, and soon after the heads of the Peshwa's columns were seen bearing down upon the Residency.* Elphinstone at once retired; forded the river, and marched his main body along the bank of the river as far as the bridge, at the same time ordering up the battalion of subsidiaries from Dápuri. A battalion of sepoys with two guns was left to guard the camp, while the rest of the force under 2,000 strong marched out, under Colonel Burr, to hold out a hand to the Dápuri battalion. In the meanwhile the Peshwa's troops, having burned the Residency,

* The Peshwa's foot were led by a Portuguese officer, Major Pinto, one wing of the cavalry was led by Bapu Gokala, the other by Moro Dakshat.

returned to their camp at Ganeskind and prepared to oppose the junction and destroy, if possible, the small bodies of British troops. As estimated at the time, the enemy's forces consisted of horse and foot in about equal shares, amounting to nearly 30,000 men; and the effect of their approach is described by Grant-Duff (who was present), as something like an elemental outbreak. "It was towards the afternoon of a very sultry day; there was a dead calm, and no sound was heard except the rushing, the trampling, and the neighing of the horses, and the rumbling of the gun-wheels." The ensuing action was equally remarkable. The subsidiary battalion, bending back a wing, received Moro Dakshat's horse in line, and drove them off with the loss of their leader; the enterprising Gokala's horse got completely round and interposed between Burr and his camp; but the tenacity of the Bombay Europeans and the ardent gallantry of the sepoys and their officers defied the rules of war. The baffled enemy recoiled, under the eye of their effeminate master who sat watching the conflict from the remote sanctuary on the top of the Parbati hill.

The day of this memorable scene was farther marked by the execution of the treaty by which Sindia agreed to join against the Pindaris and to surrender for a time the fortresses of Handia and Asirgarh. The formation of the circle round the haunts of the Pindaris was approaching completion when, about 13th November, the movements of the central divisions of the Grand Army were thrown into confusion by a short but deadly plague of cholera by which—it has been estimated—20,000 officers, soldiers, and camp-followers were swept away. During the ten days of this pestilence the hopes of the Mahrattas revived. In the north the Pindaris, took advantage of the movement of the Grand Army, which had encamped on the Betwa to escape the cholera, and moved towards the Chambal. It was, however, not likely that they could proceed very far in that direction; and Malcolm went in close pursuit, while the 1st and 3rd divisions of Hislop's army held Southern Málwa with headquarters at Ujain.

In the meantime General Smith, with the 4th division had turned back, arrived at Poona, and expelled the Peshwa, who fled towards Purindar accompanied by the brave and faithful Gokala. On the 17th November the city was peaceably occupied, and, by the strenuous exertions of Elphinstone and the General, order was at once restored. The British took the field; and war was declared against Báji Ráo who kept the command of his army, with the help of a numerous cavalry; while, to increase his claims to the support of good Mahrattas, he went to Satára and took the Rája into his camp. That helpless descendant of the mighty Siváji had for some time past been virtually a prisoner of State; but he was still the hereditary sovereign; and whatever legitimacy there was in the Mahratta Empire reposed ultimately upon this unseen foundation. Having possessed himself of this sanction to his proceedings the Peshwa turned northward, outwitted Smith, and joined the unscrupulous Trimbakji (who had caused all the trouble) in the difficult country above Poona.

While the unwarlike but ambitious chief was thus struggling, a train of his laying exploded in another quarter. It has been already mentioned that Apa Sáhib had been enabled to assume the Bhonslá sway at Nágpore, partly by British aid.* For some time he appeared sensible of this friendship, and desirous of profiting by it. But the respect for the position of the Peshwa which was so general among Mahrattas led the new Rája of Berár, or Nágpore, to lend a sympathetic ear to that intriguer's solicitation; till, at last, the Bhonslá gave audience to an Envoy, who arrived from Poona, bringing him a gift and high title. This was on the 24th November, after the attack on Elphinstone had been heard of. Mr. Jenkins,

* It afterwards appeared that he had secretly murdered his predecessor.

the British Resident, on being invited to witness the investiture, sternly declined; warning Apa Sáhib of the risk he was running of a rupture with the British. But the warning was received with scorn; and, on the evening of the 26th November Jenkins perceived that his house was being surrounded by the Rája's multitudinous forces. To the West of the Residency was the hill of Sitabaldi, with two peaks, each about 100ft. high; the city being on the further, or eastern side. Colonel Scott, who was in the neighbourhood with a couple of battalions of sepoys and a weak body of horse,* took post on these summits, where he was joined by the Resident. The Arab mercenaries led the attack, and the fight went on all night, until at last the northern eminence was captured. Many of the British party had now fallen; and the position of the survivors was becoming most critical, when Captain Fitzgerald—with unauthorised but happy audacity—charged the assailants in the plain on the westward with his small body of horsemen, broke their line and took their guns. The battle now slowly ceased; the Arabs were driven from the hill; and, finally, the Rája tendered an apology which Jenkins was fain to accept on condition of the troops being withdrawn.

These scenes, in two such remote places, were of so remarkable a coincidence that one can hardly avoid reflecting on the situations in which civil officers were liable to be placed in the earlier days of the British dominion in India; situations which, indeed, will be found occasionally reproduced, at much more recent periods. It would have been difficult for military men to have shown more coolness or more judgment than was displayed by Jenkins at Nágpore, or by Elphinstone at Poona. Nevertheless, it must be admitted that the civilians, whatever

* The 6th Bengal Cavalry and a troop of the Madras Bodyguard. Blacker says that their commanding officer, Captain Fitzgerald acted in the face of the "most express injunctions," and commends his "generous disobedience" (p. 113).

qualities they had, could have done but little without the cordial co-operation that they received from the officers in command of the troops, who appear to have obeyed without hesitation the orders issued by them. Mr. Canning, while not perhaps altogether appreciating the political difficulties which surrounded Elphinstone before the outbreak at Báji Ráo, did full justice to the manner in which he used the military force at the crisis. "Mr. Elphinstone," said the Indian Minister in his place in Parliament, "exhibited military skill and courage which, though valuable accessories to diplomatic talents, we are not entitled to require as necessary qualifications for civil employment." A baronetcy was offered, but Elphinstone was poor, proud, and unconcerned; and he refused an honour which he would "have had to share with half the aldermen of London." He would have been glad of the Bath, but it was not conferred; and the well-born Scottish gentleman disdained the hereditary honour. The services of Jenkins were rewarded by the K.C.B., but not until twenty years later. Elphinstone went to the grave undecorated.

At the same time Thomas Munro, another of the great Anglo-Indians of that great time, was equally busy in the southern Mahratta country; where he had at first commanded the Reserve. But Munro, though his ability as a soldier was of the first-class, had been long employed in administrative duties. He had been latterly charged with the settlement of the country south of the Krishna river which had been ceded by the treaty of 1817, and he longed earnestly to complete his task.

Forseeing difficulties there with which his local and administrative experience rendered him peculiarly qualified to deal, he resolved to confine himself to this branch of the coming operations, and with singular self-restraint he left the glories of the forward movement to his second-in-command, Brigadier-General Pritzler, while he restricted himself to the more modest sphere for which he conceived himself most fitted. His conduct receives generous notice in Colonel Blacker's soldierly and everyway excellent work. Nor did Munro fail of other and, temporarily at least, more important distinction. Ably supported by Colonel Newall, he reduced a number of recalcitrant forts, and pacified the country more by his own great personal influence than by the employment of his very small military force. And, in the same speech from which we have already quoted, he received praise as high as any that has been bestowed upon an officer in the House of Commons. "At the southern extremity of this long line of operations," said Canning, "and in . . . a district far removed from public gaze, was employed a man whom I should indeed have been sorry to have passed over in silence . . . than whom Europe never produced a more able statesman, nor India—so fertile in heroes—a more skilful soldier. . . . He went into the field with not more than five or six hundred men . . . and marched into the Mahratta territories. . . . The population which he subjugated by arms he managed with such address, equity, and wisdom, that he established an Empire over their hearts and feelings."

But it is time to turn back to the master of these mighty servants, and see how it fared with the Grand Army and with its coadjutor from the South.

With his troops barely freed from a frightful epidemic and his two most powerful allies making war upon his officers, or flying for their lives before his detachments, Lord Hastings may have seemed to be sufficiently provided with anxieties. Besides these, the Pindaris appeared no nearer to being caught; and were now treating with Scindia, now offered harbour in West Málwa, where the young Holkar was growing up, and where Tulsi Bai, the Lady-Regent, was making cruel enemies among the nobility. Sindia, indeed, offered friendly professions; but Lord Hastings thought it wise to preserve that chief from all temptation by hedging Gwalior with a wall of British troops. Forces from the southern army were hurried up to Nágpore, which was not occupied without considerable loss. The Rája, Apa Sahib, now professed to be very penitent, joined the British camp, and affected to forbid hostilities; but his Arab mercenaries would not surrender until they had made terms for themselves with Brigadier-General Doveton, by whose orders they were deported to Khándes, where they were left to their own devices.

While the eastern part of the line was thus employed Hislop remained at Ujain with his 1st and 3rd divisions: while the 4th was chasing the Peshwa, protected by the unflinching Gokala with such vigour that while the van of the British was hunting the Mahrattas the cavalry of the latter were sometimes pressing the rearguard and baggage of the British. During this pursuit, as in that of the Pindaris, the march of the pursued pursuers was terribly hampered by the heavy guns which it was at first thought necessary to drag along with the forces; but towards the end of December General Smith conceived the fortunate idea of leaving the bulk of his ordnance in Sirore, while he marched rapidly on Poona to protect the city from a threatened attack by Gokala. At the same moment decisive events were occurring in Málwa. The energetic and generous Malcolm, whom we last noticed at Poona, was now in command of Hislop's 3rd division, and was also in political charge. With his usual impetuous frankness he fancied he had secured the whole Durbar of the Holkar State when, in fact, the stronger party there was hostile to the British alliance. So that, when the *darras* of Chitu and Wásil Muhamad, heading back from the Kota frontier, entered the territories of Holkar, which was on or about 9th December, Malcolm found himself suddenly checked in his pursuit by powerful bodies of the State army. To all the overtures of the British officers the leaders opposed nothing but insolent threats. On the 20th they put their Prime Minister under arrest, they beheaded Tulsi Bai the Lady-Regent; and the next day engaged the two British divisions at Mahidpore on the Sipra, north of Ujain. The two British divisions, consisting of nine battalions and about as many squadrons, with irregulars and artillery, found themselves opposed by 20,000 of the best native cavalry in India, with infantry and heavy guns. The British troops, fording the river under a severe cannonade, charged up the ravines, and over the intervening plain: Young Holkar left the field on his elephant, after displaying much intrepidity. Raushan Beg, the leader of the revolution, was severely wounded, and the Mahratta loss was estimated at 3,000, with seventy pieces of cannon; the British had 174 killed, but the wounded were numerous, and their wounds generally, dangerous. Here was another of the Governor-General's unparalleled allies to be conquered; while, almost up to the end of the year, his Excellency was not sure that Sindia might not take the part of the other three.

About the same time news was received that General Dyson Marshall, the captor of Hathras, had encountered the darra of Karim Khán and captured that leader's family and baggage, near Shahabad, about half-way between Kota and Jhánsi. Soon after those Sirdars crossed the Chambal, and, for a time, joined the other Pindari bodies.

In the Poona country the chase of Báji Ráo followed its accustomed circuitous course. The princely traitor endeavoured to make terms for himself; offering to poison Gokala, an offer which the Governor-General could only reject with proper indignation. Báji has been compared with Mithridates: an injustice to the Pontic despot. On the 10th January, orders reached Elphinstone to prepare for undertaking the settlement of the territory which, once known as Baglána, had formed in later times the special domain of the Peshwas, and the central State of Maharashtra. The division of General Pritzler now joined that of General Smith, and Báji began to be hemmed in. On 20th February, he was overtaken at Ashta, a village sixty-one miles east of Satára. He was only enabled to escape by the devotion of the gallant Gokala who covered his flight by charging obliquely, and almost cutting off, a full half of the British cavalry line. Gokala, however, paid for his exploit with his life; on his fall his men were driven off the field; and the poor Rája of Satára, found seated by the wayside, fell into the hands of the pursuing victors. The son of the once formidable Ragoba, hereditary President of the Confederate States, was now a hopeless fugitive, without a home, a cause, or a champion.

On the eastern side the Nágpore troops re-assembled at Simagar, a stronghold about twenty-five miles from Narsinghpore, where they were attacked, on the 5th January, 1818, by Lieutenant-Colonel McMorine; their cavalry being charged and broken, the whole body, 5,000 strong, ran off through the town, leaving their guns behind. General Donkin pushed Chitu through the Bundi hills, where the freebooter obtained harbour for a while from one of Sindia's officers, Jaswant Ráo, Governor of Jáwad. The rest of the marauders were by this time pretty well surrounded, and tossed to and fro between various British columns. At the same time they lost the screen so long afforded by the army of the Holkar State. Scattered by the late events, that army and its chiefs were no longer able to oppose the plans of the Marquess; Tantia Jóg, the lately-imprisoned Minister, was sent to the British camp at Mandeswar; and a treaty was concluded with him, in which the State allowed itself to be seriously mulcted of territory, while provision was made, at Holkar's expense, for Amir Khán and other chiefs whom it was thought proper to reward. By that arrangement another branch was lopped off the great tree that had been overshadowing western and central India, while the British Government acquired another vassal. Lord Hastings received the tidings of this conclusion in camp on the borders of Bundelkhand, before the middle of January; but, four days later, Major General Brown was obliged to act against Raushan Beg and other officers of the State who—regardless of the treaty—had re-assembled some of the scattered remnants of beaten armies and were exerting themselves to create a new disturbance. They were, however, routed with much slaughter, and they lost eleven pieces of artillery. About the same time the best-mounted followers of Karim and Wásil were attacked by a party of native cavalry under Major Clarke, and nearly 1,000 of them killed. The two chiefs retired towards Bhopal; before the end of February these and other Sirdars surrendered to various British officers, Chitu alone remaining at large, under the protection of Jaswant Ráo of Jáwad. But Jáwad was gallantly stormed by General Brown at the end of January; and about the same time Chitu's camp was surprised by Lieutenant-Colonel Heath, as the Pindari was endeavouring to steal past Handia. The wretched marauder once more escaped, but his brother, his son, and a great number of his followers were killed.

The Pindaris being thus slain or dispersed leaderless, the Grand Army was broken up, and Lord Hastings slowly progressed towards Calcutta, by way of Lucknow. The Pindaris were, virtually, and as an institution, abolished; and—great as must have been their sufferings during the process—it must be admitted that they drew the trouble on their own heads by persistent misbehaviour. Their atrocities, when left alone, were equalled by their craven pusillanimity when coped with; for there was not one hour of their hunted existence when they tried to fight or to die like men. The fates of their leaders were curious. Karim settled down as a farmer upon land assigned him in the Gorakhpore district, where he—a few years later—had to drink out of his own cup; his homestead being attacked by a band of dacoits from Audh, and several mem-

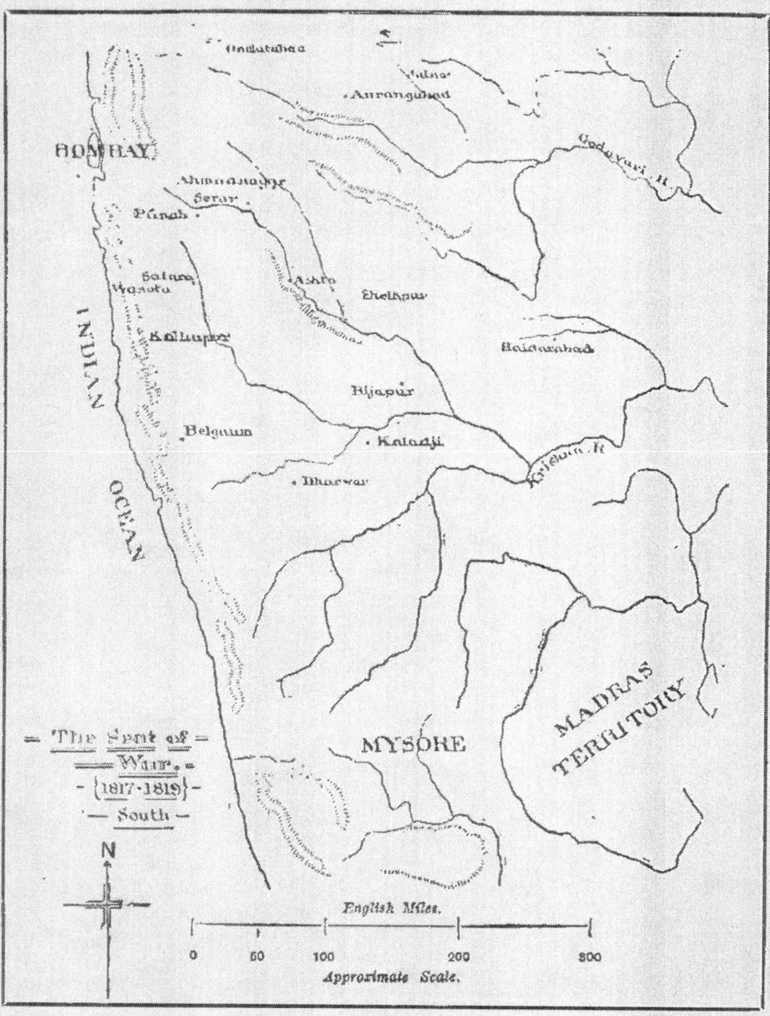

The Seat of War.
(1817-1819)
South

bers of his family slaughtered. Wásil Muhamad, who was also endowed with a farm, chafed under surveillance, and finally poisoned himself. A more romantic retribution awaited Chitu. He wandered about, almost without followers, joined some Mahratta fugitives, was attacked and chased into Málwa, about February, 1819, and finally entered a forest near Kántapore. The place was hard by the Bágli pass, leading down the Vindya range to his home at Etwás; and it seems as if some instinct had brought the hunted creature there to die. He got no farther; some troopers, finding his horse wandering about with an empty saddle, made diligent search until they discovered, among the haunts of tigers in the wooded glades, the arms, dress, and severed head of the once-dreaded freebooter.

Thus the primary object of the expedition was attained. But the British officers were like men who, searching the wood for a wasp's nest, should rouse the wolves. We must now recur to the exertions rendered necessary by the infatuated misconduct of the Peshwa and the Bhonslá of Berár.

[Same authorities. See also "Political and Military Transactions during the Administration of Lord Hastings," 1812-23. H. T. Prinsep. London, 1825.]

SECTION 2.--In the last week of February the Peshwa, Báji Ráo, forded the Godávari, hoping to get into Holkar's country, where he still hoped to find adherents. Here he found the way barred by Hislop, and turned towards the northern part of the Nizám's dominions. He was now completely expelled from his own territory; and the Pindaris had been virtually dispersed. Hislop therefore repaired to Aurangabad, and there laid down his command of the Army of the Deccan, which was partly sent into cantonments, the residue being left to aid Elphinstone and Munro in the pacification of the Mahratta country. The Peshwa, having been joined by the flower of Holkar's horse under an enterprising officer named

Ram Din, proceeded towards Nágpore to solicit help from Apa Sáhib. Here he was pursued by columns under Lieutenant-Colonel Scott, Colonel Adams, and General Doveton, the last of whom encountered him near Seoni, between Jabalpore and Nágpore; the Peshwa was completely routed, and—deserted by most of his followers—fled northward towards Burhanpore.

While the displaced ruler was thus wandering, his late dominions were being rapidly reduced to order. On the 10th February Satára was surrendered, and, a few days later, the famous fastness of Sinhgarh, twelve miles south-west of Poona, was besieged. This was the headquarters of Siváji, founder of the Mahratta Empire in the seventeenth century, and was by situation almost impregnable, standing about 2,300 feet above the surrounding plain on a steep ascent partially scarped. But the walls were old, and the south side began to crumble after a week's battering. The troops in garrison—among whom there were no native Mahrattas—surrendered to avoid an assault.* General Pritzler treated them with liberality, which was not thrown away, but had a good effect on subsequent occasions. Purindar was taken in the same way on 15th March; and on 9th April, Wasiota, the last fort about Satára, surrendered after some mortar-practice. On the following day Mr. Elphinstone went to Satára and installed the Rája—the descendant of Siváji—with due ceremony, and with an announcement that the Peshwa's reign was at an end.† He proceeded thence towards Khándes, settling the country, which he describes as much wasted, and with no cultivation save that just about the vil-

* Blacker 240, and plan 22. In the "Imperial Gazetteer" it is quite erroneously, and twice over, said to have been "stormed," which would have been a serious task; as it was, no bloodshed occurred on the British side.

† The text of the proclamation—dated 11th Feb., 1818—will be found in Wilson (Appendix to vol. VIII.).

ages, which were themselves ruinous and half-deserted. For the next nine months he continued to apply to the settlement of Maharashtra all his knowledge, wisdom, and justice. The total area of the country under his administration was estimated at 50,000 square miles—about the size of all England —with a population of four millions (it is nearly double now). Into these tracts, differing as they did in many respects, he was unwilling to introduce either the Bengal system of tenure and revenue, or the complicated "Regulations" of law and procedure. His own method, as he wrote at the time, was to learn what systems were in existence and to preserve them unimpaired. He admired the agriculturists and sympathised with their depressed condition; and he made Munro and Malcolm his models in dealing with them. He endeavoured to be on friendly terms with the officials and greater landowners, and even undertook the difficult task of conciliating the Brahmans who long formed a hostile element in the city of Poona and other large towns. The feudal holdings of the nobility presented two distinct classes. To those granted by the legitimate Governments of the past he proposed to give full recognition, making them "hereditary in the fullest sense of the word." To later grants he applied an elastic rule, recognising prescription and good conduct. The urban Brahmans were a class hard to deal with. The ex-Peshwa—whose superstition was among the less discreditable elements of his worthless character—had shown them great favour and purchased their goodwill at a cost which could not be emulated by an economic government. Elphinstone proposed, however, to maintain all permanent endowments, and to found prizes for Sanscrit learning; these—in the form of the Poona College—still subsist. In the great matter of land-settlement he did away with the system of contracts under which capitalists had been able to rack-rent the actual cultivators on paying a lump-sum to the public fisc. A light assessment was to be made on the area under plough, the amount being collected and paid by the village office-bearers. The rest of the revenue was raised from customs-dues, and other sources familiar to the people. For the redress of minor grievances he maintained the old system of *panchait*, or village arbitration, placing it under the general control of the collectors of districts. In laying these foundations he was occupied till the Spring of 1819, when he left to take up a new and well-merited preferment—the Governorship of the Bombay Presidency.

His example had been his friend Munro, a man of equal ability and benevolence; no doctrinary, and quite free from aggressive patriotism. Munro deplored the subsidiary system, and did not wish for universal dominion, observing that the inhabitants of all the British Provinces suffered for want of a career, and were "certainly the most abject races in India." Yet this wise and good man wrote the epitaph of the Peshwa's Government in these scathing terms:—

"It was fortunate for India that the Peshwa commenced hostilities, and forced us to overthrow his power: the Mahratta government from the first has been one of devastation. It was continually destroying all within its reach, and never repairing. The effect has been a diminution of the wealth and population of a great portion of the peninsula of India." And again: "All other Hindu states took a pride in the improvement of their country by construction of temples, tanks, canals, and other public works. The Mahrattas have done nothing of the kind; *their work has been chiefly* DESOLATION."

The subverted President of this organized anarchy still hoped to find a friend in the Bhonslá. But a correspondence between the two chiefs, of which portions were found by Elphinstone, and by him transmitted to Jenkins, revealed the infatuation and duplicity of the Nágpore potentate, who was at once arrested, while forces were sent to reduce his remaining strongholds. A small body of native horse and foot, with three light field-guns, was despatched at the end of March towards Chánda, a walled town and citadel, to which Báji was said to be advancing on an invitation from the Rája; while the Poona and Haidarabad divisions operated in the Peshwa's rear. Several strong places in the Nágpore country, which the Rája had agreed to give up, made more or less resistance—under secret orders—before surrendering to General Marshall; and some parts of Bundelkhand and Ságar required a show of force before they were reduced to order. Chánda was besieged by Adams; and, the town walls having been breached and stormed, the citadel surrendered on 20th May. The town is now a thriving *entrepôt* of commerce; and the citadel has been converted into a jail.

The pursuit of Báji, the ex-Peshwa, continued through the month of April, along the line of the Godávari, where he continued to baffle the British officers by a variety of artful stratagems, aided by the natural difficulties of the country. He was careful to make ostentatious enquiry as to all the routes except that which he purposed to take; and he always disposed his cavalry so as to deceive his pursuers and screen himself. Fighting was not a part of his programme, any more than it was with the Pindaris. Nevertheless, his power of mischief did not seem by any means at an end yet.

On the 12th May the Bhonslá Rája was being escorted towards Hindustan, and had arrived within a few miles of the Narbada river, when he contrived to effect his escape by the corruption of his guards, and made his way to the Chindwára forests, where he was protected by the Gonds, a Dravidian tribe who occupy that region.* His intention, doubtless, was to join the ex-Peshwa, in which case the trouble might become chronic. Fortunately, by this time, the toils were closing

* The whole (speaking roughly) of the modern "Central Province" was formerly known as *Gondwána*, from this people (see map of the Mughal Empire).

around that fugitive, who was intercepted on his way to the Narbada; and then, at last, resolved to throw himself on the mercy of Malcolm, of whose generous character he had already made trial in past days. Malcolm was accordingly communicated with, and, on consenting to an interview, was conducted to Báji's camp, near the pass where the Purna river joins the Tapti, on 1st June. As Doveton was now pressing on him from Burhánpur, and another column on the way from Mandleshwar, it might seem that Báji had not much option left; yet he still affected sovereignty, alternating a poverty-stricken display of pomp with somewhat abject appeals to Malcolm's ancient friendship. Malcolm submitted an ultimatum. After much vain haggling the terms were submitted to; including an abandonment of claims to power, and the acceptance of a handsome pension at a place of residence in Hindustan, to be selected by the Governor-General. Báji then joined Malcolm's camp on the 3rd June, being still permitted to retain some 2,000 of his troops. These men had been, for the most part, members of a body of Arab mercenaries enlisted by the murderous henchman, Trimbakji Dainglia, who was still at large. Whether they had a just grievance, or whether they only wanted a pretext for desertion, these men took advantage of Malcolm's courtesy in marching at a distance from Báji Ráo, to surround the tent of that unfortunate chief, just as he had reached Seoni, near Hoshangabad, with mutinous clamours for a settlement of their claims. This was on the 9th June, when Malcolm, hearing of the affair, hurried up; and, by a mixture of firmness and good temper, and by the prestige of his reputation, adjusted the dispute, he persuaded the ex-Peshwa to cross the Narbada to the British camp, and disbanded the mutinous mercenaries. This peaceful victory—due to personal character and conduct—has been justly eulogised as one of the General's best pieces of service. In Malcolm's company the fallen chief was escorted to Mau, where he was allowed to rest while the final orders of the Governor-General were awaited.

Lord Hastings, it soon appeared, was far from approving the liberality with which Báji Ráo had been treated. Still, those were the terms on which the ex-Peshwa had submitted, and his Excellency was far too honourable a man not to ratify the engagement. Báji was therefore escorted to Hindustan by Lieutenant Low, afterwards to be known in larger diplomatic scenes. The spot that he chose for his residence was Bithore, on the Ganges; long after to acquire a melancholy reputation by the revenge of his adopted son, the Nána Dhundu Panth.

There was now only one serious obstacle to the introduction of peace and order into the long-vexed regions of Central India. Apa Sáhib, the Bhonslá, was still at large, understood to be making his way towards Holkar's dominions, on the border of which he might hope to find a refuge. The fort of Asirgarh had been one of those which Sindia had agreed to make over as security for the fulfilment of the engagements that had been taken from him on the eve of the war; but the commandant—acting, as afterwards appeared, under secret suggestions from his lord—had refused to surrender the place, and had fired his cannon at British troops. Moreover, Apa Sáhib was at one time believed—not altogether erroneously, as appeared afterwards—to have been received there as a refugee.

In point of fact, the Bhonslá had been harboured in the Mahadeo hills until the beginning of 1819, when he marched in the direction of Málwa, and did accept the invitation of the commandant of Asir, though not for long. On hearing of this the indefatigable Malcolm started from Mau towards Asirgarh, in the middle of February; and joined his force to that of General Doveton on the 17th when they laid siege to the place. It stood on a detached spur of the Sáthpuras—the range that runs between the rivers Tapti and Narbada; the fort stood on a flattened crest, at a height of two thousand two hundred and eighty-three feet. The fortified plateau on the summit was about sixty acres in extent and contained a good tank of water fed by a spring: the rock beneath being scarped to an average depth of one hundred feet, with only two paths for access, of which the easier—on the south-west side—was defended by a double line of masonry works, with five successive gateways. On a lower plane of the hill was an outwork connected with the village at the foot. Reduced in the last year of the sixteenth century A.D., by Akbar's famous minister, Abul Fazl, it fell into the hands of Sindia at the break-up of Mughal power; was captured in 1803 by Arthur Wellesley, but restored to Sindia by virtue of the treaty of Anjangaum. The force by which it was now invested consisted of native horse and foot; something like a thousand of European infantry and horse-artillery; with two siege-trains, including eighteen-pounder guns, mortars, and howitzers. The town lying on the west was occupied on the 18th March; but a severe struggle took place there two days later, by reason of a sally of the enemy from the lower fort. Shelling went on for the next few days, and the wall of the lower fort was breached on the town-side. General Doveton began serious operations on the north and east, while Malcolm's guns continued to play on the western walls. On the 30th a column advancing cautiously found the lower fort abandoned and took possession: the garrison fired from above; but did no damage from want of machinery to depress the muzzles of their guns. On the 31st General Watson arrived from Ságar, bringing two thousand good troops, including a company of British foot, artillery, two twenty-four pounder guns, some mortars, and other ordnance. The siege operations now progressed more rapidly and it was soon ascertained that the men of the garrison were losing heart: on the 6th a new breaching-battery was opened on the western side; and on the 7th breaches began to appear in the walls of the upper fort. The commandant now asked for terms, and humane terms were offered him : but the operations were not suspended till 11 a.m. on the 8th when the commandant accepted them for himself; and at 4 a.m. of the following day announced that his men had joined in the acceptance. They were all foreign mercenaries, and were allowed to retain their private property on giving up their fire-arms. But the bird was flown : Apa had paid but a hurried visit to the fort, and had departed again before the siege began. To finish his story here, he sought an asylum in the Punjab ; but being eventually dismissed thence by Ranjit, he threw himself on the hospitality of the Rája of Márwar ; and died some years later, at Jodhpore.

The Generals now broke up the army ; Doveton and Watson returned to their respective posts, and Malcolm assumed the civil administration of Málwa where he spent the next three years in useful diplomatic action, and in taming the savage Bhils of the mountains.

The Province of Rajputána still remained to be dealt with. It may be remembered that Jaipore was considered the State most in need of protection in 1817, and that it was here that the greatest difficulty and delay were met with ; in fact no alliance was concluded until the British had shown themselves able to dispose of the common foes, unaided by Jaipore or any Rajput State. Rajputana has been accurately described as the region where the purest blood of the military Hindu classes has remained in a kind of feudal independence from a date anterior to the Muslim conquest ; the Bhattis—who claim to represent the ancient Jádu-bansi race—settling in the extreme West among the stony wastes of Jaisalmer, while the Rathors occupied the "land of death," or Márwar ; the Sisodias gathered on the Méwar plateau at the water-shed of Loni and the Banás ; and the Kachwáhas founded the principality of Dhundar on the north slopes of the Arawali range which afterwards became known as Jaipore, from its modern capital. Minor States may be traced by the names of their chief towns upon the map; Alwar, Karauli, Bundi, Kota, Jhaláwar, Partabgarh, Dungarpore, and Sirohi: Dholpur is a Ját State sprung from that of Gohad: and Tonk is a Muslim *enclave*, owing its existence to the submission of Amir Khán. Farther South, between the Chambal and Narbada, is Bhopál, another Muslim principality, founded by an officer of the Emperor Álamgir (Aurangzeb); lastly come the small States of Kechiwára, of which the chief place is Rághugarh.

With the Governments of all these arrangements, begun by Metcalfe, remained to be concluded by Ochterlony and Malcolm. In most of them anarchy had become almost an accepted state of things. Upon the departure of Wellesley and Lake the Mahrattas under Sindia and Holkar, and latterly the Pathán soldiers of fortune who had been patronised by these chiefs, treated the Rajput States—one and all—as so many carcases might be treated by wolves and jackals. Their marauding followers desolated the country, while the Rájas—instead of combining for the common protection—filled up the measure of public suffering by civil war. By the end of the year 1818, however, all the Rajput States had made treaties with the British Government, which they acknowledged as the paramount power, entitled to tribute or to military subsidy. The interweaving of boundaries, by which the Mahrattas—especially those of Holkar's State—had loved to confuse accounts and maintain causes of quarrel, were rectified by new delimitations: and, by insisting upon holding the shire of Ajmere, with its city and strong hill-fort, the Governor-General secured for himself and successors a watch-tower commanding the whole country. The general scheme, both in Rajputana and in Málwa, was the preservation of existing customs. Where the difficulty lay was in the conciliation of the claims of the feudal lords with those of the sovereign "Rais and Ranas"—to use the phrase of the old Muslim chroniclers. Popular rights were not much regarded, though it might be too much to say that they were altogether sacrificed: in a state of society such as then prevailed in Central India, peace was almost all that the humble tillers of the soil asked for, with immunity from depredation. These simple and rudimentary "rights"—if that be the proper word—they now at last obtained.

In the country to the East some further changes had been necessitated by the misconduct and consequent expulsion of Apa Sahib, the Bhonslá Rája of Berár. A grandson of Rághuji, the Bhonslá of Wellesley's time, was set on the seat of authority at Nágpore; but he was a minor, and Mr. Jenkins administered the country in his name. The districts of Ságar Nimár, Chindwara, and the Upper Narbada, were placed under British rule; and the district of West Berár—lying between the Wardha and Godávari rivers—was ceded to the Nizám.

But the greatest territorial alteration was on the Bombay side. At the beginning of the war this Presidency had authority over nothing but a part of Gujarát. By the overthow and expulsion of the Peshwa, a vast tract came into the Company's jurisdiction, which was made subject to the Governor-and-Council of Bombay. This included the districts of Poona, Ahmadnagar, Násik, Sholápore, Belgaum, Kaladgi, Dhárwar, Ahmadábád, and the Konkan, together with the rights of Holkar in Khándes. Such extension of the Company's direct authority had been no part of the original object of the war, nor were any British Statesmen ever more undesirous of such extension than the Marquess of Hastings and his advisers. But, without complicating ourselves with the mysticism of "manifest destiny," and the like, we can see that the misconduct of the Peshwa left them little option.

No other annexations took place: and the arrangements made in 1819 proved durable. With the exception of a short local campaign against Bhurtpore, which had no effect on the territorial position of the Company, no military action was needed, between the Sutlej and Cape Comorin, for nearly a quarter of a century.

[Same authorities as for last section.]

SECTION 3.—Having thus sketched, within the limits permitted by the scale of our work, the operations of the British Government against the Pindaris, the Peshwa, and the Bhonslá, we must now, with similar brevity, show the change that followed in the relations of the British with the Native States after peace was restored, and good government took root in dominions under direct British sway.

Lord Hastings was disinclined by nature to any avoidable interference in the internal affairs of other powers. At the same time he had long formed an ideal, and that ideal was now in the course of realisation. In spite of the reluctance of his councillors, and in direct opposition to the policy traced in London, he had made the punishment of the Pindaris the means of founding a new Empire of India. From the time of Warren Hastings to the end of Wellesley's administration the power of the Company, as political agent and representative of Great Britain in India, had been that of a strong and humane system setting an example, and exercising an influence among a number of other co-ordinate powers, *primus inter pares.* By the events of 1818 it had risen from this to a position of supremacy and general arbitrament that was hardly to be discriminated from complete sovereignty. Two-thirds of the vast regions south of the Sutlej, and the eastern Himálayas, had now been brought under the direct rule of the three Governments of Calcutta, Madras, and Bombay. The remaining portion was in various degrees of independence, in no case amounting to complete freedom, and presenting more or less of responsibility to the paramount power. Mr. Prinsep, writing in 1820-25, described these States as falling into three distinct classes though he did not perhaps make the distinction as clear to his readers as it was to his own mind.

The first class, the so called "independent" States, he stated to be those in which the ruler held a place somewhat resembling that of such a potentate as the King of Saxony in the modern German Empire. Sometimes paying tribute to the paramount power, always under obligations of military co-operation, the Rája, or the Nawáb raised his own revenue after his own methods, and nominated or dismissed his ministers and subordinate officials. Of such were Audh, Gwalior, or the Sindia State, Bhopál, the States of Rajputana, Bhurtpore, and the Cis-Sutlej Sikhs; and in the south, Khloapur, and perhaps Mysore. The second class, which the writer under reference calls "ministerial," was that in which a native administrator selected or approved by the paramount power, carried on the details of the public service under the general control and advice of a British Resident; and in that category, at the time under notice, were Haidarabad, Indore, and Satára, while Audh tended in the same direction. The third class, called by Prinsep "residential," included cases where a sort of sequestration, professedly temporary, led to the whole administration being directly carried on by the Resident; a method employed in various States at different times, occasionally terminating in annexation, but usually in the restoration of the native dynasty, of which the latest and most conspicuous instance is Mysore, released in 1881.

It will not, perhaps, be thought that the respective limits of these classes are very plain, and we shall see cases of States wavering between one class and another. Nevertheless, a distinction between at least two main sets of Native States long formed a part of the public laws of India, and in a later period proved to be of some importance. Modern writers are wont to class in one, the whole of what they term "feudatory States," and to call the British Government, by a still more forced analogy, "the Suzerain power." Both terms involve somewhat of a misnomer, and the first leads to serious confusion. The great States in alliance with the "Government of India" were clearly not "feudatory" in the ordinary acceptance of that word as implying that they held their territories as vassals, or held fiefs derived from the grant of a superior lord; still less could the British Government be called "Suzerain," taking the word in its proper sense of "superior tenant."* Cases like that of Haidarabad, where the ruler appoints his agents, coins his own money, and exercises without appeal the power of life and death, would hardly be called mere "fiefs" in any system, they are subordinate allies restrained by treaty from making war on each other, or on the paramount power. Nor does the paramount power hold from any one, at the present day, even if it did in 1819, for it was declaredly and absolutely the Sovereign and Parliament of Great Britain, by whose authority the Company, even then, professed to bear sway.† The relation may be best conceived by thinking of that existing between the German Emperor and the constituent States of the Empire, excepting Prussia. But there was, no doubt, a class of States which, if not precisely "feudatory," were and are wholly dependent: such was Satára, created by Elphinstone by way of corroborating the deposition of the Peshwa. The remaining Princes had been what in Europe would be termed "mediatised" as in the case of the Carnatic mentioned in CHAPTER X.

This short digression is only intended to suggest a necessary qualifying of Prinsep's classification. The difficulty which he foresaw in the case of Audh, was evaded during the administration of Lord Hastings. The Governor-General's amiable and considerate disposition prevented him from disturbing the

* SUZERAIN. *Terme de féodalité. Qui possède un fief dont d'autres fiefs relèvent*, Littré *in v.*

† The motto round the seal of the E. I. Company was "*Auspicio regis et senatus Angliæ.*"

repose of Ghâzi-ud-din, the negligent ruler of that Province, whom, as already mentioned, he even encouraged to call himself "King."* The other doubtful case was that of Haidarábád where the incompetence of the Nizám and the greed of an unscrupulous Hindu statesman brought on clouds which darkened the end of Lord Hastings's otherwise splendid administration.

But before glancing at that painful affair, let us turn to the measures taken by Hastings for the domestic welfare of the people under his direct sway, or under that of his British subordinates.

In the north-west of Bengal, the Provinces ceded by the the Nawábs of Audh or conquered from the officers of Sindia ruling in the name of the effete monarchy of Delhi, had for some time past been administered by two Commissioners of Police and a Revenue Board acting in direct dependence on the Governor-General. Thus connected with Bengal the Provinces were naturally liable to be affected by Bengal policy, and above all, liable to be brought under the Permanent Settlement of the Land Revenue. It is difficult for the general reader to understand the importance of this question. Yet the chronicles of Ireland may serve to give us a notion of the connection of agrarian policy with the fortunes of a population entirely dependent on agriculture. And this is so, not only by reason of direct bearing on the condition of the people, but also by virtue of the vast and varied influence that land-laws exercise in such cases upon the work of Government itself. From the days of Shore and Warren Hastings down to those of Thomason and Bird, most Anglo-Indians of eminence have acted on the maxim of Munro, the ablest, if not the wisest, of them all. "In India whoever regulates the assessment of the land-rent, holds in his hand the mainspring of the public

* Ghâzi wished to assume the absolute style of *Pádsháh;* in deference to the advice of the Governor-General he changed it to *Pádsháh-i-Awadh*, which recalls the case of Faustin Soulouque, "Emperor of Haiti."

peace." The only trouble has been that the strength of conviction and earnestness of purpose among those excellent men have so far militated against open-mindedness as to present the most bewildering contradictions of opinion. An ever-diminishing party has always upheld the "Zemindári," or Bengal system, whereby large estates are recognised or created, and the payments to the State-fisc settled, if possible, in perpetuity.* Metcalfe, in the case with which we are here more immediately concerned, was all for a periodical settlement with "villages," (communes having joint-responsibility). Munro consistently urged that settlements should be open to yearly revision, and denounced the principle of joint responsibility; holding that every cultivator should deal directly with the State, and be only answerable for his own field, the demand on which should be open to annual re-examination of area. This was called "Ryotwári," but it should be remarked when that system came to be introduced a few years later into the territories subject to the Bombay Government, it was with a strong determination that nothing should be revised for thirty years. Few, if any, of these divergencies were necessitated by local causes; the "village" system, perhaps, might have been found less vigorous and less suitable to actual facts in some regions than in others;† but the principle of "Ryotwári," or that of permanent demand might have been applied, either or both, to the whole of British India alike. Yet here we see men of ability, experience, and benevolence, opposed to one another on fundamental principles. Later on, we shall find a similar

* The discussion was revived about 1869, and formed the subject of a Report presented to Parliament.

† The "village," according to an experienced observer, is the universal integer of primitive Indian tenures. (Sir G. Campbell in "Cobden Club Papers"). By "village" is to be understood the institution described by Sumner Maine, Freeman, and others, as common to early Indo-Germanic Societies under the names of "Mark," "Township," and so forth. But it had lost much of its cohesion in parts of Madras and Bengal.

antagonism, in the closely similar cases of the Punjab and Audh, when one school of experts was for settling with great landlords, the other for admitting the village communities to contract directly with the State.

In the time with which we are now concerned all these ideas were fermenting. Men of great natural powers, who had come out from Europe before their minds had been fully trained, and who fell to work almost at once, each in his own sphere and among his own particular local influences, soon took their respective views, for which each was prepared to claim exclusive preference. Lord Hastings was hardly fitted by the experiences of his own early life to mediate. Probably, if he could have had his own way, he might have favoured Zamindári tenures and a perpetual assessment. But the Madras countries were by this time under the control of Munro, who became Governor of the Presidency in 1820. The Bombay territories had been too lately constituted, and the greater part of them was still too much depressed by war, and the mismanagement of the Mahrattas to allow of final measures. In the Lower Provinces of Bengal the evils of the Cornwallis system—notably the want of protection for the actual occupants of the soil and the rapid transfer of superior tenures under the operation of the Sale-Laws—had begun to attract attention even in the days of Minto; and the home authorities had begun to denounce the entire system under the influence of Munro.

The only remaining sphere was in the North-West. Here the supposed boon of a perpetual contract with "Barons" and other holders of large estates had, indeed, been promised, though never introduced; and it was now regarded as entirely suspended under orders from England. But nothing definite had as yet arisen in its place. "At first the assessments were made on no definite principle, except to maintain the revenue borne on the roll of the Native Government. New settlements were made in 1805, 1807, and 1812." ("Statement of Progress for 1874-83," by J. S. Cotton, p. 128.) These assessments were made upon anyone who was forthcoming; when there was no one else the estates were farmed to contractors, upon the lines generally followed by native Governments of the period. Rights, assumed or even created *ad hoc*, were ruthlessly sold by auction for arrears, real or pretended; and a number of auction-purchasers thus obtained a State-title under which the real occupants were little considered.

But acute observers were beginning to notice the real state of facts. A special Commission was formed to inquire into the evils that were becoming evident, and to suggest remedies. The Hercules of the occasion was found in Mr. Holt Mackenzie, one of the Government Commissioners; and the result was the cancellation of manifestly fraudulent sales, and the issue of the famous Regulation known in the Bengal Code as VII. of 1822. "Assessments," notes Mr. Cotton "were no longer to be based upon the mere statements of past collections furnished by native officials, but upon an exhaustive investigation into the circumstances of every village. In short, it was proposed to ascertain the true agricultural rent of the country and to determine at the same time the relations of all parties with regard to the soil, in subordination to the Government." ("Statement," *ut sup.*) The idea of fixing a permanent demand upon fluctuating assets was abandoned or adjourned *sine die*; but private property was to be recognised, thirty-year leases being given to the proprietors, with option of renewal on expiry. At this operation all claimants were to be invited to assist, and those who could not establish full ownership might yet advance secondary and subordinate claims. The representative of the State might then make concurrent engagements; or the superior tenants might be bought off with an annuity, and the settlement only concluded with the actual occupants. Even the non-proprietor cultivators were to have their status acknowledged and their rights—if they had any—officially put on record. The customs and by-laws of the estate were to be embodied in writing; rates estimated from produce were to be converted into money; and, after due allowance for the proprietors, the State-demand was to be calculated on that basis.

Such was the somewhat elaborate, but essentially just, scheme intrusted to the North-West Provinces officials by the Government of Lord Hastings; a scheme which really reflects as much glory upon the administration as the pacification of Central India. The social and political value of the "village system," thus happily preserved to the greatest and most important part of Hindustan may be gathered from the often-quoted description of Metcalfe. It is so vivid a picture of the state of the country that no excuse can be necessary for quoting it again.

"The village communities are little republics, having nearly everything that they want within themselves, and almost independent of any foreign relations. They seem to last where nothing else lasts. Hindoo, Patan, Mogul, Mahratta, Sikh, English are all masters in turn, but the village communities remain the same. In time of trouble they arm and fortify. . . . If plunder and devastation be directed against them, and the force employed be irresistible, they fly to friendly villages at a distance; but when the storm has passed over they return and resume their occupations. . . . A generation may pass away, but the succeeding generation will return. The sons will take the place of their fathers—the same site for the village, the same positions for the houses, the same lands will be occupied by the descendants of those who were driven out when the village was depopulated; and it is not a trifling matter that will drive them out, for they will often maintain their post . . . and acquire strength sufficient to resist pillage and oppression with success." It need only be added that the republics were often oligarchic, consisting of members of the same clan, claiming a common ancestry, and resenting the intrusions of strangers, excepting as serfs, helots, or cultivating tenants. This, which was the normal frame-work of Indian society, was obliterated in the Deccan as in Bengal; but in many parts of Hindustan and through all the Punjab it is still in vigorous existence.

How far it might have been preserved in all parts of the Madras Presidency is not easy to decide.* Ever since he was assistant, under Read in the Baṛamahl in 1792, Munro had given the whole of his somewhat narrow but powerful intellect to the development of the *ryotwári* or field-system. A commission, appointed at that time, effected a rough survey of the cultivation, the dues on which were assessed on the actual ryots. Elsewhere other systems grew up, and in the northerly portions of the country many permanent settlements were made with *Zamindárs* or with chieftains known locally as *Paligárs*. In 1800, however, Munro extended his field-settlements into Canara and Malabar; and, finally, in 1817, the Court of Directors issued orders for the adoption of that system wherever possible; and it fell to Munro to carry out these orders as Governor—which, it need hardly be added, he most willingly did. Unfortunately, the detailed labour involved in an efficient field-system was too great: the assessments had to be based upon imperfect information, and it appeared ultimately that this benevolently-intended scheme had the effect of confiscating a full half of the gross produce. There was no inquiry into ownership, no record of rights, no cohesion among neighbours. There being a yearly revision did not affect the rate of assessment; the best lands often remained untilled because the assessment was too high. There was no opening for saving, investment, or the application of capital; the complica-

* That it might have been discovered in most parts by due search seems probable from the fact that it certainly existed in the original Madras Jágir.

tion of details necessitated the employment of a multitude of officials, while the provision of remissions to anyone who could show grounds for non-payment made the collections precarious and difficult—an evil which, still to some extent, continues.* Still, fixation of demand was, doubtless, a boon.

The administration of justice was almost as essential to the welfare and development of the public, and it obtained the notice of Lord Moira at an early period of his incumbency. Here, as in the case of the land-revenue, we have already seen that it had been part of the original scheme to maintain existing institutions with as little disturbance as might be: in substantive criminal law the Muslim penal code was to be used with such modifications as were demanded by European sentiments, so that inhuman punishments were abolished and some minor errors rectified. Civil litigation, generally involving some question of a quasi-religious character, provision was made for deciding suits according to the Scriptural principles of the parties, expounded by a sort of sworn experts. But, as to procedure, native principles were found less easy of adoption by European administrators laying claim to a superior civilisation. As in the parallel case of revenue and tenure, divergency as to fundamentals soon appeared. The original "Patriarchs"—Munro and his school—would have all the minor disputes adjusted by *panchait*, citing the native adage —*panch men parmeshwar* ("God is with the Five"). But it was objected to by other and less enthusiastic observers, that the award of five elderly ploughmen might lack all divine elements; the administration of justice was a primal and inherent function of civilised rulers, who were not justified in transferring it to a crude and dilatory arbitration, only tolerable as an alternative

* From Mr. Cotton's report, above-quoted, it appears that the land-revenue of Madras was in balance, with a deficit of Rx. 336, 346 (or 8 per cent.), at the end of the financial year 1882-3.

to anarchy. A series of regulations based upon the recommendations of Munro was, however, issued by the local Government of Madras in 1818, some of which regulations are still in force. Especially fruitful has been the institution of what were called "Village Munsifs;" this has, indeed, in recent times been extended to other parts of India, to which it appears even more suited than to a region where the village—as an integer of administration—had been abolished, and where another machinery had been provided for the determination of petty suits. It is understood that the *panchait* is little more than an unburied corpse; but the petty village tribunals have flourished and become models for adoption elsewhere.*

In Bengal the want of summary jurisdiction had long been felt. In 1815 there were nearly 18,000 cases pending in the various classes of superior court, and the clearance of such arrears was estimated to demand the work of nearly six years. This was in the Courts presided over by European officers; but the Court of Directors, approving of the proposals from Bengal, proceeded to sanction the increased employment of native judges, who, in the three grades of *Munsif*, *Amin*, and *Sadr-Amin*, should dispose of causes in which the amount in suit was of small value. As this was the nature of most of the suits—and the superior Courts willingly cleared their files by sending down all the cases that could be tried in the Courts below—a sensible relief was soon experienced. The great drawback in this direction was the then scandalously slender scale of pay allowed to these native officers—the highest of which rates was *raised* to 100 rupees a month in 1824. When it is considered that the number of suits disposed of by their Courts was estimated at 300,000 annually, it may be imagined what a wide door was thus opened to corruption, miscarriage, and general demoralisation. In the newly-constituted territory of the Bombay Pre-

* v. Arbuthnot's "Munro," pp. 116. The village Munsif system was extended to Hindustan in 1892.

sidency, Elphinstone, the present Governor, and Chaplin who succeeded him as Commissioner in the Mahratta country, were both disciples of Munro, and warm advocates of the *panchait.* Yet it is noticeable that many of the subordinate officers there saw that the thing was but an effete relict of a happily-extinct era; one of them, indeed, was bold enough to report: 1st, that the people preferred the decision of a European; 2nd, that the duty was irksome to the arbitrators themselves; and, 3rdly, that the proceedings of these unpaid judges were not only slow, but liable to corrupt influence.*

In regard to criminal jurisprudence and procedure a strong controversy went on between the Governor-General and the home authorities. If the policy of the latter, as exerted or pressed at this period, were to be described with all possible brevity, it might be called "an attempt to extend Munroism into every part of British India." But, in this matter, as with the land in the North-West Provinces, the Governor-General and his councillors were quite unanimous in opposition. They could not be brought to see the advantage of Munro's favourite scheme for uniting in one person the duties of collector and magistrate; here, indeed, they were opposed not only to Munro, but to Metcalfe. They were, perhaps, on firmer ground when they objected to the employment of village office-bearers in matters of justice and police. The village, as a communal institution, had ceased to exist in Bengal, and any administrative duties that might be intrusted to the Zamindárs would be really discharged by their agents. The Darogas and Thánadars—native police officers—might be oppressive as the Munsifs might be corrupt; but, at all events, both alike were paid public servants, dependent for their bread upon satisfying the inspecting officials of the State. Nevertheless—so far as this principle could be observed—the

* Report of Collector of Khándes, quoted in Wilson II., 373 n.

Government was willing to reform, as was shown by regulations issued in 1815-1821, in which especial provision was made for the liberty of the person and the prevention of delay. Reg. VII. of 1822, already noticed, furnished means of conferring judicial powers on Revenue officers in the North-West Provinces.

In the matter of general Finance the administration is easily tested, and will be found to present signs of the same wisdom and watchfulness as were shown in other departments. The total revenues of the three Presidencies were left by Minto in a state of surplus valued at nearly two million pounds sterling. Lord Hastings, after two long and successful wars—during which he is said to have fought twenty-eight battles and captured 120 forts—and after making his employers supreme in the East, left the net surplus nearly three and a half millions (the account is to be seen in Wilson), as follows:—

1813-14	Rx.
Receipts	17,228,000
Disbursements	13,617,000
Interest on debt	1,537,000
Sent home	116,000
Net Surplus ...	1,958,000

1822-23	Rx.
Receipts	23,120,000
Disbursements	12,082,000
Interest on debt	1,694,000
Net Surplus ...	3,444,000

In regard to education and the press, his sentiments were as generous as his measures were just. He did not believe that the ignorance of the subject is the strength of the ruler;

but even if that were so, he would not buy immunity at such a price. "It would be treason," he wrote, "to imagine that it could ever be the principle of this Government to perpetuate ignorance in order to secure paltry and dishonest advantages over the blindness of the multitude." He was not only the founder of the Indian Empire but the founder of national Indian education. With regard to the freedom of journalism he laid down an axiom no less pregnant when he said :—"It is salutary for public authority—even when its intentions are most pure—to look to the control of public opinion." The power of banishing an obnoxious publicist, still, indeed, existed by virtue of an edict of the Company which he could not abrogate; but that power was never used under his administration.

Before concluding the story of these honourable labours it is unfortunately needful to say a few words about the sad events in which it closed. Events, let us haste to add, by which the honour of the Governor-General was unstained; but in which, nevertheless a certain facility of nature and a generous unwillingness to suspect others, of which we saw an example in the case of Audh, led to a deplorable blot on this page of British Indian history.

The territories of the Nizám—or what we may call "the Mughal Deccan"—had (as we saw) been pillaged and wasted, first by Haidar and his son, then by the Mahrattas. The present prince was not the man to restore their prosperity; with no strong quality but avarice he resided in his palace, "counting out his money" like the King in the nursery rhyme, while the business of the State was carried on by an astute Hindu named Rája Chandu Lal. The Court expenses, however great, would not of themselves have been ruinous. But there were other more serious burdens, the most grievous being a showy military force, under very highly-paid European officers. In that army had at one time been a half-caste named William Palmer, who had left the service and established himself as head of a Bank at Haidarábád; before long he was joined by an Englishman, Sir W. Rumbold, whose wife had been a ward of the Marquess of Hastings. The Bank prospered and made advances out of the funds intrusted to it on behalf of the administration of Chandu. These loans were to bear interest at 25 per cent., besides being secured on assignments of revenue-paying estates. They reached the large amount of Rx. 300,000 in one year; and, being specially licensed by the Governor-General, they assumed an appearance of a transaction sanctioned if not shared by the Government—an appearance strengthened by the connection between the Marquess and one of the partners. In 1820 the Bank notified the Resident that it was prepared to consolidate the debts at a reduced rate of interest; for which purpose a new loan of sixty lakhs (Rx. 600,000) was to be substituted. The Resident procured sanction from Calcutta for this transaction also; but it was not brought to the notice of the Government there that of the sum offered no more than fifty-two lakhs were to be credited to the State, the balance being absorbed by the Bank as a bonus.

In the last month of the year 1820 the Resident's post was assumed by Metcalfe, a man of equal acuteness and integrity. No sooner had he mastered the situation, than he laid before the Governor-General a sketch of the abuses that were going on, and a special denunciation of the sixty lakh loan. To his equal mortification and surprise he found that Rumbold had also written, stating matters from the point of view of the Bank; and all that Metcalfe got for his pains and zeal was rejection of his advice, and a semi-official reprimand. Stung personally and alarmed on public grounds for the future of his charge, he resumed the correspondence in a dignified style of remonstrance. He neither wished ill to the Bank nor to Chandu; but he had a duty to perform, to Government and to the people. The loss of his lordship's confidence was hard to bear, he could only seek comfort in the consciousness that the confidence might some-day be restored. Whilst thus addressing Lord Hastings in person, Metcalfe gave a qualified permission to Mr. John Adam, the senior Member of Council, to make use of a confidential letter in which he had already informed that gentleman that there was evidence of the collusion of officials lately employed in the Residency, and that sanctions to the loans might not have been so readily accorded, had not these officials been either sleeping-partners, or the recipients of abnormal rates of interest on their deposits. The letter was shown by Adam to the Governor-General; and Lord Hastings bowed his stately head; sent Metcalfe a letter of friendly apology; and, what was of more importance, gave his assent to Metcalfe's proposals. Money was advanced on the security of the territorial revenues of the Nizám's dominions at 6 per cent, the debt to the Bank was paid off; and in a twelvemonth W. Palmer and Co. suspended payment, and presently ceased to exist as a firm.

The censures pronounced in England led the Marquess to tender his resignation; and he laid down his office on the first day of the year 1823, being succeeded, *ad interim*, by Mr. Adam as senior Councillor.

[Kaye's "Metcalfe."; Prinsep *ubi sup*; "Land tenures of various countries," ("Cobden Club Papers," N.D.) Also "The Marquess of Hastings"; by Major Ross, of Bladensburg: a volume of the "Rulers of India" series, published in 1893.]

CHAPTER XV.

BURMA AND BHURTPORE.

Section 1: The war with Ava—Section 2: Disturbances in India—Section 3: Domestic Administration, 1823—28.

SECTION 1.—Mr. Adam, during the few months of his administration, had but to carry out the policy in which he had been so long associated. He applied a portion of the over-flowing resources of the Government to the cause of national education which Lord Hastings had so generously espoused. And he banished a recalcitrant journalist who had already received warnings, but who, presuming on the good nature of the rulers, persisted in pouring ridicule upon their proceedings in his paper. This paltry affair made a stir at the time, being represented as a measure of reaction, while it was in fact only the necessary working of machinery previously set in motion. Writers who chose to obey a few simple restrictions based on policy and good manners continued to pursue their calling as unmolested as before in the metropolis of British India; indeed it was Munro rather than Adam who was the opponent of Indian journalism; and the arguments employed by the Governor of Madras are cited by his biographer, and evince all the vigour of his powerful, if rather one-sided intelligence. The problem of reconciling a perfectly free commentary with a perfectly arbitrary Government, was not finally settled, as we shall see hereafter, till near the end of the nineteenth century. For the present we need only note that the undeserved obloquy that has been bestowed upon Mr. Adam formed the subject of a generous protest from Metcalfe a few years later. In the middle of the year 1835, a meeting was held in Calcutta to acknowledge the legislative removal of all special restraints on journalism, at which Metcalfe, the author of that policy, even in the elation of the moment, did not forget what was due to the misunderstood dead. "Had he (Adam) been now alive and at the head of this Government," so Metcalfe said, "he would probably have been among the fore-most to propose the abolition of those laws." And he declared in the same address, that Adam was "one of the best, purest, and most benevolent men that ever lived."

Further details will be more appropriate when we come to the brave speaker's own brief tenure of supreme power; the above quotations are all that seem requisite to place Mr. Adam's memory in its proper light. His tenure of office was professedly temporary, and the delay in the arrival of a permanent head of the Government was due to political events at home. In 1820, Mr. Canning had voluntarily exiled himself from political life owing to disagreements with the King and Cabinet. On receiving the resignation of Lord Hastings he had been offered the reversion of the Government of India, and had accepted the offer. But the continuance of exile had no charms for him; and he used so little expedition in making preparations for departure, that when the Marquess of Londonderry's unhappy decease occurred, Canning was still in England. He was ere long appointed to the vacant post of Secretary of State for Foreign Affairs, and the nomination of a Governor-General for India was still to make. The Court of Directors was at first desirous of appointing Lord William Bentinck, whose recall after the Vellore Mutiny was a natural source of remorseful regret. But the claims of Lord Amherst ultimately prevailed. He had been sent out to China as Ambassador-Extraordinary in 1816; when, although his mission had been a total failure, it was considered that he had not been to blame; and it was now arranged that he should have the Government of India by way of compensation. He accordingly took charge from Adam in August, 1823, and in less than two months had to decide on the important issue raised by an attack made by some Burmese officials upon a post belonging to his Government. This outrage proceeded from an unfounded claim to the island of Shápuri, in the district of Chitagong; it was avowedly committed under orders from the Court at Ava, and it was only the crowning event of a long course of insult on the whole of the long frontier between the two countries from Aracan to the borders of Assam and Cachár. A letter was in consequence addressed to the King of Burma, in which disavowal and reparation were demanded and due warning given that no further trespass must be attempted. At the same time a British detachment was ordered to the scene of the dispute.

About the middle of January a Burmese army arrived in the neighbourhood, and the standard of the Burmese kingdom was surreptitiously hoisted on the island, two British officers being at the same time kidnapped and sent into captivity. On the northern side, meanwhile, Burmese forces occupied posts in Assam and Manipore, while Cachár was threatened, and the alarm spread to Silhet. For many months the Court of Ava preserved a contemptuous neglect of the Governor-General's remonstrance; the kidnapped officers were indeed enlarged, but no notice was taken of the demands for redress. Accordingly in February, 1824, a British force was sent into Assam, and an ultimatum issued.

So far, all was well. The Government of India—as we may now term the Governor-General in Council—had united firmness with moderation. As it was evident that nothing but a severe lesson would teach the comity of nations to these uncivilised neighbours, the only remaining question was, how that lesson should be taught? Great difficulties at once came in view. The frontier above described was so long, and ran through so rough a country, that it was impossible to defend the whole of it, much more to make it a base of aggressive operations. There remained the alternative of an attack upon Aracan and Pegu by sea. But the Bengal army, speaking generally, was of the nature of a local militia, entitled to special allowances if sent beyond local limits—even on land—and wholly opposed to service by sea. A few corps there were, called "Volunteers," which had been raised for general service; but these would not suffice, even if all could have been sent on board and accompanied by all the European soldiers at the disposal of the Government. The only source from whence the deficiency could have been made good was the "Coast Army," as the forces at the disposal of the subordinate Presidency of Madras were denominated. Munro was still Governor there, and his well-known zeal and military efficiency left no room for doubt but that he would loyally respond to any call that might be made upon him. What, then, can be thought of the foresight or the promptitude of the Government of India when we find that—although the *casus belli* arose in the beginning of 1823—it was not until the 23rd February, 1824 that any notice was given to Munro that such a war was impending, and that he would be called upon to furnish the bulk of the forces then immediately required?

In the meantime the war had actually broken out, hostilities having been precipitated by the Burmese army, which cut up the small British detachment at Chittagong. The Bengal force was now hastily equipped, consisting only of two corps of British Infantry, two companies of Artillery, and one regiment of Bengal sepoys. But Munro did his part, and before the end of the month an army was assembled at Madras, consisting of two King's regiments and the Madras Europeans, seven native battalions, and details of artillery and pioneers. The chief command was intrusted to Major-General Sir Archibald Campbell.

A number of war-vessels conveyed the troops, attended by a flotilla of gunboats, and by the *Diana*, the first steamer ever employed in Eastern warfare. The Bengal contingent met the fleet at Port Cornwallis, in the Andamans, in April, and all proceeded to the mouths of the Irawadi, the principal fluvial avenue of Burma. The town of Rangoon was easily occupied on 11th May, and then appeared the real nature of the problem.

If it had been an error not to give Munro an earlier intimation of what was expected of him, that error had been partly retrieved by the energy of his action. The second mistake was, unhappily, irretrievable. The country was entirely deserted, yet it was found impossible to move. The south-west monsoon had set in, and the river had become an impetuous torrent, not to be overcome by sailing-ships; and the preposterous undertaking of the Calcutta Government was, for the next six months, entirely frustrated; while the men died like flies, exposed, with no proper nourishment, to the malaria of the reeking swamps of the Delta. Small forays took place, but nothing important was possible.

On the 1st December a Burmese army, under Maha Bandula, the best Native General, appeared before Rangoon: this was the same officer who had been successful against the British in Chittagong, and, on the 17th May, had actually defeated a considerable British force at Rámu, killing a number of men and officers, and taking about 250 prisoners. The task now before Bandula was more serious. Much as the British had suffered during the rainy season, they had received some reinforcements; and, with the setting in of the cold weather, and improved arrangements for victualling, the health of the troops showed a vast improvement.* Bandula was therefore not

* During the five worst months of 1824 about a third of the men had been in hospital, and the Europeans—who suffered the most—had been decimated by death.

unwelcome, and was suffered to approach as near as he pleased, until the British army—only about 3,000 strong—was completely surrounded by his stockades and pits, from which it was apparently expected that his men might fire without danger to themselves.

The action that ensued was more than a battle, and almost attained the dimensions of a campaign; the brave Burmese leader endeavouring for an entire fortnight to make the courage and numbers of his men counterbalance the inferiority of their science, skill, and armament.* At length, on the night of the 14th June, Bandula tried the effect of a conflagration. Rangoon was set on fire in several places by his incendiaries; but the flames were extinguished, by the energetic good-will of the soldiers and sailors, before any stores or ammunition had been involved. On the following morning two columns marched out against him, one of 600, and the other of 800 men. The stockades were stormed, and the main intrenchment carried with the cold steel; the enemy fled by the rear, but many were overtaken and slain by the Governor-General's bodyguard. The victory could be hardly called "decisive;" but it led to the retreat of the Burmese General; it inspirited the invaders; and it altered, permanently, the character of the war.

The Government and the European public at Calcutta were however, far from satisfied; and the plan of invading Burma by the river, which had been adopted in haste and upon insufficient information, was for a time suspended, in deference to the advice of the Commander-in-Chief, Sir E. Paget, who now recommended advancing from the landward side. Accordingly, Assam was occupied by General Richards, and two fresh

* The Burmese appear to have had abundance of firearms, small and great, although of an antiquated pattern. Havelock says the General was ridiculed for asserting that he captured 250 pieces of ordnance on the 7th, when no more than 13 were guns of any considerable calibre. But the fact of the rest being portable adds to the completeness of the defeat.

expeditions were prepared. On the northward a force of 7,000 men was sent, under Colonel Shuldham, with orders to advance through Cachár and Manipore, to Ava; but, after labouring with the obstacles of the country for about three months, Shuldham returned, without seeing an enemy, but without attaining his object, in the month of April. A second, and still larger army, left Chittagong in January, 1825, with the purpose of reaching Ava through the Province of Aracan. After three months of slow and painful marching, General Morrison, with the bulk of his force, arrived at the chief town, also called Aracan, which was taken in April, after a short struggle. Then —as at Rangoon in May, 1824—the trouble began. Surrounded by pestilential swamps, and plagued by torrents of rain, the army slowly melted away, until—towards the end of the year 1825—Lord Combermere, the new Chief of the Indian armies, withdrew the fever-smitten remainder. The Aracan fever was long remembered.

Meanwhile General Campbell found himself in a position to take advantage of the repulse of Bandula; and he began to ascend the Irawadi on the 13th February, 1825. Bassein was taken by a flank column under Major Sale, of the 13th Foot;* and, on the 1st April, the whole army began the siege of Donabew, where Bandula had taken up a strongly-defended position, from which he had repulsed an attack by General Cotton. It is impossible to say how long this siege might have endured, or with what losses ultimate success might have been bought; but during the night of the 1st April, the brave commander of the Burmese was killed by a rocket from the British batteries, and on the following day the works were carried and the disheartened defenders put to flight without much loss. The fall of Donabew broke the active strength of the enemy, and freed the people of Pegu from the oppression of the Burmese, to whom they were foreigners. The British then

* Afterwards the defender of Jalálábad.

ascended as far as Prome, which was occupied on the 27th; and here the invaders remained encamped during the rainy season. On the 17th September an armistice of one month was granted, the Court of Ava having invited negotiations for a treaty of peace. But the month expiring without any further steps being taken, except a haughty message from Ava demanding the unconditional surrender of all conquests, a further advance was deemed expedient. The armistice was broken, in the last month of the year, by the enemy, who attacked the defences of Prome with a force of 40,000 men, but met with no success. On the 26th December they opened a fresh negotiation, and a treaty was offered and accepted. But it was not ratified by the Court of Ava, and General Campbell proceeded on his way northward. On the 19th January, 1826, he came before a Burmese position at Mellon, which he captured, with a quantity of ammunition, guns, stores, etc., and resumed his advance. The Burmese made another, and as it proved, a final stand at Pagan-Myo, the ancient capital of Upper Burma, where they were once more routed, on the 9th February, 1826. The British being now arrived at Yandabu, within four days' march of Ava, the Court at last frankly surrendered, and a treaty was concluded, the captives taken by the Burmese being released, and the Provinces of Aracan and Burmese Tenassarim ceded, with the payment of the first instalment of a war-indemnity of a kror (one million of Rx.); the entire British army then evacuated the country. The total loss of life, from battle and disease, was just short of 5,000 men, in the whole war;* the money spent was 13 millions of Rx. And it need not be added that this deplorable war, which reflects credit upon no one but the brave troops engaged, has been related but briefly. It hardly forms part of the history of India; yet it was not without serious effects upon that

* Official report by General Campbell. Some writers give a much higher estimate.

history. With the exception of Madras and Bengal Proper, indeed, there was no part of India that escaped its influence. And even in Bengal itself, although the civil population and its chief men remained tranquil, yet the trials which the Government incurred by a feeble and vacillating policy led to a sinister occurrence which showed germs of great future disaster.

Lord Amherst, however, received a step in the peerage, by the title of Earl Amherst of Aracan; and, what proved in the end to be of more importance, the additional territory furnished in its perennial rice-fields, a constant and trustworthy source of food supply for the Indian community. In Assam and Cachár a still more important cultivation has arisen—that of tea; which, spreading to the Punjab on one hand and to Ceylon on the other, is now supplying more than half the consumption of the British Islands, besides furnishing largely to the markets of Australia and of Asiatic and European countries.

The occurrence referred to as disturbing the peace of Bengal was the mutiny of the 47th Bengal Native Infantry, who refused to march into Aracan with General Morrison's army in October, 1824. On the 1st November they were paraded at Barrackpore; and, on refusing to listen to the remonstrances of their officers, were treated by military execution. The artillery and British infantry first fired on the helpless mass, and when it broke in confusion, the fugitives were pursued and sabred by the Governor-General's bodyguard. The blood of these unfortunate men cried from the ground for more than thirty years.*

[The most interesting monograph of the first Burmese war is from the pen of Lieutenant H. H. Havelock, of the 13th Foot, afterwards to gain renown on a more glorious scene. Havelock

* The Court of Enquiry held on this affair found that the Sepoys had mutinied out of "despair at being compelled to march without the means of doing so."

was Assistant-Adjutant-General of Sir A. Campbell's army. His account of the three campaigns, though written in a style at once inflated and severe, is spirited and soldierly; and his description of the visit to Ava at the close of the war, paid by himself and two other officers as British Envoys, gives a striking picture of the Court of Burma as it then was, and the awe which hedged the King. (Printed at Serampore, 1828.) There is a more familiar narrative, by Captain T. B. Doveton, who served throughout the war with his regiment, the 1st Madras Europeans, which was published by Messrs. Allen, of London, in 1852. Wilson's account is (as usual) judicious and full of research.]

SECTION 2.—Lord Amherst's manifesto against the Court of Ava had, as we saw, been issued in February, 1824; and the British expedition had proceeded to Rangoon and remained there—an object of anxiety to its own Government, and of speculation to the rest of mankind—for the rest of the year.

It unfortunately happened that this was a period of unrest and reaction in most parts of India. The country was full of disbanded officers and men whose occupations were gone, and who looked anxiously for other openings. The police was without organisation; the administration of justice was in an imperfect and unpopular condition: the settlement of the land-revenue was in a crude and almost unworkable state. In the Madras country, indeed, the energy of Munro had produced a kind of torpid acquiescence; and Bengal was free from disturbing influences. But elsewhere, and wherever a Native Court existed, there was chafing, and plans of outbreak were silently shaping themselves. Local disturbances were the premonitory symptoms: from the Cis-Sutlej to the Upper Duáb of the Jumna and Ganges troops had to be called out for the restoration of order. A Pindári recrudescence appeared in Málwa, and a person calling himself brother to Báji Ráo—the ex-Peshwa—attempted to invade the Nágpore Province. The Bhils, too, broke out among the Sathpura hills; their insurrection, however, was put down without much trouble, and led to the gradual taming of their wild tribes, which first brought forward the remarkable talents of Outram,* afterwards distinguished in more important transactions.

But it was among the mediatised or reduced chiefs and princes that the most formidable symptoms of insubordination appeared. The Desai of Kittore, near Dharwar, overpowered a party of the Bombay native troops towards the end of 1824; killing Mr. Thackeray, the Collector of the District, with two of the officers of his escort, and carrying off his European assistants, who were imprisoned in the Fort. It was not until a force, including two European regiments and a strong body of artillery, was sent against him that the chief capitulated (on a promise of his life), and surrendered the prisoners. A similar affair followed in February, 1825, when the chief of Umrez, near Sholapore, resisted a British detachment, killing a subaltern and some sepoys; though he afterwards evacuated the place and made his escape. Farther north, the peace of the Bombay Presidency was disturbed by a serious rising in Cutch, abetted by the Amirs of Sindh. In this region there was a titular Rája; but he shared his authority with a number of kinsmen of the Rájput clan of "Jhareja," who were said to amount to the astonishing total of 200. Besides being notorious for the practice of female infanticide, these men were habitual harbourers of marauding bands; in the present instance they had, or affected, a special grievance in the supercession of Bharmal Ji, a claimant of the chiefship. After a short campaign their resistance was overpowered; and the small State of Nawánagar, in which they are now represented, is in these days peaceful, and purged of the practice of infanticide.

* It has been thought that the Bhils represent a pre-historic race, like the Kols, Santals, etc. They number about 750,000, and are gradually taking their place as low-caste Hindus, though preserving many of their old beliefs and ceremonies.

All these, however, were but petty and sporadic signs of disorder. It was in Upper India—the scene of Lake's victories—that the most serious peril awaited the British Government. In Machari * and Jaipore elements of evil had been long fermenting; and these were now exasperated by events that were developing in the famous Ját State, of which the capital was Bhurtpore.

It will be remembered how, in 1804, the then Rája—in violation of a very favourable treaty—had sided with Jaswant Ráo Holkar, and defied Lake. That daring veteran had a low opinion of the Ját chief's firmness, and attacked him with insufficient means. Lake failed to take the place; but he drove away Holkar and extorted a complete submission from the Rája, promising in return the protection of the British Government. This arrangement, made in April, 1805, worked fairly well for nearly twenty years. The failure to take Bhurtpore pleased the people of India, and flattered their chiefs with a feeling that the British were not omnipotent; but the Játs themselves owned the supremacy of their former enemy; and when the next Rája, Baldeo Sinh, felt his end approaching, he sought to secure the succession to his minor son by procuring for him a robe of investiture from the paramount power. Sir D. Ochterlony, the Governor-General's agent, obtaining the requisite authority from Calcutta, performed the ceremony 6th February, 1825; and Rája Baldeo died soon after, upon which the young successor announced his accession.† But, on 24th March, Ochterlony reported that Durjan Sál, the late chief's brother, had assumed the Regency, and that the young chief's life was in danger from his ambition: he had, therefore, he added,

* Now known—from the name of the capital—as Alwar, a Rájput principality.

† Wilson says the investiture was performed by "an assistant;" but the despatches show that Ochterlony visited Bhurtpore for the purpose on his way from Jaipore to Delhi.

reminded the Court and Chiefs of their allegiance, and called upon them to obey the Rája. He still hoped that Durjan Sál would abandon any project he might have entertained of claiming the succession, and content himself with ruling as Regent as long as his nephew wasa minor. Ochterlony further announced that, the better to make clear his views, he had conveyed a distinct statement of them to Durjan, and had enforced his words by calling out an imposing force of British troops from the neighbouring cantonments, under Major-General Reynell. Negotiations were thereupon begun by the usurper, who—in the course of the month of April—offered to come to Delhi on a safe-conduct and to bring his young nephew with him.

So far Ochterlony seemed to be succeeding. His prompt measures alarmed the usurper; who may have sincerely trusted that, with the Resident's support, he might obtain from the Calcutta Government an acknowledgment of his Regency, leaving the future to take care of itself. But both Durjan and Ochterlony reckoned without Lord Amherst, whose intentions are shown only too clearly in a private letter addressed to Metcalfe by Mr. Secretary Swinton on 10th April, 1825. The Government had resolved, so Metcalfe was informed, on "making some arrangement by which Sir D. Ochterlony should retire from active employment." And Metcalfe was invited to come round from Haidarábád and resume the duties of Resident at Delhi. Already, a week earlier, a reprimand had been sent to Ochterlony: the British Government had, it was allowed, been willing to gratify the deceased Rája by recognising his son and heir-apparent and future successor, but the question remained to be considered as one of political expediency—Sir David ought to have awaited the instructions of Government before taking any steps to enforce the succession: and he was now directed to "remand to their cantonments" all the troops that he had called out, to invite explanations from Durjan Sál, but to abstain from any measure likely to commit the Government to hostilities. This mandate was followed on the 15th by a further rebuke, in which his action was condemned as "precipitate and unjustifiable."

This was the "arrangement" mentioned in Swinton's letter to Metcalfe, and it produced the desired result. The old man thought that his fifty years of glorious service had entitled him to more confidence and greater courtesy. As he said, in writing to Metcalfe, he "felt himself abandoned and dishonoured;" but he did not care to enter into controversy with superior authority, or to express his "opinion of what he thought evident . . . on a comparison of letters, one authorising, the other denying the investiture." He accordingly sent in his resignation and retired to the neighbouring cantonment of Meerut, where he died in less than three months.*

Metcalfe soon avenged his old preceptor. Arriving at Calcutta in the end of August, he devoted himself at once to the study of the Bhurtpore case; and, ere long, presented to the Government a memorandum in which he declared himself in favour of vigorous action. Even if the succession were not held to be completely guaranteed, his opinion would still be that the British Government was, on every other ground, absolutely bound to interfere. Upon this Lord Amherst at once declared that his view of the subject was "materially altered." The Council presently acquiesced: and Metcalfe set off for Delhi, empowered to act upon his own judgment. On the 25th November, having proved the insincerity of Durjan by adequate offers of accommodation, Metcalfe issued a sort of manifesto, which so tersely expresses the situation that it might be taken

* Ochterlony was buried at Meerut, where his tomb is still to be seen: a monument was erected to his memory by public subscription on the *Maidan* of Calcutta. His name lives in native tradition under the strange form of "Loni-Attah," of which the literal sense is "Butter and meal," a *naif* testimony to the abundance supposed to have been bestowed on the land by his administration.

as a complete summary of the case against the usurper, who never intended to do anything less than raise the standard of resistance and supersede the rightful heir.

The late Rája's only son, Metcalfe pointed out, had succeeded his father in pursuance of his recognition as heir by the "Representative of the British Government." Durjan Sál had subsequently assumed the power, rank, and title of the principality, and the interference of the British "became necessary for the protection of the lawful Rája." Durjan Sál was therefore called on to surrender the usurped position to his nephew and to leave the territory, on a provision to be made for him. Durjan, influenced by fanatics and interested advisers, declined the invitation. They probably argued that the action of the Government earlier in the year showed that the British were afraid of renewing the enterprise of Lake and of meeting with the same want of success; and it was the opinion of Malcolm and other well-informed persons that the affair was being scanned with a malevolent interest all over India; that failure to reduce Bhurtpore would precipitate many elements of mischief; and that such failure was eagerly anticipated by many who deemed the whole strength of the Government absorbed in Burma, and insufficient even there.

If such were the calculations of ill-wishers they were soon disturbed. During the preliminary waverings General Paget had retired; the new Commander-in-Chief of the Indian armies —Lord Combermere—was a determined and distinguished veteran, who had led Wellesley's cavalry in the Peninsula, and turned the day at Salamanca by a grand charge of horse.

This experienced officer was resolved to avoid, in so important an undertaking, any danger that might be expected from insuficiency of means. In the former siege Lake had only eleven weak regiments of Infantry, the relics of a severe campaign, with six iron battering guns and eight brass mortars, of small calibre: the gunners were so few that men had to be taken from the field-pieces to work in the batteries; the engineer establishment had consisted of three junior officers with three companies of pioneers; and, although Lake afterwards received reinforcements, they were neutralised by the need of simultaneous operations against the armies of Holkar and Amir Khán, who sought to raise the siege. Very different was the force that was now collected. The Agra division, under Major-General Jasper Nicolls, comprised three brigades of infantry, four regiments of cavalry, two troops of horse-artillery, and a proportion of field-guns. From Muttra came a second army, under Major-General T. Reynell, of similar strength. The siege-train included sixteen twenty-four pounder guns, twelve eight-inch howitzers, and sixty mortars from eight to thirteen inches calibre; and in all consisted of no less than 112 guns of position in addition to fifty other guns; Brigadier Anbury commanded the engineer park, with three hundred and fifty sappers. Such was the power which, in the very crisis of the Burmese war, the British Government was able to marshal for the chastisement of Kunwar Durjan Sál.

That rash usuper, by emulating the enterprise of Raghoba in the last century, had furnished an opportunity of which, as we have seen, the Government was in much need. Jaipore and Alwar were ready to rise; Sindhia was fretting under the meshes that Lord Hastings had thrown over him; the unrest of the Mahratta country had already displayed ominous signs; "we might," says a writer of the time, "have looked in vain for one friendly independent neighbour disposed to succour or even to forbear." The usurper had conciliated or coerced all the local nobles; disbanded soldiers from all quarters had flocked to his standard; the strength of the garrison was reckoned at 20,000 stout warriors; of the armament there can be no doubt, for 132 serviceable guns were found when the place was taken, including several twenty-four pounders and thirty-two pounders, with one sixty-eight pounder; they had besides 300 smaller wall-pieces. But the great difficulty arose from the nature of the place to be attacked. The fortifications of Bhurtpore consisted of two parts, the town and the citadel, all surrounded by dense woods, and girt by a deep fosse or moat. There were two distinct lines of fortification, those of the town—nearly eight miles about—of great height and thickness, constructed of earth and almost impossible to breach by ordinary methods. On the north-west side of the citadel a castle erected on raised ground had formerly abutted on the town-wall; and it was here that Lake's unsuccessful attempts had been made. Since then the defences had been reconstructed on that side, and the castle was now completely isolated. To the north of the place was an extensive piece of water from which the moat could be filled, and it was this which had presented Lake with his most effective obstacle, being twenty yards in depth and fifty broad.

On the 10th December, 1825, the Muttra force, arriving in the neighbourhood of this lake, took possession of the dam just as the enemy's men were beginning to cut it for the purpose of sending water into the moat. A struggle took place, but the Játs were driven off by Mr. Wm. Fraser, of the Bengal Civil Service, with a party of Colonel Skinner's Irregular Horse in which corps he held the rank of Major. The result of this timely action was not only to leave the moat dry but to prevent a general inundation by which the troops would have been annoyed and impeded to an incalculable extent. The Agra division soon after arrived on the south.

Combermere's next step was to draw a cordon of his cavalry and field-artillery round the town; this he proceeded to reconnoitre with the engineer officers one of whom was severely wounded on the occasion. On the 13th and 14th the train arrived, and a letter was sent to Durjan informing him that, before the bombardment began, he would be permitted an interval of twenty-four hours in which to send the women and children to a place of safety; the bold usurper took no heed of the courtesy.

Having determined that the most suitable point of attack would be the north-east angle of the town, the British Commander took up his quarters in a garden and house about a mile distant, on that side, named after the late Rája, Baldeo Sinh. From this point the siege-works began on the 23rd December, and from that day to the 10th of the following month, the construction of the batteries went on in spite of the fire of the enemy. On the 27th December, this fire was particularly annoying, being directed by a deserter named Herbert, who laid one gun with so much accuracy as to kill a table-servant of Lord Combermere's as he was waiting upon his master.*

By the 2nd of January, the breaching batteries had twenty-five guns and sixty mortars playing on the doomed bastions; but still the breaches could not be pronounced practicable: instead of the curtains opening and the sides of the bastions forming accessible slopes, a mere alteration in the contours appeared, and the engineer officers refused to take the responsiblity of declaring an assault feasible. It was therefore determined to await the result of a sap that was to be taken under the bottom of the ditch and the revetments. On the 8th January, Durjan sent in an offer of accomodation to which Metcalfe, as Political Agent, replied that nothing short of unconditional surrender could now be received. That night a serious explosion took place in front of Baldeo Sinh's garden, where 20,000 lbs of powder were destroyed by a well-directed shot from the town, while a sortie, under cover of a very heavy fire, sought in vain to profit by the accident. There were now two main branches in the north-east angle, as shown in the diagram (4 and 5) but

* This was an extraordinary case, Herbert was an artilleryman who had served at Waterloo, and bore an excellent character: when the storm of the place was accomplished he was caught and hanged.

the engineers persuaded Lord Combermere to delay assaulting them until the great mine should be fired.

On the 17th January, 1826, all final preparations had been made. The great mine had been run under the cavalier (3) and charged with 10,000 lbs. of powder: and the cavalry and horse-artillery posted all round the walls, at distances varying from two to three miles to watch and cut off parties of the enemy who should endeavour to break out and escape. General Reynell had charge of the right breach, the left being alloted to General Nicolls; minor parties were told off to scale on the right of each. About 8-30 a.m., on the 18th, the great mine was fired; the detonation was appalling, the whole north-east bastion mounting into the air with about 400 of its defenders.* Two British Brigadiers and two other officers, who had pushed forward, were thrown down and disabled, one being severely hurt; the storming-party, however, mounted the breach, where they lost another leader. Meanwhile the lateral scalers had executed their respective tasks, and for the next few minutes there was a hand-to-hand conflict upon the top of the ramparts. The left column (General Nicolls) had a still harder struggle. No sooner had the foremost files gained the crest than they encountered a most serious check, the enemy having turned their guns to sweep the ramparts they were almost all killed, the leader, General E. Edwards, being among the slain. But the regimental officers pushed forward, the rear ranks closely followed, one by one the enemy's guns were captured, and the south-east bastion was presently crowned by the troops. Then descending, they forced the "Agra-Gate," and admitted the reserve, under General Adams; in this operation a great slaughter of the enemy took place. Adams then proceeded to clear the streets; and in less than an hour the town was fully occupied and all the gates were

* A lady who was at Agra at the time once assured the author that the shock was felt at that place, a distance of 35 miles.

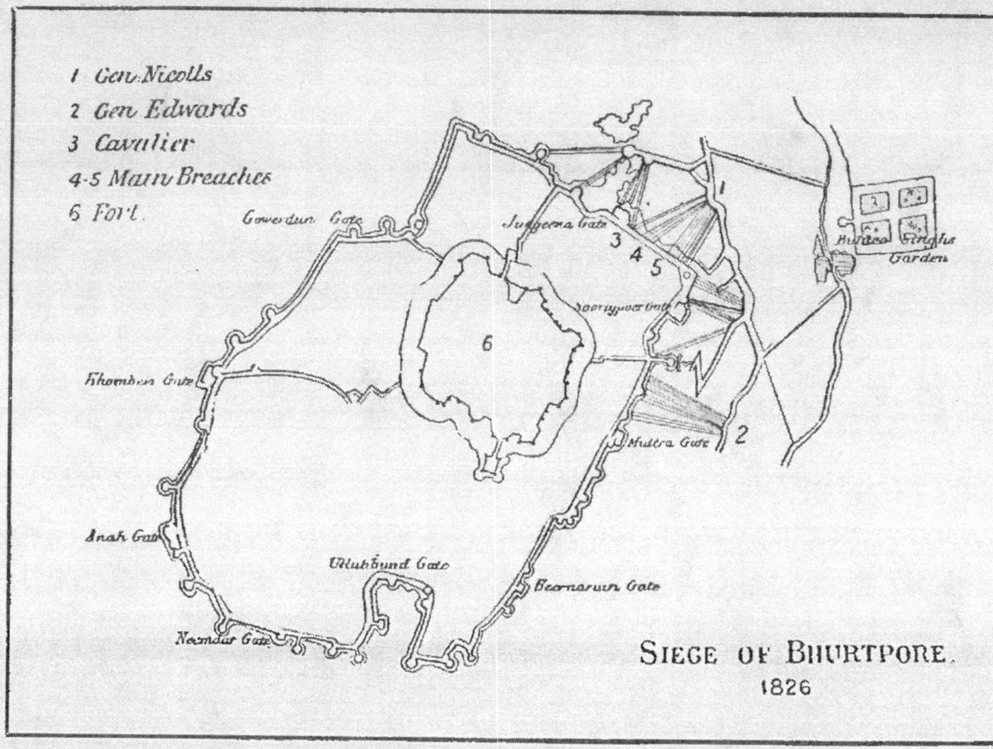

SIEGE OF BHURTPORE.
1826

secured. Before the troops was still the inner castle, about 100 ft. high, surrounded by a wet ditch, and armed with guns which continued to fire for some time.

This defence, however, proved to be no more than a temporary delay intended to cover the escape of Durjan Sál. About noon the baffled usurper succeeded in breaking through the picket set at the "Kumbher Gate," on the western face of the town, along with his family, and an escort of horse about 100 strong. As soon as the party was observed it was pursued by a troop of the 8th Bengal Cavalry, and, being overtaken, surrendered without resistance. The man whose ill-considered enterprise had caused the war was sent a prisoner-of-state into British territory. The victims of his temerity amounted to about 14,000, killed and wounded, among his own followers; the British loss was 103 killed and 849 wounded.

At 4 p.m. a white flag was hoisted on the citadel; and the siege of Bhurtpore was at an end. The other strong places of the principality were at once surrendered, and the Commander-in-Chief, having left a party to complete the destruction of the defences, proceeded towards Alwar in order to support the negotiations that were pending with that State. Before proceeding, however, to take a brief notice of that affair a word may be added in explanation of the importance which has always been attached by Anglo-Indians to the operations at Bhurtpore. They were not of very long duration; nor, indeed, beyond bringing a vast amount of prize money to the army,* was this war of one month against a petty Ját State attended by any very conspicuous direct result. Yet the credit of the British Government, perhaps its whole future fortune in India, depended on a rapid and unquestionable success. It was the belief of all contemporaneous observers that the duration and, to some extent, disastrous nature of the Burmese war had

* Lord Combermere's share of the prize alone amounted to about £50,000.

been the primary cause of the defiance of the Government by Durjan Sál; and that another failure, or even a long delay, in the reduction of a place that had once baffled the British arms might have proved a "beacon blazing forth a call to universal opposition."

As it was, the news of Lord Combermere's victory dispelled all intended hostility. The Rája of Alwar had offended by attempting to shield the author of a murderqus assault upon Ahmad Baksh, a Muslim nobleman, who had been his predecessor's guardian: he had also supplanted his precedessor himself and put him in confinement. When Ochterlony remonstrated he had refused redress and begun to strengthen the fortifications of his capital. But on the fall of Bhurtpore he lost his courage; he gave up the assassin, and set at liberty his deposed kinsman, for whom he was compelled to make provision by a grant of land.

Bhurtpore has ever since willingly adopted the position of a protected State. Nearly two thousand square miles in area, it has a population of about three hundred and eighty per mile, eighty-two per cent. being Hindus. It is well administered, fertile and prosperous; with a good number of schools and infirmaries, a mint for local coinage, and an army of 10,000 horse and foot.

A similar successful result has followed the action in Alwar. The deposed Rája ruled over his little territory as long as he lived: at his death it reverted to the principality, which has continued to prosper to the present day. If, therefore, the conduct of the British rulers of Hindustan appears to have savoured of the high-handed, we must at least admit that it has been greatly justified by its fruits. The picturesque elements, the mediæval practices, of barbarous States may appeal to the imagination more loudly than sanitation and schooling. But the ordinary tests of human welfare can hardly be applied to any community with more confidence than to the populations

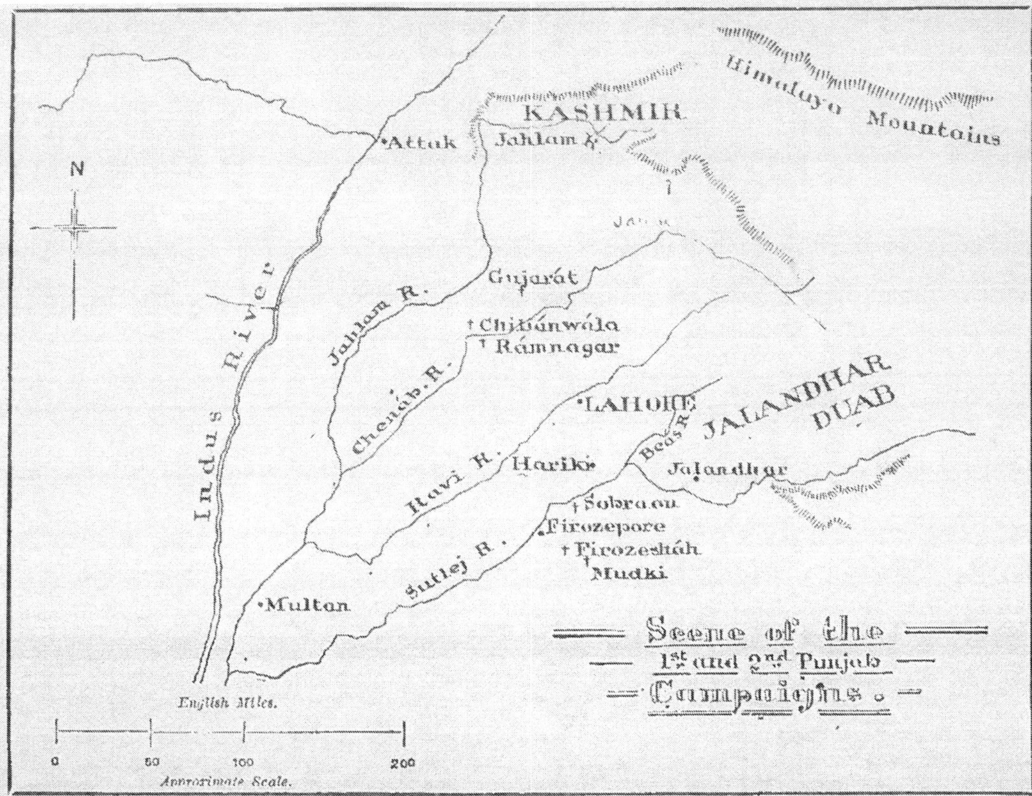

Scene of the 1st and 2nd Punjab Campaigns.

of such States as they exist in modern India: enjoying the peace and order of civilisation with much of the content and cheerfulness which civilised communities do not always find.

[For a spirited account of the siege of Bhurtpore by an eye-witness see "Narrative of Siege, etc.," by J. N. Creighton.

The political discussions and decisions are quoted from an unpublished record in the Indian Office. Other facts may be found in Kaye's "Metcalfe."]

SECTION 3.—The warlike undertakings of Lord Amherst did not leave him either funds or leisure for much civil administration until the end of the summer of 1826. Setting out from Calcutta in August, the Governor-General marched slowly towards Cawnpore, where he halted to receive the chiefs of Bundelkhand and Audh. The titular King of the latter province was Ghází-ud-din Haidar, the same ruler that had received so much kindness from Lord Hastings; an easy, timid man, but possessed of considerable intelligence. He was now approaching the end of his life; but he waited upon Amherst in November, and was soon after honoured with a return visit. He appears to have made the best of his opportunities: ascribing the unfavourable reports of his administration to ill-will and ignorance on the part of the officials who had made them; pointing to the great extent of cultivation to be seen throughout the country, and to the recent loans that he had been able to make to the Company's Government. Lord Amherst—who does not seem to have been a difficult man to persuade—acquiesced in this reasoning: and Ghází-ud-din was allowed to end his days free from foreign interference.

In January, 1827 the Governor-General reached Agra, where he held a durbar, attended by the Central India chiefs, and by Agents or Envoys, from Sindia at Gwalior, and Holkar at Indore. Holkar was still a minor, and had lately lost, by death, the services of Tantia Jóg, the able minister who had served and saved the State after the days of trouble that ended at

H 2

Mahidpore. But the post of Agent to the Governor-General being in the competent hands of Mr. Gerald Wellesley, and the minority being almost at an end, the death of the Minister was the less felt. As for Daulat Ráo Sindia, that chief was in declining health, and the affairs of the Gwalior Ráj were much influenced by his favourite wife and her brother, Rája Hindu Ráo. The lady—known to a former generation of Anglo-Indians as the Baiza Bai *— was daughter of Sherji Ráo, the obnoxious Minister whose dismissal had been one of the conditions of the pacification with Lake; and her brother lived to a period close to the revolt of '57, when his house upon the ridge was a well-known post during the siege of Delhi. A man of pleasant appearance and frank manners, he became a favourite with the British officers of the time from Bentinck to Dalhousie: and there must be many still living who have met him, at dinner or at tiger-hunts. Such was the man who now attended Amherst's *levée* to secure the favour of Government for the Bai, his sister. For in consequence of family reasons Daulat Ráo was unwilling to adopt an heir, and desired that this power of adoption with the Regency at large, should devolve, after his decease, upon the Baiza Bai. Nothing positive was concluded at the time. Among other visitors at Agra was the youthful Rája of Bhurtpore, duly grateful—we will hope—for the wild, but favouring tempest to which he owed his independence. Progressing to Delhi the Governor-General there received the chiefs of the Rajput States, and also overcome the obstacles which had prevented his predecessor from visiting the fallen Emperor—or "King of Delhi"—whom we have already noticed under the august title of Akbar Sháh.

What Lord Amherst did next was to take a step of which neither himself nor anyone else could have perceived the

* v. "Up the Country": Letters of the Hon. Emily Eden, sister to Lord Auckland, in whose company the lively lady travelled; meeting, among others, the Baiza Bai.

importance: he resolved to pass the hot season at Simla. This pleasant neighbourhood—the Engadine of India—is not far from Malaun, and the scene of Ochterlony's successes against Amar Sinh, the Gurkha, in 1815. Four years after that war a log-hut, erected by Lieutenant Ross, the Political Officer for the Hill States, was the beginning of the settlement: it is now the summer resort of the Viceroy, the Commander-in-Chief, and the Heads of Departments: the population in the season is over 14,000 souls, and the revenue of the town-council is equivalent to nearly twenty thousand pounds a year. Since the day when Amherst paid the place his first gubernatorial visit, Simla has been more and more tending to become the administrativecentre of British India.

While the Governor-General was thus setting an example for this new departure, several distinguished men were passing altogether from the Indian scene, while others were undertaking new parts. Daulat Ráo Sindia expired at Gwalior, 22nd March, 1827, prematurely aged, before his fiftieth year. With his last words he placed the question of succession unreservedly in the hands of the British Resident who attended his bedside; and, in pursuance of what was represented to be his Highness's wishes, the Baiza Bai was—without much solicitation—persuaded to refrain from *Sati*; while a young and remote relation was adopted by her, and was placed upon the seat of authority, 18th June, 1827. At the end of July, a greater than Sindia was taken; the earnest and energetic Munro, the Governor of Madras. He was on tour in the Bellary district, and had reached Pattikonda, when cholera broke out in his camp: Munro was attacked in the morning of the 6th July, and died the same evening, after a service of over forty-seven years. His Council issued a loyal and appropriate Minute on receiving the news; a statue was erected in his honour at Madras, and works of public usefulness commemorated his death and his burial on the respective sites of each. Malcolm had gone to

Europe by this time; where he busied himself in the Court of Proprietors, and became noted as a candidate for the Governorship of Bombay, about to be vacated by his friend Mountstuart Elphinstone. Among other changes was the death of Ahmad Bakhsh Khán, the ex-Minister of Alwar, which was the occasion of the Rája's pardon and restoration to darbár-honours. Ghází-ud-din Haidar, of Audh, also died in 1827, and was succeeded by his son, Sulaiman Jáh, who assumed the title of Nazir-ud-din, whose accession may be regarded as the beginning of the end which came thirty years later. Bred in a scene of unbounded self-indulgence, the new King plunged at once into the lowest company—European and Asiatic alike—in which he could find flattery for his folly and encouragement in his vice. For a notion of the manners of the Court of Lucknow the reader may be referred to a book published in London many years ago, but still worth attention.*

In the month of October, the Governor-General returned to Calcutta and turned his attention to measures that had been for some time in preparation for the improvement of the administration of justice. Ever since the publication of the Fifth Report of the Committee of the Commons in 1812, constant attention had been drawn to this subject; and in February, 1827, the Government of India—dealing especially with the case of Bengal—had addressed the Home Government an answer to several despatches issued by the Court of Directors during the interval.

Lord Amherst and his Council were strongly opposed to a portion of the arrangements recommended to them by the Directors. The influence of Munro was still strong in the India House; and one of his fixed principles had been—as may be recollected—the employment of native agency in civil justice, especially in the form of village Munsifs and Panchaits. Upon

* "Private Life of an Eastern King," by W. Knighton, LLD. The narrative is said to be derived from the information of an eye-witness.

this Amherst's Government observed that the extension of Native agency, in a regular and official form, was undoubtedly desirable, and was indeed under preparation: but that all the authorities whom they had consulted were of one mind in objecting to the other parts of the proposal. Whatever advantages might attend the employment of village courts in the territories subject to the Madras Presidency, there was no hope in North India of benefit from introduction of that system; nor indeed was there any in Bengal. It was at the same time announced that a Chief Court of supervision and cassation—such as already existed in Calcutta—would be erected at some central place in the North-West Provinces.*

As to the holders of the land and the revenue to be derived from them, Regulations had been passed since 1814: and—in the parts not under the Permanent assessment—investigations into titles and records of rights were still pending. Nevertheless it was by this time becoming clear that Regulation VII. of 1822 was an engine too delicate and minute for the work expected of it; and the enquiries to which it led were only considered to yield matter for quinquennial settlements.

The administration of Criminal Justice in Bengal was in a like experimental condition. The most seasonable reform of the period—that which had the best success at the time and has endured the most efficiently and permanently—was the extending of the summary jurisdiction of the magistrature. The principle—now so strongly insisted upon in every part—of uniting the control of criminal and fiscal administration in the same hands was still denounced, mainly on the ground that the "Collector" had too much revenue-work to leave him leisure for the functions of chief-magistrate. At the same time

* This Court went by the awkward title of "Sudder-Dewany and Sudder-Nizámat Adálat": there was one for each Province, but they have long since been everywhere amalgamated with the Crown Courts, as will be seen hereafter.

some extension of civil jurisdiction was attempted at Madras; with a somewhat premature introduction of the Jury-system in criminal trials. But these measures of reform were interrupted by the death of Munro; and his successor, Mr. S. R. Lushington,—though an experienced official—had not much time for innovation, and was, besides, fully occupied with retrenchment.

While Munro was spending his last days in endeavours to reform the judicial administration of his Province, Elphinstone was closing his generally successful period of service in a painful controversy with the Supreme Court of Bombay. That Court had been erected in 1823, on the model of the Crown Court in Calcutta; being intended for the like functions; namely, the trial of cases arising within the limits of the Presidency town and its dependencies, and also those in which European British subjects were concerned. Almost from the first the relations of the new tribunal towards the executive Government were such as to present a sinister reflection of the conflict between Impey and the Council at Fort William of some forty years before.

The Chief Justice, Sir E. West, was a man of ability; but he had an exaggerated idea of the power and importance of his Court. Elphinstone was conspicuous for serenity of temper, breadth of view, and wise circumspection. After a few preliminary attempts to identify the Governor and Council with alleged infractions on the liberty of the Press—which Elphinstone defeated by a Minute calmly recapitulating the facts—the Supreme Court entered on new and more important matter. A question had arisen, in the course of the war with Báji Ráo in 1818, as to the disposal of some public treasure with which the commandant of one of the Peshwa's forts had made away. The man was compelled to disgorge; but at his death it was found that he had made over to a Bombay Banker a claim against the Company based upon this transaction. The Banker prosecuting this claim in the Supreme Court, the Chief Justice indulged his feelings of hostility by showing on the Bench a strong anti-Governmental animus. Elphinstone's conscientious, though non-contentious, mind led him to fear that the result of this case might be to lead to many suits in which the whole of the Deccan-settlement might be exposed to hostile scrutiny. "In all new settlements," he observed in his candid, moderate, way, "there must be many faults . . . and here in particular there must be plenty . . . because we were ordered to make the experiment of a Government in the Native way, free from the technicalities of our laws and regulations." He did not, however, by any means, intend to plead guilty, nor indeed to plead at all if he could help it; being honestly of opinion that, as Commissioner of the Deccan during and immediately after the war, he had been carrying out a policy of State never intended to be tested or tried by any law but that of public safety. But his demurrers were overruled; and his Secretary was served with a subpœna to bring before the Court all the records of Government in connection with the war. Fortified by the opinion of the Advocate-General, Elphinstone offered to supply all papers relevant to the case, but if others were demanded he proposed that the Secretary should suffer himself to be imprisoned for contempt, so that the matter might be referred for the disposal of the Home authorities. This bold course succeeded so far that the demand of the Supreme Court was stopped for the time.* Chief Justice West soon afterwards died; but the embers of dispute remained, to blaze up more fiercely under a new Governor.

In the second half of the year 1826 Elphinstone tendered his resignation; the disputes with the Court had annoyed and wearied him; and his generous schemes for the education and employment of natives had met with but little encouragement

* The Court, indeed, ultimately decreed against the Government for a large sum of money; but the judgment was afterwards reversed by the Privy Council.

from the Government at home. He had completed his Code of Regulations in which a rational procedure and a humane system of punishment were introduced; a recognition of the *panchait* being made for the disposal of civil suits in the original design as introduced in the Deccan. This latter provision, however, did not find a permanent place in the Bombay Code.

He felt that his work was done. But there was one part of the task that he had originally undertaken which—though not given to him to carry out—was to be undertaken and ultimately completed by the enthusiasm of an admiring community. When it became known that he was about to retire a subscription was raised—chiefly among the Native public—to preserve his name by associating it with a College to be established at Bombay for the teaching of literature and science both in English and in the vernacular languages. This, he said, was dearer to him than a thousand statues; the foundation was formally announced to him in a warm address from "the native princes, chiefs, and inhabitants of Bombay, its dependencies, and allied territories": and on 1st November, 1827, he made over charge to Sir John Malcolm.

The great quadrilateral of Anglo-Indian statesmanship was now broken up. Munro was dead; Metcalfe was in Council, awaiting one final step on the Eastern ladder before turning to fresh fields of labour; Malcolm was beginning his last stage; Elphinstone, still on the threshold of middle-age, was retiring for ever. There must have been in the circumstances attending the foundation of the British Empire, some special influence to produce such a group of great competitors, closely followed, too, by a number of others whose names are less famous, yet whose abilities and services would have been remarkable on a less remote and unobserved scene. There have been great Anglo-Indians since those days; but their work was made the easier for them because they were preceded by Barry Close, Richard Jenkins, Ochterlony, and Holt

Mackenzie, the galaxy that shone about the brilliant fourfold constellation.

It was perhaps fortunate for Lord Amherst that he derived such a source of strength from the inheritance of his predecessors. Wellesley, Minto, and Hastings, all had helped to form or to bring forward the great men of that great day; and these were enough—with the help of Campbell and Combermere—to tide their chief over most of his difficulties. One thing, however, they could not do for him: they could not supply the lack of financial ability at head-quarters. The war in Burma had been conducted on a scale of almost unwatched expenditure; and loans of nineteen millions of Rx. (conventional £) had been required up to the middle of the year 1826. For the year 1827 the budget still showed a deficit of more than one million. The administration of Lord Amherst finally added over ten millions to the debt of British India, and even somewhat diminished the amount of the annual revenue while adding three millions to the yearly charges.

Amid these embarrassments his Excellency retired, in February, 1828, without awaiting the arrival of a successor. Mr. Butterworth Bayley, as Senior Member of Council, assumed temporary charge of the Government. He held office until July, and these six months were occupied in various useful labours by which the way was prepared for subsequent reforms. One of the most important steps of that period was the enactment of a Regulation (III. of 1828) appointing Special Commissioners of Appeal in disputes regarding the right to *Máfi*, or freehold tenures: the origin of which disputes may be stated in a very few words. The great bulk of the public revenue of those days came—as we have already seen--from the net produce of the soil, which was collected for the State subject to deductions allowed to the *málguzárs* * for the trouble of management, or

* *Málguzár* ("contributory") was a term merely indicating the person n direct relation for the payment of the revenue from an estate assessed to the Government due.

in recognition of proprietary right; and the assigning of this margin to a certain recorded person or set of persons formed the basis of a "settlement." When, therefore, an Indian land-owner asserted a freehold tenure, he was claiming the right to appropriate the whole of the net produce instead of only retaining the settlement margin: and in the infancy of British power it had been held that such a claim ought generally to be admitted unless the Revenue officers could establish its invalidity in a court of law. As the process of assimilation went on, the eyes of the rulers of British India were necessarily drawn to the injury inflicted upon the general contributories by such alienations of the land-revenue; as also to the defective nature of many of the titles on which such alienations were claimed. Summary enquiries tended to suggest that many of these Máfidárs—as the Freeholders were called—had no written titles of validity; and had, perhaps, only assumed the right of witholding the State dues on corrupt indulgence from local officials. They were often, therefore, really little better than smugglers, and smugglers on a very serious scale: and it was neither just not expedient that the revenue officers should be left in the position of having to prove a negative every time they attempted to recover the dues of the State. On the other hand, when new legislation had reversed the *onus probandi*, and thrown the burden of proof on those who asserted a right to hold land without payment, it was found that there was the danger of an undue bias, in the adverse direction, from the zeal of the revenue officers, now become judges in causes where the revenue was at stake. To counteract any such danger the Regulation under reference was passed. It gave power to the Commissioners to hear appeals from the orders of Collectors on alleged freehold titles; but this probably caused discontent among more than the directly interested parties: for the loss of income, however improperly acquired in the first instance, must alarm the loser's neighbours almost as much as it annoys the loser himself. These feelings found expression amongst Anglo-Indians of what was known as "the Calcutta (or Cornwallis) school"; the ablest exponent of which was, perhaps, H. St. G. Tucker. But the ultimate general result was to convince most people that legislative action was a welcome relief to holders of good and valid titles, at the same time that it guarded the interests of the contributory body at large.

In point of fact, nothing but the most inveterate prejudice can conceal from later generations the immense superiority of the "Mufassilite," or provincial, class of officials to those of their colleagues who never left the Presidency towns. Nothing is more remarkable than the scorn with which Metcalfe mentions the Bengal system of land-revenue whenever he comes across it in his memoirs and minutes.* Metcalfe's love for the village system was nothing new, nor was it confined to himself, Munro being the only one of the mighty four who did not approve of it for universal adoption, and he out of no love for the Bengal system, but from quite other and opposite reasons. From his earliest acquaintance with rural India, Metcalfe had derived an opinion that village settlements for long periods were the arrangements best suited to secure a revenue-demand that should be just to the State while acceptable to the Málguzárs. And the fact that, while Resident at Haidarabad, he was able to introduce that system, with success, into the Nizám's dominions certainly favours the notion that Munro could hardly have been restrained from village-settlements by purely local causes. The scene of Munro's earliest *ryotwári* work was contiguous to some of the Haidarabad territory.

After Metcalfe left the southern countries, the sinister influences he had striven so hard to weaken in those quarters soon

* "Our revenues might be improved, our civil expenses reduced. But nothing of this kind will be done as long as the caste of Bengal councillor shall remain," so writes Metcalfe in 1819. Some years later Malcolm called them the "Dowdeswells and Barlows."

revived. His successor, Mr. Martin, became as strong a supporter of the Hindu Minister, Chandu Lal, as Mr. Russell had been. The old difficulties were skilfully and imperceptibly revived; the hereditary district-officers recovered their interests, so often used with ill-effect both to the Malguzars and the State; and Martin, although he did not disturb village-settlements already conducted, yet showed himself no friend to the further extension of the system. Metcalfe had reduced the revenue-officers to their proper level; having ascertained that those who—under the general title of *Zemindár*—had charge of villages, were local agents acting under higher-grade officers—called *Talukdárs*—ostensibly in the interests of the State. Hence his object had been to keep them to that work; the villagers, he argued, would be checked by their presence, in making untenable objections to assessment; and they would form a useful supplement to the inexperience of the European settlement-officers. But that was no reason for obliterating the rights and tenures of the villagers and handing them over to these agents without protection.

Although unable to provide for the maintenance of his policy in the South, Metcalfe laid its foundations and reared its walls in that part of the Upper Provinces then called "the Delhi territory." In 1826 he recorded the results, and congratulated himself with reason on the order and prosperity that had been produced.

These and similarly important questions were now beginning to attract an intelligent interest beyond the immediate sphere to which they applied. The terrible state of the Indian finances more especially, appealed to all who were in any degree responsible. When Amherst sent home his resignation, some difficulty was at first experienced in finding a suitable successor, one who should have at once English rank and Indian experience. When at last the choice fell on Lord William Bentinck instructions were given him of which the nature may be understood from a letter which he received from Lord Ellenborough, President of the Board of Control, noted by Bentinck himself as truly sound and statesmanlike :—

"We must bring the total expenditure within the income," said the President, "and so much within the income as to be enabled to reduce the taxation. India cannot rise under the pressure of the present taxation : and to make the people of that country consumers of the manufactures of England we must first make them rich.* That object is remote indeed; but we must endeavour to attain it. . . . We have a great moral duty to discharge towards the people of India : we must, if possible, give them a good and permanent Government. In doing this," Ellenborough acutely concluded, "we confer a greater benefit upon the people of this country than if the interest of India were apparently sacrificed to theirs."

These were golden words. That the true interests of both countries were not hostile but united had been the contention of the Duke of Wellington, Sir John Malcolm, Sir Thomas Munro, and Mr. Elphinstone. "If we can manage our native army," so the last-named had written so far back as 1819, "and keep out the Russians, I see nothing to threaten the safety of our Empire—until the natives become enlightened under our tuition *and a separation becomes desirable to both parties.*"

An amicable and benevolent tutorship, in view to due wages for the present service and to ultimate emancipation, such was the generous programme of these great and good men. It was as much for the interest as for the honour of Great Britain (so they believed) that the separation, when it came about, should be a friendly parting between two civilised nations.

* This may recall the old anecdote of Impey, on landing in Calcutta for the first time, proposing to provide stockings for the bare-legged coolies. But, however easy to give such aspirations a ludicrous turn, they show more statesmanship than some other efforts of English lawyers in India.

[Consult "Metcalfe Papers," London, 1855; Kaye's "Malcolm" (Vol. II.), London, 1856; Colebrooke's "Elphinstone," corrected by Mr. Cotton's monograph in Sir W. Hunter's Oxford series. Also Dr. Knighton's "Private Life of an Eastern King" (originally published in 1855, but Messrs. Routledge have recently brought out a new edition; London and New York, N. D. Also see Wilson, Vol. III.]

CHAPTER XVI.

1828-1836.

LIBERAL BEGINNINGS.

Section 1 : Retrenchment in the three Presidencies—Section 2 : Political affairs under Lord W. Bentinck—Section 3 : Administrative reform under Lord W. Bentinck.

SECTION 1.—Lord William Cavendish Bentinck owed his appointment, partly to the friendship of Mr. Canning, who was his connection, partly to a feeling that he had been somewhat harshly treated twenty years earlier, when he was recalled from Madras in consequence of the mutiny of Vellore. Since that time he had seen military service in Spain and in Sicily, and in the latter war had held the chief command. He was a man of cold exterior, but honest and resolute, well-suited for the work of reform that lay before him. He had the full confidence and support of the Home Government.

Madras was about the same time intrusted to a new Governor, the Rt. Hon. S. R. Lushington. For many years a member of the local Civil Service, he had married a daughter of the first Lord Harris; and, on retiring to England, had been taken up by Mr. Perceval, and finally made a Secretary to the Treasury. His administration—as already mentioned—was marked by a share in the work of economic reform, and in the consequent unpopularity which such work is too likely to entail.

Sir J. Malcolm, who had been an unsuccessful competitor for Madras, was consoled by the Governorship of Bombay on Elphinstone's retirement. Although the post was considered of inferior dignity, he had hoped to find the Lieutenancy of the

Central Provinces—with which he had been so honourably connected—made a sort of personal adjunct to his charge: in this hope, however, he was disappointed; the minor charge being vested in Mr. G. Wellesley. Malcolm was well equipped, however, for the appointment to Bombay; and, in the time of trouble that awaited him there, acquitted himself so as to fulfil the warmest expectations of all who knew his noble nature. He, too, had to apply the pruning-knife to the tree of official expenditure; but his genial and buoyant character enabled him to avoid the personal animosity which annoyed the Heads of other Governments. Nevertheless, there was one enemy whom even Malcolm was unable to conciliate; and he encountered hostility from professional pedantry which left wounds of which the scars—as we are told by his biographer—never quite disappeared.* The quarrel arose from the seeds sown by Sir Edward West, the antagonist of Elphinstone: but the matter had so little ultimate bearing upon the general history of India that we must be content with a very brief summary here, referring those who desire details to Sir John Kaye. Chief Justice West died a few months before the revival of the dispute between the Court and the Government, leaving his extreme opinions and pretensions as a legacy to his brethren of the Bench. The Court attempted to issue writs beyond the limits of the City (to which, except for European British subjects, its jurisdiction was understood to be confined), Malcolm, supported by his Council and advised by the Advocate-General, ordered that the local authorities should resist the enforcement of the writs. Sir. J. P. Grant, the acting Chief Justice, declared from the Bench that the Court "knew no equal, and no superior but God and the King. The East India Company and all those who governed their possessions must be told, as they had been told ten thousand times before, that in this Court they are entitled to no more favour and prece-

* Kaye's "Malcolm," Vol. II., p. 540.

dence than the lowest suitor." This tirade was excited by a letter, in which the Governor and his Councillors had respectfully acquainted the Court with the reasons for which they had held themselves constrained to decline obedience to the writs. And Grant, carrying his indignation into private life, refused to allow his family to visit at Government House. The matter being referred home, the views and action of Malcolm were warmly approved by Lord Ellenborough; and the Privy Council gave judgment that the writs had been improperly issued, being directed to persons beyond "those limits in which the Court had a general jurisdiction," and against a person not personally subject to its jurisdiction. Thus was this important principle at last established by an authority from which there was no appeal; and the people of Bombay—as of the rest of India—were for the future spared the troubles arising out of conflicting claims on their obedience. The remainder of Malcolm's brief administration was mainly absorbed in measures of financial economy, in which productive expenditure was carefully exempted from reduction. In spite of money-pressure, the making of roads and the cultivation of cotton were pushed on; and something was done to aid and advance the opening of steam-communication with England by the "overland route." On the 10th November, 1830, Malcolm officially opened the "Great Bhore Ghat," by which—to use words of his own—the wall between the Concan and the Deccan was broken down; "the road," he truly said, "will prove a creation of revenue." On the 5th of the following month he left India, after a service of half-a-century; his successor being an Irish nobleman, the Earl of Clare.

In the meanwhile the Governor-General was earning disfavour and annoyance on the wider scene of Bengal. The instructions of his employers left him no alternative, it is true; but it was thought at the time that he might have shown a little more sympathy with the victims of retrenchment; a little less

I 2

of the suspicious watchfulness which, in his view of duty, had to be extended to subordinate officials.* The Civil Service was the first to feel the shears; a committee having been appointed to suggest the means of curtailing the expenses in that direction. The salaries of the civil officers were so extravagant that, after all savings suggested by the committee were carried into effect, the aggregate sum, divisible amongst the four hundred or so of whom that body consisted, still amounted to nearly a million of Rx.—then equivalent to pounds sterling.

The Committee which enquired into military expenditure had far less margin to work on. Some of the higher appointments were well, though not too lavishly, endowed: the pay of the regimental officers hardly sufficed for their subsistence; and the peace universally established throughout India left little prospect of increase from prize-money. There was, however, a system of extra-allowance which—under the Anglo-Indian appelation of "Batta"—had to some extent made up for the deficiences of the pay. This was an *ad valorem* grant, originated in Lord Wellesley's time, and at first intended to provide free quarters, as the officers did not reside in barracks. Orders had been repeatedly issued by the Court of Directors for the suppression of this allowance wherever house-room could be found for the officers; but Hastings and Amherst had both contrived to stave off the unpleasant duty of curtailing the incomes of their poorest but most indispensable servants. Athough the Committee had no great reductions to propose on their own account, yet Lord William had no choice but to obey the orders, again reiterated, for dealing with the Batta question: and a notification was accordingly issued, in November, 1828, to the effect that no more than half-Batta

* On his first tour up the country he asked a collector whose office he was inspecting, whether his balance-sheet always corresponded with the exact state of the cash in the Treasury? "It must," answered the official, sternly; "because you see, my Lord, I keep the key myself."

would henceforth be issued to officers quartered within 400 miles of Calcutta. This, of course, was tantamount to a reduction of the allowance by fifty per cent.; and, whatever be thought of its abstract justice, it was but natural that those affected should view with indignation so considerable a diminution of the income which they had expected on entering the service. General, though fruitless, was the remonstrance that ensued, headed by the Commander-in-Chief, Lord Combermere. The argument of the officers, that the whole result of this oppressive act only added £20,000 a year to the revenue, was met by the obvious retort that every other interest affected by retrenchment of the like amount could plead similar objections. But it was never shown that this particular addition to the resources of a great State could not have been made good without injury and annoyance to a body to whose skill and courage that State was indebted for its very existence.

Next in danger to hostility from a large and important part of the Army was anything like a wide-spread dissatisfaction among the Company's Asiatic subjects. It has been already observed that the order for investigating freehold titles had been issued by the Acting-Governor-General, Mr. Bayley, before the arrival of Bentinck; and that it had been objected to by the landed classes in Bengal, and by Mr. Tucker in the Court of Directors, of which he was now a member. But the measure was really one of justice; and its ultimate result was a permanent increment of about £300,000 a year without active opposition.

Altogether—inclusive of military establishments reduced by orders from London—arrangements were made which were expected, as they gradually came into effect, to result in a total saving of nearly two millions sterling a year.* But mere

* Rx. then equalled British sterling. By a recent reform of the currency a general rupee for India had been struck, with the head of the British Sovereign on one side. It was, at that time, worth one-tenth of the pound sterling.

diminutions of expenditure were not deemed sufficient : it was also deemed necessary to increase the receipts. The chief item of revenue was that derived from the land: which in 1829 amounted to about $\frac{11}{19.5}$, or more than half, of the total income of the State. The settlement in Bengal being fixed in perpetuity, and that of Madras subject to annual revision, no great improvement could be looked for in those Provinces; Bombay was still in the most backward and experimental condition. According to appearances, it was in the "Ceded and Conquered Provinces," now beginning to be known as the North-West, that the best results were to be expected. The results anticipated from Reg. VII. of 1822, had not indeed ensued. Partly owing to its own complexity and partly to human infirmity, few if any of the settlement officers had been able to master the elaborate rules of that enactment, or to apply them to practice; and when the Governor-General began, in 1830, to give his personal attention to the affairs of the North-West, it became apparent that—in all the preceding eight years—no substantial progress had been made.

Very important innovations were necessary to make this department less costly and more efficacious. But such details as can be given in this chapter will be found in their more appropriate place in the concluding section: whatever retrenchment may have been derived from Lord William's interposition being quite subordinate to the great improvement in speed and administrative progress. When the subject first attracted the attention of the Government no one expected that the work would be complete in much less than a generation, and many estimated a duration three times longer. By the new system the whole province under revision was, in fact, dealt with in seven years.

Another department overhauled was that of the opium revenue, one of great importance to the Indian contributory; in fact only second to the land-revenue. So much of the income of India as can be derived from the sale of opium to foreigners, is evidently so much saved from internal taxation. But the production of the drug was not—nor is it yet—confined to the poppy-fields of British India. Although inferior in marketable value to the article prepared under Government officials in Bengal, the article produced in the Native States of Málwa was—if only by reason of its relative cheapness—a formidable rival of the Government manufacture; while the expense of the various systems and establishments contrived at one time or another for bringing fiscal claims to bear on non-British opium were productive of results altogether incommensurate with the inevitable friction and expense. Before Bentinck's arrival the attention of the Government had already been drawn to this matter; and the acting Governor-General, Mr. Bayley, had issued orders for an enquiry into the means of checking frauds on the revenue caused by opium-smuggling in Western India. It was ultimately resolved to refrain from all attempts to enforce treaty obligations entailing interference within the limits of Native States; and to substitute a system of passes, such as—in substance—still remains in force. In one year the net revenue was raised to a tenfold increase.

All these measures—if we except the "Half-Batta" order (for which Bentinck was by no means to blame)—were sound, statesmanlike acts, calculated to bear more and more fruit as time went on. It has already been hinted, in preceding chapters, that this character of durability is the true criterion of extraordinary public service. It undoubtedly happened that Bentinck—like Cornwallis before him, and Hardinge at a later date—did not mark his administration by conquest to anything like the same degree as many other Governors who were not of the military profession—such as Wellesley, Ellenborough or Dalhousie. But conquest, however it may dazzle the multitude, is not the only test of a great ruler.

One of Bentinck's merits—and perhaps not one of the least

of them—was the equanimity with which he encountered the tempest of obloquy and insult to which his discharge of duty exposed him. Men whose incomes were universally affected—and this meant an indefinite prospect of prolonged exile—were not in a mood to discriminate between the man by whom the deed was actually done and those by whose injunctions he had been set in motion. Such public opinion as then existed in British India was the opinion of two-high spirited local services and that of the officers of the Royal Service, and Presidency lawyers, mostly ignorant, but sympathetic. The feelings of the natives might be of more importance; but they had no means of organisation, or even of expression in ordinary times. When therefore, the Governor General, after making the retrenchments required of him by his employers, proceeded on his way from the Presidency to visit the Upper Provinces, the Europeans at the places which he visited withheld from him the courtesies of civilised society, almost the common dues of humanity. When his barge grounded on the river-bank, no help was afforded; when he halted no one attended his receptions; the whole of the officers of a regiment that had been distinguished at Bhurtpore, to a man, refused his invitation to dinner. On this occasion, however, nature and dignity asserted themselves; for the military secretary informed the officers that the invitation was tantamount to a Royal Command, any neglect of which would expose the offenders to suspension from rank and pay, pending a reference to the Court of Directors in London—in those days a matter of a twelvemonth. The officers then submitted

The European discontent was shared by the troops. When the camp arrived at Cawnpore a review was to take place before Lord William. "It is supposed," wrote the wife of a civilian, "that he will if possible, avoid this: the soldiers are in so discontented a state that he may perchance *receive a bullet on parade.*" As the lady expressed no disrelish of the prospect, it may be perhaps concluded that she, and the class to which she belonged, would not have been displeased to be among the spectators of such an incident.

In a Calcutta newspaper of that day it was stated—amongst other imputations upon the illustrious reformer—that his arrival at Agra had been the occasion of a startling combination of parsimony and vandalism. Lord William, it was solemnly announced, had sold the inimitable "Pearl Mosque" of the Imperial Palace: the very price was minutely stated—£12,500. It was added that his Excellency was in treaty with a well-known and devout banker of Muttra, for the sale of the Taj at Agra, in order that the marble of that lovely mausoleum of a Mughal Empress might be applied to the construction of a Hindu Pagoda.

Such was "public opinion" in India two generations ago.

[The materials for this section are chiefly derived from Parliamentary papers, and from an article contributed by the author to the "Calcutta Review" in 1878. See also Wilson Vol. III.]

SECTION 2.—Like other Governors of India of the military profession, Bentinck shrank from war, and avoided adding to Empire by conquest. A few cases, nevertheless, arose in which the misconduct of native chief or tribe was such as to seem intolerable to the paramount power, and then followed the usual consequences.

The new relations with the Burmese involved the trouble which is almost certain to arise on the first official contact of barbarism with civilised government. After the first shock of conquest is over, the wild freedom of the conquered, or the suspicious fears of their immediate neighbours, may give occasion for uneasy, tentative movements which are easily, and almost by any accident, turned into open hostility. Especially is this likely to happen in parts where the success of the conquerors has been least conspicuous, and where a number of disbanded soldiers, with empty stomachs and short memories, linger on the scene.

The first trouble of this sort occurred at the extreme north-east of the newly delimitated frontier between Bengal and Burma. Here the district of Asam proper, or the valley through which the Brahmaputra flows after leaving the mountains, had been ceded to the Company by the treaty of Yandabu. But a Shan tribe—the Sing-foo—having carried away a number of Asamese as slaves, it was found necessary to send a small party against them. The expedition was successful; and the Sing-foo were driven across the Patkai range, in 1830. A more serious affair had already occurred in the Khási hills, to the south, where an attempt to make roads had alarmed the simple minds of the half-savage inhabitants. The *Siem*, or chief, of the petty state of Nong-Khlao attacked the intruders with the whole militia of the country-side, on the 4th April, 1829. Two British officers and some sepoys were massacred; and, though a punitive force was at once sent to the neighbourhood, its operations were impeded and delayed by the difficulties of the country, interspersed by mountain ranges and rushing streams. For three years the highlanders gallantly maintained the unequal struggle; in 1832, however, they consented to pay tribute, and the chief soon after surrendered on promise of his life. He was deported as a State prisoner to Bengal. The hill-country is now peaceful and prosperous, with good roads, education, and justice. The little State of Nong-Khlao is still governed by its *Siem*.

The adjoining hills of Cachar and Jaintia were, however, annexed in 1830-32; the former at the desire of the inhabitants —who dreaded falling into the hands of the Rája of Manipore —the latter by the surrender of the Rája. In Upper Asam an endeavour was made to set up a Native dynasty; but it was not successful; and that region also came under direct British management, but not until 1838. The whole together, from the Surma river to the borders of Bhutan, forms the modern Province of Asam, administered by a British Chief-Commissioner from Shillong in the Khási hills.

On the opposite side of what was then the northern frontier of British India, a powerful State had been by this time formed, under the strong hand of Ranjit Sinh, Maharája of Lahore, with whom Metcalfe had made the treaty of 1809. Since that time the Rája had pursued the calls of his ambition in a career which had no serious check. Debauched, treacherous, not even gifted by nature with the talents of a great master of war, he had yet, by patient labour and a choice of subordinates that never failed him, become head of the Sikh confederacy and ruler of the whole land of the five waters, from Multan to Kashmir, and from the northern bank of the Sutlej to the borders of Afghanistán. He paid but little attention to the civil administration of these wide dominions—exceeding in extent the whole area of the modern Empire of Germany—but he surrounded himself with good and able officials, who saw to the maintenance of order and the punctual payment of the revenues. In military affairs he was a true reformer; and the British Government had to learn, a few years later, what a machine of war could be made out of the stolid yeomen of the Punjab, "so unemotional, so ready to take the good and the evil of military service with an equal mind."* When the Maharája first emerged into power, the soldierly merits of the Sikhs were by no means conspicuous; like the Mahrattas, they had been known chiefly as feudal cavalry, following their various local chiefs with antiquated weapons and sorry steeds. But Ranjit had made them into a standing army, raised by voluntary enlistment, established on the basis of high pay; and comprising a fair artillery, besides a force of regular infantry under French and Italian officers bred in the school of the great Napoleon. Guided by the advice of his able

* Griffin: (Ranjit Singh, in "Rulers of India" series).

councillor, the Bokhariot Azizuddin, he had maintained his fidelity to his engagements with British India, and at the time of which we are speaking could offer to the Governor-General the alliance of an absolute monarch secured in his vast and various Empire by an obedient and disciplined army of 30,000 men.*

Already, in 1827, Ranjit Sinh had made overtures of friendship on the occasion of Amherst's visit to Simla; and a present of horses had been sent in return for a tent of shawls which he had offered for the acceptance of the King of Great Britain. This incident deserves notice because the horses had been forwarded to Lahore in charge of Lieut. A. Burnes, whom they thus furnished with his first introduction to Indian "politics."† It was now deemed advisable that the old alliance should be further cemented by a personal meeting between the Maharája and the head of the Indian Government. In the summer of 1831, Burnes waited on the Governor-General, who had by that time reached Simla; he reported what he had seen of Sindh and the Punjab in the course of his mission, and was despatched on a fresh journey to Afghanistán. At the same time proposals were sent to Lahore, the result of which was that arrangements were concluded for an interview, at the end of the rainy season, between Lord William and Ranjit Sinh.

The name of the able and ill-starred Burnes is of one of sinister augury. It is not indeed to be supposed that a Bombay subaltern could have suggested a complete policy to the Governor-General at that stage of India's foreign relations. Nevertheless, there is reason to believe that the condition and

* Inclusive of local levies it has been estimated at 80,000 strong; but those levies were only a sort of *landwehr*, much inferior in quality to the disciplined veterans of General Ventura. The artillery consisted, nominally, of about 376 guns; but a great part was unavailable for field-service.

† In India, "political affairs" signify diplomacy.

future of the Kábul Amirate formed a principal object in the plan of conference. Diplomatic policy was never one of Bentinck's strong points; and it is probable that the germs were now formed of that fatal system of action, the full discredit of which has been since reserved for Lord Auckland and Lord Ellenborough. We have seen that, more than ten years before, the progress of Russian arms in Central Asia had begun to cause disquiet in Anglo-Indian circles. Since then, many things had happened to foster and enhance such feelings. On the other hand, it was known that Sháh Shujá, the *de jure* claimant of the Afghán sceptre, was a refugee in the Punjab; and that he was negotiating for a restoration with the Maharája, always ready to make trouble for his Muslim neighbours. In the matter of Sindh, at least, there can be no reasonable doubt as to the nature of Burnes's advice, nor much as to its influence. The opening of the Indus to British navigation was certainly suggested by his voyage; it terminated as we shall presently see.

On 25th October the two potentates met at Rupar, on the river Sutlej, forming the border-line of their respective territories. The Sikh ruler was attended by 10,000 of his chosen horsemen and 6,000 regular infantry, many of the former in coats of mail and burnished morions; the chiefs fluttering their crests of heron's plumage and scarfs of brocaded silk, the foot being clothed in close imitation of British infantry. The escort of the Governor-General was less numerous and less showy; but it included the gigantic troopers of the body-guard, the stalwart 16th Lancers, a troop of Horse-artillery, and two *Risálas* of Skinner's famous "Yellow-Boys," or Irregular Horse; together with a regiment of the King's infantry, and two sepoy corps. No circumstance was omitted that could give life and splendour to this Field of Cloth-of-Gold. Presents of great value were exchanged; the troops on both sides were paraded and reviewed, and the horsemen of each army vied with one another in feats of skill, in which the Maharája, in spite of his years, bore a distinguished part. What were the more serious occupations of the two rulers can only be conjectured from the subsequent events. The movements of the Russians and their recent successes in Persia, we may be sure, were not forgotten, nor the threatened attack upon Herat by the son of the Persian King, assisted by the Russians; and what wonder if a scheme for providing both India and the Punjab with a friendly outpost came under discussion? With Sháh Shujá enthroned at Kábul, grateful for the past and hopeful for the future, there would be a strong barbican on the north-west, held by a trusty guardian.

While the Governor-General was thus occupied, a number of minor disturbances were occurring in various parts of India. On the western border of Bengal a sanguinary outbreak of an aboriginal population known as Kols, had occurred in Chutia Nágpore. They belonged to the races mentioned at the beginning of this book* as non-Aryan, the dregs—perhaps—of the neolithic population spread over so many countries. Like their neighbours the Santals—another race of the same kind—the Kols had held aloof from Hinduism, or only stood towards it in the light of helots. But about the end of 1839 the cup of their affliction seemed full. Their lands had been enroached upon, the Minister of the local Rája oppressed and plundered them; if they went into British territory they fell into the hands of rapacious officials, and under the shadow of mysterious law-courts: the European officials more than once interposed, and the simple savages for a while listened to their explanations. But soon the lesson was taught them, by interested instructors, that it was from the Government those officers served and represented that their troubles came. Then despair seized upon them; armed with bows-and-arrows, and with clubs, they

* Chapter I. Section 2.

wandered forth—like the "Jacques" of mediæval France—to wreak on all who were better off than themselves revenge for intolerable though unaccountable suffering. The fields of the intruding Hindus were wasted; their villages were sacked and burned; nearly one thousand of them were massacred, before any steps could be taken in defence. At length, in 1832, a force of Native troops of all arms having been assembled from the nearest cantonments, a campaign was made in which —with little loss to themselves—the sepoys slew some of the insurgents, taking others captive, and sweeping away the insurrection. Happily the trouble was not all in vain; for the Government taking a just and benevolent view of the whole case, pardoned the prisoners and redressed the grievances of the Kols. The insurrection spread to the neighbouring districts, but was found to have similar causes. Manbhum and Sinhbhum were pacified, after a short campaign; and when order had been completely restored—which was in April, 1833—the root of mischief was destroyed by a special Regulation. The action of the Courts was abolished; and the Kol country—including Chutia Nágpore, and Sambhalpore, with a population of equal numbers to that of Scotland—was made over to the benevolent despotism of a Commissioner, whose will was to stand for law. That arbitrary method is more intelligible to a backward race than a system of appeal, control, and check: and it may be inferred that the benevolence and capacity of the local despot have been well provided for by his employers, at least, the Kols have been quiet ever since.*

More serious trouble arose in other quarters. It has been already observed that Bentinck was less successful in what Anglo-Indians call "political" affairs than in some other parts

* Colonel E. F. Dalton is the best known of these Commissioners. See his book, "Descriptive Ethnology of Bengal," Calcutta, 1872; where indeed is contained almost all that is known of the Juangs, Kols, Mundas Sántals, and other Kolarian tribes.

of his administration. A certain vacillation and an occasional inconsistency were shown, especially in dealing with the older States; and this perhaps was chiefly owing to the maintenance of the "non-intervention" policy in the instructions of the Home Government. In all the States which Wellesley and Hastings had brought within the circle of British influence and protection, one or other of two classes of question was for ever arising. Theoretically independent, were the rulers of those States *in esse* or *in posse* to regulate the succession according to their pleasure; and were they at liberty to choose their own Ministers and their own methods of administration? At first sight it would appear as if both queries demanded an unchallenged affirmative: an enforced surrender of those powers was so obviously a surrender of independence. Nevertheless, the objections of the Anglo-Indian "Politicals" were not devoid of plausibility. In the position to which events have forced us, they would argue, we cannot allow misrule or usurpation: "having become the paramount power in India we are the supreme guardians of general law, tranquility and right."* These arguments convinced Amherst, although he had at first condemned Ochterlony's action in 1825. The present Governor-General was of another order of mind, and had a strong will of his own which led him to follow the orders of the Board of Control in London, rather than the advice of his agents and counsellors in India. But the results were not always happy, either for the parties intended to benefit, or for the reputation of the British in India: and it generally appeared in the end that intervention was inevitable after all.

In Rájput countries the non-intervention policy had always prevailed, since the days when old Lake differed with Barlow: and nowhere had that policy been less justified by events. The chiefs were indolent, the barons proud and quarrelsome,

* Metcalfe. See the whole matter, argued in detail, in his paper on the Bhurtpore case. Kaye's "Metcalfe Papers," p. 122.

disputed successions, caused endless disturbance, marauding and civil war were almost universal. Udaipore in particular, was for many years disturbed—as Bengal had been—by dissensions between the Hindus and non-Aryan tribes; and the assistance of the British was from time to time invoked, with negotiation or in arms. In the year 1827 positive orders from England caused the cessation of armed intervention: the troops being withdrawn, the Rána was unable to restrain the tribes, and disorder became universal. The principal trouble arose from the Bhils, a race whose gradual reclaiming under Outram has been noted above, but of whom many tribes remained in a state of lawlessness between the Vindya and the Aravalli. Before the end of 1827 the British had once more interposed, and when the aged Rána died, in the following year, order seemed restored. But no sooner were the British troops once more withdrawn than the elements of disorder immediately reappeared. Finally the British agency was entirely withdrawn in 1830, but instead of evil happening the result was most fortunate. Left to himself the Rána applied himself earnestly to his duties; and from that day Mewar has been unmolested and faithful.

More serious at one time, appeared the situation in Márwar —or Jodhpore as the State is commonly called—a half-insane ruler, named Mán Sinh, always either fighting his Barons or coerced by them, was long left to his own resources. At last a chief named Dhokal Sinh came forward as a claimant to the Ráj; and, being supported by sympathisers from neighbouring States, was enabled to collect an army of 7,000 men and march upon the capital. Lord William, being appealed to by the Rája, decided that this was "foreign invasion" and a legitimate case for interposition: but aid was only afforded on a promise that the case between the Barons and the Rája should be submitted to British arbitration. Dhokal Sinh withdrew on the orders of the Governor-General being made known to him, and a reconciliation was temporarily effected between Mán Sinh and his unruly Barons. Mán Sinh himself, however, began soon to cause trouble to the Government, and he was only brought to reason, in 1834, by the arrival in his territory of a strong force of all arms under Brigadier General Stevenson. He then executed a treaty which included submission to all demands, with compensation, indemnity, and provision for the pay of a special body of troops under British officers.

In the country of the Rája of Jaipore, between Márwar and Delhi, trouble had been brewing ever since Metcalfe succeeded Ochterlony as Governor-General's agent at Delhi, and representative of the British in Rajputána: it arose out of the opposition of two irreconcilable parties in the State; and it was the more conspicuous and annoying from the nearness of the scene. The Ráni—mother of the minor Rája—favoured a Jain financier named Jhota Rám who, in the double capacity of a plebeian and a dissenter from Hinduism, was much disliked by a section of the aristocracy headed by Ráwal Bhairi Sál. Metcalfe, on taking charge of the Agency, referred the dispute to a council of the nobles: and, on a small majority voting for the views of the Rána, Bhairi Sál was dismissed to his estates, and the banker became actual ruler of the State at about the end of Lord Amherst's administration. When Bentinck became Governor-General his arbitration was invoked, but he declined to interfere in what appeared a domestic dispute; and the consequence was that the Jaipore country was filled with disorder. In 1830 the Agency was detached from the Delhi office and transferred to the more convenient station of Ajmere; upon which occasion advantage was taken of the presence of Stevenson's force—originally collected for the coercion of Márwar—to send a strong detachment to restore the authority of the Rája in the Shaikhawáti division of his territory, in 1834. Jhota Rám's conduct on this occasion had the appearance of collusion on his part with the Shaikhawáti rebels; and when, in the beginning of 1835, the young Rája died—very suddenly—suspicion and discontent against the Jain banker became too strong to be neglected. Major Alves, the British Resident at Ajmere, proceeded to Jaipore to hold an enquiry, of which the result was the disgrace of the banker, and the return to power of Bhairi Sál. In June, 1835, a rising was organised in Jaipore city by the banker's friends; in the course of which Alves was wounded, and his assistant, Mr. Blake, murdered. Intervention of the sternest kind was now necessary: a permanent resident was accordingly stationed at Jaipore; the murderers were hanged; and the troublesome Jhota Rám and his brother were deported to British territory and imprisoned for life. Much scandal and suffering might have been prevented if the Governor-General had taken advice tendered by Metcalfe ten years before, and if the same vigour had been then shown as was at last found necessary. Since those days the State has continued peaceful, prosperous, and faithful: and the city of Jaipore is now one of the finest and best administered of Indian towns, with a population of 150,000 souls, a School of Art, hospital, college, and public garden, the streets lighted by gas, and amply provided with hydrants fed from extensive water-works.

In the neighbouring State of Gwalior dynastic disputes had followed on the death of Daulat Ráo Sindia, which ultimately led to important consequences; but all that belongs to our present period may be very briefly stated. In 1833 the Baiza Bai was compelled to lay down the Regency, and leave the country, with her brother Rája Hindu Ráo; the Government recognised the boy whom she had adopted; and the Bai retired to her private estates in the Deccan.

Such were the main fruits of "non-intervention" in the principal Hindu States. In the two great Muslim States affairs went on in a less conspicuous, though not uninstructive manner. The ultimate settlement in Audh, or rather the last before the end, was made in the early years of Bentinck's incumbency. The Province had long been the subject of discussion; the British officials asserting that it was ruined by misrule, the Natives pointing to the wide extent of cultivation and the preponderance of immigration from adjoining districts under British rule. The truth was to be found midway between those extreme statements: Audh was not a pattern of earnest energetic administration, neither was it a pandæmonium of iniquity and suffering: it was governed very much as Oriental States are generally governed; and many of the inhabitants preferred a laxity with which they were familiar. Nasir-ud-din was, doubtless, a crapulous young ruffian; yet, so long at least as he had a capable Minister, the Province was in a condition of fair prosperity. That Minister, however, fell into disgrace in 1833; and he was succeeded by a man far his inferior in ability. The civilian Resident, Mr. (afterwards Sir Herbert) Maddock—who had been a systematic depreciator of Audh administration—was, about the same time, succeeded by the resolute and yet moderate Major (afterwards General Sir J.) Low; and Bentinck contented himself with warning the "King" that the Home Government had authorised intervention—even to the extent of his Majesty's deposition, should such measures appear necessary. At the same time, however, he made of the affair an occasion for a very noble expression of opinion for the behoof of the Home Government. Acting in the specially fiduciary character imposed upon the British by all their past dealings with Audh, it was their duty, he thought, if they took the Province into their own hands, "to frame an administration entirely Native . . . The only European part of it should be the functionary by whom it should be superintended": that superintendence ought, nevertheless, to cease as soon as the incapacity of the present Prince should cease, whether by his reformation or by his death; and in the meanwhile, "the whole of the revenue should be paid into the Oude treasury." That was the utmost interference Bentinck could bring himself to deem desirable even in the case of Audh: which was a very special one, seeing that the kingdom was the creation of the British, who thought—whether rightly or wrongly—that it could not stand for a month without their support.

This just and salutary policy unhappily found no favour; and the wretched Nasir went down the rapids without any farther attempt to save him. Meanwhile the great Viceroyship of the South was equally abandoned to its own resources.* The British officials left by Metcalfe being removed, the native "Zemindars" resumed their exactions. Uncontrolled by a non-intervening Resident, Chandu Lál took to his old courses; the farming system revived—so dear to slothful rulers; "and all, save evil, slumbered in the realm." It may be noted that Metcalfe—the best and most moderate of the "political" school—recorded a Minute in 1829 in which—while admitting that the aim and ideal of the British Government in regard to this case ought to be the restoration of the Nizám's independence—was yet of opinion that the time for such restoration was still far off; and that, in the meanwhile, it was the duty of the British to maintain a check upon the Minister and to abstain—for the present, at least—from any steps tending "to withdraw our interference in the management of the Nizám's country." The writer of that Minute was at the time a member of Lord W. Bentinck's Council; but his advice was not followed; and perhaps, in the sequel, he was not sorry for the neglect. For he returned to the subject some six years later, when—for a moment—he was himself Governor-General: and the experience of those years combined, with the sense of that great responsibility, to work a considerable change in his opinions. He now confessed that interference could only be

* The Nizám was still professedly a Sovereign Prince, the "ally" not the vassal of the Company.

justified in extreme cases: and he spoke of it as an evil in itself, only to be incurred as a protection against greater evils. He affirmed himself to be now convinced by experience that "interference ought to be avoided": only if it was not avoidable it was to be exercised with decision and to the full extent requisite for the object sought. One may almost fancy that Metcalfe owed any change that may be here observed to the influence and example of Bentinck, whom—though at first repelled by coldness of manner—he had learned to respect and love. Uncertain and inconsistent as that stateman's actions sometimes appeared, he was capable of decision and even sternness on occasion. The year 1832 was marked by two considerable annexations, both in the extreme South. Mysore was sequestrated in consequence of a general insurrection caused by incorrigible misgovernment and only allayed by the presence of considerable bodies of British troops and by the inquiries and promises of British officials. The treaty of 1799* was enforced, the Rája being deposed and pensioned, while the State was left to be administered by a Commissioner with three European subordinates.† This was altogether a favourable instance of intervention: the country soon returned to peace and order; the heir was educated for his future station; the British guardianship was gradually relaxed; and after the lapse of nearly fifty years the principality, prosperous and law-abiding, was surrendered by it temporary custodians.

In the lovely highlands of Coorg, adjoining Mysore to the south-west, a somewhat different set of events led to a more permanent occupation. The Rája showed an inveterate ferocity, treating with insolent contempt all the remonstrances addressed to him by the Resident. Four columns were accordingly marched into the hills, which—after some checks—succeeded in cap-

* v. *sup.* account of overthrow of Tipu Sultan.

† Colonel Morrison was the first Commissioner, succeeded soon after by the celebrated Mark Cubbon, who held the post for nearly thirty years.

turing the chief town, Mercara. In compliance with the alleged desire of the people, Coorg was annexed, and has been a part of British India ever since.*

From this hasty record it may be seen that Metcalfe's generalities were very much of the nature of academical propositions: and what the story of Bentinck's political action seems chiefly to teach is that—however honourable an Indian ruler might be—there was a period in British progress when each case of the kind came up for separate treatment on its own merits. If any general rule at all may be thought to have been established it can only be that great care and great unselfishness were required, at such a period, in order that the paramount power should judge rightly and righteously where to interfere and where to abstain. It may be further concluded that the period under consideration has now passed away; and that all Native States within Indian limits are now "protected" and bound to render obedience in return for that protection; while States beyond those limits enjoy less protection and owe less obedience. But it is a delicate subject; and it might puzzle an expert to say on what clause of the law of nations is based the authority to coin money enjoyed by some States; to say what facts distinguish Kábul from Cashmere; or to state why there is a British Resident in Nepal but not in Bhutan?

[Books already cited, or referred to marginally.]

SECTION 3.—Whatever elements of goodwill and sound judgment may be observed in Lord W. Bentinck's foreign policy, his strong and upright character is most clearly shown in the record of his internal administration and reforms.

First, in order of time as of humanity, was the prohibition of "Suttee," or widow-burning. This word, as usually spelt, is a variation of *Sati*—"true," or "chaste": and the Hindus

* The little Province was at first administered by Lieutenant-Colonel Fraser.

applied it to a woman who cremated herself on her husband's funeral-pile. Many causes conspired to make this cruel practice general; and all attempts to abolish it had hitherto failed.* In 1829 Bentinck called for opinions as to the reasons of this failure and the way in which they could be dealt with. He found good grounds for believing that the right was no integral part of the Levitical law of the people; and he ascertained that it was not practised by the sepoys nor by the poorer classes who formed the bulk of the population. These were two strong encouragements to take a final step.† Previous Governments had so far interfered as to put the practice under magisterial control: requiring district officers to take cognisance of every case, so as to be satisfied that no poor creature was immolated against her will. Such a regulation, however, was open to the great objection that by prohibiting forcible cremation it gave an implied sanction to cremation that was voluntary; but it had one beneficial, though undesigned, consequence. By recording each case as it occurred it showed how rare the practice was among the sixty odd of millions inhabiting Bengal —where the rite was most prevalent—for it appeared that, in the year 1828, only 420 cases had occurred, and that number was not much more than half of what had been recorded ten years before. Regarding the rite, therefore, as a moribund luxury of the few, and fortified by the concurrence of the Sudder Court and all the best authorities—including many pious and influential Hindus—the Government promulgated an edict by which all who should in future take part in or abet a case of Suttee should be punishable on a charge of culpable homicide: similar edicts were at the same time issued in Madras

* The desire to avoid payment of jointure was among the causes of the the practice, which was always most prevalent in wealthy families, and—especially—among the great landowners of Bengal.

† Metcalfe had already abolished the practice in the Delhi territory when he was Resident there.

and Bombay. Little agitation followed, except that the fanatical school organised a petition to the Privy Council, by which it was unanimously rejected. The cruel practice—which was, perhaps, already dying out—disappeared under legislation with which humanity sympathised. Even in countries beyond the operation of British law the practice is condemned: the last known case of Suttee was in 1877, when the late Sir Jung Bahadur died in Nepál.

Another outrage on humanity which claimed the spurious support of religion was the practice of Thuggee (Thagi), or robbery by garrotting. A sort of caste, or guild, had arisen, during the anarchy or misgovernment of the past, having for its object the strangling of travellers. Though the ultimate end of these crimes was the acquisition of plunder, an attempt was made to give them a sacred character. The protection and aid of the goddess, Káli, was invoked at the beginning of an expedition: on the return of the robbers her shrine was enriched and decorated with a part of the proceeds. In the Native States they found harbour and immunity; sometimes the official servants of the State actually participated in the spoil that the garotters brought back from their expeditions; and where things did not go quite to that length the murderous marauders got safety from the weakness of the administration. Their practice was curiously efficient. The young people and recruits were employed as scouts, spies, or decoys; all had a slang dialect with which they maintained internal and secret communication; outwardly they conformed to social and religious observances, and counterfeited any tribal manners that suited their purpose. When they heard of any unwary company of pilgrims or other travellers they fell in with them as if by chance, affecting to be of their own caste. For days they would associate with their intended victims, disarming suspicion by pleasant conversation and friendly offices. At last they would find their opportunity. Some evening, at the end of a march, the party would be seated, in unguarded intercourse, preparing their simple meal under the trees by a well. Suddenly the past-masters of the trade would throw the lasso, each round the neck of a particular friend near whom he was sitting, and the lives of the whole party were choked out of them in a few moments. It has been said that such was their dexterity that no instance of failure was ever recorded.

The extirpation of this terrible organisation was a public service as great as the suppression of the Pindaris. Their head-quarters were known to be in the same sequestered regions, the wild country of Central India. The task was, therefore, intrusted primarily to the Agent of the Narbada Territories, with whom were associated officers of known activity and skill, provided with tents, travelling-equipage, and general warrants to override all local jurisdictions. The best known of these officers was Major (afterwards Sir William) Sleeman, whose various reports and unofficial publications are the source of nearly all our knowledge of this nefarious society. The initiatory ceremonial, the system of oaths, and the secret language, combined to surround investigation with peculiar difficulties; but by persevering and ubiquitous pursuit, by disregard of legal pedantry, and by a judicious practice of pardon for information, the society was so far broken up that two thousand of the members had been taken within five years from 1830 to 1835; and the sacred remainder driven to abandon their calling or pursue it on a vastly reduced scale.*

Bentinck did not confine his exertions to the abolition of

* A similar, though less deadly, practice is still known; that of causing stupefaction to travellers by the introduction into their food of powder made from the seeds of the thorn-apple (*Datura tatula*) and their subsequent spoliation. The drug is not intended to cause death—though it sometimes does so—and those who use it are believed to be individual thieves not enrolled in any secret confraternity.

evil; he also aimed at whatever might make Indian life more interesting and elevating. In doing so he was not innovating, but rather wisely adopting the principles of the great Anglo-Indians of whom we have already seen something. Greatly as they differed on many points, Munro, Malcolm, Mountstuart Elphinstone, and Metcalfe had always concurred in asserting that it was a positive and urgent duty to extend the opening of official careers to the natives far beyond the narrow limits imposed by Lord Cornwallis. To the generous arguments by which this doctrine had been heretofore supported were now added the twofold considerations of improving the administration of civil justice and relieving the overstrained finances; one of Cornwallis's least successful experiments had been the crection of Provincial Courts of Appeal and Circuit, and they had become nests of delay and inadequacy. It was resolved—with the entire concurrence of Metcalfe*—to sweep away the Provincial tribunals, increasing alike the numbers, pay and jurisdiction of the local Courts of first instance, and vesting the appellate jurisdiction in District-Judges controlled in their turn by officers of greater experience. Two details of this measure were afterwards reconsidered: it had been originally intended that the local Courts should always be held by Hindus or Muslims; and it was proposed that the primary control of the District-Judges should vest in the Divisional Commissioners. It was ultimately settled that the mixed population that was gradually arising—Half-caste, or "Eurasian"—should have their share in judicial employment; and it was found better to vest the control of the District-Judges exclusively in the Sudder Court at the Presidency, a second Court being constituted for the Western Provinces.

The final arrangements for the settlement of those Provinces afforded another opportunity for the employment of Native

* "Papers," p. 169. Also Council-Minute of 13 April, 1831, *ib.* p. 287, and 29 Oct., *ib.* p. 290.

civil officials on a scale of considerable extent. It has been already stated that Holt Mackenzie's arrangements—though the principle was entirely approved—were found of too intricate and dilatory operation. The new Statute, Reg. IX. of 1833, which is still the foundation of settlement-work in Upper India, was calculated to facilitate and expedite the application of Mackenzie's principles. The duty of carrying it out was intrusted to the Board of Revenue, of the North-West Provinces of which the head was Mr. Robert Mertins Bird; and although —as Metcalfe showed in a masterly Minute*—Bird was at first hasty in some of his generalisations, yet the due knowledge soon came to that earnest and able observer; by whom settlements were formed through which the revenue and the rights of the yeomanry were alike placed on a secure basis. On one point only have these operations been seriously impugned—it has been urged that Bird and the eminent disciples whom he trained, were insufficiently attentive to the interests of the Talukdárs, or holders of the rights of collection on groups of estates. If this was an error it proceeded from high considerations. As men like Bird and Thomason began to study deeply the condition of the rural classes, they found that the real proprietary interest in the land had been for ages—in very many instances—vested in the co-possessors of joint village-communes. But these had often fallen under the power of contractors or usurping landlords, who rendered no corresponding services either to the land or to the Government. Hence, official patronage of the peasantry arose with a certain tendency to ignore the landlord class, or to pension them off with annuities. This policy, extensively carried out in the North-West Provinces settlements, was to bear somewhat bitter fruit, years afterwards, when the Province of Audh came into British hands.

Nevertheless, even supposing that the Talukdars had hard

* See "Metcalfe Papers" (29 November, 1832), p. 255.

measure in the North-West Provinces, the Settlement was generally a great boon to the country, and amongst its advantages must always be reckoned the creation of a most valuable class of Native public functionaries—the Deputy-Collectors—without whose help the work could never have been accomplished.

A short explanation of the new system is all that can be here attempted, but it should be borne in mind that it extends to a country equal in area to Italy, Austria and Hungary combined, and peopled by nearly 68 millions of human beings, of whom almost all are dependent for their subsistence upon agriculture.

It used to be supposed that the State in Hindustan was entitled to so much of the gross produce of that agriculture as could be obtained; and there was, even at the time of which we are now speaking, a small division of Hindustan—in the very heart of the Company's dominions—where a resolute attempt was made to enforce that principle. The lands held by the Begam Sombre, at Sirdhana, came under examination on her death in 1836; when it was found that the Begam had been in the habit of subjecting the fields to an annual "*ryotwári* settlement," in which she took 33 per cent. more per acre than was demanded in the adjoining British villages; the tenantry were constantly emigrating; and those who remained were sometimes compelled to cultivate by armed soldiers, stationed in the fields for the purpose. To go back to an earlier date, it was a matter of record that Akbar had limited the State-demand to one-third of the gross produce, and that this limitation was regarded as a benevolent and memorable act. Mackenzie proposed to go on a similar system; to discover by actual experiment the value of the produce and the cost of production; and, after deducting the latter to divide the balance between the *Málguzár* and the State.

The reform of Mr. Bird consisting in disregarding elaborate

processes and scientific theories of rent.* The true course appeared to him to be far simpler. He substituted a rough appraisement of the actual "assets"; ascertaining the rent really paid, or, if the land were not rented, the rent paid by similar land in the same *pargana*, or fiscal union. He was then empowered, by the new Regulation, to assess the Government-demand for the next thirty years, by fixing it at a share of these rental-assets varying according to the degree of confidence felt in the appraisement and other concomitant conditions. The share to be so fixed might fluctuate between sixty-five and seventy-five per cent. We see that, if the Begam took thirty-three per cent more than the neighbouring British collector, there was ample justification for the reluctance of her Highness's ryots to pursue so unremunerative a calling. The share of the Government has now been limited to fifty per cent. of the assets, exclusive of rates for roads, schools, etc.

The weak point of the new system undoubtedly lay in the difficulty of getting at the actual rent, especially in a country where the land was mostly cultivated by yeomen paying no rent at all. That this difficulty was far from imaginary may be seen from the experience of the present day, when the progress of society must have enlarged the extent of the renting-system. Enquiries made by the Famine-Commissioners of 1879 and reported in the following year, showed that the ratio of assessments to gross produce in the North-West Provinces averaged nearly 8 per cent; so that some approach to Mackenzie's ideal had at length been found possible. But in the beginning it was not so; and how was a valuation to be made solely on the basis of the rental in a country where, according to the same authority, twenty-four per cent., of the cultivated area is still

* It may be remembered that Ricardo's theory of rent had been propounded in 1817. Like many of the so-called "laws of Political Economy" it was chiefly academical; and had little or no bearing on a country like India, where some rents were rack-rents, others customary.

in the hands of peasant proprietors themselves, and over thirty-six per cent. held by privileged tenant, only 38·5 per cent. (a little over one-third) being let to tenants-at-will and presumably charged with a real market-rental? It was not wonderful that Metcalfe should have doubted of the success of such a method. "It is not clear," he wrote, "what is meant (by the Board) to be described as land-rent, It may mean a rent received by an intermediate landlord; or it may mean that portion of the produce which is termed rent in the technical division of produce under the term 'wages of labour, profits of stock, and rent?' In either case it would be more correct to define the land-revenue of Indian Governments as consisting of a portion of the gross produce, for such is the fact." But of course to act on this would have been to return to the old delays and difficulties of 1822; and it was fortunate that Bird persuaded the Governor-General to give him his rough-and-ready way. The first settlements under his system were far from scientific accuracy, and the *pargana* rent-rates must have been little better than more or less lucky conjectures. But the rights of individuals and the customs and by-laws of communes were publicly ascertained and recorded; a tolerable field-map was put up with papers of each village; and the rental estimates and assessments were generally accepted and successfully worked.

Such is a very meagre outline of the state of the question in the days of Lord W. Bentinck, and of the way in which it was disposed of by his Government. There was no great addition to the revenue immediately possible, if indeed such had been desired, which it was not. The Government was content that the people of the Western Provinces should continue to pay no more than they and their fathers had, or ought to have, paid; but the payments were in future to be strictly limited on one side and quite punctual on the other. The total amount at the present day, shows an increase of about twenty per cent.

on that of the first thirty years' settlement; but it is all, or almost all, realised with but a trifling exercise of coercion.* The Málguzárs have the full benefit of all extensions and improvements of the cultivation pending the duration of the settlement; and are not liable to surcharge on any intermediate enhancement of the assets; only at the expiry of the thirty years can there be any increase of demand, and then it is to be strictly proportioned to the unearned increment proceeding from State improvements or the diminished value of the monetary standard.

In finance, generally, Lord William made great reforms. Profiting by a commercial crisis in Calcutta he reduced the rate of interest on Government loans; so that persons who now shrank from speculative investments were enabled to get the benefit of State-security with the not unremunerative interest of four per cent. The effect of all his economies combined was to convert a deficit into a surplus, and to provide a handsome margin for the Home-charges of the Government.

All the pains taken to improve the prospects of Native aspirants for State-employ supposed a due provision for their education. A new college was accordingly opened at Agra, and a definate solution given, both there and in the Presidency, to the important fundamental question what should be the medium of instruction; *i.e.*, should it be English or some learned language of the East? The scale was turned in the direction of English by the earnestness and eloquence of Macaulay, then a Member of the Governor-General's Council under the new Constitution given by Parliament to British India.

The Company's Charter, as was shown in treating of the events of 1813, had thrown open the monopoly of Indian trade while reserving that of China. That Charter came to an end

* In Madras the balances uncollected at the end of year run from three to four per cent. of the whole demand; besides extensive remissions. The demand appears to increase year by year.

in 1834, when the Reform Act had been passed, and a general spirit of innovation was abroad. But the Select Committees had been appointed in 1830, and much of the material of the new legislation had necessarily been collected before the Reformed House of Commons met. It was evident, at once, that the Chinese trade could no longer be preserved; but when the question of territorial Government came up the Company was able to make out a stronger case. The Ministers of the Crown found nothing in the evidence taken by the Committees to alter their disinclination to add the Government of India to their other duties; and consequently the political powers of the Company were extended for another period of twenty years. Some negotiations took place as to the guarantees of the interests of the Company under the new order of things; and it was in addressing the Court of Proprietors in support of the proposed arrangements that Sir John Malcolm got his mortal stroke. He made his last speech on the 22nd April, 1833, and died on 30th May of the same year.

Among the chief improvements introduced by the new Charter was the provision for future legislation. Up to the date each Presidency had been indebted for its laws to the fiat of the Governor-in-Council, the Governor-General, in the matter of law-making, acting solely in the capacity of Governor of Bengal and its dependencies. It was now arranged that the Governor-General should have the aid of a Legislative Council, with authority to pass Acts for the whole of British India; and from the year 1834, we hear no more of "Regulations," save as unrepealed edicts of the previous period may be referred to; and Bills are framed and passed into Acts (subject to the control of the Home-Government), by three regular stages as in the Imperial Parliament.

The better to regulate the drafting of these Bills, and with a view to codifying and otherwise improving the existing laws, a Member, especialy qualified, was to be attached, for this purpose, to the Executive Council. The first Law-Member was Mr. (afterwards Lord) Macaulay, whose influence in the Education question has been already mentioned. Under his impulse was also begun the long labour on criminal jurisprudence which, matured by Sir Barnes Peacock and supported by a rational system of Procedure, has given the *Indian Penal Code* its high and well-deserved reputation.

A further most sound and salutary reform was the erection of a separate administration for Upper India, henceforward to be known by the title of North-West Provinces, which we have already sometimes used by anticipation. Power was indeed taken in the Act, to make a fourth "Presidency" and there was a proposal to appoint Metcalfe to be the first Governor of Agra. But the reproduction of the expensive and, perhaps, effete machinery of Madras and Bombay was happily overruled; and Metcalfe was satisfied with the more modest, but not less substantial position of Lieutenant-Governor; he did not however, hold it long. Bentinck found his health failing, after seven years of constant conflict, travel, and labour. For the past 18 months he had discharged the duties of Commander-in-Chief of the Indian army, in addition to his proper duties: during his long tenure of the Governor-Generalship he had personally visited almost every part of India; he had challenged and beaten down the misconduct of chiefs, the resistance of rebels and malefactors; he had encountered the hostility and hatred of many persons, and whole classes, from whom he might have expected help and service. He felt that his work was done; and in March 1835, having set all the new machinery in motion, he made over charge of his office to Metcalfe. A statue provided by public subscription and adorned by an inscription from the pen of Macaulay attests the "veneration and gratitude" of those by whom it was erected.

[Consult the Lives and Papers already cited: also "Bentinck," by D. C. Boulger, in the "Rulers of India" series—Oxford, 1892. The article in the "Calcutta Review," for 1878, mentioned above, contains a description of the prevention of an attempt at widow-burning in 1825, near Calcutta. The woman leaped from the pile when she felt the fire; the assistants struck at her and tried to force her back: but the Europeans present rallied the police, charged the mob, and rescued the victim. It proved to be a question of property. The scandal of such encounters was a minor reason for forbidding the rite.]

CHAPTER XVII.

THE AFGHANISTAN BLUNDER.

Section 1: Shah Shujá, his friends and foes. The Lucknow succession—Section 2: Occupation of Afghanistán—Section 3: Kábul, Sindh, and Gwalior.

SECTION I.—Metcalfe, who had influenced Indian affairs as Member of Council for the past nine years, was now in possession of the supreme power, with some slight expectation of permanency. The Court of Directors resolved that it would be inexpedient to make any other arrangement at present. This was explained by Tucker to mean that they hoped to prevail on the Government to issue a substantive commission to Metcalfe. But the maxims of State were against him: it was an Anglo-Indian—Mr. Edmonstone—who had first formulated the notion that no one of his class ought ever to be Governor-General, and the doctrine was too agreeable to London politicians not to receive a ready welcome. Whatever might be thought of the merits and services of Warren Hastings and Lord Teignmouth, the Ministers of the day were unable to resist the opportunity of providing for an old supporter or banishing a troublesome friend. A show was indeed made, on the receipt of Bentinck's resignation in 1834, of tendering the post to Mountstuart Elphinstone, of whom the Duke of Wellington had a very high opinion. But the tender was insincere: Elphinstone had already assured the Chairman that he would not accept. An attempt had been made in 1829 to get Elphinstone to go back to Bombay on Malcolm's retirement.* Then he was asked to undertake a mission to Persia, but answered plainly that "nothing should ever induce him to go to Asia again." So that his rejection of Lord Ellenborough's present offer was a foregone conclusion. The post was then—according to Greville—offered to Sir James Graham, who had lately seceded from the Whigs; but, if this offer was made, it also came to nothing. Charles Grant, the President of the Board of Control, was himself a candidate; but the Court had just appointed his brother to succeed Clare at Bombay, and thought that enough had been done for the family.

In the meanwhile Metcalfe went on with his work. In great measure this consisted in carrying out projects in which he had been already engaged with Bentinck. The Minute recorded by him on 16th May, 1835, some six weeks after he received charge of the Government, is remarkable for a view of the position of the British in India, which—while somewhat differing from that expressed by the late Governor-General in respect of its dangers—yet takes in all the doctrine which the writer had always been wont to maintain and express. The late Governor-General's Minute had been put on record on 13th March; in had made somewhat light of the disaffection of which he did not deny the existence, and had endeavoured to point out that the only way of safety, either against the natives or against invasion from without, lay in improved military administration. Metcalfe hereupon undertook the task of showing; first, that the dangers were greater than was supposed; and, second, that the military reforms proposed were either uncalled-for or impossible. Wise after the event, we can now see that neither of

* "The Duke asked what I was going to do about Elphinstone. *I considered he had left India altogether*. . . . I then mentioned Clare. The Duke thought . . . he had not a very strong mind. . . . I have a great regard for him . . . but I have *a little hesitation as to his fitness*." —Ellenborough's "Diary" (*ann.* 1829). It is but fair to add that Clare did nothing to justify these misgivings.

these able statesmen was wholly right; yet there was more than a grain of truth on each side. Metcalfe's proposition turns out less paradoxical than at first appears; Bentinck's ideas have, to a considerable extent, obtained the sanction of Time, the great tester of men's plans. Nevertheless, the two summaries, whether they agree or whether they differ, are both full of instruction as showing how matters then looked, to the most responsible observers.*

Bentinck's main object had been to make much of the danger of Russian invasion, and of the steps necessary to put and maintain the Indian army into a state of normal efficiency, so as to be ready at all times to meet such an attack with the internal resources of the country. He urged that the European garrison should be at all times equal to one-third the strength of the Native army; he advised the abolition of the Bombay army, and the arguments on which he based the advice went far towards a case for abolishing the Madras army as well. Metcalfe joined issue on the general question, and demurred to some of the details also. As to internal weakness or strength, he admitted that the British rule in India was a stronger power than any one power that might assail it; but he asserted that this was not enough. So far from having any hold on the affections of the people, they would find in time of trouble that the people were universally disaffected. Some said that India was held by opinion, some that it was held by force: the fact being that the only opinion that was of any benefit was the opinion that the force was sufficient. Instances were taken from the late intestine troubles: as soon as things seemed to be going wrong in one place, revolts broke out in others. Each was put down in detail, it was true; but how if all had taken place at once?

Still worse would be the state of affairs if a whole series of such insurrections were to occur simultaneously during a Russian

* See "Metcalfe Papers," p. 191; and Boulger's "Bentinck," p. 177.

invasion. Yet such perils were not to be conjured by tinkering and tampering, by reducing the number of British officers or raising the number of British troops, still less by absorbing the armies of the minor Presidences. To us, who have seen the strength of the British garrison in India raised to more than double of Bentinck's proposed increase, while the number of white officers in a Native corps has been reduced to six or seven, and who know that the Bombay and Madras armies are no longer exclusively recruited there, such fears must needs appear groundless. But the gist of the policy was not this; and when Metcalfe went on to say that the real defence of British India against foreign invasion lay in the twofold maintenance of national strength in England and national justice in India, he attained the highest level of statesmanship, and laid down truths that are as important to-day as they were then.

One danger that Bentinck had predicted was from increased knowledge, but Metcalfe repudiated the notion. Ignorance, not knowledge, was the danger to be feared; opinion that was expressed was not formidable, but opinion that was suppressed was a volcano.

In conformity with this enlightened view, Metcalfe went much further than recording a Minute. He passed an Act. Next to the constant effect of good Government, there was nothing to which he looked for the removal of disaffection so much as the spread of knowledge and the free utterance of public feeling. "The time is passed," as he added, in the Minute above cited, "when the action of the Press could be effectually restrained—even if that course would be any source of safety."

Even though these convictions of his were to be regarded as no more than a repetition of the doctrine of Lord Hastings and an approval of the practice silently adopted by that great man's successors, they would still be remarkable, coming from one who had been in India ever since his boyhood, and had never shared in the movement of liberty in Europe. But with Metcalfe the liberation of the Press was neither an academical theme nor a matter of tacit sufferance. He determined to do all that in him lay to hedge it with the protection of positive law. One of the earliest Acts on the new Statute-book is one repealing all regulations for the special censorship or control of unpublished matter, leaving published matter to the action of the ordinary law-courts. The Act was received with enthusiasm in Calcutta; a meeting was held to do honour to the large-minded ruler—whose generous testimony to his predecessor, John Adam, has been already quoted. Only twice, during the succeeding half century, was it found necessary to interrupt this policy, and it is still in complete operation.

But the feeling of the Court of Directors was not the less unfavourable. Not only was any lingering chance of the Governor-Generalship lost for Metcalfe, but the Governorship of Agra was reduced to a lower status when it was conferred upon him.

After Elphinstone had refused the post of Governor-General, the Directors had made a nomination (January, 1835) which had been accepted by the new Tory Government, though the nominee was "totally unconnected with them in party politics" (Tucker). "My maxim," added the Chairman, "has been that India ought to be of no party." Sir Robert Peel endorsed the maxim by accepting the nomination of Lord Heytesbury, who, as Sir W. A. Court, had been a member of the unreformed House of Commons, and had been created a peer for diplomatic services. He had lately returned from an embassy to the Court of Russia, and would, in all probability, have proved a wise and capable ruler of India. But an adverse fate, and the selfishness of party, deprived him of his post after he had made all his preparations, and even attended the farewell dinner always given on such occasions by the Court of Directors. In April, 1835, fell the short-lived Conservative ministry

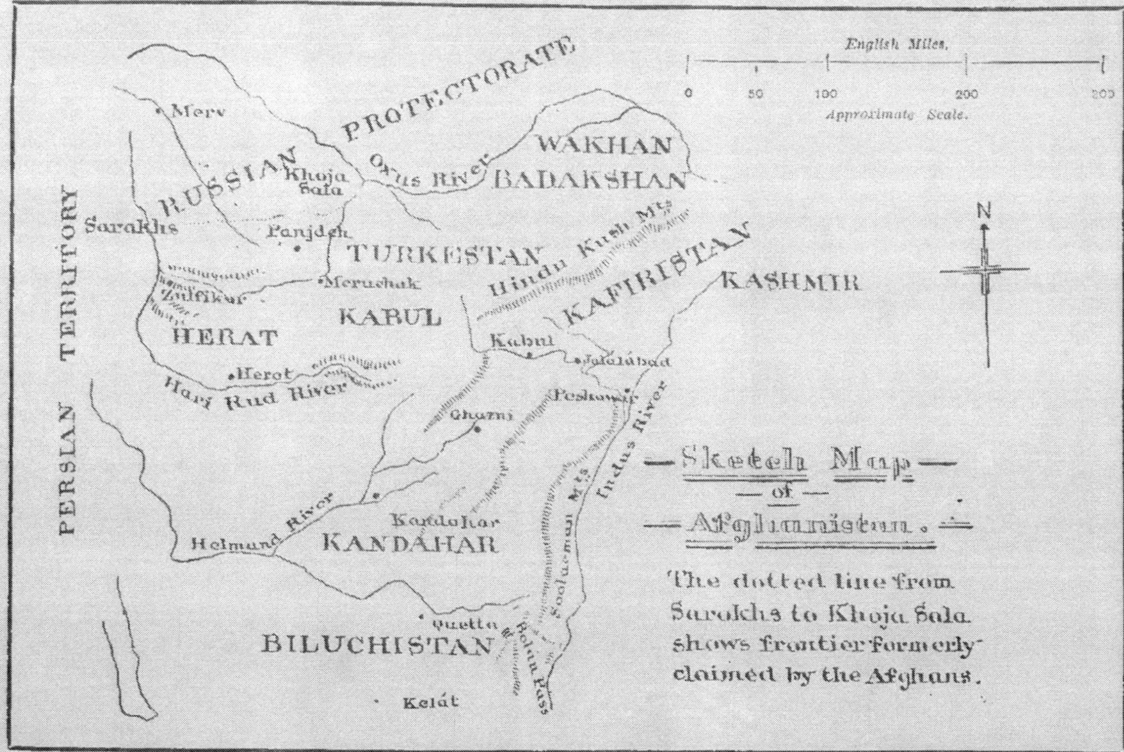

—Sketch Map—
—of—
—Afghanistan.—

The dotted line from Sarakhs to Khoja Sala shows frontier formerly claimed by the Afghans.

formed by Sir R. Peel at the desire of King William IV., and Lord Melbourne's Government lost no time in cancelling the appointment and nominating Lord Auckland, in spite of an earnest protest of the Directors. The nomination proved the Nemesis of party-interposition; but the penalty fell, not upon the offenders, but upon the innocent inhabitants of British India.*

George Eden was thirty years of age when he succeeded to the peerage which had been conferred on his able and distinguished father. Since then he had been one of the small body of reforming members of the House of Lords, and had held one or two subordinate offices, rising to First Lord of the Admiralty a few months before the *coup d'état* of 1834. When his friends returned to power, he was at first put back into the Admiralty, but apparently preferred the more showy part of politics; and the supersession of the unoffending Heytesbury seemed the best escape from difficulty. A moderate and well-meaning man, Auckland left England with the best intentions, assuring the Directors that he "looked with exultation at the opportunity of doing good to his fellow-creatures."

He took charge on 20th March, 1836, leaving to Metcalfe the option of retiring altogether or of accepting Agra shorn of its status as a Presidency. Metcalfe patriotically chose the latter alternative, hoping to be recompensed by the Governorship of Madras upon the approaching departure of Sir Frederic Adam, the Governor. But it was at once declared at the India-House that his recent action in regard to the press had cancelled all his claims to consideration. Metcalfe on this tendered his resignation, and he soon after left India for ever. He found, however, in other and still higher employment the means of usefulness and honour which were denied

* Grant went to the Colonial Office, being replaced at the India Board by Sir John Hobhouse, a man of ability but wanting in discretion, who had once been imprisoned for breach of privilege.

him by those whom he had served so ably for nearly forty years.*

It has been well observed by Sir J. Kaye that Metcalfe left India at a conjuncture when his services were more needed than they had ever been before. Ever since 1830 his pen had been employed in recording warnings against measures which could hardly fail in compromising the British Government in war beyond the Indus. In 1833, after the meeting of Bentinck and Ranjit, the exiled Sháh Shujá had departed on a futile attempt at restoration, and the Government of India had begun to form plans for posting a mission, under Burnes, at the Court of Kábul. Metcalfe at once repeated his former warning. A commercial agent would, necessarily and at once, tend to become a political agent, he said; and to the extension of political relations beyond the Indus he perceived enormous objections, It would be an interference in the political affairs of Afghanistán, attended with far more danger and difficulty than any such interference in the Native Courts of India.

But the warnings were unheeded. In 1834 Sháh Shujá had returned, utterly defeated, from his endeavour to overthrow the power of Dost Muhamad, the *de facto* ruler of Kábul. In the following year Ranjit took possession of Peshâwar which henceforth became a province of Punjab. At the same time the Daurâni chief who held Herát was embroiling himself with the Persians, who appeared likely to invade the western frontier of Afghanistán, and Dost Muhamad, alarmed at finding himself threatened on both sides, made his first appeal for the support and friendship of the Indian Government. Lord Auckland replied by announcing that "a commercial mission" was about to proceed to Kábul; but informed the Amir at the same time that "it was not the practice of the British to inter-

* He was made Governor of Jamaica in 1839; and in 1842 became Governor-General of Canada and a peer. He retired in 1846, in which year he died, unmarried.

fere with the affairs of other independent States." In July, 1837, the Sháh of Persia set out for the siege of Herát, with 50,000 troops, and accompanied by a Russian envoy and some officers and troops of that nation. The news aroused universal excitement in British India, in the midst of which Lord Auckland took leave of his Council and set out for Simla, accompanied by his Foreign Secretary, Mr. (afterwards Sir William) Macnaghten and one or two junior civil officers of more ability than experience. At the same time the "commercial mission" appeared at Kábul, headed by Captain Burnes, who had been there and made the acquaintance of the Amir in 1833, after the mission to the Court of Lahore, which has been already mentioned in these pages.

But before entering upon this disastrous affair it will be well to turn to an item of internal politics, which came before Lord Auckland in 1837. The succession in Audh, though of less temporary prominence, was destined to even more tragic issues than that of Afghanistán.

In the early part of July, 1837, the wretched Nasir-ud-din died at Lucknow, poisoned by some of his own kindred. A stormy scene ensued. Colonel Low, the Resident, was informed about midnight of the 7-8, that the *Bádsháh Begam*, the mother of the late King, was advancing on the palace at the head of an armed force with the intention of establishing the succession of a boy named Manna Ján whom she asserted to be the deceased King's son and heir. As in the case of Vazir Ali, in 1797, the British authorities were persuaded that this youth was not the son of his putative father.* It was, therefore, intended to elevate a collateral to the protected royalty. Low, on hearing of the Begam's move, sent across the river, to the British Cantonment, for the assistance of a body of troops; and in the meantime proceeded with his

* *Sup.* Vol. I., p. 311. It is curious that a similar situation was on the eve of appearing at Lahore, as will be presently explained.

candidate to the palace. The young claimant, with his putative grandmother, took possession of the *Lál Báradari*, which was a sort of "Westminster Hall" of Lucknow; and on Low appearing about 3 a.m., addressed him from the throne with a demand for recognition and homage. The hall and its annexed apartments were filled with armed men, swords and spears clashed, blunderbuses were fired, answered by the discharge of artillery from the surrounding streets, while a bevy of nautch-girls whirled before the throne to barbaric music by the light of smoking flambeaux. Imperturáble amidst all the confusion, Low presented to the Begam his remonstrances upon the inutility of her conduct: threatened and hustled, the intrepid officer persevered in refusing to do homage to the usurper, till a friendly noble led him outside. By this time day was breaking, and by its welcome light appeared five companies of regular troops led by the Brigadier in person. Low now announced that the troops would do their duty if the hall was not cleared in a quarter of an hour; and as the infatuated lady still maintained her position there was nothing left but to open fire when the term of grace expired. After a few rounds of grape had been fired by the guns without, the order to storm the hall was given to the 35th Native Infantry, soon to be employed in more glorious service. The sepoys obeyed without hesitation, and the Begam's followers fled, leaving fifty of their party dead or wounded on the floor. The British candidate was at once produced and mounted the throne—by the title of Muhamed Ali—under a royal salute, at 10 a.m. on the 8th July. Low's proceedings were approved by the Government, but it was determined to curtail the future power of the King, On the 10th November, 1837, a treaty was offered and accepted whereby the new ruler of Audh undertook to allow the Resident all support in measures for "remedying the existing defects in the administration," on pain of sequestration and direct British management. The sequel is noteworthy. There was a feeling at home, amounting to something like conviction, that the alleged defects in Audh administration had been grossly exaggerated; and that, such as they were, British interference, so far from being an appropriate cure, was partly answerable for them, if not their chief cause. So far back as 1834 Mr. Tucker wrote to Metcalfe a letter from which the following is an extract:—

"When I visited the Province" (1807) "it seemed to be prosperous enough, though not particularly well managed by Lucknow Tehsildars whom *Baillie had introduced*; the villagers appeared comfortable . . . But when the late Mr. Scott Waring brought" [newly-cultivated] "land upon the rent-roll, and taxed it, the same high rate of assessment could not be paid; *and the province has rapidly declined*." When the Chairman of the Court of Directors, himself an experienced revenue officer, could thus openly attribute the decline of the Province and its agriculturists to mistakes of British revenue-management, we may fancy the reluctance that may have been felt in Leadenhall Street to act upon or confirm the treaty of 1837. Still more serious is the reflection that Lord Auckland did not think fit to communicate to Muhamad Ali that the treaty had been disallowed.* At the end of 1837 Auckland went from Calcutta to Audh and Delhi; being everywhere met by sad signs of the famine of which this was the second year. It was this experience that led to the preliminary surveys which ended in the great Ganges Canal, finally constructed under Hardinge and Dalhousie.

The feelings and wishes of a more important Native Court

* Aitchison's "Treaties and Sanads," Vol. II. The treaty provided that if the Province had to be taken over it would continue to be ruled on Native principles, and all surplus revenue be paid into the King's Treasury. No intimation of its disallowance having been given, the successive Kings may have thought it binding, and that this was the worst that could befal them.

than that of Lucknow were now to be treated with even less consideration than what was shown to Audh. But, before proceeding to consider the relations of the British Government towards the Amir of Kábul at the period we have now reached, it will be proper to look for a moment at the scene and personages of the impending drama.

The country now called Afghanistán is a composite region, about twice the size of the British Islands, lying between the Persian Province of Khorásan and the Punjab Provinces of British India; bounded on the south by an artificial frontier from Biluchistan, and by a similar line on the north from the Uzbeg countries now dependent on Russia. But, down to recent times, the three Provinces of which it consists had a somewhat diverse history; for while Kábul and its northern dependencies formed part of the Mughal Empire, Herát and the Hari Rud Valley belonged to Persia, while the basin of the Helmand (including Kandáhar) was a debatable land, sometimes ruled by one power sometimes the other. The general character of all parts is very similar, being determined chiefly by the great altitude at which the interior portion stands :* the principal access is by the passes made through the mountain walls by the rivers which flow to all points of the compass from the central water-shed. When Nadir Sháh, the Persian usurper, died (1747), the whole became united under Ahmad Sháh, head of the Abdáli tribe, the name of which he changed into Dauráni, by which name the tribe is still known. We have already had occasion to say something of the Abdáli in connection with the check of the Mahrattas in 1761; and we have also seen how his grandson Zamán Sháh made peace with the youthful Ranjit of Lahore in 1797, and what an influence was produced on the India of Lord Mornington's time by the hopes and fears that his name and supposed intentions were

* Ghazni, the central town, is over 7,000 feet above the sea level, and the winters are severe and long.

able to excite. Zamán Sháh being overthrown in a rebellion and deprived of his eyesight, had sought refuge in the Punjab; and Sháh Shujá—his younger brother—was reigning in his stead, when Mountstuart Elphinstone was sent in charge of a mission to the Court of Kábul. Elphinstone met Shujá in 1808, at Peshávar, and endeavoured to obtain from him a promise to hold his mountains as a barbican against invasion by a Russo-French army. While the negotiations were pending at Peshawár a revolt against the Sháh broke out under another brother, named Mahmud; the Sháh abdicated after being worsted in a brief struggle; and he joined his blind brother in exile in 1809. This revolution led to a break-up of the "Empire" of Afghanistán. The Daurání tribe was divided into Khails, or clans; the ruling clan being known as Populzai. But the Vazir and principal supporter of the new ruler was a man of another clan, the Bárukzai; his name being Fateh Khán. After some years Mahmud became tired of the Minister's preponderance and had him put to death. His brother the afterwards famous Dost Mahmud, avenged the murder, and in 1826 made himself master of Kábul. But his hold on Kandáhar was more precarious, while Herát continued under the Daurání dominion.

In 1837, Herát was ruled by Sháh Kamrán, a member of the Populzai clan, when the Persians, as above stated, undertook the siege. It was thought—and so far almost universally—that an integral part of the old Afghán country might indeed be held by a separate Afghán prince, but could not safely be exposed to foreign conquest. While, however, the Governor-General was debating on the best means of warding off the attack of the Persians—who were believed to be acting in the interest of Russia—it occurred both to Lord Auckland and to the Cabinet of London, that use might be made of the Maharája of the Punjab, with whom negotiations had been going on since the Rupar interview in Bentinck's time, and without whose permission it might be difficult to march an army to the possible seat of war. For that war was possible, nay imminent, there could hardly be any doubt. Informed of what was going on in Persia by their Envoy, Mr. (afterwards Sir John) McNeill, the British Cabinet had already addressed a remonstrance to St. Petersburgh. The Czar had sent a diplomatic answer, saying that his representative—Count Simonich—had exceeded his instructions: and the Count was ultimately recalled, though not without significant claim on the part of the Czar's Government to support Persia, and an invitation to the British to do likewise, which had a ring of irony.

The danger, thenceforth, was deemed pressing. The capture of Herát by the Persians would bring the power of their allies the Russians, into the most vulnerable part of the frontier State. Ranjit Sinh, for his part, did not wish for a strong, united Afghanistán under the able rule of his old enemy Dost Muhamud; lastly, each of these—Ranjit and Dost—wanted the Pesháwar valley. It was for the Government of India—acting on the information of Burnes—to advise the Cabinet of London as to the course to be pursued. Unhappily the advice of Burnes was constantly neutralised by Captain Wade, Agent in the Punjab, through whose hands Burnes had to send all his communications. Wade was as much in favour of Shujá as Burnes was friendly to the Dost.

It will probably never be known how much of the blame of supporting the Sháh belongs to Auckland. Up to the end of 1837 his action seems open to no censure. As the Duke of Wellington observed in the following year, it could not be said that "while the siege of Herát continued, particularly by the aid of Russian officers and troops, the Government of India could have done otherwise than prepare for its defence" (the defence of India, not Herát). But the defence of Herát was also memorable; partly due to the skill and gallantry of an

Indian officer—Lieutenant Eldred Pottinger—partly to the effect produced on the minds of the hostile leaders by a small naval demonstration. "The policy of the Persian Court," the Duke said in the same letter, "has of course been influenced by its fears of Russian invasion. . . . The invasion by the Persian Gulf was a make-weight against Russian influence, and certainly had an effect; and—if I have been rightly informed—affected the Russian Government more than anything else that could be done." *

The Persians, while engaged on the siege of Herát had not neglected the resources of diplomacy. They sent envoys to negotiate a treaty with the Bárukzai chief who held possession of Kandahár, while a Russian officer made his appearance at Kábul, bearing a letter which professed to be written by the Czar's own hand. These apparent menaces really offered a last place of penitence to the British authorities; for Burnes persuaded the chiefs of Kandahár to dismiss the Persian Envoys; while the Dost wrote to Auckland proposing to do the like to the Russian emissary, if the Government of India would promise support. Whether influenced by fear of Ranjit, or swayed by instructions from home, Auckland made a cold and unfriendly reply to the offer of the Amir, advising the Amir strongly to relinquish the idea of obtaining the Government of the Pesháwar territory. Apparently from that time the Great Design pursued its fateful course. A certain school of writers asserts that this was solely due to Lord Auckland and his advisers: on the other hand the late Sir Vincent Eyre always declared that Auckland was all along secretly adverse to the war.† And we have some confirmation of this suspicion from Mr. Tucker, who wrote to the Duke of Wellington, at the time, that:—

* Kaye's "Tucker": p. 500. Two ships from Bombay had landed some sepoys on the island of Kharak.

† "The Kábul Insurrection," by Sir V. Eyre: London, 1879. v. also final note to the present volume.

"Much has been suppressed; and, although there are strong reasons for believing that the late movements have been directed from this country, the whole responsibility would seem at present to be thrown upon the Governor-General." It is doubtless difficult to see how a subordinate officer with ordinary duty could have penetrated the secret views of the Governor-General; but the above statement was repeated in 1879—after Eyre had risen to high distinction.*

In any case we have the Blue-book of 1859, containing the full text of Burnes's letters to Auckland, and those of Auckland to the Home Government.† From these, truly, the complete story does not emerge: only two of the despatches sent out from the India House at the bidding of the Board of Control are given—much less is there any trace of correspondence with the Minister at the Court of Teheran, McNeil. But Auckland's letter to the Secret Committee (p. 273 f.f.) shows that, as late as February 1838, he was willing—if not hoping—to hear of the "adjustment by any mode acceptable to the parties of the differences," between Ranjit and the Dost, provided that the latter kept clear of the entanglements likely to "disturb the existing state of affairs in Central Asia" (par. 9). And this was written after the arrival of the Czar's letter which, says, the noble writer, "was reported to me semi-officially, by the Envoy of Her Majesty in Persia, early in the month of January." In the month of April again, he wrote another short letter, in which he said that the decision to which the Dost had come was "satisfactory." That decision had been reported by Burnes from Kábul on March 7th, and involved an assent to all that Auckland had demanded, save that the Dost begged—

* "The Kábul Insurrection," etc.

† "Papers on Cabul, etc."; Printed by order of Parliament, with omitted passages in brackets. This publication was due to a debate in the Commons. (v. Trotter's "Auckland," Note to Chap. V.)

as a salve to Afghán feelings—that the Sikh garrison should be withdrawn from Pesháwar, which should be held by an Afghán Governor, "under the orders of the Maharája" of Lahore. It only now seemed to need a firm attitude towards Ranjit to persuade him to accept the proferred compromise.

Again the veil falls; but enough can be seen to make it probable that the Dost—or his advisers, for it must be borne constantly in mind that the Dost was not an absolute monarch—began to be very nervous at the continuance of the siege of Herát, and the possibility that the Persian army might not only capture that place but come on to Kandahár. The Dost complained that the British were abandoning him and turned to the Russian envoy. Burnes then availed himself of the provisional order of recall which he had already received, and had a farewell audience of the Dost on 25th April (Bluebook p. 221).

On May 22nd, the Governor-General sent home his declaration of war; and, on 13th August, reported having devolved on Captain Wade "the duty of promising the ratification and interchange of the tripartite treaty with the Maharája and the Sháh Shooja-ool-Moolk," having for its object the restoration of the Sháh and the deposition of the Dost, who was to be offered an "honourable asylum in the Company's territories." His first letter was received at the India House, 26th October, where—strange to say—a despatch authorising a similar policy was lying ready signed, though it was not sent out until the following day.

Auckland's letters assumed the full responsibility: "of the justice of the course about to be pursued, there cannot exist a reasonable doubt. We owe it to our own safety to assist the lawful sovereign of Afghanistán to the recovery of his throne . . . . I have, in adopting this step, been deeply sensible of the responsibility which it places upon me . . . . and look with confidence for your . . . support to the plans on which, in the exercise of the discretion confided to me, I have resolved."

The lawfulness of the Sháh's sovereignty was here assumed. Personally, his claims were weak: he had been driven out of Afghanistán when young; he was now sixty, stamped with the brand of failure, and particularly unpopular on account of his haughty manners. The Dost, on the other hand, could point to many years of successful rule, though only as Amir, without exercise or claim of absolute sovereignty. The only parallel to Auckland's policy was Louis XIV. endeavouring to expel William of Orange to make room for James Stuart. Yet of this policy a Liberal English Cabinet approved warmly.

Moreover, the Dost was frank, manly, and urbane; a stout, and usually victorious warrior, apt for business and surrounded by the magnetism of an able and successful chief. It is difficult to understand on what ground anyone, excepting perhaps the ruler of the Punjab, could desire to see the former substituted for the latter, as Amir of Kábul and Kandahár.

But reasons were forthcoming, or had to be found. In a manifesto dated at Simla, 1st October, 1838, the Governor-General (still without his Council)* set forth a view of the matter which—as was observed by Tucker—might have been supposed to emanate from the Chancery of Lahore. Tucker wrote to the Duke that the Tripartite Treaty on which it was founded—was "evidently of *Native* origin . . . . but we have made some fearful additions to it for Runjeet Singh's *sole benefit*."† Several Afghán towns and provinces, on which the Maharája had lately laid hands, were guaranteed to him and his heirs; the Nawáb of Baháwalpore and the Amirs of Sindh were placed entirely at his mercy.

Before the proclamation had been issued the siege of Herát

* It has been even asserted that the Council at Calcutta—by whose assistance he was supposed to have arrived at his decision—refused to record the declaration when it was sent to them for the purpose.

† "Tucker" p. 501. Italics in the original. The Treaty is dated 26th June.

was raised, and the baffled Persians were in full retreat. The alleged object of the movement had ceased to exist; but the movement was not slackened—having in truth another motive, namely, the deposition of the Dost, and the substitution of the Sháh, by foreign force. The unfortunate Pretender was to exemplify the proverbial difficulty of maintaining a seat supported only by bayonets.

[The most accessible authority on the origin of the war is the volume of Correspondence published in 1839. Much, as Tucker said, was suppressed, and the defects are but imperfectly supplied in the Parliamentary "Papers" of twenty years later which contain, indeed, the passages previously suppressed, but with two unimportant exceptions, no despatches from the Secret Committee. It is, however, quite plain that in passing through the hands of Wade, the pleas addressed by the Dost to Burnes were constantly blunted. As Amir, or President of an ill-cemented oligarchy, the Dost was bound to conform to the feelings and wishes of the chiefs who represented the Afgháns in his Durbar. These included claims on Herát and Kandahár, as well as on Peshawar, and he was only in a position to throw himself heartily on the British alliance if the British would promise him some support in regard to all three. The MS. papers to which the present writer has, for the first time, been permitted access, show that the Secret Committee acted merely as the organ of Sir J. C. Hobhouse and Lord Palmerston, who again acted on information from McNeill at Teheran. These statesmen were of opinion that a "King" of their own making would rear a stronger barrier against the Russo-Persian menace than a loose federation under the Dost. Burnes, on the contrary, thought that it would be better to forward a strengthening of the federation under the Dost alike "for commercial and political ends."

An interesting debate (March 19, 1861) is recorded in Hansard; a motion for a Select Committee on the mutilation of the papers, was lost by a majority of 101 in a house of 208 Members.

For a good account by an eye-witness of the first campaign see "Durand's First Afghán War," 1879, (chaps. 3, 4, 5.)]

SECTION 2.—Lord Auckland has been described by a stern but able critic as "cold, cautious, and reflecting, but infirm of purpose," and the same writer, who had good sources of information, assures us that it was only by gradual means that he was brought to espouse the cause of the Pretender.* It must not be forgotten that even the prudent and non-interfering Bentinck had given some sanction, and even money-help, to Shujá's unfortunate attempt in 1834, and that the Tripartite Treaty was much based on the lines which ruled the Treaty concluded on that occasion between the Ranjit and the Sháh. The official who negotiated the more recent instrument was Mr. (afterwards Sir William) Macnaghten, who had formerly been distinguished as a scholar and jurist, but had entered the diplomatic department in the time of Lord W. Bentinck, and was now appointed Agent with the Sháh.

The plan originally contemplated was in fact a mere reproduction of that of 1834. The Sháh was to renew his attack on the Bárukzai republic with co-operation from the Punjab, ceding to that power all claims upon Peshávar and Kashmir. But Burnes, on his way back from Kábul, meeting Macnaghten at Lahore, convinced him that such an attempt would fare no better than the first, and then the scheme was enlarged so as to admit the presence of a few British corps, to give stability to the movement. But here the military authorities were necessarily taken into council, and the Commander-in-Chief, Sir Henry Fane, without expressing political opinions, at once declared that if British troops were to be sent, they must be in sufficient numbers to take care of themselves; thus the wise and the foolish conspired to ensure disaster, and the Governor-

* Durand, pp. 43, 67.

General, unwilling to recede from his plans, and still under the fear of Russian aggression, was led to make more extensive combinations. A column was now ordered to move from Bombay upon Sindh, and four others, from various parts of Hindustan, were directed to converge upon Firozpore, on the southern bank of the Sutlej, and proceed thence through Baháwalpore to Sindh. The news of the retreat of the Persian army from Herát—though it did not cause the abandonment of the design—led to a diminution of the "Bengal" force, as it was called; and Fane—who had already made arrangements for resigning his command—made over the charge of that portion of the expedition to Sir Willoughby Cotton. Fane proceeded with a flotilla down the Indus bound for Europe; but the army, moving by land in the same direction, continued for some time to have the benefit of his advice and support. The proclamation, of which mention has been already made, had declared that these forces were only intended to "support His Majesty the Sháh against foreign interference and factious opposition," and that they would be withdrawn so soon as the independence and integrity of Afghanistán had been established.

Sindh was chosen as the route of advance, partly in deference to the feelings of Ranjit who appeared unwilling to allow his allies to march through the Punjab.* It consisted ultimately of 9,500 fighting men, besides a separate force, raised for the Sháh's service: this was 6,000 strong, commanded by British Officers, and it attended the person of the Sháh, accompanied by Macnaghten, a man personally courageous, who had been for a short time in the Madras army before he entered the civil service.

* An intelligent staff-officer of the day, afterwards to acquire glory as a General, thought it might have been sent *viâ* Dehra Ismail Khan and through the Gomal Pass; but Durand points out objections, apart from the jealousy of the Maharája which might no doubt have been overruled. (Havelock, Vol. I., p. 65).

These two bodies marched down the left bank of the Sutlej, crossed the Baháwalpore territory—where they received helpful treatment—and arrived near Rohri, on the left bank of the Indus, towards the end of January, 1839. In the meantime Sir John Keane—who was to command in chief on Fane's final departure—was threatening Haidarábád, the chief town of Lower Sindh, and awaiting the arrival of reinforcements from Bombay.

Sindh was at that time under a confederation, much like Afghanistán, only that all the Amirs were of one clan: the northern part of the Province was under Rustam Khán, of Khairpore, the southern—or lower—part being ruled by some of his kinsfolk of whom Nur Muhamad was chief. By the direction of the Government, Burnes—who now held the substantive post of Agent with the Khán of Kelát (the leading chief of Biluchistan)—negotiated with the Khairpore Amir, while the dealings with the Amirs at Haidarábád were in the hands of Colonel H. Pottinger, the accredited Resident in Sindh. The latter had a difficult task, unwilling as were the southern Amirs to aid the Sháh or own his supremacy. The Khairpore chief proving more amenable, Cotton obtained the cession of the island-fort of Bakkar, and began to march down the Indus with the view of co-operating with Keane in the South: but the demonstration sufficed; the Haidarábád Amirs submitted, and Cotton returned to Rohri and resumed his preparations for crossing the river. This operation, in fact, had already been commenced as regards the artillery-park: and by the 18th February the whole army had crossed without accident.

These matters were only preliminary to the war; but they have to be taken into account for they show the initial difficulties of the Great Design, at the same time that they prepare us to understand what we shall find taking place in Sindh only a few years later. By the treaty then existing the Indus had been neutralised, a special clause authorising the navigation being guarded, by provision against the use upon those waters of any vessel carrying troops or munitions of war. The possession of Shikarpore was, by the same instrument, guaranteed to the Amirs; and nothing was said of the payment of tribute to Afghanistán. Now, however—on no ground but that of the convenience of the strongest—a demand for money was made on the basis of a claim to arrears of an obsolete tribute; a merit was made and credit taken out of the non-retention of Shikarpore; the place believed to command the possession of the whole land—Bakkar—was seized; the valley was filled with armed men and virtually made a British Province. The sequel will soon appear.

When Cotton and his force had crossed the Indus they marched forward towards the Bolán Pass; reaching Dádar on 11th March, whence the engineers were sent forward to improve the road. The Bombay column, under Keane, followed, arriving at Dádar, 5th April: and Cotton was ordered to halt at Quetta, and there await the orders of the Commander-in-Chief. The forces experienced all sorts of difficulty and hardship: the country was an almost unbroken desert; the tribesmen of the surrounding hills drove off their camels, plundered their convoys, and killed their foragers. On arriving at Quetta, Cotton found that no depôt of supplies had been formed: and in obedience to Keane's orders, his force was kept there, on half-rations, for eleven days, idly consuming the scanty provisions that remained, while the strength of the horses diminished, and the non-combatants starved. Keane, however, arrived to assume the command on 6th April; and immediately decided on an advance. After crossing the Khojak chain the forces would find themselves on a much lower level than that of Quetta: the heat was intense by day, while the country proved deficient in wood, water, forage and provisions. On the 13th April, the Pass having been sufficiently smoothed, the troops began to descend, though complete advance was not found feasible until the 20th. The Bárukzai chiefs then slowly retired; and, virtually unmolested except by the marauding mountaineers, Keane reached Kandahár on 26th April, where he was joined a few days later by the reserve of Bombay troops under General Willshire. The Sháh was still behind; but he presently arrived at Kandahár, and was duly enthroned on 8th May. The advance of the army, however, was long delayed by the need of rest for the animals, and the supply of provisions; the time was occupied by Macnaghten and Burnes in political operations with the rulers of Kelát and Herát; and in endeavouring to arrange for the Sháh's peaceful occupation of Ghazni and Kábul.

But evil omens were already showing themselves to persons of ordinary observation. "This will never do," observed the Khán of Kelát; "you may keep the Sháh on the *masnad* for a time by force; but as soon as you leave the country he will be expelled."* A British officer wrote in a private letter:—"proceeding more like a beaten than an advancing army . . . we reached Kandahár . . . With the people I have been disappointed . . . mean, avaricious, treacherous, cowardly, filthy; generally thieves, invariably liars, and withal extremely religious . . . It is a pity Dost Muhamad was not selected as our puppet King: for Sháh Soojah is neither a soldier nor a gentleman, and highly unpopular with his subjects who, but for our support would soon knock him off his perch." A political officer, writing to the Governor-General's sister, admitted that to most people the Sháh's case seemed impossible. Nevertheless, the writer went on to say, that it was all coming right; the "populace are the finest race of Asiatics; they greet the Sháh with every demonstration of joy, and declare that Dost Muhamad will fly without resistance."†

* Havelock, Vol. 1. p. 261.

† "Wanderings of a Pilgrim," by Fanny Parkes. London, 1850. "Up the Country," by the Hon. Emily Eden; 2 vols. London, 1866.

So determined an optimism almost deserved success, if events could have been controlled by courage. But all was against the politicals and their schemes. On the 27th June, 1839, died Ranjit Sinh, Maharája of Lahore, refusing to the last to consult a physician sent to him by the Governor-General. The Punjab Provinces, so long kept together by the pressure of his hand, broke, before long, into a tangle of anarchy. On the same day Keane set forth from Kandahár, imprudently leaving his heavy guns in charge of the garrison there. The Sháh followed with his contingent the next day, and Willshire brought up the rear with the Bombay reserve. On the eastward the mouth of the Khaibar was held by Wade with a heterogeneous levy of Punjab troops; but they did not attempt to ascend the Pass.

On the 20th July, Keane's column arrived within a march of Ghazni, which was held against them by Muhamad Haidar Khán, one of the Dost's sons. A careful reconnaisance showing that all the gates of the fort but one had been built up with solid masonry, while the unfortunate abandonment of the guns had left the General without a battering-train; it was therefore found necessary to fall back upon the antiquated methods of Lake. The northern gate of Ghazni had been left open as a means of escape: but the British forces marching round the town, cut off this egress. On the afternoon of the 22nd they beat off a body of *Ghάzis* (aspirants for martyrdom) who had descended from the hills in the hope of raising the siege; and on the following night the doors of the gate were blown in by the Engineers, and the storming-parties, gallantly led by Dennie and Sale, occupied the town. The citadel surrendered, and Haidar Khán was made prisoner. The victors only lost seventeen by death, but the wounded were 165, amongst whom were no less than eighteen British officers.*

* Sir J. Keane's general order of the 23rd July bears testimony to the "skill and cool courage" of the Engineer officers, Captain Thomson, of

Dost Muhamad, on hearing of the fall of Ghazni, called in the troops under his son, Akbar, from the Khaibar, which was immediately occupied by Wade. Concentrating 13,000 men, with thirty guns, about half-way between Kábul and Ghazni, the Dost attempted to oppose the advance ; but Keane marching out of the last-named on the 30th, reached Shaikhábad on the 2nd August, and there learned that the Dost, alarmed by frequent desertions, had fallen back on Bamián, This was the easiest Pass over the Hindu-Kush range, and the escape of the Dost into the lands of the Uzbeks on the other side was considered so undesirable that a flying column was detached in pursuit, commanded by James Outram, above mentioned as the civiliser of the Khándes Bhils. The raid was unsuccessful, but the invaders were able to secure the Dost's guns and ammunition, which had been abandoned on his sudden flight. On the 7th August, 1839, the Sháh re-entered Kábul, after an absence of thirty years. The attitude of the populace was one of curiosity rather than of sympathy; and the British officers, having conducted him in military pomp to his palace, offered their respectful congratulations, and left him to his reflections.

The moment was critical for himself and for his supporters. The declaration of the 1st October, 1838, had—as we saw—made a promise of withdrawal as soon as "the Sháh should be secured in power." The political officers were responsible for pronouncing on the signs of the times. With much hardship the army had restored the exiled Pretender, bearing discomfort and danger with courage and forbearance. The politicals affirmed that the Dost was a fallen tyrant, and the population was in ecstacies at his overthrow.* What, then, made them

the Bengal Engineers, and Captain Peat, of Bombay, as also Lieutenants Durand and Macleod. Durand (afterwards the Hon. Sir H. M. Durand, Lieutenant-Governor of the Punjab) is the author of the book to which we have been already indebted, and shall refer often hereafter.

* Even Havelock—who was at that time aide-de-camp to Sir W.

delay the announcement that, the object having been attained, the troops should leave the popular Sháh to the support of his subjects, aided, perhaps, by the troops of his Contingent and the possession of all the great strongholds of the country?

It was because the Envoy was not prepared to back his opinion. He did not dare to recommend the course which was the logical conclusion of his arguments. He preferred to give advice to the Government whose servant he was which involved India and Britain in expense and disgrace, and rapidly made good the prediction of the Khán of Kelát. Nor were the measures with which Macnaghten began the new reign of a kind to benefit the King whose protection he assumed. Aware, as he was, of the weakness of the ostensible sovereign in a country long parcelled out amongst a proud nobility, his first attempt was the raising of a mercenary body of troops recruited from all the more lawless of the local tribes. The Afghán nobles were disgusted at this new policy; and a chief, who affected to side with the invasion, remarked about this time to Outram:—"I am hated for my friendship to the English; next to the Sháh, I am the most unpopular man in the country."

We must pass lightly over the events of the next twenty-four months, which belong rather to the history of Afghanistán than to that of India. In November, 1839, Keane left Kábul, telling Durand, who accompanied him, that "it would not be long before it would be the scene of a signal catastrophe." Keane was rewarded by a peerage, Auckland was made an Earl, Macnaghten received a baronetcy, Wade was knighted, as Burnes had been some months before. In November, General Willshire, on his way back with the Bombay column, stormed Kelát, whose Khán was not considered to have acted loyally in the matter

Cotton—shared the general opinion on this subject. See his second vol., p. 118. He says that the Sháh had not the *personal* popularity of the Dost; but that the Afgháns thought that the British support was a guarantee for better Government.

of supplies, and was now slain, fighting valiantly in the breach. The Bombay column was, for the time, detained in Sindh.

The winter of 1839-40 passed quickly; Cotton was in command of the army of occupation in the north, with his headquarters at Kábul; the southern force being under General Nott, at Kandahár. In April, 1840, occurred the first outbreak, the revolt of the Ghilzais, a hardy tribe inhabiting the mountainous country between Kandahár and Kábul, with the western slopes of the Sulaiman range. Columns sent out from both the northern and southern divisions, reduced the Ghilzais to temporary submission, which was confirmed by the promise of a small annual stipend. Biluchistan continued to be disturbed all through the summer, so much so as to threaten Nott's hold upon the Bolán Pass by which alone he could communicate with Sindh. In July, Kelát was recaptured by the son of the deceased Khán; in the following month the Biluch insurgents defeated a British detachment and took three guns on the north of the Bolán. On 3rd November, Nott re-occupied Kelát, fresh troops marched up from Sindh, and communications were once more secured. The same period witnessed attempts by Dost Muhamad and his partizans in the north and west of the country, which ended for the time in the Dost riding into Kábul and giving himself up to Macnaghten, by whom he was sent to India. On arriving in Calcutta the deposed Amir was received with the respect due to a fallen but manly foe. Sir Willoughby Cotton, who had resigned his command, accompanied the Dost to Calcutta.

General Nott might now reasonably expect to fill the vacant post of Commander of the forces in Afghanistán; and his appointment was recommended by Sir Jasper Nicolls, a veteran who had succeeded Fane as, Commander-in-Chief of the Indian Army.* But the outspoken way in which Nott was wont to

* Nicolls had served in the second Nepal campaign, and had led one of the divisons at the siege of Bhurtpore. (v. *sup.* CHAPTER XV.)

express himself stood in the way of his advancement; and General Elphinstone, a well-born but worn-out officer, was sent up to Kábul.* Nott, therefore, remained at Kandahár, with Rawlinson for his political adviser.† During the early part of the year 1841, these two excellent officers did all that they could for the pacification of the country, and sent repeated warnings to Macnaghten at Kábul. That brave but infatuated man persisted in making light of every symptom of danger. Nevertheless, the eyes of the authorities at home were beginning to be opened; and one final opportunity of retreat was offered by the withdrawal of the Russians from Transoxiana, and by the despatches of the Secret Committee commenting upon the growing cost of the prolonged occupation. But Macnaghten protested against the "atrocity" alike of doubting and of abandoning the Sháh; and Auckland was easily persuaded to let the troops remain, even when it was clear to everyone else that the only chance in the world that the Sháh could have must be in the removal of his foreign friends.

But the expense of the war was beginning to be felt in India where it was believed that some economies could be combined with the maintenance of the occupation. Foremost among these was thought to be the cessation of the allowance made to the tribes, who immediately resumed their predatory habits. Akbar Khán, son of the captive Dost, arrived at Bamián from the northward, and began to correspond with the Ghilzai leaders with whom he was connected by marriage. The top of the mountain road to India was blocked at Khurd Kábul;

* As the old guardsman passed through the Governor-General's camp on his way to Kábul, Miss Eden's quick eye noticed his broken strength: "He is in a shocking state of health, poor man; one arm in a sling and very lame . . . he hates being here; he is wretched because no one understands his London topics. He went off with a heavy heart." ("Up the country," by Hon. E. Eden.)

† Major General Sir H. C. Rawlinson, now one of the few survivors from those days.

and a party of sepoys with two guns was sent under Colonel Monteith to clear the road for Sale who was marching towards Pesháwar. In Broadfoot's biography will be found a very interesting note descriptive of the march of this detachment and throwing a lurid light on the situation of the British officers left at Kábul. Elphinstone was such a sufferer from gout as to be unfit for any kind of duty. Macnaghten, who had been appointed Governor of Bombay, was winding up affairs previous to taking his departure. Burnes was reckoning on taking up the duties of Envoy and Minister. Orders were hard to get, and when got were far from clear or sufficient. Monteith was mobbed in the upper pass; and Sale, going to his relief, had to fight and negotiate his way to Gandámak. Macnaghten heard of these operations on 21st October, and expressed much disappointment, though the fault was perhaps his own as much as Sale's.* Fortunately, Broadfoot, who commanded a corps of Sappers, had insisted on being well provided with intrenching tools before he started.

The approaching departure of Macnaghten, and the sense that the British were neither infallible nor invincible, were factors of the growing discontent. Sale reached Gandámak on 30th October, pursued not only by swarms of local tribesmen but by many retainers of the Kábul aristocracy. On the 1st November, the chief conspirators met and made their last arrangements while Burnes was visiting and congratulating the Envoy. On the following morning a mob came to Burnes's house in the city, murdered him, and plundered the treasury of the Mission which was hard by. The last act of the drama had begun.

* Durand gives an interesting extract from Macnaghten's letter (p. 338). The Envoy hoped to leave on 1st November, and thought Burnes the fittest man to be his successor. But he thought Sale might have acted against the tribes in a more decisive manner—as to which he was probably right. The evidence seems strong that there need have heen no negotiation. But the Envoy had also said "there would be no fighting."

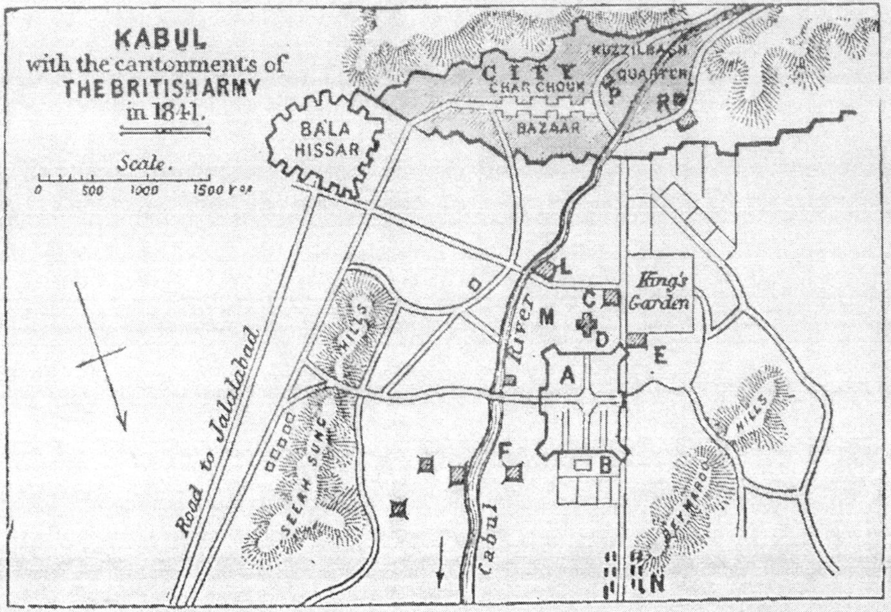

A. Cantonment.
B. Mission Residence.
C. Commissariat Fort.
D. Magazine.
E. Mahomed Shereef's Fort.
F. Rikabashee Fort.
H. Zulficar's Fort.
L. Mahmood Khan's Fort.
M. Spot where the Envoy was murdered.
N. Village of Beymaroo.
P. Sir A. Burne's House.
R. Anquetil's Fort.

There was no want of courage among the officers on whom had fallen this fiery crisis. But the angry fate of an evil design seemed to throw about their councils a mist of doubt and delusion, till they fell into confused wrangling, and could do nothing right. A reference to the plan* will show what might have been attempted, and explain how fatally the real performance fell short. Brigadier Shelton was indeed sent with a respectable force to the Bála Hissár; but he did nothing when he got there; and the armed multitude of insurgents occupying the plain between that citadel and the cantonments, placed the British defence in two separated positions, and speedily captured the small forts in which the stores were kept. Nott and Sale were now addressed with orders to hasten to Kábul; but the former was prevented from compliance by valid causes, while the latter, taking the responsibility of disobeying, lost as fine an opportunity of doing signal service as ever a British Commander threw away. It is the opinion of the best military critics that if he had returned to Kábul, or if he had only remained encamped at Gandámak, he might have averted the impending disaster.

On the Envoy's part there was no want of energy. Aided by Mohan Lál, an intelligent Hindu secretary, he endeavoured to stir up strife among the leaders of the rebels, two of them presently died,—assassinated as men said by some of the British agents. Fighting went on, in which the British did not always show to advantage. On the 22nd, Akbar Khán arrived at Kábul, and the Envoy finding that all his efforts were vain, unwillingly began to negotiate. It was at first proposed that the army should be peacefully withdrawn on promise of the Sháh continuing to reign. But ere long the provisions failed, and the season of snow was beginning; no time for choice, no ground for treating would soon be left. Thus pressed, the Envoy went out to meet Akbar Khán upon the plain, on 23rd

* In Eyre's book.

December. After a brief dialogue the Khán slew him with his own hand, and the last shred of the veil of diplomacy was torn away.* The force—over 4,000 strong—set off on January 6th, giving hostages for a peaceful evacuation. Akbar proved unable or unwilling to protect them from the tribes; the road was deep in snow; food failed, baggage animals succumbed; the women were sent to Akbar's camp with the General and a few companions; ringed by incessant fire from the hillsides, the soldiers fell in the snow, and there were soon only 20 officers and 25 soldiers left to reach Gandámak, where they made their last stand. Here they were overpowered; and on the 13th January Dr. Brydon, the sole survivor staggered into Jalálabad.

[For the early part of the war, Havelock is an excellent authority; being on the General's staff he saw all that a combatant officer could see of the "Bengal" column and its operations. His book is much superior to that which he published on the Burmese war; free from artificial solemnity, and pleasantly lighted by a cheerful humour. On political matters a safer guide is to be found in Durand, who was equally able to testify from personal observation, but who had the advantage of being private secretary to Lord Ellenborough before his narrative was completed. These two books furnish the testimony of able and soldierly eye-witnesses up to the time when Keane left Afghanistán. For the subsequent events consult the works of two other military participators:—Vincent Eyre, "The Kábul Insurrection;" and Broadfoot, "The Career of Major G. Broadfoot, C.B.," London, 1888. With these may be coupled Hough's two works: "The Army of the Indus," London, 1841; and "The British Force at Cabool from November, 1841 to January, 1842," Calcutta, 1849.

* The Envoy was killed in the heat of a passionate struggle; and Akbar protected his companion Mackenzie. Akbar's general conduct appears to show a chivalrous, and even humane, character.

Mohan Lal (who died a convert to Islám) left some books, among them a "Life of Dost Mohammed Khán," two vols., London, 1846. See also Stocqueler's "Memorials of Afghanistan," Calcutta, 1843.]

SECTION 3.—By a singularly fortunate compensation the countries of India proper were at peace while these painful scenes were going on between the Indus and the Hindu-Kush mountains. The settlement operations went on in Hindustan; Bengal was developing improved methods of transport by road and river; Bombay was witnessing the first attempts of "overland" communication between India and Europe.* In the Madras Presidency alone was there any appearance of trouble; and the "Coast Army"—which was to remain so loyal and so useful in 1857—was displaying the last sign of that tendency to mutiny which had formerly led to so much alarm. A general gloom had naturally spread over men's minds in all parts of India; but it had not, in any part but the southern regions, taken an active form; and in the beginning of the year it became known that the weak and wavering Auckland was likely to be soon removed in favour of an abler Governor. The Court of Directors had, on the last day of 1840, addressed the Indian Government in a serious tone of warning; but their instructions had been neglected. Nevertheless, the constant drain on the financial resources of India could not be long neglected; and the result of the General Election in July having been to give the Conservative Party a majority of nearly 100 in the House of Commons, the Government resigned, and Lord Ellenborough was appointed to supersede Lord Auckland as Governor-General of India. On the 4th November, his Excellency was entertained at the usual banquet, when he made an emphatic declaration of his intention to rule "on peace principles."

* "The August overland mail arrived on 3rd October, quicker than ever." (Miss Eden *ub sup.*)

Meanwhile, Lord Auckland seemed morally paralysed. On 3rd December, he wrote to Sir Jasper Nicolls, in the advanced British post of Ludiana, begging him to consider the means of "retiring with the least possible discredit." Nicolls at once concerted measures with Mr. (afterwards Sir George) Clerk; and on the 13th January, 1842, Brigadier Wild appeared at the mouth of the Khaibar, but was unable to advance on Jalálabad owing to a bad spirit among the Native troops.

Sale was known to have reached that station on the 12th November, and it could only be hoped that his small force would be able to hold out until General Pollock should arrive with a force sufficient to force the pass. The Council of War at Jalálabad received on the 9th January an order, signed by Elphinstone, for the surrender of the place to Akbar Khán. To this it was resolved to pay no attention. The garrison engineer was George Broadfoot, already mentioned.* On the 13th, when Dr. Brydon arrived with his dreadful story, Broadfoot reported to Sale on the state of Jalálabad, pointing out that, unless he was prepared to hold the place to the last, he should march out immediately and fight his way down to Peshâwar. Sale determined to remain, and wrote accordingly to Nicolls. But on the 26th—having learned the news of Wild's failure—he concerted with Macgregor, the political officer, a scheme for a possible convention with Abkar Khán, which they proceeded to lay before the Council. Besides himself and Macgregor, he assembled the Commandants of corps:—Colonels Dennie (13th Foot), and Monteith (35th Bengal Native Infantry), Captains Abbott and Backhouse (Artillery) and Oldfield (Cavalry), with Broadfoot as garrison engineer. Broadfoot and two others opposed all projects of negotiation; but, in conformity with the votes of the majority,

* Broadfoot—though only a captain of Madras Native Infantry—was Commandant of the sappers; and we have already noticed his fortunate providence in bringing down engineering tools from Kábul.

a letter was sent to Kábul stipulating for a safe-conduct with hostages. In justice to all concerned it must be added that a letter had been laid before the Council in which the Governor-General declared that all the Afghanistán forces should be withdrawn; moreover, there were many British ladies, officers, and soldiers of all ranks in the hands of the enemy, whose lives might have been compromised by a hasty refusal. Captain Abbott, a man of ability and proved courage, asserts that the proffer of convention was only intended to protect the captives and to gain time.* In due course, however, a letter, in the name of the Sháh, called upon the officers to prove their sincerity by affixing their seals to the agreement; and Broadfoot then availed himself of the apparent doubt cast on their sincerity to persuade them to send a reply politely closing the negotiation. The wisdom of this bold course appeared the very next day, when news arrived that relief was at hand. By the end of February the defences of Jalálabad were finally completed in spite of an earthquake which threw down the works first erected.

The other garrisons now remaining in Afghanistán were two, Colonel Palmer with his regiment—the 27th Bengal Native Infantry—was in charge of Ghazni, where he was immediately invested and put under a strict blockade by the Ghilzais; and Kandahár Fort was more effectually occupied by five corps of sepoys, with artillery, and some of Skinner's Irregular Horse. In the adjoining cantonments were posted H.M.'s 40th Foot, two more Native Infantry corps, and a regiment of the Sháh's Cavalry under British officers. General England was understood to be advancing with reinforcements from Sindh. Rawlinson, the political agent, and the Shahzáda, Taimur Khán,

* "Journal and correspondence of the late Major General Augustus Abbott, C.B." For the Governor-General's letter, v. p. 269; this was apparently the "French letter" referred to by Broadfoot. One of the hostages demanded by Sale's first Council was Abkar Khán!

attempted to engage the co-operation of the neighbouring Dauránis, under their able chief, Mirza Ahmad Khán. On first hearing of the insurrection at Kábul, Nott had attempted to send succour to Elphinstone; but the snow drove back the reinforcements before they could reach Ghazni; and by the middle of December, 1841, Nott's forces were concentrated at Kandahár. It was well that it was so; for, what with the treachery of Mirza Ahmad and the Dauránis, and what with the defect of the Afghán levies, Nott and Rawlinson were soon hard pressed. England being opposed at Haikalzai retired upon Quetta, and left them for the present to their own resources. These, however, were adequate to the needs of the case; the insurgents were not only resisted but attacked; and the Afgháns had a second lesson that the unfortunate Elphinstone was not to be taken for a type of the British leader. The exploits of Nott were on a remote scene; but what he did during the spring and summer of 1842 has been said by good judges to put him on the first rank of English Generals.* We have only here space to add that by his victory of 29th May, General Nott broke up the paradoxical confederacy between the Ghilzai rebels and the friends of the Sháh, thus pacifying the Southern Province and preparing to co-operate with the troops in the Punjab, as soon as it should be known that they were advancing.

Active and brave as were Nott and Rawlinson, they were unable to relieve Palmer, who yielded Ghazni in March, after sustaining a blockade of more than three months. The officers were sent to swell the numbers of captives at Kábul, the sepoys being distributed as slaves among the Ghilzai villages, where over 300 of them were found and rescued later in the year. In the latter part of April, however, after another action on the ground of his former action at Haikalzai, England succeeded in effecting a junction with Nott at Kandahár. But the move-

* Nott's despatches will be found in Stocqueler's collection.

ments of the latter General were still impeded by uncertainty: and the Government of Calcutta held for some time to the scheme of withdrawing the Kandahár troops through the Gomal Pass by the help of the Sikhs.* As for General England, his presence was required in Sindh, whither he retired in good order, taking with him the Shahzáda Taimur, and the women, children, and superfluous stores.

Auckland—after issuing a tumid but vague announcement of an intention (or, at least, a desire) to be revenged on the Afgháns—contented himself with consulting Nicolls as to the best means of bringing the troops away. But that officer, encouraged by Mr. Clerk and his assistant, Captain H. Lawrence,† began to push troops forward to Peshávar. On February 15th these officers received authority to do what they could for the relief of Jalálabad; but General Pollock, to whom the execution of the task was intrusted, at the same time received instructions to fall back on the Sutlej when it was accomplished, thereby leaving the Punjab exposed, and abandoning the captives to the mercy of the Afghán leaders, of whom the murderer of Macnaghten was the most humane.

Such were the last instructions of the expiring Government. But on the 21st February Lord Ellenborough arrived at Madras, where he became informed of the state of affairs in northern India. He also found Lord Elphinstone's Government there in much anxiety. A regiment of Native Infantry had mutinied at Haidarábád—the capital of the Nizám—and two corps that had been ordered to embark at Madras to reinforce General Gough in China had refused to go on board. Ellenborough lost no time; he announced that nothing should interfere with Gough's operations: at the same time he sent home for more European regiments; pacified the Madras sepoys by a resolute attitude; and hastened to Calcutta where he took charge on the 28th.

* Durand, p. 419.

† Afterwards famous as Sir Henry Lawrence.

His first care was to provide reinforcements and instructions for Gough in China; and then he turned to his internal difficulties. Leaving the Madras authorities to deal with the insubordination of their men, he took up the question of the instructions to be given to Pollock. The force of which that able officer took command in February was ample for the services that were, or might be, required of it.* But the spirit of the sepoys was low. On March 14th Pollock reported that they could not be trusted to advance without solid support; and he asked for more guns and British soldiers. He was also in great need of the means of transport, as may be judged from the one fact that more than 14,000 baggage animals had to be finally provided before he could move.

On 14th March the new Government issued to Nicolls, Pollock, and Clerk the first announcement of its views: the Council then consisting of Messrs. W. Bird and Thoby Prinsep, C.S., and General Sir W. Casement. It was laid down that all attempts for a permanent occupation of Afghanistán must be abandoned, and that military measures alone would guide the course to be adopted. The objects were declared to be the relief of the British then in the country, "and the re-establishment of our military reputation." In the circumstances nothing more could be profitably said. The Punjáb was uneasy, as also were Nepal and Bundelkhand: six Indian regiments were absent in China. All that the Government could do was to point out the objects and to leave to the officers on the spot the task of obtaining them with the smallest amount of risk.†

* H. M. 3rd Light Dragoons, 1st and 10th Bengal Light Cavalry, a troop of Horse Artillery, two field-batteries, H. M. 9th and 31st Foot, and seven regiments of Bengal Native Infantry. Some Sikh troops were to co-operate; though—as General Avitabile said—"the very sight of the Khaibar gave the Sikhs colic." Under Henry Lawrence, however, they were to do good service.

† See the entire despatch of 14th March in "Durand," p. 437. Between that time and the middle of the year the Governor-General kept the Duke

As soon as the necessary arrangements had been effected Pollock forced the Khaibar, and reached Jalálabad on 16th April. Here he found the garrison in high health and spirits, having repulsed all the assaults of Akbar Khán and provided themselves with supplies. Meantime the Governor-General's orders assumed a more cautious tone: indeed it is apparent from Ellenborough's letters to Wellington that doubts of Nott and England were swaying him to wish that Nott's forces might withdraw—like those of England—by way of the Bolán. With the approval of his illustrious correspondent negotiation was tried for an exchange of prisoners; but the Duke pointed out that this would not be successful without a forward movement involving some risk and much expense. On July 4th orders were finally issued for an advance on Kábul alike to Nott and Pollock, who were now fully supplied with both cash and carriage.

There is little more of this blended story of good and evil to be told. Ellenborough issued a spirited order, in which he gratified the hearts of the soldiery by commenting on the behaviour of "the illustrious garrison"; and prominently selected Broadfoot for honour and preferment.* The luckless Sháh was murdered at Kábul on April 5th; his son Fateh Jang being, for the moment, put in his place, though the opposition to the British operations continued to be directed by Akbar. That wild but chivalrous Chief did his utmost to oppose the advance of General Pollock from Jalálabad, which began

informed of all his anxieties which were evidently very great. Amongst other things he thought that Pollock was too much influenced by the advice of the "political" Captain Macgregor, whom he at length removed from employment in that capacity. The carriage-difficulty, too, was long in getting dealt with.

* He had been severely wounded in a most successful sortie on March 24th. The Infantry of the garrison consisted of all that was left of H. M. 13th Foot and the 35th Bengal Native Infantry. Colonel Dennie was, unhappily, killed in the last sally, April 7th, a misfortune that was generally debited to General Sale's arrangements.

in August. Nott at the same time marched upon Kábul from the other side—where he was distanced in the generous race by having to occupy the evacuated forts of Ghazni and collect the sepoys of the 47th from the villages where they had been made slaves. These men having been collected, the walls of Ghazni were mined and blown up by Nott's orders on September 19th. Meanwhile Pollock fought his way to Kábul, being joined on his way by Fateh Jang, the Sháh's son. Arriving there on the 17th, he enthroned the young Sháh, and planted the British colours on the Bála Hissár. On the 21st the captives came in, having bribed their guardian: amongst them were Ladies Sale and Macnaghten, General Shelton and the survivors of his regiment—the 44th Foot—together with Colonel Palmer, Vincent Eyre, and the gallant political E. Pottinger, to whose skill and vigour they were indebted for their escape. On the 30th Istalif—where the chief of Burnes's murderers was harboured—succumbed to General McCaskill after a brief defence. Meanwhile Nott had brought his little army to Kábul without loss: and, after destroying the central market-place as a final mark of victory and punishment, the combined forces turned their backs on Kábul, October 12th, and reached Peshávar, without serious trouble, on November 6th.

Thus ended Auckland's melancholy undertaking, after adding nearly twenty millions to the public debt, creating a deficit of two more in the accounts of his final year, and permanently lowering the respectful awe which the British power had hitherto commanded in India and in Asia. Mr. Tucker, on behalf of the Company, recorded a spirited protest, saying that the real quarrel was with Russia which made it a European question; that the policy had never been sanctioned or approved by the Court of Directors; that it was not needed for the protection of India; and that the people of that country ought not be charged with the cost. But his plea met with no attention.

Of the war in China nothing more need be said but that it was carried on from first to last by the British Government, and only belongs to Indian History so far as the service of Indian troops is concerned. In that respect it did nothing to detract from the reputation of the army; and at its conclusion General Gough came to India to begin a new and distinguished career in that country.

Lord Ellenborough gave the returning forces a splendid reception at Firozpore, and liberated the captive Amir Dost Muhamad, who returned to Afghanistán and at once resumed the chieftainship, displacing the Daurâni dynasty for ever. Pollock and Nott were knighted,* and a medal was struck bearing the inscription, *Pax Asiæ restituta.* In a few weeks a new war was begun by the irony of Fortune.

But in order to understand what now ensued we ought to look for an instant at events in Sindh since the time of the Kábul disaster. Sir H. Pottinger had been sent to China, as political commissioner; and Outram was Resident in his room. The command of the Bombay Army had been given to Sir C. J. Napier, a brave and intelligent, but extremely combative, officer, who had served with distinction against the French in Spain.

Napier arrived in Sindh, 9th September, 1842, armed with full military and diplomatic powers. It was a period when the civil authority in India had been much weakened by recent events, and the position of political agents—even if originally members of the military service—was somewhat unfairly discredited; indeed there is reason to believe that both Napier and the Governor-General were influenced by that feeling. It might be thought that Outram (as indeed his future career was

* As General Pollock's name will not often occur again, it may be here noted that he was ultimately made a Baronet. He was also created a Field Marshal and Constable of the Tower, which was the first time of such honours being bestowed upon a Company's officer.

to show), did not deserve to be made a scapegoat for the errors of judgment that men were disposed to attribute to Macnaghten or to Burnes. Be this as it may, misunderstandings soon arose, and Outram lost the confidence of his fiery chief.

The conduct of the Amirs had been generally wise, if not positively loyal, since Rustam Khán had ceded Bakkar to General Cotton, and Nur Muhamad had submitted at Haidarábád, as mentioned in the preceding section. Outram's personal influence, and the constant presence of troops going and coming, not only prevented hostile action but ensured a certain amount of help in the matter of camels and supplies. But Outram found more reason to complain of the Amirs after the Kábul disaster; and he contemplated a new treaty by which their conduct should be steadied and British hold on Sindh secured. Ellenborough and Napier agreed that this engagement ought—in fairness to the general population—to be such as to provide for an improvement in the whole administration. Napier accordingly went to Haidarábád, and, while, there, received from Outram proof that old Rustam of Khairpore had been detected writing to the new Maharája of Lahore proposing a combination against the British power. This information Napier at once forwarded to the Governor-General with a proposal for some modification of the treaty previously contemplated, and naming certain posts to be demanded of the Amirs, by way at once of precaution and penalty. He further proposed that the leading men among them should be called on to sign the treaty. On November 12th, the Governor-General's answer arrived, enclosing draft of a new treaty, not, however, to be offered for signature until Napier should have satisfied his mind as to the alleged treachery having been really committed. Now, Napier had many high qualities; but a judicial temper was not among them. He did not know anything of the Asiatic character; he could not make allowance for any sort of double-dealing; of the Amirs he had a prejudiced opinion. Assuming their guilt, therefore, without making the enquiry suggested, he, in a half-unconscious way, resolved upon their overthrow.* On their part, resistance was not seriously contemplated, and they offered to sign the treaty—though, of course, without admission of guilt. But their followers were not equally submissive; and the result was that, early in 1843, a mighty host of hardy Biluchis was collecting in Lower Sindh, watched by a small body of British troops of whom about 900 only were Europeans. In such a scene of general mistrust and preparation for hostility a spark was all that was wanting to cause explosion; and that spark soon fell. On the 4th February, old Rustam came to Haidarábád, and Napier had no further legitimate ground of complaint. All the Amirs signed, with the exception of one who was away; but Napier—who had left Haidarábád—continued his military preparations, and, in his absence, Outram could not give any pledge as to what he would do. The Amirs were bewildered; their Biluch followers swore to defend them in arms. On the 15th Outram was forced to escape from the Haidarábád Residency by the violence of a mob; but he made his way by water to Napier's camp. This was a *casus belli*, and on the 17th was fought the battle of Miáni, where 30,000 brave but undisciplined mountaineers were routed, with heavy loss, by a body of soldiers not more than a tenth of their number, but led by British officers and encouraged by a handful of British comrades. One more battle, on March 21st, decided the war; Napier was not dealing with a nation of patriotic highlanders like the persistent Afgháns; and the alien Amirs and their clansmen could do no more. Napier became Governor of Sindh; and the opposition of Outram was inadequate to save the Amirs from deposition and banishment. It only remains to be added that order

* "We shall annex Scinde," he noted at the time in his diary.

and a revenue settlement were introduced, though the crude machinery worked creakingly at first. Public works received an instant impetus; and the port of Karáchi—which was inaccessible to ships for half the year—was cleared and protected by a breakwater, and is now considered the fourth seaport of Indian trade.

Neither argument nor subsequent success can justify these proceedings; but those who will take the trouble to weigh the temptation in one scale and human nature in another will see that justice is due to Napier and Ellenborough as able and benevolent men dealing with a problem of which the conditions were imperfectly known. The Governor-General trusted too much to his ardent subordinate; and it is evident from Napier's private papers that the subordinate was never quite free from the glory-thirst which misleads almost all great soldiers. The conquest, described by the gallant conqueror himself as "a humane piece of rascality," was condemned by the Court of Directors in Resolutions passed in August, 1843; and there can be no doubt but that the condemnation was fatal ultimately to Ellenborough's tenure of office.

In September, 1843, the Maharája of Lahore, Sher Sinh, was assassinated; and the condition of the Sikh army, or Khálsa, as it was called, became a source of alarm, both to the chiefs of the Punjab and to their neighbours. Organised Committees took the virtual command out of the hands of the legitimate leaders; and the worst days of the Roman Pretorians were apparently being reproduced. There was no knowing when these brave and well-trained troops might be thrown across the frontier of Hindustan by the panic-fear of the aristocracy or by their own restless audacity. In the midst of this anxiety a source of trouble, similar if not so formidable, arose in the State of Gwalior. The army of that State was less numerous than that of the Punjab, and not quite so highly trained, but the spirit of political dictation was hardly less strong among them.

The Rája adopted by the Baiza Bai on Daulat Ráo's death had died, leaving a childless widow and an adopted son who was a minor. A question of Regency arising, the army refused to recognise the nominee of the British Government, and the Resident consequently removed to Dholpore, on the frontier, about the end of the year. The Governor-General, who had come to Agra, moved down a force of 12,000 men under Sir Hugh Gough; and, failing to meet the Ráni, crossed the frontier on Christmas Day, having already reviewed the state of affairs in an able minute. The terms which he offered to the Durbar were, briefly, the restoration of the Regent and the reduction of the strength of the army, which was out of all proportion to the wants of a protected State. Failing to obtain any satisfaction on these subjects, the Governor-General slowly advanced towards Gwalior, and on the morning of the 29th December, arrived at Maharájpore, fifteen miles from the city. Here he unexpectedly found the Gwalior army strongly posted. Having left his heavy guns at Agra, Gough was obliged to storm the enemy's intrenchments with the bayonet: the enemy fought well, and the field was not won without some difficulty and loss. On the same day General Grey, coming up from Bundelkhand, met and routed another army at Panniar, twelve miles south-west of Gwalior. Eighty guns were now seized, and the numbers of the army were reduced from 30,000 to 9,000; a "Contingent" under British officers being afterwards added. This latter step was to prove disastrous; otherwise Ellenborough used his success with wisdom and moderation. Nevertheless, having completely lost the confidence of the Court of Directors, he was recalled before the middle of the year; and the verdict of general opinion was that, however able and upright, he had done much to justify the measure by imprudent language and flighty ways.

His administration is only otherwise marked by a tendency

to employ military men in civil work, and by a development of the subordinate police-service. He left the Sikh problem to be solved by his successor.

[v. Colchester; "Administration of Lord Ellenborough;" London, 1874. Kaye; "Memorials of Indian Government;" London, 1883. "Conquest of Scinde," Outram, Edinburgh, 1846; Ditto., "Sir W. Napier" (2nd edition), London, 1857. The letters (to the Queen and Wellington), published, without comment, by Lord Colchester, form an ample picture of an ardent will, with a vigilant and generally far-seeing observation. Of course, Ellenborough made mistakes; and the mistakes of such a mind—though not so dangerous as the errors of a weak man who, having once gone wrong knows not how to recover himself—are sure to be conspicuous, and a cause of alarm to official superiors.* For an extreme view of Ellenborough's conduct, and of possible peril to which it might lead, Tucker's "Memorials" may be consulted. Tucker was also without question an able man; but he was more a man of business, perhaps, than a statesman; age and experience, too, produced in him a caution, which may have been somewhat in excess. It is, however, to be noted that the Duke of Wellington, in February, 1843, sent Ellenborough a strong warning as to the use of "caution and temper."]

* The proclamation about the alleged "Gates of Somnath," has become a bye-word. The destruction of the Cantonment of Karnál, the grant of the China medal, the re-organisation of the police, and the wholesale removal of the officers of the Ságar Commission, were all acts of unnecessarily arbitrary character which might have been referred home for approval without injurious delay.

CHAPTER XVIII.

A SOLDIER'S RULE.

Section 1: The Punjab, 1839-46—Section 2: Material prosperity and progress of India under Hardinge—Section 3: Retrenchment, Finance, etc.

SECTION 1.—Sir H. Hardinge—like Napier, a distinguished Peninsula warrior—arrived in Calcutta, July 23rd, 1844. He landed with the usual pacific intentions, and was at once confronted with the usual call for warlike preparation.

Ever since the murder of the Maharája in 1843 the Punjab had presented a great and growing problem; and Ellenborough had not been granted time for its solution, though he had been quite aware of its urgency. He had not only had it in his mind in his action against Gwalior but had taken other preparatory measures, such as the examination of the defences of Delhi; the arrangement for cantoning troops at Firozpore, Ambála, and Kasauli; and the ordering pontoons to be got ready on the Indus, whence they could, if necessary, proceed to the Sutlej.

In other parts of the Empire the arrangements of the late Governor-General, however despotic, had been mostly attended with success. Rawlinson had been sent to look after Indian interests in the Persian Gulf—on the other boundary, Broadfoot had taken the place of an unsuccessful Commissioner in Tenasserim. The Nizám's affairs were in a bad condition, and Ellenborough had contemplated the possibility of the administration of the State being assumed by the British Government, but at the eleventh hour the Nizám had agreed to introduce all the desired reforms. Henry Lawrence had been sent as Resident to Káthmándu; and, after a sanguinary political crisis, "order reigned" in Nepal.

In Audh, Pollock was resident in the room of Low, promoted to Haidarábád. The "King," whom Low had enthroned on that memorable July night,* just seven years ago, had died and been succeeded by a son of the Nasir-ud-din breed, under whom all went to ruin. One of Hardinge's first duties was to address to this worthless ruler a warning which was completely, though silently, ignored. This matter will be more fully noticed hereafter.

Outram had been provided for in the Southern Mahratta country, where he soon had an opportunity of showing his qualities, doubted or denied by Napier and Ellenborough.

By the time of Rája Sher Sinh's murder (1843) the active and able British agent, George Clerk, had been transferred, as Lieutenant-Governor, to Agra; and his successor was a less competent man, in bad health besides. The new Government at Lahore was weak and distracted; carried on nominally by Jindán Köur, mother of the infant Maharája, Dulip Sinh, under an opposition on the part of Ghuláb Sinh, the Rájput Chief of Jammu, whose nephew—Hira Sinh—was, for the time, in power as Prime Minister. Anxious to furnish the Pretorians of the Khálsa with distant and dangerous occupation, Hira Sinh marched the bulk of the army towards the Sutlej. The agent addressed Lord Ellenborough in terms of exaggerated acerbity against Hira Sinh, and the Governor-General wisely resumed the preparations already briefly noted. Other misunderstandings followed, in which the British officials unfortunately gave the Sikhs some grounds of just complaint; and while these dis-

* See CHAPTER XVII., Section I.

putes were still pending, Col. Richmond – the agent in question —took sick-leave, and Broadfoot was sent to relieve him.*

On the 1st November, 1844, the new agent assumed charge of his post, and he had a conference with the Envoy of the Lahore Government a few days later. It was soon evident that the Durbar was in great trouble, both with the Sikh aristocracy and with the army; and that there was a disposition to urge the grievances above noticed, yet without any apparent wish for war. But Jindán Köur, known as "the Ráni" and mother of the boy Maharája,† was restless and secretly planning the destruction of the Minister, Hira Sinh. There were, in fact, three parties: the Rájputs of Jammu—of whom the Minister was one—had the apparent and legitimate power; the Sikh nobles formed a regular opposition; but the arbitrament was likely to lie with the Army-Committees. This the Ráni had found out, and was beginning to act upon her discovery.

Before the end of the year these plots developed, so that the Minister was attacked, and forced to fly from Lahore. He made for Jammu, the mountain-home of his family, but was overtaken and killed before he had got many miles on the way. For some time the Ráni profited by his death; for his uncle, Guláb, was too intimidated to leave the hills; while the army was quite willing to leave to others the semblance of power so long as there was double pay to be had. The Ráni, who was personally popular, governed through her brother, Jowáhir Sinh.

The next few months were full of anxiety; for her, and for the British. It is wearisome to have to repeat the old story of involuntary aggression, but from the correspondence of the period one can hardly avoid the conclusion that both Hardinge

* Richmond was soon after transferred to Lucknow, vice Sir George Pollock, promoted to be military Member-of-Council at Calcutta.

† It is said by Sir L. Griffin to be doubtful if she was the mother of Dulip, and certain that Ranjit was not his father ("Ranjit Singh," Rulers of India).

and his agent on the Sutlej were really using great exertions to avoid a collision to which there could be but one end.* Nor does it appear that the nominal rulers of the Punjab—Jowáhir Sinh, the Ráni's brother, and her favourite Lál Sinh—had originally any feeling of personal hostility, or violent desire to enter upon a struggle with the British Government, a course opposed alike to the traditions of the late Ránjit, and to their own sense of inferior means. Yet the Ráni's secret mind was already unfavourable to peace. The Treasury at Lahore was becoming exhausted; Jowáhir Sinh had no popularity, nor administrative experience; Guláb Sinh was not likely to remain long quiet. On the British side there was much reason to mistrust the sepoys of the Bengal army, who saw a host on the other bank of the river extorting double pay from their employers, and had for some time shown a spirit of insubordination in their own ranks. In such circumstances it would have been worse than idle to neglect preparations; and Hardinge gradually increased his forces at Meerut and Ambála, and caused the train of boats, provided by his predecessor, to be moved from the Indus to Firozpore. These movements were, of course, observed by the Lahore Government and the Sikh army. To the former it seemed natural to appeal to the power which had been allied with old Ránjit for protection against Pretorian violence. To the latter it was, by many supposed to be indifferent how soon matters came to a crisis with troops to whom they knew themselves superior in numbers, and may have believed themselves not unequal in other respects.†

* Hardinge's maxim was:—"The Punjab must be either Sikh or British." But he preferred that, if possible, it should be Sikh.

† The Khálsa army was returned at the time as 88,662 men with 484 guns, while the Governor-General had accumulated a force about 40,000 strong with 100 pieces of artillery, between Delhi and the Sutlej. The Sikh troops were insubordinate: but their military discipline was high and their spirit that of a dominant class.

Nevertheless, no one seemed anxious for war; and the best observers—both at the time and ever since—have agreed that the Governor-General's preparations were the least that could be made, for purely defensive purposes. He was consistent in refusing to lend his troops to the Durbar; and he kept the members clearly informed of his intentions to hold them answerable for their own misconduct.

So passed the summer of 1845. Napier continued his energetic course of action against the marauding clans of Upper Sindh; where, however, his operations on the Multan border are believed to have added to the difficulties of the situation. Elsewhere tranquility prevailed North of the Narbada and the Máhanadi: it seemed as if all Hindustan was occupied in watching the gathering clouds on the north-west horizon. That they might burst in storm was probably the general idea, even though those best informed could hardly feel quite certain as to the time or manner. From the letters written at the time by Broadfoot and his Assistant at Firozpore—Captain Peter Nicolson—it is clear that a pacific course was followed, tending to the maintenance of a "buffer-State" between the Sutlej and the Indus, even if such a policy should involve the ignoring of petty affronts.

The abiding anxiety arose from confused rights upon the left—or British—bank of the river, where the Durbar asserted inadmissible claims to sovereignty over lands which were inextricably included in British districts although left in Ranjit's possession by the Treaty of 1808. Over these an undisturbed ownership had been always allowed, but the claim to rule was necessarily repudiated by the British. Yet this alone would never have led to war, which was, moreover, deprecated by the most enlightened Punjab statesmen, from the astute Rája of Jammu to the cultivated Muslim Councillor, Fakir Azizudin. But Jowáhir Sinh was a drunken *parvenu* on whom no considerations of wisdom or of honour had any effect and he now began to listen to the arguments of his able but unprincipled sister, the Ráni, who was actuated only by a desire that the army should be employed away from Lahore, if not destroyed by the British. *Dux fœmina facti.*

About the middle of the year the Governor-General resolved to visit the North-West as soon as the rainy season should be over; in the meanwhile he received from Broadfoot a warning sent by Rája Guláb Sinh, to the effect that there would be war after the Dasahra.* The wily Rájput was already planning to make interest for himself with the power against whom he saw the Sikhs would soon be dashed—to their own destruction—in spite of the warnings of their wisest counsellors, and even in spite of their own occasional misgivings. The soldiers, at one time, even turned on their tempters; and, on the 21st September, slew the Ráni's brother, the drunkard Jowáhir. The ruthless woman continued her course: weeping over her brother in the open street, reviling the soldiery with unveiled face, she never ceased to blind, inflame, and mislead the dull-witted janisaries. As a contemporaneous English writer observed, the Ráni yielded to the army, "encouraged its excesses; called its madness reason; and urged it on in the hope of guiding it to destruction. History scarcely records a conception more bold and able."†

Reports were now continually reaching the British officers of attempts to seduce the Sepoys from their allegiance; and these attempts were probably the work of the Hindustánis in the Sikh army, who were able to tell their countrymen and kinsmen in the British service of raised pay and relaxed control. To a British officer on the frontier the warning was

* The autumnal feast was usually regarded as the opening-time for military operations in India. This is believed by the Hindus to be the day on which Rama set out on his great campaign (v. sup. pp. 15, 23). The war did not, in this instance, begin till a month later.

† Herbert Edwardes: "Calcutta Review," No. 46.

about this time addressed by a native gentleman, "to send for plenty of Europeans, and to remember that no reliance could be had in regard to the Hindustáni forces."

At last, in the third week of November, Broadfoot was able to assure the military authorities that the army had swallowed the bait and threatened the chiefs with destruction unless led immediately across the Sutlej. On the 24th Fakir Azizudin uttered his last warning; and the old high priest—Rám Sinh—solemnly adjured Rája Lál Sinh to recollect that the whole Sikh nation would be held answerable for the follies of the army; but the Rája—who was then at the head of affairs—could only reply that if he did not lead them on the soldiers would kill him.*

On the 5th December the death of Azizudin was reported; and Rájas Tej Sinh and Lál Sinh with anxious hearts moved towards the Sutlej, which they began to cross on the 8th. The crossing was complete by the 15th, when Lál Sinh, leaving his associate to mask Firozpore with sixteen battalions of foot and twenty squadrons of horse, threw his main body into an intrenched camp at Firozsháh, and advanced to meet and—if possible—surprise Sir H. Gough who was marching somewhat negligently up with a British force of 11,000 men, including some cavalry and light field-batteries. Lál Sinh came upon them at the village of Mudki as they were sitting down to breakfast on the 18th. The British cavalry, attacking the enemy's horse on both wings, laid bare and enveloped the flanks of the infantry; and Gough's line, pushing on with the

* The Rája was afterwards a political prisoner in the author's charge. He was a handsome, agreeable-mannered man: not personally brave. Neither he nor Tej Sinh was by birth a Sikh. There was a general idea at the time that the chiefs had been bought by the Government of India; but there is no evidence in support of this view. Guláb, indeed, had endeavoured to negotiate, but the Governor-General did not send him any reply. The conduct of the other two is explained by their not being Sikhs, nor secure of their lives from the army.

bayonet, drove them back with the loss of seventeen guns out of twenty-two that they had brought into the field.

After this battle—in which the victors had 215 killed, inclusive of Sir R. Sale* and Sir J. McCaskill—the army halted for two days, during which three fresh regiments arrived, and the Governor-General had his name put in orders as second in command to Sir H. Gough. On the 21st the British moved up to the west of Firozsháh† to meet Sir J. Littler who was directed to march down from Firozpore; and with him a junction was effected, about 3 p.m., a short distance from the west front of the Sikh intrenchment, near the village of Báh. As in so many of Gough's actions, conditions were untoward: the columns did not move against the enemy's works until late in the afternoon of the shortest day in the year; one attack failed because the troops were thrown into alarm by an unauthorised (and injudicious) order—but not until the 62nd Foot had lost nearly 200 men—no durable impression was produced on the enemy; and the British troops were left, some in one spot, some in another, without food or shelter, through the long winter-night. Next morning, however, they took the Sikh intrenchment; and, although Tej Sinh came up with 10,000 fresh troops, he did not dare—or did not care—to attempt its recovery. The British lost 2,200, killed and wounded; among the killed being the able and intrepid Broadfoot. The Governor-General—in writing to Ellenborough—spoke most disparagingly of the native troops, attributing all his success to the Europeans.‡ The news of these events

* Sale's extraordinary career, of over half-a-century, included Seringapatam, Mauritius, Burma, and the whole of the Afghán war. He was struck by a grape-shot on the field of Mudki, and died the same day.

† So named from a local saint; the title of "Sháh" is sometimes given to Muslim devotees.

‡ "Our Native cavalry did not behave well. . . . The British infantry carried the day. I can't say I admire sepoy fighting." After the war he asked Lál Sinh whether the Sikhs had orders to spare the sepoys?

caused much anxiety at home, and measures were taken to enable Hardinge, should he deem it necessary, to assume command of the army in the field. The battle of Firozsháh was of that kind that—as the Governor-General himself observed—another such victory might shake the Empire. Technical difficulties, joined to Hardinge's own delicacy, delayed the supercession of Gough until the necessity had ceased.

In point of fact—as is well observed by a modern historian—that ambiguous action was, in fact, decisive.* Had the Sikhs repulsed the British from the intrenchment and captured the cantonment of Firozpore, there was nothing to prevent them from raising the country and becoming masters of Hindustan. The consequence of their defeat, on the other hand, was to leave them with no chance but to get back to their own land as best they might. Like the stout soldiers that they were, they would not accept this position without another struggle; but their failure was a foregone conclusion. Having, on January 28th undergone another defeat, from Sir H. Smith at Aliwál, they resolved to make a stand upon the Sutlej; and Gough—who was awaiting heavy guns and other reinforcements—was constrained to give them time to intrench themselves there. The position which they selected was near the village of Sobraon, to the east of Firozpore, where they covered the ferry of Hariké, joining both banks of the Sutlej by a fortified bridge-of-boats.

Gough moved upon their works in the dawn of the 10th February, 1846: they were garrisoned by 20,000 men; the left and centre had sixty-seven guns in battery, the right, otherwise the weakest fortification, was only protected by *zamburas*, or culverins; but batteries of heavier metal commanded the

The Rája answered, "Whoever comes against the Khálsa is treated as a foe; but with those who do not come, what is there to be done?" The Rája related this to the author with his own lips.

* Malleson: "Decisive Battles of India."

position from the right bank of the river. A force of cavalry, amounting to 10,000 men, under Rája Lál Sinh held themselves in readiness higher up the stream near Hariké, the chief command within the works being under Tej Sinh. The British force, when joined by the troops from Ludiána, amounted to 16,000 men, with an effective battering-train and twenty troops or companies of field-artillery. After three hours' bombardment from the heavy guns had failed to subdue the fire of the works, a division of all arms, under Sir R. Dick, attacked them on their weak point, the right; while Generals Smith and Gilbert marched against the better-protected left. After a stubborn fight, in which each column was in turn repulsed and rallied, the British entered at all points; Tej Sinh fled, breaking the bridge-of-boats; there was a hand-to-hand fight of two hours' duration within the works, and then all was over. Dashing into the stream the Sikh soldiers were followed by the horse-artillery where, as the Commander-in-Chief said in his despatch, they "suffered a terrible carnage." Their total loss has been variously estimated, the highest number stated being 8,000.* The British lost 320 killed—among them being Sir R. Dick, killed as he was entering the intrenchments, and sixteen other officers. The wounded amounted to over 2,000, of whom 146 were commissioned officers. The Governor-General had directed the operations in the hottest of the fire.

But the spirit of the Khálsa was broken at last.† Advancing to Kasur the Governor-General was met on the 15th by Guláb Sinh and the chief Sikh Sirdars, with whom he negotiated the preliminaries of a treaty, shortly afterwards concluded formally at Lahore. By that agreement the Durbar ceded the Jalandhar Duáb—or tract between the Sutlej and the Biyás—

* Edwards alone suggests a higher total.

† When the Ráni first urged the army to march against the British they refused, saying they would be rushing upon certain death ("Hardinge," 81).

and also Kashmir, the Government of which was made over to the wily Rája of Jammu on his advancing the kror of rupees—one millions Rx.—which had been claimed as war-indemnity, but could not be furnished from the exhausted Treasury of Lahore. The Ráni was left in the position of titular head of the Regency during the minority of young Dulip; Lál Sinh being Vazir, and Henry Lawrence—who had, on Broadfoot's death, been summoned from Nepal—was appointed British Resident. This application of the dual system began in March, 1846, but did not last very long.*

One of the servants of the Sikh State was a Muslim named Shaikh Imám-ud-din, the Governor of Kashmir. When the Rája of Jammu attempted to take possession of the valley under the treaty this man refused to acknowledge the Rája's authority; but, when Lawrence took up some battalions of sepoys supported by Durbar-troops, the Shaikh at once submitted, pleading that he had been acting under orders of the Durbar; and, producing a *parwána* bearing Lál Sinh's seal, in proof of the assertion.† Lál Sinh was brought to trial before a court presided over by Currie, the Foreign Secretary, and being found guilty of treasonable practice was deported into Hindustan by orders of the Governor-General.

This affair, combined with a number of general considerations, shook the confidence of Lord Hardinge in a scheme of administration never very hopeful. It was now proposed that the country should be avowedly put under the control of the British Resident, and a new treaty was accordingly offered to the Durbar which was concluded before the end of the year

* Hardinge and Gough were made Viscounts, and minor honours were bestowed on other officers. The troops received a gratuity of twelve months' pay.

† Lawrence was accompanied to Kashmir by General H. M. Wheeler, afterwards to do and die, almost by his side, in a still darker hour of treason.

1846: the form of a Sikh Council of Regency was maintained, and an annual payment of twenty-two lakhs of rupees was fixed as payable by the Durbar for the expenses of the British troops in the Punjab. The Ráni was obliged to retire on a handsome allowance, and English officials took the place of most of the Native chiefs in the internal administration of the country. In addition to these was the Resident's brother John, who was appointed Commissioner of the Jalandhar Duáb, where he at once set to work to introduce a revenue settlement.

At the time of the war it had been estimated that the population of the Punjab proper was about three millions, of whom not more than one-sixth had been Sikhs; that confraternity being one of religion, not of race, so that the son of a Sikh father is not a Sikh until he has undergone the initiatory rite. Now, in no part of the country had the Sikh religion been propagated with more success than in the Jalandhar Duáb; and, in no region had the evil results of military domination been more apparent, one-half the gross-produce was often taken from the Gentiles, besides cesses and transit-dues, under which production and distribution alike staggered. The Rájput, we are told, was an especial object of Sikh oppression; and all of them, who had any pretence to wealth or influence, were mercilessly crushed. The Sikh idea was to recognise nothing higher than the actual tiller of the soil, and whoever was not a member of the creed and militia of the Khálsa was only valued as a yielder of revenue; the view, in a word, once taken by Alá-ud-din Khilji. Such was the system which encountered the British administrators in the southern Punjab, and such the need of some reasonable and humane plan for the encouragement of industry and other latent resources.*

Meanwhile the Sikhs were far from real submission; and the plots against order, which are to be regarded in India as among the most honourable dangers of civilisation, were

* Ibbetson. For Sultan Ala-ud-din and his view, v. sup., Vol. 1, p. 76.

working far and wide beneath the surface. At Patna—under the rule of Sir Herbert Maddock, Deputy-Governor of Bengal—rumours were found to be rife, aimed at unsettling the minds of the people, Hindus and Muslims alike; while the sepoys of the neighbouring cantonment were being tempted to desertion and mutiny. In Lahore itself the slaughter of horned cattle—always a sore subject with Sikhs as with ordinary Hindus—was worked as a grievance by agitators, who persuaded the chandlers to close their shops, and thus inflict on the Government the clamours of a public deprived of food.* The example was followed by the trade in Jalandhar, but it was put down at both places by a mixture of firmness and conciliation.

Still, on the whole, Henry Lawrence thought that the Punjab was settling down. In January, 1848, he accepted an invitation to return to Europe with the retiring Governor-General; his place as Resident with the Lahore Regency—in point of fact Governor of the Punjab—being transferred to Currie, now Sir Frederick by virtue of a baronetcy.

[The best account of the first Punjab war is that furnished by Sir H. Lawrence to the "Calcutta Review" and included in a collection of his "Essays written in India," published as a book in 1859. See also the "History of the Sikhs," by Captain J. D. Cunningham, of which the second edition appeared in 1853. The "Career of G. Broadfoot" contains much interesting correspondence; some remarks on the war, from the standpoint of a young staff-officer, will be found in "Memorials of Herbert Edwards," Vol. I. Most of these events are skilfully summarised in Trotter's "History of India, from 1836 to 1880," Vol. I. (Captain L. J. Trotter, served with the 2nd Bengal Fusiliers from 1848). For social, industrial, and fiscal facts,

* This is one of the curious forms of negative resistance learned by the Hindus from centuries of alien oppression. It is not often used against the British, and appears to be dying out by slow degrees.

refer to Sir L. Griffin's monograph on Ránjit, already cited. "Hardinge" (in the same series) is an interesting narrative, by the present Lord Hardinge, who was by his father's side at Firozsháh and through the entire campaign. Some facts—such as the proposed supercession of the Commander-in-Chief—are made public for the first time in this very skilful little book.]

SECTION 2.—It is remarkable how much has been done for India by Governors who took office at an advanced age, and after a long service as military men. The administrations of Lords Cornwallis, Hastings, and William Bentinck are all instances of soldier-rulers—who though driven into defensive warfare—abstained from aggressive policy, and devoted as much attention as they were able to command to the business of peaceful reform. Hardinge was conspicuous in the same honourable and useful field of labour. His political work requires brief notice before considering his domestic administration.

A contemporary writer observed that, if the Punjab had been a recent difficulty, yet the chronic difficulty of Indian administration was always Audh.* No Native State had greater, or more long-standing, claims upon the attention of the Government: the princes had, ever since the days of Warren Hastings, abstained from all appearance of hostility, while their Treasury had always been open to the Company's service in the time of need; the people, on the other hand, remaining liable to a certain amount of oppression which they might have resisted had it not been backed by British bayonets. Hence the constant problem—to support the ruler yet provide for honest rule—was, perhaps, worse than difficult, and must have often appeared insoluble. The reader may remember Ben-

* "Calcutta Review," 1847. (Afterwards included in Sir H. Lawrence's Essays, cited at the end of the last section.) Lawrence was much opposed to the remedy of annexation, advocating Bentinck's principle, and protesting against a rupee of Audh revenue going into British hands.

tinck's attempt to deal with this, and the omission of Auckland to inform the "King" of the fact that the treaty, in which Bentinck's leading principle had been embodied, was not confirmed by the authorities in London. That principle—it may be recollected—was that all interference should be limited to the control of a European superintending functionary ruling—as far as possible—through native officials, and accountable to the Audh Treasury for the entire surplus revenue; and even that amount of control was to be withdrawn so soon as the requisite reform had been effected and its continuance secured. Such was also the idea which governed Hardinge's original arrangements in the Punjab; and though in that case it broke down, as we have seen, yet there was no reason why it might not have been tried in Audh. Hardinge, however, did not wish to go even so far as that with so helpless, yet so friendly, a State. The harmless old man whom Colonel Low had enthroned, had died in May, 1842, having been succeeded—as observed above—by Amjad Ali, one of the old school of debauched princes who quite neglected all public duties. The revenue was collected by contractors and grantees, and spent in fireworks and the building of seraglios. At the outset of Hardinge's administration the British Resident at the court of this potentate was Colonel Richmond, the predecessor of Broadfoot on the frontier; and he soon had to invoke the support of the Government to his remonstrances. The Government at that time, indeed, contented itself with friendly advice. The maladministration—so "His Majesty" was reminded—was extreme, and must be repaired. An apparently capable Minister had been dismissed, contrary to the expressed desire of the British Resident. Warned that this course of conduct could not be approved, the King reinstated his dismissed Minister; but a good deal of ground for complaint continued to arise, and unfortunately Colonel Richmond had not strength of character or influence for its removal. At length, in April,

1847, a scandalous scene occurred within the very precincts of the palace, in which the Minister was attacked by armed men and held to ransom. The offenders were, indeed, arrested; but the Resident—who had actually been an eye-witness of their violence—assured them that they might escape if they pleased; or, if they elected to stand a trial, that their lives should be spared. The Governor-General was naturally displeased: the word of a high British official must be kept; but he determined to go to Lucknow in person, and to take security against the recurrence of such events; while immediate beginnings should be made in the reform of the revenue administration. It was a generous effort, and gave one more proof—if such were needed—of the goodness of heart which was a prominent characteristic of Lord Hardinge. As matters were to turn out, we may, perhaps, be allowed to regret that no one remembered Bentinck's treaty: if the principle of European control, with a competent Resident, could then have been adopted, the people of Audh might have been saved much suffering, and a doubtful page of British Indian History been otherwise written. But Hardinge contented himself with once more repeating the old warnings; and the King, with ready tears, made the usual promises of amendment.

A yet more serious matter arose in South Orissa; where the British officials had, for some time past, been engaged in endeavours to put down the barbarous practice of human sacrifice, once—it is believed—wide-spread, if not general, but of late confined to the Khonds, or Kandhs, of that region.* These barbarous people, depending on vicissitudes of season for the narrow margin between living and starving in their remote

* v. *sup.* p. 46. The Kandhs, Khands, or Khonds, are said to be an aboriginal tribe, and their ideas and customs are interesting as probable factors in the evolution of Modern Hinduism, which was, perhaps, indebted to them for its sanguinary Deity, Siva (or Mahádeo in the darker aspect).—v. "Imperial Gazetteer," in Vol. "Kandhs."

forests, were in the habit of propitiating the powers of Nature by the rite known in their language as "Meria." The meaning of this was, in a word, the immolation of captive youths; who—on the day appointed—were either decapitated at once, or, in many cases, bound to a stake before a crowd of Khonds, each of whom, at the priest's signal, cut off a slice of the flesh from the trembling and shrieking victim until death came to his relief. The pieces of human flesh were then carried off, and being buried in the fields were held to cause fertility. It was reported that as many as twenty-five young persons—of both sexes—had been thus sacrificed at a single festival; and ever since the year 1836 British officers had been employed, with partial (but not complete) success, in making war upon this senseless and cruel custom. The beginning was made by Major Campbell, of the Madras army, from whose memoir we derive our knowledge of the subject. Other districts, under the Madras Government, were also partly inhabited by these wild clans; who were, however, most numerous in the border-State ruled by the tributary Rájput Chief of Bod. The Khonds —though barbarous—are a proud and aristocratic race, brave and generous. The best results were obtained, among them, after Campbell had left on account of his health. His successor was Major S. C. Macpherson, who lived among the Khonds until he won their trust. As a proof of respect and confidence, they gave him several hundreds of captives destined for the Earth-god; and, while, accepting this curious present, Macpherson not only prevented any further kidnapping, but persuaded the Khond priests to teach their followers that the flesh of goats or buffaloes would be equally agreeable to a hungry Deity. He had, however, to undergo many vicissitudes; some of the wilder clans rebelled and attacked his camp; he was at one time removed from his post on the ground that rebellion had been provoked by his measures. But he obtained a complete success at last, and having at the expense of his own comfort got a footing among the simple savages, he addressed himself most honourably to their tenderest point—their sense of the necessity of impartial justice. When the Khond clans saw that the white chief and his assistants could hear and decide honestly between contending villages, that craving for order, which is a primary want with all high-minded people, caused them to yield, to Macpherson's wishes, a compliance which they had been too proud to give upon compulsion. This noble conquest of a noble race was almost completed before Hardinge laid down his office, though Macpherson was not entirely exonerated until the next administration.*

Nor was the reformation of these brave savages the only effort of Hardinge's Government. The rite of Sati, widow-burning, which Bentinck had put down in British India continued to be practised in States beyond the limits of direct British rule; while the wholesale extermination of girl-babes was widely prevalent in both classes of territory among the higher classes of Hindus. In the former matter the Government of India could only interpose by way of remonstrance: but in such things all depends on tone; and the remonstrances of Hardinge's Government were so conveyed as to produce obedience. It was not otherwise in the matter of female-infanticide; for even in British India the Government did not think coercion was likely to do good in such a delicate business; nevertheless care was taken to let it be seen that the practice was highly repugnant to the ruling power; and a keynote was thus struck which has never since ceased to vibrate.†

* A Meria sacrifice is recorded as having taken place, in Vizagapatam district, so late as 1849, when three victims were killed. They had been sold by their parents for sixty rupees.—"Imperial Gazetteer," in Vol. "Bundaré."

† The custom consists rather of refusing to preserve life than of actual bloodshed; and is founded on the difficulty of providing for girls in later life. Side by side has grown up a system of buying kidnapped female infants, both practices are being gradually restrained.

In this, and in many other instances, notice was given to all who had the necessary power of perception, that a new era was beginning for India. Despite a most perilous and momentous war, in which the Governor-General of more than sixty years hazarded himself like the common soldiery, the work of moral change continued to be steadily pressed upon the country.

In the Punjab and Hindustan resistance was in proportion to the hardness of the popular fibre.* The Lahore Durbar, indeed, acquiesced in the disgrace of Lál Sinh and the deposition of the Ráni; but they knew well enough that the Khálsa, though subdued for the moment, was by no means cowed or tamed. In consequence of their earnest prayer the new treaty of December 1846, now made provision for the presence in the Punjab of a force of British troops, ostensibly as a garrison for Lahore: this had been formerly refused, but the objections to it were now removed because, under the new arrangement, the jurisdiction of the British Resident was to be supreme, so as to avoid the unseemly spectacle of Native misrule backed by European military power. The treaty, concluded at Bhyrowal, on December 26th, inaugurated the new order for the land of the Five Waters.

In the North-West Provinces, too, there was a sense of coming transformation, like the breath of early spring. The inquiries set on foot by Regulation IX. of 1833, had led to organic changes in the tenure of land. It was found that during the past two generations many titles had arisen which seemed opposed to the prosperity of the people. Under the Mahratta anarchy usurpations of all sorts had encroached on the right of the fisc; while the British conquest had brought in a system of transfer by auction-sale under decrees of court which were not only opposed to popular sentiment but often collusive and fraudulent. The Lieutenant-Governor who

* v. CHAPTER I. (Vol. I. p. 7.)

succeeded George Clerk was T. C. Robertson, whose name first occurred in these pages when we were dealing with Lord Amherst's negotiations in Burma. This experienced and high-minded official did all that he could to restrain the zeal of his Revenue-Board; but during the administration of Lord Hardinge he retired, and was succeeded by an official of the opposite school. Mr. James Thomason was the son of a pious Bengal Chaplain; and was himself a man of strong convictions, inclining, in civil affairs, to the verge of Benthamite Democracy. He did not see the use of the various kinds of encumbrances which had arisen like parasitic growths in the darkness of the past. And when he found that claims of this kind were supported by false testimony and forged deeds, his sometimes pedantic benevolence became righteous indignation, which perhaps extended to a whole class blame due for the fault of a few individuals. It became the rule for the Settlement-Officers to cast all the burden of proof on the Talukdar, and if his title were not quite convincing, to refer him to a Court of law, unless he agreed to accept the terms offered; these, broadly stated, were equivalent to a rent-charge of 18 per cent. on the balance settled on the estate. Thus, in an estate of which the net-produce was reckoned at Rs. 1000, if the Government demand were fixed at 600, the remaining 400 would be charged with an annuity of seventy-two to the Talukdar; and if he were dissatisfied he was told to plead his already-discredited cause in a Civil Court. To the credit of the District Judges, let it be added that they often decided these cases against the known disposition of the Government; but the Talukdars as often prejudiced their own cases by the evidently fraudulent nature of the evidence which they thought it necessary to produce.*

* True averments supported by false evidence make one of the chief obstacles to the administration of justice in India—criminal no less than civil.

In the matter of auctions of landed property Mr. Thomason had less chance of carrying out his philantropic intentions. It was doubtless most painful to him to see the families of the yeomanry reduced to the status of predial serfs, for no greater fault than lack of prevision, or simply of punctuality. But there was no remedy excepting what might be afforded by enjoining caution and forbearance on the European District-Officers. When the interest of the *málguzárs* (revenue-payers) had been converted into "property" it had to be clothed with all the attributes and conditions of property, as much when these were opposed to the wishes of the owners as when they were obviously to their advantage. Thus does the introduction of civilised ideas disturb long-established barbarism.

The only cure for these "growing-pains" of society is the slow remedy of knowledge; and for this Hardinge introduced preliminaries in the very outset of his rule. On October 10th, 1844, he issued a resolution which, mild and almost commonplace as it may now appear, came upon the men of that day as a beneficient revelation, announcing that in future preference would be given, in first appointments, to candidates educated in the Government Schools. The effect was instantaneous; in a community that is undergoing social transformation there is a fatal tendency to seek employment of the more dignified appearance; and India is not the only country in which the service of the Government, whether for that or for more ignoble reasons, has peculiar attractions. To the quick-witted and crowded. Bengali population the Minute acted as if the millennium had opened; and a well-attended meeting of Baboos, in the month of December testified to the gratitude of the Calcutta gentry by a written address of thanks to the Governor-General.

Nor were these symptoms of improvement entirely artificial or due to the action of an alien Government. Following the example of Ram Mohan Rai, several Hindus overcame the influence of caste-rules and the fear of the "black-water" so far as to visit Europe. Of these, the one most remarkable alike for his wealth, ability, and the premature close of his courageous experiment, was Dwarka Náth Tagore, who went to London in 1845 to make arrangements for the training of Hindu medical students. The noble innovator died in the following year, aged 51, and was interred at Kensal Green. His memory was honoured in Calcutta by the foundation of an educational endowment, to be known by his name and applied to scholarships for Hindus at the University of. London. Among other such spontaneous movements was one in which some generous reformers entered into a league in behalf of Hindu widows; but the feeling against re-marriage was too strong and general for much practical effect at the time, beyond a suggestion to the Hindu mind that its trammeling prescriptions were not laws of nature.

Calcutta had gone far ahead of the rest of India. Nevertheless at Madras also a note of progress was audible. Lord Elphinstone, the nephew of the great Anglo-Indian bearer of the name, on laying down the Government of Fort St. George, was honoured by the Native public with a proposal that some educational foundations should bear his name in the Presidency College. Up to that time education of the higher sort had been almost entirely confined to the schools and colleges of the missionaries in that region; and the efforts of these good men had occasionally appeared more energetic than discreet. In the Tinnevelly District, about this time, serious riots had been thus caused, during which many villages of native Christians were sacked and the inhabitants maltreated. The dispute gave rise to a serious judicial scandal, one principal result of which was the production, in the popular mind of an impression that the British Government, by that time under Lord Tweeddale, was taking side with the missionaries, and leaning in the direction of propagation more than became the administration of a non-Christian land. In all the three "Presidencies" of which British India was composed, questions of this kind were beginning to form topics of discussion in the newspapers, which was sometimes conducted with more zeal than knowledge.

In the Upper Provinces Mr. Thomason took another step, with the cordial approval of the Governor-General, in the foundation of a College of Civil Engineering at Roorkee, near the Hurdwar gorge. So far back as 1837-8 the attention of the Government of India had been directed to the project of utilising the water of the Ganges for purposes of irrigation, that year having been marked by a drought of long duration, and consequent dearth of great severity. Major (afterwards Sir Proby) Cautley was deputed to examine the Ganges at the point where it breaks into the plains, and on receipt of his report, a committee was appointed to discuss the best means of carrying out the work with as little detriment as possible to the drainage and water communication of the country. It was at length resolved to make a navigable canal, taken on the highest line of land in the neighbourhood, and the work was begun by Cautley, and carried on during his absence on leave, by Colonel Baker. The erection of workshops and foundries at Roorkee, suggested the plan of the College, which was designed by Captain Price of the Bengal Army, and opened in 1847 under the charge of Lieutenant (now General) R. Maclagan, of Engineers. It soon became the most important institution in the country, and may be said to have created an indigenous school of Civil Engineers, who have furnished the operative staff to whom India owes almost all her modern constructions. There is also at Roorkee a meteorological observatory, and it is likewise the headquarter station of the corps of Bengal Sappers.

The opening of the Ganges Canal took place in the time of Hardinge's successor, but like many other matters of that period, owed its inception to the previous administration. Great credit is doubtless due to Lord Dalhousie for the measures of internal progress with which his name is popularly connected, but the student of history will not forget that it was the war-worn Hardinge who set on foot the due preparations for the telegraph and for the reform of the Post-office, as it was Hardinge who began the system of State-aided railroads, and who set going the surveys for the ascent of the Bhore Ghat and the Great Eastern Railway.

[In addition to books already cited see "Directions for Collectors, North-West Provinces," Agra, 1846; and "Directions for Settlement Officers," ditto, Calcutta, 1852. The author has been also aided by his own professional recollections, and by a paper contributed to "Blackwood's Edinburgh Magazine," in 1862.]

SECTION 3.—The financial year ending March, 1846, saw the North-West frontier enlarged and an estimated future addition to the land-revenues; but the immediate result was a deficit of nearly one-and-a-half million of rupees.

The courageous and conscientious veteran who was at the head of the Indian Government had seen but little of business, nor had much occasion to study the science of finance. But he saw that the time for retrenchment was come, he understood that economy must be undertaken, and he set about the duty in the manner most germane to his experience. In so doing he justified the estimate taken by one who knew him well. "Hardinge," said the Duke of Wellington, "was one who undertook nothing that he did not understand." His present task was the reduction of the Indian army, especially of the large branch of it belonging to Upper India, and known, not very accurately, as the army of Bengal.*

* This odd nomenclature has persisted from the time of Clive to that of Lansdowne, so that the army which holds Peshâwar and Lahore is still officially described as that of the Bengal Presidency.

In any measure of army reform Hardinge was of opinion that two obligatory points were to be firmly kept in view. The European portion of the force must be maintained in full strength, and the whole army must be so distributed as to leave no point on the North-West frontier unguarded or unwatched. Since the fateful year 1837 the forces had been gradually increased by 120,000 men, but whatever might be the new duties involved by the treaty with the Punjab Durbar, it was a matter of absolute necessity to relieve the budget of some part at least of this heavy load.

Hardinge had already asked the Home Government to relieve him of his office before the end of the year 1847. But he did not think it either fair or expedient to leave the carrying out of these retrenchments to his successor; and he knew that his experience as a military administrator would give him a real advantage in dealing with the matter for himself.

The plan that he adopted enabled him to reduce the rank and file of the army by about 50,000 men, without creating suffering or complaint. It consisted in offering a bonus to every man willing to take his discharge, and anticipating the invalid-retirements by a twelvemonth. In this way the reductions proceeded until the number of men in an infantry battalion stood at 800, at a peace-footing, and the strength of a corps of cavalry was brought down to 420. Yet, since no diminution took place in the number of officers to each corps, the ranks could be expanded on the approach of war: the efficiency therefore of the army was not reduced in the same ratio as the expense.

The total sum saved amounted to Rx. 1,160,000. The sum payable by the Lahore Durbar—as tribute or subsidy—was Rx. 220,000; and the revenue derived from the districts ceded under the treaty was Rx. 500,000. The total relief to the finances has been estimated at two millions; so that, when Hardinge laid down his office, there was a surplus, the first since the time of Lord W. Bentinck.

The army was redistributed so as to leave some spots unguarded where the stationing of troops appeared wasteful, while important garrisons were reinforced. After the war there were 54,000 men between Delhi and Amritsir, with a battering-train and 120 field-guns.* Two moveable columns, complete in carriage and equipments, took especial charge of the Punjab, where a recrudescence of the mutinous spirit of the disbanded, but not disarmed, Khálsa troops might at any moment occur. Each of these columns was, in fact, a perfect brigade, composed of a battalion of the British Line, three regiments of Native infantry, and one of cavalry, with twelve field-guns: the first was commanded by Colin Campbell—afterwards Lord Clyde—and the second by Colonel H. M. Wheeler. Four battalions of Foot, with 20,000 Native infantry, three regiments of cavalry, and seventy guns, were available as reserve. The whole force was under the command of Major-General Sir John Littler.

The health and comfort of the British soldier at the same time received a first instalment of that solicitude which, by a most remarkable improvement in health and reduction of the death-rate, has perhaps doubled the efficiency of this indispensable bulwark of the Empire. The loss in the European army, annually, is now less than fifty per thousand—inclusive of death and invaliding—what it was in the first half of the century, there are no means of discovering, because no one paid any attention to the subject.† But the present extraordinarily low rate would never have been reached but for three reforms, all introduced by Hardinge; the establishment of an increased number of convalescent depôts on the

* These details are taken from Lawrence to whom they were furnished by Colonel Wood, Military Secretary to Lord Hardinge.

† From 1870 to 1883, the rate diminished by twelve in the 1,000. From this one can conjecture what the diminution may have been during the previous twenty-three years between 1847 and 1870.

hills; the allowance of ice for hospitals; and the provision of *punkhas* to be worked in the barracks night and day throughout the hot weather, at the public expense.

Another important work to which Hardinge attended—greatly to the benefit of the general public as also to the comfort and despatch of military movements—was the Grand Trunk Road, from Calcutta to Delhi. Now that good railway accomodation is complete over the whole of this line of country, that route is chiefly valuable for local transport: but a broad road planted with trees and provided with rest-houses, and wells, was a work of equal use and humanity at the time; and its maintenance should never be neglected. A rebellion may easily cause interruption to railway communication; but a good road is less easily destroyed; and it was seen in 1857 how essential it might be to the despatch of small but important detachments. The postal-reform above referred to was devised and sent home for sanction under the orders of Lord Hardinge; and transit-dues were abolished by him over the interior of the country. He watched and forwarded that noble undertaking, the Grand Trigonometric Survey of India: while his artistic taste and spirit were displayed in the preservation of great monuments of former rulers; including the famous "Taj Mahal," which he found going to ruin on his visit to Agra. The health and self-respect of the citizens of the modern capital received their greatest impetus during this administration, under which an Act was passed through the Legislative Council whereby Calcutta was endowed with a Municipal Council. Under progressive developments this has now expanded into an elective body providing for the water-supply, drainage, and general management of the city; and spending annually somewhere about half a million. But whatever be the nature of the expansion in the constitution and usefulness of this body, its first origination is due to Lord Hardinge; and to his forethought may be fairly ascribed the fact that what was once a haphazard collection of houses upon a pestilential swamp has become a capital worthy of a great Empire; with 160 miles of good roads, a population of near three-quarters of a million of human beings, and a general death-rate of thirty per 1,000.*

Finally must be mentioned what may have seemed at the time little more than an interesting experiment. By encouraging the plantation of tea on Government estates, Hardinge founded a virtually new industry.† In 1890 the total exportation of tea from India was valued at five millions and a quarter; and the British Islands took more tea from India than from China.

And now the time approached when this good and able public servant should lay down his heavy burden. He was now in his sixty-fourth year, having spent nearly half a century in continuous and often arduous service. He returned to Calcutta from his last tour in November, 1847. Those who can remember that period will connect it in their memory with commercial disaster and the ruin of many a fair reputation. But they will also bear in mind the universal respect that attended the wise and unselfish veteran. All classes of the Calcutta community combined to pay a farewell tribute to the man who had ruled India with unsurpassed firmness, courtesy, and devotion; whose honourable exertions—for ten hours a day during three and a half years—had advanced their moral and physical well-being, and brought them prosperity and peace.

On the 24th of December, a meeting was held at the Town Hall of Calcutta, to give expression and effect to these feelings, and the Natives present brought forward an important amend-

* The European death-rate of Calcutta is about fifteen per 1000, lower than that of most European cities: and this in a locality known a century ago as "Golgotha."

† The Assam tea-plantations began before his time, but did not take their final development until some years later.

ment to the proposed address which was ultimately incorporated, with some modification. This clause especially dwelt on the obligations conferred on India in the direction of the encouragement of education. In acknowleging this address the Governor-General prominently referred to "the united voice of the Native and European inhabitants;" and begged his hearers to recollect that the welfare of the country must depend upon the identity of interests among all classes. A fine equestrian statue, by J. H. Foley, R.A., on the plain in front of the Vice-regal Palace, perpetuates the gratitude and admiration of the people.

CHAPTER XIX.

THE CLOSE OF AN EPOCH.

Section 1 : The second Sikh war.—Section 2 : Annexation.—Section 3 : Internal administration.

SECTION 1.—The undiscriminating admiration of force has led men to single out Lord Wellesley as the ideal ruler of India and to talk as if Lord Dalhousie alone, in later days, came up to the Wellesley standard. Perhaps a calm and attentive study of the facts briefly summed up in these pages may tend to modify that view. We may even think that we come to see that much of what we had been inclined to attribute to those able statesmen was prepared, and even affected by other hands. Most of all is it likely that we may learn to dilute the strength of our belief in the unaided power of any individuals, however intelligent or highly-placed ; and to see that their work has been mostly confined to the shaping of details: while the great current of History—in India and elsewhere—has been formed by the needs of man and the natural process of evolution.

Thus, when we think of Dalhousie as fixing the future destinies of British India, by bringing the frontiers into contact with Upper Burma, with the Chinese Empire, and with Russian Turkestan, we ought not to forget that all those approaches had already begun, in the wars of Hastings, Amherst, and Auckland. The part of Dalhousie's political conduct which was original has, indeed, been condemned by many good judges, and, partly, by the logic of events, while his solution of the Punjab problem—which is less open to dispute—had been foreseen and prepared by Hardinge, his immediate predecessor. How that solution was precipitated will now be briefly shown.

Lord Dalhousie landed in Calcutta on January 12th, 1848. He was in his thirty-sixth year, already distinguished as an adminstrator, having, as President of the Board of Trade, been engaged in the recent development of railway-work in the British Islands. He was welcomed by Hardinge with the assurance that all was peace in India; and so confident of this were those best qualified to judge that Colonel Lawrence was one of those who embarked with the departing ex-Governor on the 18th.

On the 23rd February, Lord Tweeddale was relieved of the charge of the Madras Government by Sir Henry Pottinger, formerly Resident with the Amirs of Sindh, while Sir G. Clerk was retiring from a short tenure of Bombay, to be succeeded by Lord Falkland. In Sindh Mr. Pringle ruled in the room of Sir Charles Napier, while Sir F. Currie acted as Resident, and virtual head of the Regency, at the Court of the youthful Rája of Lahore.

Suddenly the bolt fell from the cloudless sky. Many of the Punjab districts besides those in the Jalandhar Duáb were under charge of British officers, who were engaged in drilling local levies and making tentative land-settlements and other beginnings of orderly administration. Among other regions yet administered by Native Chiefs was the district of Multan, on the Sindh border, where stood a famous fortress taken from the Patháns in 1818 by Ranjit Sinh. Since that time the fort and country had been held by Diwán Sáwan Mall, one of Ranjit's best adminstrators; and, on his death, by his cruel and unprincipled son, Mulráj.

Towards the end of 1847 Diwán Mulráj, dissatisfied with the

new system of Government, had tendered his resignation; he was asked to reconsider it; but when the winter was over he repeated his request to be relieved, and a Sirdar named Khán Sinh was accordingly sent to take charge, accompanied by Mr. Agnew, of the Civil Service, who was to be "political" adviser, and who took as his assistant, Lieutenant Anderson, of the Bombay army. It seems now to be pretty well established that the whole thing was an intrigue, devised to give occupation to the British authorities while the emissaries of the Ráni raised the Sikhs for a general revolt.

On arriving at Multan the new Názim and his European associates were received with apparent friendliness, and shown over the fort; but on leaving the city to return to the camp, outside, they were attacked by a murderous soldier in the service of Mulráj. The Diwán turned his horse's head and rode to his suburban villa; but his escort turned back—apparently by his orders—to join in the attack. Agnew and Anderson were carried off, covered with sword-cuts; and, their dwelling-place being made as defensible as possible, they sent word to Banu, the nearest point where a British officer could be hoped for, and awaited events. But all in vain; for the escort was soon corrupted and persuaded to desert, and then the baggage cattle were driven off. By the evening of April 19, Agnew and Anderson were alone, but for the company of a few faithful followers, and the loyal Sirdar, Khán Sinh. The mob now approached, and the building was violently invaded by armed men. Quietly and simply the helpless young men awaited their murderers; their heads were struck off, their bodies mutilated and at last buried with ignominy. But they had told their murderers they would not die unavenged; and the vengence was soon to come. There was another young Briton in the neighbouring district in Banu, who heard of the attack on Agnew and hastened to his relief. Mulráj came out to stop him; and a spectacle was presented worthy of the world's wonder. On one side one of the richest men in Asia, strong in a position inherited from a powerful father, with thousands of veteran soldiers, artillery, and all munitions of war; on the other an isolated alien with two indifferent guns, and no followers but what he could raise and drill as he marched. But one fought for his country the other for himself alone, and the English officer, Herbert Edwardes, beginning the campaign with his improvised levies, soon obtained help from General von Cortlandt, of the Sikh army, and from the Nawáb of Baháwalpore, already mentioned as friendly in 1838. In a long and trying engagement on the Chenáb he was left to himself by the Baháwalpore troops, and only joined by Cortlandt after seven hours of desperate endurance; but at the end of the day the men of Multan were in full retreat. That was on the 18th of June; Edwardes was soon after joined by another young officer —Lt. E. Lake of the Bengal Engineers—in whose hands the Baháwalpore contingent gradually became more trustworthy; On July 3rd, the associated forces were close to Multan. Here they were again confronted by the enemy, near the suburban village of Sadusám; but Edwardes was no longer alone or obliged to maintain a long defence. Aided most ably by Lake he led his men from point to point. Mulráj was unhorsed and scared off the field; in the two actions the enemy lost ten guns; after the second Mulráj and his men were cooped up within the walls of Multan.

But there the tide of success seemed to have lost its power, and a long ebb succeeded. In vain did Currie implore the Commander-in-Chief to send British troops to Multan. Lord Gough, so rash in action, now had a long relapse of prudence; and Edwardes would have been unsupported and exposed to be overwhelmed, had not Currie, on his own responsibility, despatched a brigade to his assistance. This was the more meritorious because by this time the general disaffection of the Sikh was becoming too plain to be any longer ignored. Fifteen conspirators had been arrested in Lahore alone, and the Rani, being identified with the plot, was deported to Benares. Perhaps, however, as has been hinted by a careful writer, Currie was not sorry to get rid of so dangerous a body of troops with their Sikh officers, and their doubtfully-affected Sirdar. Currie sent a British brigade afterwards, having at length obtained the consent of Lord Gough. Tej Sinh, the betrayer of the Khálsa, seemed the only Chief of distinction who remained true to the British connection; and the survivors of his victims, assured that they had not been beaten by fair means, were eager to try conclusions with the British once more. From Jalandar to Pesháwar, the subterranean current was traced; and in Sikh villages the word went forth, so that all the adult males sharpened their swords, and stood prepared for action. But in the course of August, Currie sent off the Lahore brigade to reinforce the leaguer; and on September 4th, the brigade from Firozpore also joined the camp before Multan, a heavy battering train being added. Eleven days later the Sikh contingent under Rája Sher Sinh deserted to the enemy, on which the siege had to be raised, and the small British force was invested in its turn in its camp at Suraj Khund, on the Chenáb. The resistance of one fortress had developed into the rebellion of a Province, for Chatr Sinh, who was raising the Trans-Indus was a prominent member of the Council of Regency, and Sher Sinh was his son. The family came from Atári, and their influence extended to the Sutlej.

British interests in the Punjab were at low-water mark, indeed, by the end of September. The defection of Sher Sinh had been due to the rebellion of his father, Chatr Sinh, the Governor of Hazára. On the other side of the Indus, the brother of Dost Muhamad, Amir of Kábul, had expelled Major George Lawrence, the Commissioner, and the Major and his family were prisoners in the hands of Chatr Sinh. Only a few of Henry Lawrence's disciples —Herbert, Nicholson, James

Abbott, and Raynell Taylor—still maintained a precarious footing in their Districts: in the hills north-east of Jalandar John Lawrence had to take the field.*

The keen political instinct of the new Governor-General penetrated to the heart of the problem. Hardinge's well-meant scheme had failed, as indeed he had always feared it might; the rude soldier-government of the Sikhs could not be fused with a civilised system of administration. "There is no course open to us," so he wrote to the authorities at home, "there is no course open to us but to prepare for a general Punjab war, and ultimately to occupy the country."

In pursuance of this clear and bold policy, which met with no opposition from London, Dalhousie ordered up a strong column from Sindh to reinforce General Whish before Multan. On the other side of India the garrisons of Meerut and Ambala, the convalescents from the hill-depôts, and the remainder of the brigades of Firozpore and Jalandar concentrated at Lahore. The brave old Commander-in-Chief began one of his blundering campaigns in the beautiful month of November. Men and officers were sacrificed, even guns lost on this and that side of the Chenáb river; the "extensive combinations" of Lord Gough had no success beyond interposing between Sher Sinh and Multán—if indeed, the Sirdar had any desire to relieve that fortress. But the doom of the blood-stained stronghold approached. On the 21st of December the column from Sindh arrived, with a force increased to 17,000 British troops, exclusive of irregulars and Patnán allies, and more than sixty siege guns: the General began the attack in earnest on December 27th, by 4 p.m. on that day the suburbs had been all won. Next day the batteries opened on the city walls, the bombardment continuing throughout the night; on the 29th, a sally of the garrison was

* Abbott and Taylor held their posts throughout. Herbert had to surrender the fort of Attak, and join the other captives. Nicholson rode for his life and got safe into Lahore.

repulsed with slaughter, Henry Lawrence who had now returned from home with a Knighthood-of-the-Bath, taking part in the action side by side with the gallant Edwardes. On the 30th, a mortar laid by Lieutenant D. J. Newall, of the Bengal Artillery, exploded the chief magazine of the citadel with 500 of the garrison, but when the explosion was over the cannonade recommenced on both sides. On the first day of the year 1849, the breach by the Delhi Gate became practicable; and it was carried on the following morning by a column of Bombay troops led by Captain Leith. The capture of the city was, however, not completed until next day; when siege was immediately laid to the citadel, where Mulráj, disheartened but desperate, held out with about 3,000 of his most trusted followers.

While this citadel still held out, Lord Gough had completed his preliminary operations in the fearless old fashion above described, and on January 10th, found himself operating in the plains between the Upper Chenáb and the Jehlam, with a system of strategy hardly superior than that with which Alexander had manœuvred against Porus on the same scene more than twenty centuries before.* Sher Sinh was encamped behind the village of Chiliánwala, covered by the heights of Rasul, with his rear protected by the river Jehlam. The strategic objective of the British General was to prevent the junction of Chatr Sinh, and beat the son before the arrival of the father. Sher Sinh on the other hand had less to gain by an immediate engagement, for he outnumbered the British by more than two to one, while he held a position naturally strong, and it was defended by no less than sixty guns. So far, then, Lord Gough was apparently justified in forcing a battle. But all that he did afterwards was hastily conceived, and unskilfully executed. On the morning of the 13th he moved down, and

* v. *sup.*, CHAPTER II., Section 2. Alexander fought a battle with Porus, whom he completely routed, on or near the field of Chiliánwala.

leaving his right exposed to a flank movement, marched on the point fronting Chilianwála. There he saw the Sikh outposts, which he drove in about mid-day, at the same time bringing his left forward till his line faced that of the enemy. The lessons of Firozsháh might then have come into the veteran's mind, and some at least of the errors of that fatal field might have been avoided. But some men never learn, and Gough was almost, if not quite, one of these. At 3 p.m. of a winter afternoon he sent his infantry across a mile of jungle to capture the Sikh guns, which was effected with much slaughter on both sides; on his right a fearful rout was caused by an unauthorised order of retreat; when the daylight was gone, the troops were withdrawn from the field they had so hardly won; the British wounded were abandoned, and out of forty guns taken from the enemy, all but twelve were lost, besides four belonging to the British. The killed amounted to 600, the wounded were over 1,600. The enemy retained his position under Rasul, where he fired a royal salute in honour of his victory. A few days later Chatr Sinh came up, and the Sikhs tried to negotiate on equal belligerent terms through the mediation of George Lawrence as captive. Under strict orders from the Governor-General, however, Sir. H. Lawrence rejected the offer of negotiation, and sent his brother back to the rebel camp with a message to the effect that nothing would be listened to short of a total surrender.

While the two armies were thus employed the siege of the citadel went forward at Multan. On January 4th it had been completely invested, and in less than a week every building within the precincts had been unroofed by the fire of the British guns and mortars, so that Mulráj had no shelter for his head but a bomb-proof archway. On the 12th the garrison attempted a sally; but it was repulsed at once. On the 18th the counterscarp was blown in by the explosion of a mine on one side; and the operation was repeated on the other three days later. Then the rebel's heart failed him, and he sent a messenger to beg mercy for his life. The stern reply went back that he must surrender unconditionally by the morrow's sunrise, or take the consequences. Accordingly, on the morning of the 22nd, the garrison, filing out, piled arms before the British Commander, followed by the surrender of the traitor himself. The British loss in this well-managed affair was about 1,200 killed and wounded. The mangled bodies of Agnew and Anderson received honourable sepulture, and Mulráj was sent to Lahore to take his trial on charges of treason and abetment of murder.

The month after Chiliánwala was not otherwise a busy period. On the night of February 12th the enemy decamped silently from Rasul, and on the 13th had marched round the British as if to fall upon Lahore; but on the following day Gough learned that the Sikhs had fallen back on Gujarát by the Chenáb, having been prevented from present mischief by the convergence of British columns, while the garrison of Lahore was on the alert, and Whish approaching from the direction of Multan. On the 20th this General arrived at headquarters, within three miles of the Sikh camp, strengthening Lord Gough's army by a welcome reinforcement of 9,000 men.

On the 21st, at 7.30 a.m., while larks were singing in the clear sky and the glacier-peaks of the Himála made a distant background, the British marched to the attack, 23,000 strong, with 90 pieces of cannon. By a judicious use of superior artillery Gough was enabled to advance his foot until they got near enough to charge. The left of the Sikh army was then rolled back upon the centre, while the right was cut off by the advance of General Colin Campbell; their cavalry—numerous in itself, and swelled by a reinforcement of Afghán horse—was intimidated and neutralised by the horse-artillery: by 1 p.m. the last Sikh army—estimated at 50,000 men, with 60 guns—was scattered and in full flight. The standing camp and almost all the guns fell at once into the victors' hands;

the pursuit was urged by Sir Walter Gilbert with remorseless vigour; by the 13th of March the whole remnant of the Sikh army was captured and disarmed, the European captives were free, the Afgháns galloping to their stony homes.

It only now remained to dispose of the destinies of the Punjab, since the country could no longer be left at the mercy of the Sikhs. In spite of the disapproval of Sir H. Lawrence the Governor-General held that no other course was open but the direct introduction of British administration; and, judging by subsequent events, most persons will probably be of the same opinion. There never would be peace, Dalhousie thought, till all power and means of making war were permanently denied to the Sikhs. Even his sagacity could hardly have forseen that the benefits of annexation could have been so wide and deep as they have been—that a once barbarous people would have become, in the course of one generation, such willing and valuable subjects. Thus, apart from all debateable cases, the annexation of the Punjab stands by itself, a hard necessity justified by all results.

The only weak spot in the affair was the unavoidable deposition of the ten-year old boy, whom Hardinge had been constrained to regard as son of Ranjit and legitimate ruler of Lahore. Dalhousie wrote of this as a thing painful, but necessary. The crown lands, the treasury, the jewel-house, of the Ráj were confiscated; but a yearly sum of "not less than four, or more than five, lakhs" was set aside "for the support of Dulip Sinh, his relatives, and the servants of the State." The boy's personal share of this allowance was at first £12,000 a year, raised at his majority to £25,000; and, on this question, many an ignoble wrangle has since ensued.*

The only other warlike incident of this period was the

* It was on this occasion that the "Koh-i-nur" diamond came into British possession, and so ultimately became part of the national regalia in London. (*sup.* p. 101.)

termination of the Meria campaign on the Mahánadi. Colonel Campbell had returned, and with a force commanded by Colonel Dyce was pacifying Gumsur, where abuse of authority, wrongly—as it proved—attributed to Macpherson, had prolonged the excitement. In 1848 a brigade of Sepoys with four guns had to be marched against the Rája of Bod; the stockades of the rebels were easily taken, and the refractory Rája was led captive into British territory. Campbell then applied his intelligence and his local influence to persuading the Khonds that it was better for themselves to give up their cruel and senseless practices; before the middle of the year the last rebel had been hunted down, and the whole stock and store of Merias, kept for sacrifice, had been surrendered to the authorities.

It only remains to be added that Mulráj, having been found guilty on the charges arising out of the deaths of Agnew and Anderson, was sentenced by the Governor-General to imprisonment for life, and disappeared for ever from the scene of Indian History July 21st, 1849.

[Lawrence's "Essays." "Parliamentary Papers." Edwardes's "Year on the Punjab Frontier." Bosworth Smith's "Life of Lord Lawrence." "Dalhousie," by Sir W. W. Hunter ("Rulers" series). Campbell's "Adventures among the Khonds." Malleson's "Decisive Battles of India." Trotter's "India under Victoria" becomes very interesting for the campaign ending with Gilbert's pursuit of the Sikhs and Afghâns; Capt. Trotter having taken part in the most stirring and important events of the time. For the story of the Koh-i-nur see article "Diamonds," by Mr. E. Streeter, in "Chambers' Encyclopedia.]

SECTION 2.—We have next to consider a class of annexations of a more debateable kind, which form the main characteristic of Dalhousie's administration as usually regarded.

In the India of that era the old antagonism of East and

West had reached its extreme point. Individualism and apathy had taken hold of all classes of Native society: the Muslim left all to Destiny, while the Hindu—having long ago exhausted his moral inheritance—had come to look upon life as an unprofitable burden. How reconcile these conditions with the bustling activity of foreign rulers, who regarded material prosperity as the object of united and disciplined exertion; or, if they blended with that object any spiritual ideal, put such ideal into a shape which neither Hindu nor Muslim was able to understand? The Anglo-Indians believed in the God of Battles, the Deity of the Puritans; a sort of practical heavenly-king that encouraged energy and favoured the endeavours of those who kept their powder dry. Accordingly they showed a sort of aggressive benevolence, of whose conscientious motives nothing appeared to the subject races but a determination to have the largest possible revenue punctually paid, together with the smallest possible minimum of festival, ancestral usage, or mortmain. The members of this governing class were bent on taking their mission so seriously amongst communities whose evolution had been determined by events and influences of which that mission could take no account.

British-Indian statesmanship had, in a word, entered upon a phase undreamed of by the precursors of the Empire. From Warren Hastings to Bentinck, the rulers of India, taking counsel from such advisers as Colebrooke, Elphinstone, Metcalfe, and Munro, had looked on the laws and creeds of the people with indulgence if not with respect: as things, not perhaps very good in themselves, yet needful to those who had grown up in them. But such a way of looking at matters could not endure; and the time was coming when the "paramount power"—asserted by the Marquess of Hastings—was to pass beyond bodily sway and concern itself with the direction of the mind. We saw, in the last chapter, with how much effervescence the Time-Spirit of Western progress was already entering into the long dream of the Oriental World. And now the brilliant Scottish nobleman, young in years, but mature in administrative skill, was to bring his ability and earnestness to a farther instalment of the same process. Himself a member of the Presbyterian Church, he was seconded by some distinguished subordinates of equally decided Puritan principles. No direct official intercourse, indeed, took place between governors and governed in which a spirit of proselytism could be clearly detected; yet it came to be felt that—politically if not religiously—the Government was inclined to go beyond its hitherto understood sphere.

Most signally was this new departure shown by the application of what has been called "the doctrine of lapse," as to which the following explanation may be found of service.

Among the Hindus one of the fundamental principles of society was—as mentioned in an early part of this work—the continuation of the family by virtue of the presence of deceased fathers, ministered to by the heirs.* For the due provision of that ministration a childless man was allowed—nay encouraged—to have recourse to adoption, whereby a son was grafted on to the barren root, ceasing thenceforth all connection with his own natural kindred. The adopted son now became, to all intents and purposes, a member of the new family, with the same rights of succession as if he had been born there. In regard, however, to political successions a qualifying rule had been laid down, which may be best stated in the actual language of a despatch of the time.

"There is no validity," said the Court of Directors, "in an adoption conveying succession to . . . the rights of sovereignty, *in a dependent principality*, unless the adoption shall have received the sanction of the supreme power." †

* *Sup.* CHAPTER II. Section 1.

† Letter of Court, d. Jan. 26, 1853, par. 4. The rest of this paragraph —which is of equal importance—will be referred to in another connection. See also Minute, by Sir C. Metcalfe, in Kaye's "Papers."

This rule, if regarded as a feudal ceremony, was open to no objection. There were States—though perhaps the term "sovereignty" was too strong to be strictly applicable to them —in which a certain power of rule and management had been conferred by the central Government; such cases only differed from a purely official lieutenancy in that the post was hereditary; and the Government, as answerable for the welfare of the inhabitants, might maintain a certain supervision over the succession. But Dalhousie made it the basis of a regular system: "I cannot," he wrote, "conceive it possible for anyone to dispute the policy of taking advantage of every just opportunity for consolidating the territories which already belong to us by taking possession of States which may lapse in the midst of them . . . and for extending the uniform application of our system of Government to those whose best interests—we sincerely believe—will be promoted thereby." It was a generous idea, not a sordid greed; yet the most generous idea that a man may form is not necessarily just. If the people were so incurably habituated to maladministration that they preferred it to civilised governance, had the British rulers any right to interfere?

This, then, was the doctrine of lapse. If a Rája died leaving a son there was nothing to be done. But a son substituted by adoption would never be allowed to succeed; for to allow that would be throwing away a "just opportunity" of introducing a "system of Government" which was good for "the interests" of the inhabitants—whether they thought so or not. The doctrine came to be applied to several principalities during Dalhousie's adminstration; although all of his annexations were not made on the same ground. The first case—earlier even than that of the Punjab—occurred in Satára, where Elphinstone had been permitted by Lord Hastings to acknowledge a descendant of the founder of the Mahratta Empire. In 1839 Lord Auckland had deposed him for insubordination, making his brother, Appa Sahib, chief in his room. Appa died in

1848, leaving an adopted son; and Sir G. Clerk, then Governor of Bombay, recommended that he should be recognised as successor. The Governor-General, on the other hand, looked on the State as a lawful windfall; the Government—he wrote—was, in such a case, "bound to take that which is justly and legally its due." In so saying he was acting upon a precedent established by Lord Ellenborough, and even followed by Lord Hardinge: though not perhaps quite to the present extent. For whereas it had formerly been held that the acknowledgement of adoption, in dependent States, was an act of grace and favour, Dalhousie looked upon it as the sacrifice of "rightful opportunities to acquire territory and revenue." Disregarding the protests of men of the old school, of whom the most distinguished was H. St. G. Tucker, the Home-Government yielded to Dalhousie's arguments; and Satára was annexed—without any attempt to ascertain the feeling or desire of the subjects.

The next State to come into the net was the petty principality of Karaoli, in Rájputána, whose chief died in 1852, having adopted a son with the knowledge and concurrence of the British Resident. Here, again, the Governor-General pressed his doctrine of lapse; but the Court of Directors held out firmly. The State was not "dependent," wrote the Court—in the despatch cited above—it was "a protected ally": and Dalhousie was further informed that it would be difficult to conceive a case in regard to which his doctrine would be less applicable. The distinction was a very fine one; Satára was also a State—or the remnant of a State—which had existed before a British Factor had ever exercised political authority in India. Nevertheless, whatever was the real scruple, it prevailed. The State of Karaoli was spared, to render good service in the Revolt of 1857. It is to be added that Dalhousie himself expressed some hesitation in the extension of his favourite principle to this case.

The next important annexation was that of Nágpore, which, however, presented the peculiarity that there had been no formal adoption of an heir before the Rája's death.* The territory was of considerable extent—larger than the whole area of the British Islands—the acquisition of which would open out the best cotton-lands of India and an unbroken communication between Calcutta and Bombay. The ladies of the family were known to be prepared with a candidate to the succession; and Mr. C. G. Mansel, the Resident, warmly supported their design. When the case came before the Governor-General in Council, the same line was adopted by the military member, General John Low, whose intrepid conduct on a somewhat similar occasion at Lucknow has been described in the last chapter. He pointed out that the recent action in regard to Satára had already given a shock to the public conscience; and affirmed, as the result of a long and varied experience, that the aristocracy was not the only section of the Native community whose feelings were opposed to the extension of direct British administration. But his arguments were to no purpose; his plea was over-ruled; Mansel was rebuked; and Nágpore became a British Commissionership, where no claims of birth or talent could obtain for any Asiatic a post of £1,000 a year.

Altogether, the doctrine of lapse was applied by Dalhousie in eight cases, great or small; besides the cases of the Punjab and Audh, which rested on other grounds. It is easy now to point to the troubles that were prepared by many of these acts; the violent resentments that they caused to be displayed during the Mutiny of the Bengal Army showed the error of the principle. But it should never be forgotten that—were but

* There was a similar instance in 1849, when the chief of the State of Sambalpore—to the south-east of Nágpore—died without issue or adoption, and the State lapsed, in conformity (as asserted) with the deceased's own wish. It was afterwards the seat of considerable disturbance.

that principle once granted—Lord Dalhousie's policy was consistent, and benevolent enough. Taught by the logic of events, the Queen's Government inaugurated the abolition of the Company's political power by a general and complete concession of the right of adoption. No annexation has since occurred; nay, one large territory has been restored to its Native dynasty; and the evils of what was called "power without responsibility" have been avoided by other and less objectionable expedients. But, once for all, let it be recorded that the hard things said of Dalhousie were as untrue as they were unbecoming. No man of higher mind or purer integrity ever ruled in India.

The annexation of the Punjab has been mentioned in its proper place. Our present limits only allow us to add that, under Dalhousie's wise and strong control, that once turbulent country was completely disarmed and pacified. The two Lawrences, Henry and John, acted there together for some four years; during which the revenue-administration was reformed, the power of the Sikh Barons curtailed and rendered harmless, trade freed from transit-dues, while great public works were set on foot. But the two great brethern were not always actuated by the same ideas; and about 1852 their differences became accentuated to such a degree that the Governor-General found himself obliged to choose which of them was to administer the Punjab. In February, 1853, John Lawrence was appointed Chief Commissioner, while the chivalrous, but at times somewhat unpractical, soldier was transferred to the Agency of Rájputána.

Before noticing the annexation of Audh, it will be proper to say a few words about an addition to the Indian Empire due to conquest. It may be remembered that in 1826, Lord Amherst had made a Treaty with the humbled Government of Ava, by which the Company obtained possession of Arakan and Tenasserim. Since then the despotic rulers of Burma and their satraps had continued an uninterrupted course of muffled hostility; until at length the Government of India was aroused to repressive action by a memorial from the mercantile community of Rangoon, in September, 1851. Commodore Lambert was sent with a man-of-war, to investigate these complaints on the spot; but representations which he was led to make were neglected; and his officers being treated with gross indignity by the Governor of Rangoon, the Commodore became engaged in hostilities with the forts on the river.

Such transactions in Asia can have but one issue. Dalhousie announced his intention to punish barbarian insolence and protect the commercial interests assailed. Issuing his declaration of war in February, during the absence from the capital of the Chief of the Army, he personally and rapidly organised an expedition provided with the means of occupying Rangoon before the break of the monsoon, and of establishing a basis of operations there for the ensuing cool season. The land forces, nearly 6,000 strong, were commanded by General Godwin (who had taken part in the former war), and supported by a fleet of steamers armed with 159 guns. As the Burmese refused to so much as receive the Governor-General's ultimatum, Rangoon was assaulted on April 11th, and captured under a fierce artillery-fire from the Burmese; whose army, however, on being defeated, presently dispersed. The British troops, being comfortably hutted and well looked-to in every respect, suffered but little from the climate; when the rains ceased, they advanced on Prome; and the people of Pegu—the Province of which Rangoon is the port—gladly accepted a conquest which freed them from oppression. The prosperity and progress of the ensuing thirty years were almost beyond belief. The trade of Rangoon increased six-fold; in the ten years alone, from 1871 to 1881, the population of the surrounding district increased 81 per cent. The progress of trade was only limited by the exactions and molestations which the barbarous Court of Upper Burma was still able to exercise, till it was finally overthrown by Lord Dufferin.

The last great annexation was that of Audh, and it is necessary to consider this with the more care, both by reason of the past connection of the Province with British India and of the influence it was to exert upon future events.

We have seen the perennial difficulties of the case, the unratified treaty of 1837, the visit and warning of Hardinge ten years later. Since then matters had been by no means improving, and all the experts were now convinced that no improvement was to be expected. Why Audh was so much more hopeless than other Native States, or what special circumstances made it more impossible to allow revelry and negligence at Lucknow than at the Courts of Haidárábad and Indore, were questions that were not asked, and might have been hard to answer.* But it cannot be denied that the so-called "Kings" had received abundant warnings, and had persisted in their idiotic courses with a full knowledge of the probable consequences. Thus, when Dalhousie received assurances from Sleeman, specially commissioned, and from Outram, who succeeded as Official Resident, that the Government could no longer, with regard either to its reputation or its duty to the people, "forbear to take over the administration," he had, it must be allowed, strong reason for action. Unhappily, no one seems to have thought of the treaty of 1837, which, nevertheless, morally bound all parties. It can be scarcely questioned that the Native politicians of Audh, who had never heard of the view taken at the India House, believed that the treaty was in force; and that the worst that could happen would be that the King would be relieved of all vestiges of responsibility, that the Resident would administer through Native agency, and that the surplus revenues would remain in the local treasury.

* For an able and sympathetic examination of the special causes of mal administration in Audh, consult Sir H. Lawrence, "Essays," 129. f.f.

Sir Henry Lawrence was, after General Low, the most accredited member of the old school of Anglo-Indian diplomacy. More than ten years had elapsed since he had admitted that the Government was "authorised by treaty to assume the management" of all the Province; but he had been careful to add that it should be assumed, under the rules laid down by Bentinck, "let the administration . . . as far as possible, be Native"; he said "*let not a rupee come into the Company's coffers.*"* Dalhousie and his "honourable masters" are not to blame for the conclusion that a treaty ought to be offered to the incompetent "King of Audh," nor even for deposing him when he refused to be relieved of power. But where was the necessity of declaring the Province a part of British India? That was, truly, the offence to good faith, to the public conscience, to the Fortune that frowns upon imprudence. When, after a scene of tears and childish murmurs, the last of the Nawábs was deposed, the annexation of the Province was completed (Feb. 13th, 1856) by the introduction of British officers and British codes, and everything calculated to make the people happy according to British ideas, and humiliated according to their own. "Millions of God's creatures," the Governor-General thought, "would draw freedom and happiness from the change." The gratitude of those millions took a strange form.

The rest of Dalhousie's doings with Native States was of the like complexion. In the case of the Nizám he had a problem somewhat resembling the case of Audh, a Muslim Court, and the sort of administration that was most likely to offend fastidious Western critics. In one respect matters were even worse: not only was the country distracted by the feuds and wars of the Tálukdars and the rapacities of an unpaid soldiery; but there was an old-standing debt due to the Company, and ever accumulating at compound interest. In course of time

* Italics in original.

this debt, principally accruing on account of the pay of the "contingent," had swollen to three-quarters of a million of R.x; and in 1851 the Nizám, under long pressure, paid off more than half, and promised to make up the balance by cessions of territory. In November of the following year Gen. Fraser, the old Resident, retired, and was succeeded by General Low, who used all his influence to persuade the Nizám to redeem his pledge, but met with no success. At length a new treaty was imposed upon him, whereby the numbers and organisation of the force were somewhat altered, and a temporary assignment was made of districts estimated to yield R.x. 500,000, for the pay of the officers and men. The financial strain at once ceased, and the establishment of a body of disciplined troops under European officers ensured the maintenance of order in the remainder of the Nizám's dominions.

The arrangements with the descendant of the other great southern feudatory, the Nawáb of the Carnatic, who had been so important in the preceding century, were characterised by what may be called by some a scorn of shams, by others a pedantic rigour. The empty title, with a considerable allowance of yearly stipend, had been enjoyed for three generations since the treaty made by Lord Wellesley in 1801. When the last lineal heir died the doctrine of lapse was applied, and the dynasty was pronounced to have came to an end. A similar decision was pronounced in regard to the Mahratta chiefship of Tanjore, where the Rája died without an heir of his body. The like also happened in Upper India, at Bithur, where the the once troublesome Báji Ráo, who had been pensioned in accordance with Malcolm's promise, left an adopted son, Dhundu Panth, better known some ten years later as "the Nána Sáhib." The Government refused to continue the pension.

A similar spirit of levelling-down entered into the relations of the Government with the faded Court of the Mughal at Delhi, the representative of the once mighty and all but universal Empire of Akbar and Aurangzeb. Mr. Simon Fraser, the Commissioner of Delhi, was directed to arrange that, after the death of the existing incumbent, the ex-Imperial family should vacate the Palace of Sháh Jahán and retire into private life.

Such were some of the dragon's teeth, sown by doctrinarians, to spring up but too soon, in the usual crop.

It would not be right to conclude this section without mention of the treaty with Dost Muhamad, the Amir of Kábul, due to the active brain of Herbert Edwardes, but cordially taken up by the Governor-General. It was concluded in March, 1855, on the principle of letting bygones be bygones, and proved of the utmost service during the troubles that were soon to come on Upper India.

[See books cited at end of last section, also "The Marquis of Dalhousie," &c., by Ed. Arnold, 2 vols., London, 1862].

SECTION 3.—If we have had to speak something doubtfully of the rapid pouring of new wine into old bottles by the Government of Lord Dalhousie in its "political" capacity, it is a pleasure to be able to treat more positively of his administration of the purely British part of the Indian Empire. To the very sweeping claims, indeed of the extreme admirers of the Marquess, it has been seen that a limitation may be taken. Neither canals, railroads, nor postal reform can be justly claimed for him as original devices; though the credit due for loyal and enegetic conclusion of the plans of others may be, in itself, no small thing. The Ganges Canal (opened 1854) had —as has been shown—been a long time in hand; the railway surveys and the new postal arrangements—borrowed from England—had been prepared and submitted to the Court of Directors in 1846. The conception—so far as it was original at all—was due to Mr. H. B. Riddell. Other items, again, are to be attributed to the general progress of evolution, or to the results of Parliamentary discussion or Ministerial policy at home.

Yet in all is to be traced the steady energy of a very superior intellect, working without rest or haste, and giving to principles —whether derived from without or from within—a character of enduring strength.

In some of his reforms, Dalhousie was evidently aided, if not prompted, from London. The Company's Charter was renewed—for the last time, as it proved—in 1853. Until the seal is removed from Dalhousie's papers, it cannot be known with certainty how far he may have influenced the discussions and conclusions. But, ostensibly, and so far as the published evidence goes, the changes—premonitory of the great final reform—were the work of English politicians. During 1852, both Houses of Parliament appointed Select Committees to take evidence and report upon the question. On June 3rd, 1853, the Bill that resulted from those enquiries was brought into the Commons by Sir Charles Wood (afterwards Lord Halifax). The Court of Directors was to be maintained, as a Board (or screen); but the members were to be cut down from 24 to 18, and one-third of the number would, for the future, be nominees of the Crown (*i.e.* the Cabinet). The appointment to the civil and military services of India were to be made on the basis of competitive examination; and the Government of India was to have the aid of a Legislative Council for making Statutes. The reform of the existing laws of British India was to be considered by a special Commission in England. Bengal was to have a Lieutenant-Governor, as in the North-West Provinces; some changes were initiated as to appointments in India, with a view to a more extended and lucrative employment of Natives. There were hostile speeches and amendments on the first and second reading; Mr. Bright particularly distinguished himself by the vehemence of his criticism. The third reading having been carried on July 28th, the Bill went to the Lords, where it was severely handled by Lord Ellenborough; but it went back to the Commons with slight alterations and received the Royal assent in due course.

The institution of a partly nominee Court, and the omission of any fixed period of duration for the new Charter, gave the Company a valetudinarian, not to say moribund, character; and the days of the old system were evidently numbered. The next important step in administration came openly from the Board of Control which, in July 1854, sent out a despatch on national education, of which the Governor-General declared that it was wider and more comprehensive than the local authorities could have ventured to suggest.* The "Department"—such is the Anglo-Indian phrase—was created by this measure, which has continued ever since to form the fundamental Charter of vernacular instruction. A practical attempt, however, had been already made by Thomason in the North-West Provinces, where the hedge-schools of the people had been put under official inspection and schooling provided which, if not compulsory, was gratuitous. The number of educational institutions dealt with by the Department (maintenance or aid, with inspection), was 134,710 in 1890; and the percentage of scholars was constantly increasing; over two and three-quarters of a million (R.x.) being spent on the work.

In the attraction of capital to India, the plans matured under this administration were most fortunate. It is true that the Natives did not, as a rule, invest in the works—mainly railways—which now received so great an impetus; but the money, if not raised in India, was spent there, and must have given employment to much Native labour, skilled and unskilled; raising the standard of employment and of civilisation. Trade with other countries (chiefly the British Islands), also received an immense development; the exportation of cotton and bread-stuffs was multiplied three-fold, and the total export trade rose

* The drafting of this memorable paper was ascribed to Mr. William Edwards, who had been in the Foreign Secretariat in Hardinge's time.

from thirteen and a half millions to twenty-three. The import trade rose still more—from ten and a half to twenty-five and a quarter millions; but this does not altogether indicate increased use of imported goods, as more than four millions of bullion or treasure are included among the imports of any year of the eight.*

One great instrument of progress—the telegraph—was entirely originated by the Government, and the ability with which it was carried out shows how judiciously the agent was selected and employed. In 1852, Dr. O'Shaughnessy—afterwards known as Sir William Broke—was deputed to London to lay before the Court of Directors his scheme for erecting electric wires over the length and breadth of India. On his return with the requisite sanction, he went to work at once and by November, 1853, a temporary line had been laid from Calcutta to Agra.†

Railways could not be laid so fast as posts and wires of the telegraph could be erected, and the system of guarantee which was long applied to main lines was probably unfavourable to speed, as it certainly was to economy. But in 1856—only ten years after the completion of the first surveys—there were 200 miles open for traffic, and progress was beginning to be yet more rapid.

The necessity for abridging the vast distances of India was receiving emphasis from recent events. The recent

* Of course this is no measure of the modern increase; Indian exports now rise at a rate of six and a half millions annually, and the whole volume of trade will soon be near 200 millions, if that figure have not been already attained (1893).

† When the Ganges Canal was opened at Rurki (April, 1854), the present writer was employed to send intimation, by relays of mounted police to the Telegraph office at Meerut, whence the message was wired to Dalhousie in Calcutta. The Governor-General's reply, by the same means, reached Rurki while the company were at dinner. The distance to Meerut and back was over 130 miles.

Punjab wars and the annexation of the Lower Indus had begun to dislocate the centre of political gravity; the cantonments of Bengal were being transferred from the banks of the Ganges to those of the Jumna and the Sutlej; the Government of India was coming to be carried on at Simla for nearly half the year. All these things combined to form a peremptory claim for improved transit, and the completion of the Grand Trunk Road on one side, of the steam navigation on the Indus on the other, gave an immediate reply.

Science, too, made useful advances. Under Colonel,—afterwards Sir Andrew—Scott Waugh the Great Trigonometrical Survey of India extended its works over the newly-annexed Provinces; while Colonel—afterwards Sir Henry—Thuillier pushed on the topographical operations which form the necessary complement of the other and more purely scientific survey. The coasts of the Empire, from the Persian Gulf to the Bay of Bengal, were surveyed and charted by the officers of the Indian Navy.

One great danger of such a rule as that of Dalhousie was that of precipitate introduction of measures either irritating or nugatory. His idea, and that of most generous minds of the time, was that a benevolent despotism could—and indeed must—reform by simple edicts the thoughts and customs which had grown up from the ancestral conditions of ancient races. Thus, following up a premature attempt of his predecessor's, he passed an Act providing that a Hindu should not forfeit his succession to ancestral property because he gave up the Hindu creed. In what has been said in these pages on the subject, it has been shown that such an innovation must needs strike at the very foundation of the Hindu Law, which regarded the devolution of family property as a preservation of the continuity of the family, and a means of propitiating the ancestral spirits and providing for their welfare in another state of existence*. Another well-meant effort of legislation was an

* v. *sup.* VOL. I., p. 26.

Act "to remove all legal obstacles to the marriage of Hindu widows" which, though introduced under this administration, did not become law until Dalhousie had left the country.

The danger here adverted to had its share in the state of the public mind which was soon to lead to political disaster. It has since then been much mitigated by an organic change in the law-making process, of which the end has not yet been seen, but of which the beginning was made in the Charter of 1853. The Governor-General of India is now aided, and at the same time controlled, by machinery at once more complicated and more powerful than the Executive Council which was once his only check. Public opinion, too, is more carefully consulted; and a new Act, even after it has received the assent of his Excellency, does not become law until it has been referred to, and approved by, the Secretary of State in London.

Less questionable were the innovations of the period in matters of purely administrative character. Something has been said above of a Department of Public Instruction, though the title is somewhat of a misnomer: in spite of the large allotment for educational objects made from Imperial Funds, the work was not centralised; each Province having its own Director-General. But in the reform of Public Works an immense step was undoubtedly taken when the "Military Board" was abolished and a central authority appointed, with greatly increased resources, for the control of all those undertakings for which the country was now, most wisely, considered to be ripe. Something has already been said of the provision for irrigation rendered so necessary to the welfare of an agricultural country peculiarly exposed to climatic vicissitudes.* At least fifteen millions of acres are now, in one part of India or another, secured against failure of rain: and, although neither the conception or inception may be

* CHAPTER I. Section i. p.p. 5-10.

due to Dalhousie, the greater part of the existing works of irrigation originated during his administration or immediately before.

All these undertakings, the telegraph, the aid to railways and education, the development of the resources and famine-insurance, while preparing a boundless future of material progress and prosperity, necessarily involved a prodigious outlay; to say nothing of the wars in the Punjab and Burma. It is the more remarkable therefore that a full half of Dalhousie's eight years were years of financial surplus, though no addition was made to the burdens of the taxpayer. The revenue rose, during this period, by nearly 20 per cent., but the increase was chiefly in established items—such as the land revenue—and was due mainly to the natural progress of affairs and to improved efficiency in administration. It more than sufficed to balance the increase of civil and military expenditure.

In army reform the period with which we are here concerned, was by no means remarkable; and the terrible explosion by which it was immediately followed is enough to throw upon it the most dreadful shadow. As a wise statesman the Governor-General could not but have a sense of coming catastrophe; and this supposition derives all needful confirmation from his own words, uttered on his last public appearance in India. We have learned, he said to the citizens of Calcutta, how an apparently slight difference will breed a storm of war; we know how insurrection may arise in which people of the most gentle manners may be led to commit bloody excesses: and "remembering these things no prudent man will venture to give you assurance of continued peace." *

This peril, then, Lord Dalhousie suspected, if he did not quite understand: but the preparation to meet it was never

* Address of February, 1856, cited (from "The Friend of India") in Hunter's "Dalhousie," p. 223.

made; when so much had been done to alarm and offend Native opinion, common prudence should have dictated an earnest strengthening of the defences. If it cannot be said that Dalhousie deserves the full blame of neglecting this, yet there has seemed to many (made wise by after events) that he might have taken up the question of military reform earlier and with more vigour. It appeared as if all his annexations, his new laws, his often wholesome but disturbing reforms, might have been postponed until he had been provided with irresistible strength for their enforcement. We have seen how Hardinge, after the Sutlej campaign, had reduced the Native Armies, seeking to approximate them to the standard of 1838: but his successor had been led to restore their strength until it had almost returned to the figures of Hardinge's earlier years; viz., near on 240,000 besides the Punjab Frontier Force (which was under the local administration) and several contingents paid by Native States, yet disciplined and commanded by European Officers. There were seven battalions of "Company's Europeans," as the white troops raised for Indian service were called; and some part of the local artillery was also manned by European gunners. The remainder were British—or "Queen's"-Troops, put for a time under the orders of the Indian authorities, and intended mainly to give tenacity to the Native Forces in action: but these troops had another use; namely to set an example of discipline, and keep the Sepoys steady in obedience. On several occasions, since the Sindh war of 1843, the men of the Bengal Native Infantry had shown the suspicious temper and uncertain faith of mercenaries; and the presence of British troops had aided the Government in meeting these dangers, as it had still earlier at Barrackpore in 1826.*

These things had however been variously interpreted. Sir C. Napier, the conqueror, and for a while administrator of

* v. *sup.* CHAPTER XV.

Sindh, had a high opinion of his own statesmanship, and was ready to show resentment when restrained. In May, 1849, he succeeded Lord Gough as Commander-in-Chief of the Indian armies, and soon began to display these characteristics. In the month of July he heard that two sepoy corps had shown symptoms of insubordination at Ráwal Pindi; and he at once sent orders to Colin Campbell, the General of the Division, which that good officer had already anticipated. Descending however from Simla with his wonted energy, Napier made a tour of the Punjab and satisfied himself that no less than twenty four regiments were ripe for revolt. Then the 66th Native Infantry broke into mutiny at Govindgarh, and attempted to seize the fort there. Napier at once disbanded them and supplied their place in the army list by a Gurkha battallion. Towards the end of the year he recorded a minute declaring that the whole of the army of the Punjab, 401,000 strong, was in a general state of mutiny.

About a month later he inconsistently affirmed, in a general order, that "he had never seen a more obedient or honourable army"; and he at the same time granted the matter in dispute. As this affected the finances of the Empire, over which, as Commander of the Army, he had no control, he was promptly called to account by the Governor-General. On a reference to the Duke of Wellington, Napier was convicted of inconsistency; and being pronounced to be altogether in the wrong, he immediately threw up his appointment. The personal question was one of merely temporary interest, but it deserves notice here as showing that the Governor-General was not duly informed of the spirit of the Native Army by the subordinate whose duty it was to discover and report it with no uncertain sound. Nor, indeed, is there reason for supposing that the fractious humour and lax discipline of the sepoys were brought to his notice by anyone else.

Years passed, and the attention of the Government was otherwise engaged. The new Commander-in-Chief was Sir

William Gomm, an accomplished man, who had been Governor of the Mauritius, and under his mild sway there was no further friction. Much was done for the conciliation of the sepoys, with more or less of wisdom. That the alarm created by past occurrences had not wholly died away, is shown by the efforts made by the Governor-General to call the attention of the authorities in London to the weakness of the European portion of the Indian army. In 1854, the Crimean war broke out in Europe, and Dalhousie lost no time in entering his protest against the propriety of withdrawing British troops from India. In spite of his remonstrances, two regiments were ordered to embark for Europe before the end of that year, and the ratio of one or two which has been since considered proper, had sunk till there were at least five sepoys to every British soldier.*

On the eve of laying down his powers, Dalhousie transmitted to the Court of Directors a series of Minutes on this subject; they were entirely neglected, and the neglect was before long to be expiated by the abolition of that distinguished but effete body. The retiring Governor-General pointed out the loss of military reputation that the Empire had incurred by the Crimean war; the failure to make the Indian armies keep pace with the great increase of territory; the possibility of trouble from external enemies: and he proposed remedies which ought at least to have been considered. It has been asserted that these proposals had not even been noticed at the India House until they were called for in the House of Commons after the Mutiny. Whether or no they would have completely prevented that disaster, whether or no that disaster

* The figures given by Mr. Holmes, citing the authority of the Duke of Argyll, are—Native troops, 232,224; Europeans, 45,522. But the roll of sepoys did not include the large local levies, such as the Contingents of Sindhia, the Nizám, etc., and the Punjab force mentioned in the text. It has been affirmed that, in Bengal, there was but one British soldier to twenty-one native sepoys. ["Indian Mutiny," p. 62].

was "a disguised blessing," are irrelevant questions in comparison with the slur that the whole case throws on the failure to take them into consideration.

Dalhousie's proposed reforms would have, at least, restored the proper proportion of British troops in the dominions of the Indian Government. There does not, it is true, seem to be any indication that Dalhousie or any one else perceived the true sources of the coming peril, or that he took any notice of the great likelihood of the contingents of the Native States feeling and displaying sympathy with the discontents and aspirations of the Company's sepoys, often men of their own kindred. He did not advert to the great extent of the Native element in the Indian artillery, always the strong point with the Indian soldiers; neither did he notice the faulty arrangement by which the regiments of the Bengal regular army had been rendered homogeneous in composition. With a large nucleus of Audh men, irritated by the annexation of their country, each corps had a few Sikhs and Patháns, not in sufficient numbers to hold their own, and a spirit of professional brotherhood had so far overcome dissidences of creed, and of nationality or class, that what was felt by each one of such corps, was sure to be communicated to all the others, like the shock of earthquake passing through kindred strata.*

If Dalhousie's preventive measures were thus, for various reasons, ineffectual to reform the army, it cannot be fairly claimed that the rest of his military administration was completely wise or beneficial. Among the evils that affected the Native troops, some were within his power of correction, and some actually of his own causing. The European officers

* A remarkable confirmation of this view was soon to be afforded. The regiments which proved the most completely indifferent or hostile to the mutinous movement in the Bengal army were *each throughout of one class;* the 66th (Gurkhas) and the 31st (all high-caste Brahmins) who bit the cartridges and used them freely against the mutineers.

were characterised by a distinguished soldier as "the refuse," on the ground that all who could possibly get away from regimental duty were away in staff-employ, while their less fortunate comrades were without interest in their work, and regarded it as penal.* The Native officers, mostly old men who had risen by long service, were charged with almost all the duties of discipline, aided by European sergeants. The men had reason to be dissatisfied with a number of reductions and petty grievances, while their heads were turned by flattery and relaxed discipline. The powers of Commandants and Courts-martial were sapped by the facility of appeals to Headquarters; and the pension rules had become so strict that a soldier could not retire until he was quite worn out, and unable to enjoy his retirement.

None of these things was in itself a sufficient cause of the Mutiny, and of the partial popular revolts which followed. The 31st and 66th, who remained faithful, had the same grievances, most of which were shared by the Bombay army, which proved mainly loyal, and the "Coast" or Madras army, in which there was no disaffection at all. Nevertheless, it must be confessed, that when, on the 29th of February, 1856, Lord Dalhousie retired from the post that he had so long and honourably filled, he left British India in a somewhat volcanic condition.

He was advanced to the dignity of a Marquess for his services, and lived, a hopelessly broken man, about four years longer, dying after the catastrophe of Fifty-seven and unable to defend himself against charges arising out of that event which were not all very just, and—many of them at least—wholly ungenerous.

* To be sent back to regimental duty was an ordinary punishment for short-comings and offences on the part of officers holding administrative posts. Under the present system, on the contrary, employment with a Native regiment is itself a staff-appointment, requiring positive proofs of capacity.

[See works cited under previous sections; also "History of the Indian Mutiny," by T. R. E. Holmes, 4th edition, London, 1891: this work is based on laborious research, most carefully and impartially utilised. The epithet of "refuse" was applied to the officers of the Bengal Army by Lord Melville who as General Dundas, had served with them at the siege of Multan, and the battle of Gujarát. Lord Dalhousie's papers are withheld from publication under a special clause in his will, and will not be available to the historian till the year 1910, when their interest (it may be feared) will have grown somewhat cold. In the meantime, much has been done for the vindication of his policy. See "India, etc.," by the Duke of Argyll, London, 1865; "A Vindication, etc.," by Sir C. Jackson, same date. Sir W. W. Hunter's able monograph, already cited, contains original matter, and has had the advantage of aid from Dalhousie's family and friends.]

CHAPTER XX.

THE FALL OF THE COMPANY.

Section 1: The Revolt of Fifty-seven—Section 2: The restoration of order—Section 3: The first Viceroyalty.

SECTION I.—When Lord Dalhousie's health broke down under work and weariness, the Ministry of the Queen named as his successor the son of the famous Statesman who had been similarly designated nearly thirty years before. Lord Canning had inherited his peerage from his mother, had served under various Governments, and had declined an offer of the Private Secretaryship to the Governor-General when Ellenborough went out in 1842. The Directors accepted the ministerial nomination; and on August 1st, 1855, Canning attended the customary banquet where he made a speech in which he showed forecast, and a dignified sense of the seriousness of his position. "We must not forget," he said, "that India was a country in which anything might happen, however quiet things might seem." There were still discontented races there, and the temper of subsidiary States might render it impossible to forbearance itself to command peace. If, in spite of all efforts a blow should have to be struck, why it should be so struck that "the struggle would be short, and the issue not doubtful." He went to the country by the Overland Route, which was now regularly established; and he landed in the end of February 1856. A man of calm and reflective character, he seemed, with massive marble manners, and the novelty of the conditions, evidently made his initiation slow, so that he was for a time dependent on the experts about him for all his information.

It was not long before he was called to act with decision, and that in a matter which had often been uncertain and difficult for his predecessors; the perpetual trouble arising out of the vague relations with Persia was the cause of Canning's first anxiety. It may be remembered that Herát, the frontier-city of Afghanistán had been held by the Saduzai chiefs, while the Bárukzais had obtained a fairly secure supremacy at Kábul; but in 1852 the Sháh had begun an expedition for renewal of the endeavour to include Herát within Persian limits, and from that enterprise he had only desisted on the earnest remonstrance of the British envoy stationed at his Court. Then came the Crimean War, in which the politicians of Western Asia saw the power of three nations engaged against Russia, apparently without success; and they drew their own conclusions. With characteristic inefficiency, however, the Persian Government did not move at once; but at the end of 1855, the British Envoy was driven to leave Tehrán by studied contumely, and in the following year Herát became a Persian city. Lord Palmerston urging immediate action, the Governor-General somewhat reluctantly sent a squadron of the Indian navy with a small division of troops—mostly Native—to lay siege to the fortified places on the northern shore of the Persian Gulf. The question of Kábul simultaneously presented itself, and resource was again had to the energy and skill of Edwardes at Peshawar. The treaty which he had made on behalf of Lord Dalhousie in 1855, was now renewed; the Dost became a friend indeed, and admitted three British officers to reside at Kandahár pending the duration of the war. Of this negotiation there was, indeed, no direct result in the way intended, but in other respects it proved most important; the officers deputed were in every way wise and able, and the Amir rigidly restrained his tribesmen from interference on the border all through the severe trials that were soon to come.

The Persian war proved an easy matter: Outram and Havelock distinguished themselves as leaders, no less than, during many previous affairs, they had done in subordinate positions. Bushire was taken; a Persian army was put to flight at Khusháb on the Shiráz road; and the sea-forces gallantly silenced and stormed some strong works at Muhamra at the mouth of the Euphrates. On April 1st the last shot was fired, and shortly after the news of the peace of Paris came out, ratifications of which were exchanged at Baghdad on May 2nd. The Shah agreed to recognise the independence of Herát, to abstain from interference in Afghanistán, and to receive back the British Envoy with all honour.

The troops at once embarked for India, where their presence, and still more the presence of their leaders, had become urgently desired. The march of events, and still more the effervescence of opinions and emotions, were rapidly precipitating a critical movement in the greater part of that country. The Madras Presidency, indeed, under the mild wisdom of Lord Harris, presented no cause for anxiety; but Lord Elphinstone, the Governor of Bombay, was recalling his Europeans from Persia,* while Canning was receiving in Calcutta almost daily proofs of the rapid approach of an immeasurable tempest.

It has already been suggested that the pouring of new wine into old bottles had been of late too rapid. The two main classes of the Natives were by no means in an uncivilised condition. But their civilisation was that of the earlier stage of human development. The ideas and practices of Christendom were thus unpopular because unintelligible. Things that appeared matters of course to a British nobleman, the

* Harris was grandson of the conqueror of Tipu; and Elphinstone nephew of the great Mountstuart who had once held the same post.

inheritor of European evolution, seemed to the millions of Hindus and Muslims as monstrously unreasonable as the Gospel did to Josephus or to Lucian.* The law regarding the marriage of Hindu widows, which, prepared in the last administration, was now enacted, is a case in point. Among other things of a like tendency, was a Bill introduced into the legislature for curtailing polygamy amongst certain classes of Brahmins. Then came a decree that, in future, all Native recruits should undertake "general service," *i.e.*, should declare their willingness to embark for over-sea campaigns, as the six "volunteer" corps did already; to the Audh sepoys, already fretting at the annexation, this was a fresh annoyance, either interfering with an ancient privilege, or else throwing open the ranks to humbler and less scrupulous classes, who might be less afraid of the black water.

To all these causes of alarm in the Native mind but little attention was paid by men in authority. A number of Hindus, especially at Calcutta, the Bábus, a section of Hindu society nearest and most familiar to the governing Europeans, were in apparent sympathy with the reforming movement. But this fact, while helping to hide the danger, also did something to intensify it. The Hindus of the old school were alarmed and disgusted to see their young men attending debating societies, or drinking beer, and eating beef, in European houses; while the followers of the Prophet, even if less directly concerned, felt like a man whose neighbour's party-wall is burning.

Many causes combined, indeed, to constitute a special feeling among the Muslims of India. One of the most distinguished of that community, the wise and benevolent man who then and even since, has displayed his loyalty in so many ways,†

* S. Paul (I. Cor. i., 23). As already hinted, it was not in the direct propagation of religious opinion that the Government erred, but in well-meant attacks upon practice.

† Sir Sayid Ahmad, K.C.S.I., founder of the Aligarh College. (v. "Life etc.," by Colonel Graham. Edinburgh, 1885.)

indeed, maintained that Indian Muslims are neither required nor even allowed, by the sacred law of Islám, to rebel against the British. But when the Indian Muslims saw the King of Audh deposed, the King of Delhi threatened, the Hindus alarmed with fear of proselytism, high employment closed against them, freehold grants resumed, great houses going to ruin, and none prosperous but usurers, they did not always stop to take counsel of the sages. And a general state of discontent and distrust thus arose, with animosities that were both social and political, fortuitous combination of so many causes rendering the condition of the Bengal army at once dangerous and weak.

All such elements of discontent combined at the moment when the sepoys of the Bengal army had attained the exact stage which prepared it to be an instrument of revolt. Pretorianism is an evil, and insubordination common to all ranks and classes of the civil population is an evil. While each of these may be dealt with in detail, or one played off against the other, the ruling power is safe; but in the case where the two combine, an explosion is bound to follow. Thus we see that the chemistry of Destiny was preparing the new India with effervescence and tumult; and we find how great was the error of those who regarded the revolt as due to any one single class or cause whether political or purely military. The wrath of the Nána who was refused the pension of his adoptive father, the ex-Peshwa; the fears of the royal family of Delhi, threatened with degradation to private rank; these were but factors. But, when to these were added the superficial observation of such men as Azimulla Khan—the Nána's emissary—and the disappointment of the Lucknow Queen-mother, who went to England to urge a vain protest against the annexation of Audh, we can the better understand the political situation. Azimulla and the Begam, in correspondence and sympathy with the Mughal at Delhi, were also in communication with the titular Peshwa, representing the former Vicegerent of the Empire.* And here was the genesis of a germ which acted on the nidus of disorder furnished by the condition of the army.

Reference has been made in previous pages to occasional instances of ill-temper among sepoy-regiments, by no means confined to the army of any one Presidency, or caused by any one form of discontent. Now, for the first time, religious temper, spiritual anxieties, alarm on account of temporal interests, Pretorian pride, political disaffection, had combined to form a mine of explosive matter which only awaited ignition. The spark was communicated by a Muhamadan intrigue.

The vegetarian scrupulosity of the Hindu sepoy was alarmed by a rumour that the ammunition for the rifles in course of issue was greased with cow's fat. The Levitical pedantry of the Muslims was equally excited by the information that the fat used was that of swine. Whichever were the fact, it was made plain to sepoy-intelligence that by biting such polluted cartridges a man must, as a matter of course, instantly become a Christian. An able and active religious teacher (afterwards known as the "Maulvi") itinerated from Audh to Calcutta, preaching and keeping men in agitation by sending mysterious cakes about through ignorant village watchmen.

The alarm about the cartridges arose in Bengal in January, 1857. Two regiments had mutinied in that Province by March. Before the end of that month symptoms of insubordination appeared at Ambála, where incendiary fires became matters of almost nightly occurrence during April; and about the same time, on the gate of the Cathedral Mosque of Delhi was found a proclamation announcing that a Persian army was

* The writer saw the letters taken at Bithur. One was a draft from Azimulla to a prominent European politician, dated at the outbreak of the Persian war, and showing extensive hopes and speculative combinations.

on its way to India, and calling on all faithful followers of Islám to stand prepared to join the friendly invaders. On the 4th May, the sentences on the Bengal mutineers were, after deplorable delay, made public; a few days later an attempt was made to enforce discipline at Meerut, one of the great cantonments of the North-West Provinces, where two corps of sepoys and one of Native cavalry were watched by a force of Europeans of all arms, and almost greater strength. Some men of the 3rd Cavalry there, being ordered to use the cartridges without touching them with lips or teeth, refused, and were in due course imprisoned by sentence of court-martial. On the evening of the next day—Sunday, May 10th—when the British soldiers were getting ready for church, the comrades of the prisoners broke into the jail and set them free. In the ensuing darkness and confusion the mutineers got away to Delhi, and the criminal classes of the town and vicinity sacked and burned the officers' bungalows at Meerut. Next morning the troops in garrison at Delhi joined the mutineers from Meerut in a Saturnalian feast of blood and rapine. The revolt of the Bengal Army had begun. Henceforth the homogeneous structure of the corps made it easy for them to be wrought on by the rebellious committees and agitators, for whatever excited one battalion was certain to have the like effect on all that were similarly constituted. Lavish terms were generally offered in the name of the King of Delhi: every regiment that murdered its officers marched to the Mughal capital, under Native officers wearing the titles and uniforms of the slain; and the conspirators hoped—or tried to hope—that the rule of the Frank would disappear from Upper India, if not from the whole peninsula.

They sent a manifesto into the Punjab, reproaching the Sikhs for having hitherto failed to unite with the movement that was to reform their common grievances. They spoke, of course, of religion endangered, but they added the more tangible charges of exacted land-revenue, and public careers closed to native learning; and they dwelt upon the erection of toll-bars upon the public roads as if it were an act of oppression equal to the alleged attacks upon the popular belief. Such a statement may seem to bear on its face the evidence of insincerity, but it is plain that it found ready acceptance in public credulity—at least among the soldiery. An officer going his rounds one rainy night came upon the wall of a shed where his guard were sheltering, and heard the end of a conversation to a very similar effect.*

Many special books have given details of those tragic times. Cawnpore was occupied by mutineers in the interests of the Nána who, on June 25, offered a free passage to Allahabad to every one of the white people who had not been connected with the acts of Lord Dalhousie.† On the morning of the 27th they were conducted to the river as if to be embarked; and some did, in fact, reach the boats. Then the Nána and his men opened fire on them; and were enabled to kill all but 150 women and children, who were made prisoners, and four strong men, who swam down the river and escaped. On the 30th the Nána was proclaimed Peshwa; the male prisoners were shot, and a Belshazzar feast set in that lasted a week. When the rebel chief heard that the avenger was at hand he caused the unhappy prisoners to be slaughtered in cold blood.

Meanwhile, Henry Lawrence—the tender and true hero whom men of harder fibre had sent from his old place of work and honour—had been "trying to do his duty" as Chief Commissioner in Audh. When even he failed to keep the

* "The Franks," said one of the men, "have ruined respectable landholders, and given their estates to shopkeepers; there is no prestige (*ikbál*) about them; they will neither make an Emperor themselves, nor allow anyone else to be Emperor; and now they are trying to destroy our Faith."—("Etawa Report.")

† *i.e.*, In the confiscation of his pension.

misguided sepoys any longer faithful, he went into the old "Residency," a group of dwellings clustered round a large central palace, and enclosed in a masonry wall. The whole Province rose in arms; the place was invested by myriads of rebels with heavy guns, and defended by 600 British soldiers, 89 gunners, 100 officers, the survivors of many mutinies, 153 civilians, and 765 faithful sepoys. The siege began on the 1st July; on the 2nd the illustrious Lawrence was killed by a shell, and his civil authority devolved on Major Banks; while Colonel Inglis, of the 32nd Foot, became Commander of the garrison. Several causes conspired to make the revolt of Audh universal throughout the province. The annexation —and, still more, the circumstances and manner of the annexation—had offended high and low. The great land-holders were injured, in their property, in their privileges, and their pride. Over 50,000 of the flower of the yeomanry had been discharged from the army without compensation. The removal of the Court from Lucknow had been a blow to local trade. And now all these interests were angrily surging round the frail breastworks of the Residency grounds.

As already stated, the policy of Dalhousie had led to the advancement of the British garrisons to the north-western extremities of the Empire; and the negligence of the Court of Directors had left the Calcutta Government without the means of filling the gaps: consequently troubles occurred at Dinapore and Benares, while there was great delay in relieving Allahabad. The Lieutenant-Governor of the North-West Provinces was shut up in the fort at Agra with a newly-raised regiment of Company's Europeans, and a handful of Volunteers. Before Delhi a few thousand men were collected, just enough to watch the northern angle of the vast enceinte, and guard their own encampment against attack. The Punjab alone, a Province which had been a scene of so much tumult not ten years before, was held by a British army duly proportioned to the numbers of the sepoys, and supported by local levies of whose fidelity, however, there was, as yet, no certain proof. In the first week of June the exasperated Ráni of Jhánsi had raised the country to the side of the mutinous troops quartered there, and had betrayed and massacred the small party of Europeans. The Gwalior contingent, mutinying on June 14th, advanced on Agra, which became insulated in the universal tide of war.

Colonel Neill meanwhile had entered the fort of Allahabad; and on the 18th prepared to advance on Cawnpore with a force of about 500 men, chiefly of his own regiment, the 1st Madras (Company's) Europeans; but on the 30th Havelock—whose name has already appeared frequently on these pages—arrived at Allahabad, and took up the preparations.*

The clouds now began to lift, and a little light broke on the gloom of the time. Ságar was saved by the loyalty of a corps of high-caste sepoys, the 31st Bengal Infantry; and an outbreak at Nágpore was quelled by the loyalty of the Madras troops and the decision of Mr. R. S. Ellis. Haidarábád in the the Deccan was kept from open rebellion by the steady loyalty of the Nizám's great Minister, Salár Jung. The relief of Wheeler at Cawnpore proved impossible; but Havelock, constantly re-inforced by driblets of Europeans from the eastward, drove the Nána before him, occupied the place of blood (17th July), and began his arrangements for relieving the Lucknow Residency forty miles on the other side of the Ganges.

Meanwhile the Punjab remained faithful. The brave Sikhs, beaten in two hard campaigns, and ruled, since then, by firm and just officers, were in no mood to join with Hindustáni traitors. Disarming the sepoy garrisons, and scouring the country with flying columns, John Lawrence made his Province a place of arms, whence to despatch reinforcements to the

* For some of Havelock's past record, see the First Burma War, the advance from the Indus in 1839, and the defence of Jalálabad in the First Afghán War.

leaguer of Delhi. In the Bombay Presidency Elphinstone and Frere showed equal energy and devotion; as did also Harris at Madras.

The supreme value of the Punjab was now to appear. All the strength of the mutiny was concentrated at Delhi, where successive arrivals had brought the garrison up to a strength of 50,000 good troops, with 114 heavy guns (besides field-artillery) and a large arsenal, behind walls 24-ft. high, brought up to modern requirements by modern science. But when the mutineers there heard that Lawrence was sending down reserves and a siege-train their hearts failed, and they began to leave in such numbers that it was rumoured that no more than 20,000 men of all arms remained in the doomed city. On the 8th September the tracing of three batteries began upon the northern glacis; and before dawn of the 14th the Kashmir gate was blown in, and the great breach carried by storm. For six days the small force of the besiegers worked their way through murderous street-fighting, in the course of which the illustrious John Nicholson got his death-wound. On the 20th the palace was stormed, but the King and his family had fled. They were, eventually, followed up and captured by Major Hodson.

This feat—one of the greatest in all military history—was performed by a body of 3,000 British soldiers with a few Native allies; fighting under every possible disadvantage, of numbers as well as climate. The entire loss during the four months, since the leaguer began, amounted to 2,151 Europeans, with 1,686 Natives. About the same time another almost equal exploit took place at Lucknow, whither Havelock had advanced on being reinforced by Outram, who—though entitled to command—voluntarily put himself under his distinguished junior. Here, too, the most audacious street-fighting was requisite; by September 30th the small force had made its way to the Residency, where they added to the strength of the defenders, if they did not altogether raise the siege. Banks was dead, and so were half his followers; but the survivors had never lost hope or heart; and the event might now be awaited, with trust, if not with patience.

[Kaye and Malleson's "History of Mutiny" (cabinet edition), 6 vols., 1889; T. R. E. Holmes's "History of Mutiny" (4th edition), 1891; Sir H. Cunningham's "Canning," (Rulers of India, 1891.)]

SECTION 2.—Thus, in less than half-a-year, had the stress of the great revolt been stemmed, by the courage and ability of a few good officers, without the help of troops from home. The complete suppression of disorder—amounting almost to the conquest of Hindustan—was a matter of considerably greater cost, both in men and time.

Early in October fresh troops arrived from the Cape, and within the next fortnight more followed from England. The new Commander-in-chief was that Colin Campbell, whom we saw commanding the left division at Chilianwála and Gujarát; a cautious, experienced old soldier, who had risen slowly by his own merits and without help from family connections. On October 27th he set out from Calcutta, a veteran of just half-a-century's service, determined to spare no effort to effect a real relief of Lucknow, and bring away the non-combatants. The situation appeared to the veteran in a more sombre light than what was thrown on it by less experienced and less cautious people. The Nána had been joined by the Dinapore mutineers; and was expecting the arrival of the Gwalior contingent; elements that presented themselves, to Campbell's mind, as most hopefully provided against by leaving a detachment at Cawnpore while he pushed forward with the bulk of his force to Lucknow.* In taking that view Campbell had to disregard the advice of those—including the chivalrous Outram himself

* This detachment consisted, at first, of only 1,000 men, but received reinforcements during the course of a few days. It was commanded by General Windham an officer who had distinguished himself in the Crimea.

—who would have had him destroy the rebels at Cawnpore before proceeding further. The result was somewhat disastrous.

The defenders of Lucknow had extended their works since Outram assumed the command, and had established an outpost in a walled garden, about two miles from the city, on the Cawnpore road. They held their own, countermining the enemy and often sallying out to spike his guns—but they had few comforts, and even necessaries were failing; the need for their relief was becoming a matter of days and hours.

On October 30th General Hope Grant crossed the Ganges with the 9th Lancers and some Punjab Cavalry with which he took post and awaited Sir Colin at the village of Banthar near Unao. The infantry and guns followed ten days later, and the whole force—about 3,400 strong—marched to Alambágh on November 12th. On the 16th they advanced on another walled garden, east of the Residency, called Sikandrabágh, which they carried by storm, putting to the sword the entire force of 2,000 sepoys by whom it was guarded. Supported by the sailors of the "Shannon," under Captain Peel, they then captured another strong post, the Najaf,* where they bivouacked for the night; and next morning, after six hours' more fighting, they cleared the way to the Residency, and were met by Outram and Havelock. Contrary to the wish of those leaders, Sir Colin insisted on the evacuation of the place, so long and so heroically guarded. The non-combatants and sick were removed during the next few days, and by the 23rd all were safe in the park of Dil Kushá. Leaving Outram in command at Alambágh, Campbell set out for Cawnpore with about 3,000 men and the rescued women and children—all that were left! On the 24th, however—before they started—a loss had fallen on the party, which was felt not only there, but wherever the

* In the jargon of the day, "Sháh Najeef;" the true word being *Najaf Ashraf*, which was the title of the mausoleum of Ghází-ud-din, the first "King."

English tongue was heard; the war-worn Havelock sank under the burdens he had borne so long.*

Otherwise, all had prospered. But a scene of disaster awaited Campbell at Cawnpore, on the 27th. Windham had been attacked by some 15,000 men and driven into the intrenchments: Cawnpore was once more in the hands of the sepoys. Nothing could be done until the helpless people whom Campbell had with so much difficulty saved could be started on their way to Allahabad. This being accomplished, Campbell turned upon the foe. From the 6th to the 8th December he continued to punish the Gwalior contingent, whom he chased out of the Duáb. On the first day of the new year he fought them again; on January 6th he was joined by Walpole and Seaton, and—under positive orders from the Governor-General—addressed himself to the conquest of the rebels in Audh. In this campaign the Nepalese co-operated from the north, while Outram kept the British flag afloat in the Alambágh with about 4,000 men, though threatened and attacked by foes who have been reckoned at 120,000.

Feeling the necessity of a decisive success, Canning urged the Commander-in-Chief to advance upon Lucknow with all possible strength; and on February 28th one of the most formidable British forces ever seen in India was assembled at Hope Grant's former station of Bunthar: it comprised seventeen battalions, twenty-eight squadrons, and thirty-four pieces of battery ordnance. Brigadier-General R. Napier—afterwards Field-Marshal Lord Napier of Magdala—was Engineer-in-Chief. Besides the Nepalese—9,000 strong—General Franks presently came up from the eastward with his Division and swelled the force.

* Public mourning was made for him, both in England and in the United States. His son, the present Sir H. H. Havelock-Allan, was with him to the last. Havelock's body was interred in the Alambágh enclosure.

In the meantime a more venturous leader than Campbell was operating from the South to "give a hand" to the Army of the Ganges. Sir Hugh Rose had won his honours in European diplomacy; he was now to show—as so many Indian "politicals" had already done—that the use of the brain need not affect the action of the heart and hand. The country between the Narbada River and the Vindhya range was, for the time, as full of dangerous—if partly latent—hostility as it had been in 1818; and Rose, when his two brigades were at length ready to march from Bombay, had serious work before him. He duly arrived at Indore—the capital of Holkar, whom the energetic Durand had kept fairly loyal—and thence, without waiting for General Whitlock who was bringing up a third brigade from Madras, Rose set out for Ságar on the 16th of January. Having relieved the Europeans there, he set his face resolutely towards the taking of Jhànsi, where the brave but treacherous Ráni was in command of 10,000 mercenaries and 1,500 mutinous sepoys, and in daily expectation of reinforcement from Tantia Topi, with the remains of the Gwalior contingent whom Campbell had expelled from the Duáb. In despite of discouraging advice from the Commander-in-Chief and the Governor-General, Rose began the siege of this strong and important place on March 21st. Day and night his artillery battered the defence, answered, shot for shot, by the guns behind the walls. On the 31st, Tantia appeared from the North and challenged an action. Sir Hugh, however, was quite ready for him: and the rebels' best "General," the vanquisher of Windham, was driven off the field, after a stubborn contest, with the loss of 1,500 men, besides his stores, guns, and munitions of all sorts. Jhánsi, being breached, was taken by storm on April 3rd and 4th, though the intrepid Ráni escaped for the time.

While Rose was thus asserting the might and majesty of discipline in the lands south of the Jumna, the Commander-in-Chief was proceeding in his careful way towards the recovery of Audh. The rebel city had been much strengthened since he withdrew the non-combatants and retired on Cawnpore in November; and now the side on which he had formerly attacked was a really formidable fortification, with the canal for a moat. But by sending Outram across the Gumti and enfilading the works; by making good use of his heavy guns; and by trusting greatly to the scientific mining work of Napier and his engineers; he gained his point, occupying the suburbs, and—finally—the city, with a loss of no more than 772 killed and wounded in three weeks continued fighting. The last attempt at resistance ended on March 21st, and then Outram, as Chief Commissioner, published the Governor General's proclamation about which there was to be such a stir. As originally worded this document confiscated all the great estates in Audh; but on Outram remonstrating a clause was added implying that great consideration would be shown to all who, even at the eleventh hour, should make submission and ask for grace. This edict led to the last public appearance of the able but impulsive President of the Board of Control, whom we once saw playing his brief part in India, but recalled by the Court of Directors. Lord Ellenborough now caused the Secret Committee to address the Indian Government in terms of severe, almost of sarcastic, rebuke. Inspired by the imperious Minister, the Court of Directors pointed out that it was both impolitic and unjust to destroy the title-deeds of a Province, which it was their interest to conciliate, for a rebellion which British blundering had done much to cause; and the Government was bidden to mitigate in practice the severity of its decree. Now, whatever opinion may be entertained of the manner in which the censure of the Ministry was conveyed—for the Cabinet was of one mind on the matter—it cannot be denied that the addition of the clause of March 10th put the Proclamation in a light not perceived at the time when the Despatch was penned. Canning and his friends were able to say that if a little patience had been used, with a little readiness to give him credit for prudence and good faith, he might have been spared so public a reproof, and one so likely to encourage the rebels. No great harm came of the matter in the end. Ellenborough resigned his post; and the Talukdars of Audh made their submission—sooner or later—receiving back their estates with a greatly amended title. The incident, however, served to show how easy it would be for English party passions to disturb the course of Indian adminstration.

Meanwhile Sir Colin, preparing for an advance on Rohilkhand, judged that the fall of Jhánsi made a demand on him to protect his left flank by completing the communication with Rose. Accordingly Brigadier (afterwards Sir G. V.) Maxwell was sent to Kalpi with his corps, the Connaught Rangers, and a few other troops. On the other side Rose advanced fighting his way through vast hostile masses and intense heat.* On the 19th May, the combined forces defeated a sortie from Kalpi with so much success that the enemy evacuated the place during the night; and the British troops obtained shelter and repose which had become matters of necessity. But not for long: on the 1st of June, they heard that Tantia and the Ráni had driven Sindhia out of Gwalior and taken possession of that almost impregnable rock. Like most of the Native Princes, Sindhia had been loyal to the British alliance, and there was no question as to the duty of hastening to his aid. Rose arrived near Gwalior on June 16th; next day he fought his way nearly to the foot of the rock; the Ráni of Jhánsi fell in a cavalry-charge. On the 19th, another still and fiercer action was fought, and Sindhia was received in the British camp. That night the fort was mastered by the happy audacity of two

* The thermometer ranged from 107° to 110° Fahrenheit, scarcely falling to 100° at night. Hardly an officer or man was fit for duty; and Rose himself was ordered home by the doctors.

young officers, one of whom unhappily lost his life in the exploit. The Central India campaign was now at an end; nothing remaining but to hunt down Tantia Topi and hang him after he had been convicted on a fair trial, of having been a leading actor in the Cawnpore massacre.

Rose's campaign is one of the finest in history. Practically ensured, by the results of that piece of daring and devotion, the Commander-in-Chief was enabled to proceed—in his slower way—to the pacification of Rohilkhand and Audh. On May 4th, he reached the neighbourhood of Bareilly with 7,500 good troops and nineteen guns. After a smart fight of six hours the rebels evacuated the place—which was unfortified—and retired into Audh, where for the present they were not molested. At the beginning of the cool season the Chief proceeded into Audh, at the same time calling up a converging column from the south-east. The Nána and his brother took refuge in the jungles at the foot of the Nepal Hills—where they are supposed to have perished by malarial fever—and the last body of mutineers surrendered at discretion in November. The only formidable non-military revolt in the North-West Provinces had already collapsed in April by the death of its able leader, the Talukdár Kunwar Sinh.* Of the chief advisers of the Nána, in addition to Tantia, one was taken and hanged in northern Audh; the other—Azimulla—was never heard of more.

The revolt had caused a vast amount of suffering, sorrow, and expense. But the benefits to which it led were such as could hardly have been bought at any cheaper rate. By cruel but salutary operation it relieved the body politic of disorders for which a milder cure might have been sought in vain.

In the first place it removed the incubus of the Court of Directors; an institution which, good work as it had once

* Kunwar Sinh's property lay in Bihár, and his grievance was with the authorities of the Lower Provinces. But he ably operated in the Eastern portion of the Upper Provinces also.

done, was by this time a sham and an incumbrance. On February 13th, 1858, Lord Palmerston submitted to the House of Commons a scheme for transferring the direct Government of India to the Crown—so far as regarded the home-administration, which was to be intrusted to a responsible Minister assisted by a Council. That day week he was defeated, on the Murder-conspiracy Bill, and next day resigned office. The new Cabinet at once took up the lapsed thread; and Mr. Disraeli produced a similar bill on March 26th. His Bill, being thought to contain certain fantastic elements, was after a short discussion withdrawn in favour of a scheme, proposed by Lord J. Russell, whereby a Committee of the whole House took up the matter by way of Resolutions. On June 7th a Bill was drafted on the basis of these proceedings, which was read a third time on July 8th, and which passed the Lords' with trifling amendments, and received the royal assent on August 3rd. Some natural sentiment apart, those best qualified to judge were of Lord Palmerston's opinion that it was time to abolish an institution which had ceased to fulfil its original functions since 1813, and which was, by the logic of events, convicted of failure. As was unanswerably shown in the course of the debates, the India Bill by which Pitt subjected the Directors to Ministerial control was provoked by the misrule of the Company; and since that time the Government of India had constantly improved. The Afghán war was an exception more apparent than real; having been only rendered possible by the faults of the system.—(Speech of Sir G. C. Lewis.) Indeed, to those who could have observed the conduct of the Court in the matter of Dalhousie's army reform Minutes, the abolition caused by a military mutiny may well have seemed an appropriate though lenient punishment.*

* Dalhousie's Minutes were so successfully pigeon-holed at the India Office that two of them were totally and irretrievably lost.

The reorganisation of the Native Army was a question which had also become insoluble had not the largest and most dangerous section committed timely suicide. The overwhelming preponderance of the Hindustáni element in the forces of Bengal, and—to a less degree—in those of Bombay, was now to be rectified; and the low ratio of European to Native soldiers, having been so fearfully accentuated, would no more be allowed to occur.

A third germ of disorder, which Dalhousie had, indeed, perceived though he did not remove it, was the condition of affairs at Delhi. The expulsion of the descendant of Akbar from his ancestral palace, the discrowning of a fallen potentate from whose patent the Company had derived its only legitimate title, had—we have seen—been contemplated: yet, so long as the King (or "Emperor" as he ought, strictly speaking, to be called) gave no serious offence, his deposition would have been a scandal exceeding even, in Native eyes, the annexation of Audh. This problem also was solved by the events of Fifty-Seven. On January 27th, 1858. Bahádur Sháh, having been taken prisoner by the enterprising Major W. Hodson, was brought to trial before a Court of British officers; Major Dawes, of Afghán renown, being President. The old Mughal affected nonchalance; but a defence was made on his behalf, in spite of which, after a long and patient hearing, the Court found that he had sympathised with the rebellion and failed to use his authority to save the lives of refugees and captives in his jurisdiction. Sentenced to be transported, he was sent to Rangoon, where he died after a lenient arrest of nearly five years.

By the end of the year order was substantially restored.* A royal proclamation, revised by the Queen herself and translated into twenty of the Indian tongues, was read in every

* The present writer travelled from Rurki to Allahabad and back in January, 1859, without meeting an enemy or seeing a sign of disorder.

British Indian city and cantonment on November 1st, 1858; and Canning received his appointment as her Majesty's first Viceroy. An amnesty was offered to all but those convicted of actual murder, subject to the exception that those who had actively abetted murder or rebellion should be guaranteed nothing but their lives. All others were invited to resume their avocations of peace without fear of molestation or question. It was a great political step, making known to the Princes and peoples of India that their persons and property were safe under a strong and clement rule. The sepoys who, in the beginning of the war, excused their mutiny by saying that the Government would not make an Emperor expressed the desire of the Oriental for a concrete representation of power. That desire was now gratified. The analogous habit of looking to a powerful landlord which was supposed to have been shown, in Audh especially, was at variance with the prevailing Western idea of the greatest welfare of the greatest number: and here too some concession to popular sentiment was made. Visiting Lucknow, Canning promised consideration to the Talukdárs; and the subject has continued to receive attention almost ever since; though it is to be feared that there are some laws of nature that are too strong even for the Government of India. Every act of grace to Zemindárs in Bengal had only produced the effect of making their property more valid as security for raising money; when debts have reached a certain limit they must be paid even should payment involve foreclosure of old estates; and thus the reign of the frugal trader is but too likely to supplant that of the spendthrift landlord nor is it easy to see why Audh should escape the general process. What the shock and shame of the great revolt certainly did was to sweep away some anomalies and correct some delusions. To the former some reference has been made. The high-caste Hindustáni army, with its overwhelming preponderance of men and its discontented officers, was one anomaly; the "Great Mogul" of Delhi was another; the Company in Leadenhall Street was the greatest of all. As for the delusions, again the reader of these pages will not be without information. The propaganda of Western ideas was checked; the "doctrine of lapse"—as will be presently shown —received its quietus. It was impossible to avoid the unmistakable lesson which the terrible year had taught. The greatest troubles of the British had taken place wherever their presence had been greatest and their influence most direct. Their best friends had been found where their interference had been least exerted. In Bengal, Bihár, Hindustan; in the lately annexed territories of Audh, Jhánsi, and Nágpore; in the Bengal army with its imitated European order and organisation, and appearance of discipline; in all these were trouble and disaster. In Haidarábád, Málwa, Rájputána; in countries where the Government had abstained from minute interposition; among chiefs in armies more irregularly managed, and Princes who had been left the freest hand in their own States; there was found active loyalty, or, at least, quiescence. Even in the Punjab, nearly half the country was still under Native chieftains; and in the rest of the Province the hand of the British Government had been only felt in benefit and friendly service.

[In addition to books already cited the reader may be referred to "Fifty-Seven" (by the present writer) London, 1883; and Sir O. Burne's "Clyde and Strathnairn"; a soldierly account of the Sepoy war in "Rulers" series].

Section 3.—Among the items of expense by which the new India of the first Viceroyalty was purchased the actual pecuniary cost is one of the most obvious. The loss of life, the interruption of business, the suspension of all friendly feeling between the European community and vast sections of the Native population; all these were, undoubtedly grievious additions to the price of regeneration. But after all, the immediate question was how to arrest the hæmorrhage of the Treasury.

Something like 100,000 British troops had been poured into the country; civil officers had been raising levies of Native militia; in many places the sources of revenue had, for the time, been dried up. What with the Mutiny and its suppression, and what with the consequent disorganisation of society and of administration, an enormous deficit appeared in finances never thought to be very elastic. Measures must needs be promptly taken to check expenditure on one hand, to increase supply on the other. The former of these two requirements was more within the competence of the Governor General and his subordinates than the latter. The issuing of peremptory orders for disbanding all the extraordinary levies sufficed to curtail the one evil; but the relief—however, needful—could not count for much. Briefly stated, the late war had caused a deficit of thirty-six millions, only a very little short of a whole year's net income: with all possible economy the expenses of 1860 were estimated to exceed the revenue by many millions. The credit of the Government was low; and new loans were raised with difficulty. The customs-duties had to be raised, to the detriment of the trade of the country; exports as well as imports were affected. The proposal to impose a licence-tax on trades and professions was received with universal outcry.

Such were some of the difficulties which the Viceroy had to lay before Lord Stanley, the new Secretary of State. The reply was to send out, as Extraordinary Councillor, an expert London financier, the Right Honourable James Wilson, late Secretary to the Treasury and editor of the "Economist." In company with Lord Canning, the Finance Minister made a tour in the winter of 1859-60; and on his return to Calcutta, Wilson laid before the Legislature—soon to be reinforced by some distinguished Native Members—his proposals for new taxation. Great opposition arose: even the official class was hostile; and Sir Charles Trevelyan—who had succeeded Harris at Madras—recorded an able protest which found its way into the public prints. This was regarded as an indiscretion demanding the Governor's recall; but the protest had not been made in vain. The obnoxious budget was revised; two of the proposed taxes withdrawn, and the third—an income tax of four per cent. on incomes above five hundred rupees a year, with a lower rate on smaller ones—was recommended as an experiment for five years.* To this tax there were serious objections; however excellent, in theory, might be the idea of making the prosperous contribute to the support of the Government to whose protection they owed so much, the idea of taxing incomes under five hundred rupees a year was felt to be preposterous. All but some ten per cent. of the heads of Indian families were agriculturists, already paying more than half their net rental to the State. Their other sources of income could not be accurately ascertained; and the attempt could not be made without demoralising investigations. Almost all Native Indian incomes were so low that it was to be feared that these dangers and consequent unpopularity would bring in but little compensating profit; and the Queen would be shown as inaugurating her reign in India by causing a maximum of evil for a minimum of advantage. The last part of these objections, at least, has been made good; even with the subsequent addition of a licence-tax—and one on official salaries—the amount from these assessments was never much more than two millions (R.x.) in one year. Wilson introduced many reforms into the machinery of finance administration,† but did not live to see the good of his labours. He died in August, 1860, and was soon after

* Mr. Wilson did the author the honour to consult him as to this impost; the difficulties were pointed out and the decentralisation of finance suggested as an alternative revenue. Some arguments of the same tendency were also orally submitted to Lord Canning: but years were to pass before that simple reform could be adopted.

† One important reform was substituting scrutiny *before* expenditure to the vicious system of post-audit, which had almost entirely failed as a check upon extravagance.

succeeded by Mr. Samuel Laing, who passed the Income Tax Act.

But before the arrival of the new Finance Minister an event had occurred of such wide and beneficial effect that it deserves a special record. In spite of all the embarrassments of the Treasury it was Canning's laudable desire that no time should be lost in showing honour and favour to the princes and nobles who had befriended and served the cause of order during the past troubles. Among these, in the higher rank, were the Cis-Sutlej chiefs, Patiála, Jhind, Nábha, and Kapurthala; The Rájas of Jaipore, Udaipore, and Karaoli; Sindhia and the Nizám above all; together with their enlightened Ministers. On all these grants of territory, honorific titles, and similar favours were bestowed; but what made the best impression of all was the issue, to the somewhat less exalted chieftains whose possessions were of the secondary, or "dependent" class, of patents acknowledging the right of such chieftains to adopt heirs. Thus the "fatal doctrine of lapse" was buried out of sight; and a policy of justice was substituted for a policy of of annexation. The objection that indulgence to chiefs was not justice to their subjects was seen to have been greatly overdone; and whatever truth it might contain was met by the more excellent way of holding the chiefs personally responsible for the humanity and efficiency of their administration.

Besides the changes at Madras other official moves marked the first Viceroyalty. The Punjab became a Lieutenant-Governorship in which Lawrence was soon to be succeeded by Sir Robert Montgomery.* Mr.—afterwards Sir Charles—

* Delhi (city and district) came under the new government; and the former centre of Empire was at once punished and rendered harmless by being made the appendage to an outlying Province. There could not have been a more signal proof given to India and to the world that a new Empire had been established.

Wingfield became Chief Commissoner of Audh in succession to Outram: Mr.—afterwards Sir George—Edmonstone, was made Lieutenant-Governor of the North West Provinces; Sir J. P. Grant assumed charge of the Lower Provinces; Elphinstone retired from Bombay where Sir George Clerk—once Resident at Lahore—became Governor. The constitution of the Legislative Council also underwent an important change. The Judges, whose criticisms had often disturbed the repose of the official mind, were excluded; but an opening for a vital reform was made by the admission of distinguished Natives. Other legislative chambers were at the same time erected in the minor Presidencies. It is only fair to add that the old Legislative Council did some notable work in the last years of its existence. Three Universities—one for each Presidency-town—had been incorporated by law in 1857, during the very storm and stress of the revolt. Two years later was passed the famous Act x. of 1859; the Magna Charta of the millions of argriculturists who were not possessed of proprietary rights, and the indispensable corrective of many abuses and oppressions which had grown up since Cornwallis introduced his settlement in 1793. Farther steps have since been found necessary; but the direction and nature of the policy were clearly laid down at the time under our present notice. For tenants-at-will, indeed, little or nothing could be done then; but occupancy-rights could be recognised, with fixity of tenure at fair rent-rates; and the period of limitation borrowed from civil law was taken as giving to such rights the benefit of prescription.

But, if the Judges of the Supreme Court were to be debarred from taking part in the making of laws, their more legitimate field of usefulness was immensely extended by their amalgamation with the principal Courts of the country, the "Sudder Adálat" as it was called. This measure was one of the far-seeing plans of Warren Hastings, destined, like most of that great man's ideas, to bear permanent fruit, even if not realised in his time. One High Court was now chartered for each Presidency, to be a Court-of-Record, and still partially manned by lawyers sent out from Home: but with these would now be associated a certain number of "Civilian Judges;" members of the civil service who had been District-Judges; while other members might be selected from the local Bar. The scheme has worked well; with a few exceptions the Benches have been competent, impartial, and able; while the printing of their decisions, combined with a general controlling action, has tended to give efficiency and consistency to the working of the Courts below. In criminal administration, at least, the process has been much forwarded by the enactment of the Indian Penal Code which, drafted by a Committee presided over by Macaulay, and finally completed by Sir Barnes Peacock, has worked, in various ways—direct and indirect—more good to the country than any other measure that could be mentioned. It not only instructs the officials, but educates the people; preserving them from arbitrary caprice and forming a standard of uniform, thought and conduct.*

Another amalgamation, less generally approved, took place in the Army. In July, 1858, a Royal Commission was issued to a number of statesmen and soldiers to report upon twelve questions of military organisation; especially in connection with the number of European soldiers that ought to be retained in India, and on what footing, whether as a separate force, or as an integral part of the Imperial Army subject to periodical reliefs. The result of their enquiries and deliberations was a recommendation that the white garrison of India should be fixed at 80,000 men of all arms, furnished from the ranks of the Imperial Army, which was, however, at that period recruited on the "long-service principle." It was understood that this was the system personally preferred by her Majesty,

* The code is said to be a text-book of study in the schools of Native States: v. Note on Indian Law at the end of this Volume (App. II.)

and the Prince Consort. A Bill to this effect became law in the middle of 1860.

At the same time a new Native army was raised in Bengal, one or two sepoy corps which resisted temptation, or being out of its reach, continued to serve, though with necessarily changed "numbers." The rest of the rank and file consisted —with the exception of a few faithful individuals—of men from new social and ethnic strata; Sikhs, Patháns, Gurkhas, and low-castes, enregimented in different companies if not in different corps. The number of European officers to each regiment was reduced to six—with a few probationers—all regimental employ being in future regarded as staff-employ bestowed, as a reward, upon special proof of fitness. Officers who chose might retire upon special terms; the remainder being without any but "General Duty," such as was involved in the Committees and Courts that might from time to time be called for in Cantonments.

On the whole these measures have stood the test of time. There has, it is true, been no great war, since then, in India: and therefore they cannot be positively pronounced a complete success. For example; if in a very long and arduous action, or campiagn, there were a serious loss of officers, we cannot feel quite certain how it would fare with a corps left entirely uncommanded: yet in a case where an abnormal amount of leading was required, it is to be feared that six officers might be soon put out of the way by death or wounds. The constant reliefs of time-expired European regiments, again, may cost more than a local Army would; and it must be a bad thing to lose the bulk of your men just at the moment when they have got over their acclimatisation and become inured to the conditions of Eastern service. On other points of military reform there could not be the same room for doubt. The preponderance of *Purbias*, ("Men from the East") was put a stop to; as was also the hotch-pot of other classes that used to be blended, in like proportion for each regiment. Each race now formed its own battalion or company, so that a spirit of competition and rivalry took the place of the Pretorianism that had once been such a source of danger. The system of class-companies became known as "building the regiment in water-tight compartments:" for it was held that by such a system, contamination—however introduced—would not spread beyond the part affected. This, though an undoubted advance upon the old hotch-pot way, came ultimately to be considered insufficient. In looking back upon the Great Revolt it was perceived that it was not class-companies, but class-corps which had, in a few cases, been the means whereby the plague was stayed: and the true remedy against future combination, of an unlawful and mischievous kind, was seen to be the creation of rivalry, if not actual antagonism, between entire regiments: for under any other rule the sense of solidarity and common employment might in time undo the work of caste, creed, and race.

Lastly, with the exception of a few mountain-batteries, there is now no Native force of artillery; all guns are intrusted to British gunners; and thus, a great temptation to mutiny has been taken away from the Native Army. In the forces of the minor Presidencies there was less immediate call for reform; but a similar spirit actuated the changes eventually introduced there also; and on the whole it must be admitted that, in the old British manner of "slow and sure," a most wholesome change was made in military organisation and management.

Turning again to civil affairs we shall see that the changes already mentioned were accompanied by others not less important. While the composition of the legislative machinery had been altered, attention had been also turned to the eminently faulty constitution of the interior Cabinet of the Viceroy, substantially similar to what had been devised by Pitt in 1784. Under this scheme every proposed measure—great or small—had to be brought before the whole Council and decided by the vote of the majority. By the Indian Councils Act (24, 25, Vict. c. 67) the more complete division of labour was introduced which—leaving the joint responsibility of the whole Council intact—makes each member answerable, in the first instance, for the current work of some one department more especially in his charge, subject to the approval of the Viceroy, who thus fulfils the ideal of a British King before the time of George I. The special Department of Finance and Account was at the same time completely reorganised; but the first Finance-Minister of India died before his great task had been accomplished.

We have already seen that Mr. Laing revised and amended his predecessor's budget. The necessity was great. The military charges still touched eighteen and a quarter millions; the cash balance was dangerously low. Twenty millions were urgently needed for railway extension; the interest of the new loans had increased the annual expenditure by two millions; the new taxes were only yielding a million and a-half, yet they pressed upon the poor in a manner which the Government regretted and desired to amend. Such, however, was the skill of the new Minister, loyally seconded by the Viceroy and heads of departments, that a total of three and three-quarter millions was retrenched from the civil and military expenditure. The restoration of order effected the rest by raising the receipts; and the last year of Canning's troubled rule ended with the unwonted spectacle of a surplus. The proverbial stagnation of Indian finance was now at an end; and it was conclusively shown that, with skill and prudence, it could have as elastic a character as that of most countries.

Unhappily, there was another element in those days—perhaps not entirely eliminated yet—which might for a time baffle the best efforts of a benevolent and able rule. Mention has been made, in an early page, of the vast forces of Nature in India, and their uncertain action.* The year 1861 was a period in which these dangers were exemplified. In the central belt of the country, from the south of the Ganges to the Godávari Valley, the monsoon-rains fell in torrents; the rivers overflowed their usual limits, and flooded vast tracts of country, carrying away roads and bridges, and frustrating the hopes of many myriads of husbandmen. Further north, the monsoon failed, causing famine and pestilence to an extent that was not beyond control, yet which caused distress that will not be forgotten by those who witnessed it.†

One of the last great measures of the period was the consolidation of all the Provinces of British Burma under one head. The first Chief Commissioner was Colonel—afterwards Sir Arthur—Phayre, an eminent officer who had held the office of Provincial Commissioner of Pegu since the annexation. The former territory of the Bhonslá was made into another similar charge, and Mr.—afterwards Sir Richard—Temple went to Nágpore as Chief Commissioner; the first of the series of high offices which he was destined to fill.

The Chinese war of this period only belongs to Indian history so far that several Sikh regiments made part of a force despatched from India, under the gallant Sir Hope Grant, which took part in the reduction of the Taku forts, and the subsequent reduction of Pekin, an event followed by the Convention of October 24, 1860. In the succeeding year, Sikhim—a small mountain chiefship between Bhutan and Nepal—was annexed for the foolish contumacy of the Rája.

In the opening of the year 1861 the East Indian Railway from Calcutta to Allahabad was opened, and the traffic was so

* CHAPTER I., Section 1.—The spread of canals and railroads has minimised these perils.

† It is on record that four millions of the peasantry in the Upper Provinces were ruined by this famine. The deaths were very numerous. The subsequent outbreak of cholera more than decimated some of the British garrisons of Northern India.

large as to yield the full rate of the guaranteed interest—five per cent.—in its first year. Soon after, other lines began working in the South: altogether, 1,360 miles were opened at this period, and 3,000 more were in course of completion. The great canals of the State were also beginning to be remunerative; though it should not be forgotten that financial profit was no more than a secondary object of these beneficent works.

In all directions the country began to show that the havoc of the revolt and consequent calamities was at an end. The total commerce of India had risen from sixty millions in 1857 to eighty millions in 1861; a full half of the increase being due to Bombay and Karáchi; and the peasantry obtained a share of the enhanced prosperity caused by the exportation of cotton, jute, and tea. A foundation was made for the preservation of timber and the extension of plantations, which was soon to develop into the Forest Department, so long and ably directed by Dr. Brandis. The introduction of cinchona-growing also dates from this period; twenty years later the profit had more than doubled the cost of the plantations.

In the midst of these peaceful and beneficent exertions the Viceroy's noble life was rapidly wearing out. The dilatoriness, the apparent coldness, of his first period were forgotten by a public which had learned to do justice to his calm temper, his imperturbable sense of duty. But his strength was spent. In the month of March, 1862, he made over his charge to his old friend, James Bruce, Earl of Elgin, and went home, to die, a broken man, like his illustrious predecessor.

[Same books as already cited in Sections 1, 2.]

CHAPTER XXI.

THE NEW ERA.

Section 1 : An unfinished career—Section 2 : The great Civilian—Section 3 : Peace and Progress.

SECTION 1.—Lord Elgin was a contemporary and friend of Dalhousie, Canning, and Harris; and was exactly fifty years of age when he accepted the burden of Indian Government. He had already governed Jamaica and Canada, in which colonies his tact and talent had given satisfaction to all. While on his way to China, in the character of plenipotentiary extraordinary, he halted at Singapore; and there, hearing of the outbreak of the Indian revolt, boldly took upon himself to divert the expedition, and take his troops up to Calcutta. The original mission, nevertheless, was only delayed for a short time; and its objects were obtained in the following year by the Treaty of Tien-tsin (26 June, 1858). In 1862 Elgin was rewarded by the Indian Viceroyship, the greatest post under the Crown in respect of trust and power. The minor governments passed into new hands about the same time, Madras being given to Sir Henry Ward—succeeded soon after by Sir William Denison, R.E.—and Bombay to Sir Bartle Frere; while Sir C. Beadon became Lieutenant of Bengal, as Mr. Edmonstone already was of the North-West Provinces; the administrative capital of the last-named being transferred from Agra to Allahabad. Mr. Laing laid down the office of Finance-member, which he had so ably held under the first Viceroy; and he was succeeded by Sir Charles Trevelyan.

The policy of Canning's later years was continued by Elgin and his Council, although the recent promotions and changes had left but one old member in his place. The letters of Lord Elgin, which have been preserved and published, show how strongly the new Viceroy was impressed with the sense of continuity, and especially determined to avoid interference with Native States and the introduction of taxes to which the people were not accustomed. In this latter policy he was particularly sure of the support of his Finance Minister. Trevelyan was an old civilian of the Metcalfe School, wary and experienced; he knew that the public mind was not sufficiently advanced to look upon taxation as anything but a form of rapacity: and he acted as if there were a tacit compact between rulers and people, that the traditional sources of revenue should be made sufficient for the services of the State.*

Lord Elgin, like most Viceroys, kept the "Foreign" Department of the Government in his own hands and acted with justice and discretion in the one important affair that came up for decision. The aged Dost Muhamad, by turn enemy and friend, was bent on a hostile expedition to Herát, where the local Governor, Sultán Ján, was acting insubordinately: Elgin refused to be in any way party to such proceedings, and even withdrew his Native agent from Kábul for the time, lest the presence of such an official might give rise to misunderstandings or misrepresentations. The Dost soon after died—in May, 1863—and the Viceroy made arrangements for sending a Vakil to congratulate the new Amir.

Three months earlier Lord Elgin set out for a tour in Northern India; no longer in the pompous and—to the

* The writer may state from his own experience that the up-country Natives of that period thought that the produce of the Income Tax went as tribute to England. "Take whatever is fitting, once and away, as a fine for the losses of the Mutiny; but do not punish us for ever:" such was the often repeated comment.

people at least—oppressive manner of the past, when a swarm of camp-followers with herds of oxen, elephants, and camels, marked every march with devastation, but as a passenger by the East India Railway. At Benares, on the 7th, he held a formal Durbar; and at a dinner in the evening, showed that he was alive to the expensive nature of the present railway system, and looked forward to the introduction of purely private enterprise.* On the 11th, the graves of the Cawnpore victims were consecrated by the Bishop of Calcutta, in the presence of Lord Elgin and a distinguished assemblage of Europeans; and the Viceregal party proceed by rail to Agra. Here was held a grand Durbar where, on the 17th, almost all the Chiefs of Central India and Rájputána appeared in full state. In medieval pomp the Ránas and Rájas gathered to the camp, mounted on elephants and escorted by squadrons of mounted men-at-arms; almost as in the days of the great Emperors. But not Akbar himself could have made them an address more full of dignified sympathy than what awaited them in the great Durbar tent of the British Viceroy. Speaking as the representative of their common Sovereign Lord Elgin assured his princely hearers of the profound interest felt in their concerns by the Queen, of which he exhorted them to show themselves worthy by acting in a similar spirit to their respective subjects. For his own part, added the Viceroy, he was ready to extend encouragement and friendship to all who laboured for the good of India. The speech was short, not on that account less welcome; and it was remarkable as striking the keynote of

* Under the guarantee-system every shareholder had a certainty from the State of 5 per cent.; and so good an investment proved fatal to economy. The East Indian line is believed to have been built at a rate equivalent to £16,000 a mile; and that in a country where unskilled labour is not paid much more than one-tenth of English wages. The whole cost of the six thousand miles of guaranteed lines was over ninety-five millions Rx.

unity, in a manner more decided than theretofore it had been ever struck.

On the 27th March, a final assembly was held at Ambala, where the Sikh chiefs and other Punjab notables were received; and thence the Viceroy proceeded to pass the hot season upon the green and breezy heights of Simla.

While the Viceroy was engaged in these peaceful occupations another of those little clouds was rising, from which, in India, the political horizon has been so rarely free. To the north of Pesháwar, between the Indus and the Jhelam rivers, a spur of the Hindu-Kush abuts on the British District of Hazara: it is known as Mahában ("great wood") and its summit attains a height of 7,400 ft. above sea-level. On the slope of this mountain was a place called Sitána, a nest of Muslim fanaticism ever since the days of Ránjit Sinh, and the subject of a small punitive expedition in 1858. Here had gathered the dregs of the Muhamadan ferment, sepoys escaped from the war, and irreconcilable Wahhábis; and here—precariously supplied with men and money from centres of disaffection in Hindustan—a colony of fanatics was formed ready for an opportunity to carry war into British territory. The focus of the agitation was, however, traced to Patna, in the country subject to the Lieutenant-Governor of Bengal. In the course ot an inquiry, held by Sir Herbert Edwardes, the extent of the mischief was found to be serious if not alarming and it became a question how to abolish the danger. Lord Elgin was naturally unwilling to stir up strife so near the road that led to the Afghán Amir's capital. On the other hand it was felt that a sharp decisive blow, struck at once, might avert the risks of a larger and more difficult undertaking hereafter. Accordingly, in the month of October, a British force of all arms, 6,000 strong, was sent into the mountains, under Sir Neville Chamberlain. The tribes unfortunately resented the intrusion and blocked the Ambaila Pass through which the advanced column was making way into the country. The opposition was so serious—being supported, it was said, by 60,000 men—that reinforcements were thought necessary; and it was not until the middle of December that aggressive operations could begin.

In the meantime, the able and industrious Viceroy was no more; Lord Elgin, on a tour through the hills west of Simla, expired at Dhármsala November 20th. His post was temporarily assumed by Sir William Denison, then Governor of Madras, on whom it devolved by virtue of seniority, pending the arrival of a new Viceroy from England. Denison had originally opposed the expedition; but now, as a scientific soldier, he perceived the necessity of doing all in the power of his Government to enable Chamberlain to extricate himself with honour. Having received the needful accession of strength, the expeditionary force stormed the defences on the night of December 15th; and the tribes not only desisted from further resistance but undertook to destroy the strongholds of the fanatics unaided. Chamberlain had been by this time severely wounded and had been constrained to make over the command to General Garvock, who—while gladly accepting the professed services of the tribesmen—judged it prudent to insist upon the presence of a British force on the spot. On the 22nd, the place was utterly consumed by fire, in presence of a British column; the fanatics having escaped in time. On the 25th the British left the country once fatal to Akbar's friend Bir Bal; and the shrewd comment of the acting Viceroy was, that if a lesson had been read to the enemy, it was not without its use as a warning to the Government also.

India had now, in rapid succession, devoured three distinquished public men.* Lord Palmerston resolved to break through the traditional bar and send out a seasoned Indian official.

* Dalhousie, December 19th, 1863; Canning, June 17th, 1862; Elgin, November 20th, 1863.

["Letters and Journals of James, 8th Earl of Elgin," T. Walrond, 1872. "India under Victoria," L. J. Trotter, (Vol. II.), 1886.]

SECTION 2.—Originally laid down by Lord Cornwallis, the maxim that the Governor-General of India should always be a distinguised man of rank, who had graduated in English politics, had been endorsed by high authority, both at home and in India. At first sight it might appear a too sweeping generalisation that excluded the whole class which had produced such men as Warren Hastings, Munro, Metcalfe and Elphinstone. It was now, at all events, to be contravened in the person of one whose claims were inferior to those of no member of the local services. Ever since he had been District-officer of Delhi, at the time of the first Punjab war, John Lawrence had been a man of mark. After the battle of Sobraon, Hardinge had selected him as Commissioner of the newly-acquired Jalandhar Duáb, and the work that he did there had enhanced his reputation. If he lacked the sympathetic elements of character which made his brother Henry a personage of irresistible magnetism, if his culture had suffered for want of the training of a University and Parliamentary life, he had at least a knowledge of Indian details, and a force of will that admitted of no question or competition. Above all, he had the prestige of having made the Punjab, taken Delhi, and saved the Empire.

When, therefore, the situation of Chamberlain's force at Mahában appeared to threaten incalculable consequences, while the cares and labours of three men of distinction had been emphasised by premature overthrow, and the fate of Dalhousie, Canning, and Elgin had thrown a deeper gloom over the terrors of exile and climate, Lord Palmerston only gave expression to public sentiment in offering the post of honourable peril to the illustrious Civilian. Without a moment's hesitation Lawrence accepted the charge, and used such speed as to land in Calcutta within two months after his predecessor's decease (January 12th, 1864). He found there a group of able coadjutors prepared to give advice which he was not always, perhaps, equally prepared to appreciate. Denison was at Madras, though he presently returned to Europe, leaving the Presidency of Fort S. George in the temporary charge of Mr. E. Maltby; Sir Bartle Frere was promoted to the high post of Governor of Bombay. Sir Hugh Rose was Commander-in-Chief of the Indian army; Sir Robert Napier, afterwards Lord Napier of Magdala, was Military Member of the Council; the Finance Minister was Sir C. Trevelyan; Mr.—afterwards Sir H. S.—Maine had the charge of the Legislative Department. According to precedent Lawrence himself undertook the Foreign, or "Political" Department, and it is to this branch of administration that our attention will be first directed.

The Mahában expedition had completed its task, and returned to India before the new Viceroy entered his duties. But the North-West Frontier naturally continued to receive careful attention from one who had been for so long himself Warder of that outpost. By a mixture of trust and menace, by a judicious combination of road-making for the use of punitive columns, and schooling for the boys of the tribes, a kind of civilisation suited to the case was gradually introduced, until the Border of the Trans-Indus became as nearly quiet as that of the Tweed had been two centuries before. In the latter part of this administration a somewhat serious attack on the British side, was made at the instigation of the Khán of Agrore, a petty chieftaincy on the Hazara frontier. An expedition was sent against the tribes in the autumn of 1868; the Khán was carried off a prisoner, and the tribes made due submission. On the other side a serious question arose out of the death of Dost Muhamad and the disputed succession. Sher Áli had assumed the office of Amir, it can hardly be dignified with the title of throne; because, since the fall of the

Saduzai dynasty, Afghanistán had become a federation of chiefs, among whom the Amir was little more than a leading chief, first among his peers. But even that supremacy was now challenged, and Sher Áli soon became involved in defending his position against his own brothers and nephews. Lawrence, acting, it is said, on hints that had been given by the Dost before his death, resolved that he would not interfere, but would acknowledge the successful competitor, whoever he might be, as the *de-facto* Amir.

On the other extreme of India's mountain rampart she touches the marches of the Chinese Empire. The point is less vulnerable than that of Afghanistán, where the invasions of ages have poured upon her plains. But here, too, vigilance was called for, not so much from the Chinese, who are too far away, and too much exposed to the maritime power of Britain, as from the mountaineers whom, with the best intentions, China may be unable to control. The Nepalese, indeed, were friendly, and Sikhim was a small State, and one which had been thoroughly coerced. But there remained the Bhutanese, a people of Mongol origin, on the eastern verge, commanding the entrance into Assam, and even of Bengal. Their country is as large as England, and they had been in the habit of paying a small annual tribute to the rulers of Assam, though acknowledging the Thibet Lama as their legitimate overlord. But after the first Burmese war they ceased to pay tribute and began a system of foraging which led to the closing of the Dwárs ("doors") which opened from their mountains into British territory. On January 4th, 1864 a British Envoy, the Honourable Ashley Eden, was sent by the Government of India to attempt the formation of a more regular and permanent understanding with these turbulent neighbours, who hastened to forestall his arrival by assurances of their unwillingness to receive him, and their entire indifference to the objects of the proposed mission. It seems, indeed, that the moment was ill-chosen for diplomatic operations, to which there was this initial obstacle, that there did not happen to be in Bhutan at the time any sort of regular government with which to treat. The Rája had been virtually deposed, and an insurgent chief, known as the Toungso Penlo, was endeavouriug to make himself master of the State. There were, doubtless old-standing grievances on either side, the Bengal Government complaining of raids on account of which the stipend promised to Bhutan had been sequestered, and the mountaineers complaining of the sequestration. But the negotiations might have stood over to a more convenient time, for the force of the State was contemptible, and a little strengthening of the frontier posts would have afforded all necessary protection. The people are to this day in a low condition of savagery, and far from numerous, while the surface of their country affording all varieties of soil and temperature in abundance, they are under no pressure to seek expansion, especially in the vaporous heat of Bengal and Assam.

Such was the nature of the adventure to which Lawrence found himself committed by the impatience of the Bengal Government. Bad news soon reached him from the camp of the Mission. The Envoy was surrounded by difficulties to which he could only oppose his indomitable resolution. Crossing torrents by frail and oscillating bridges of twig and rope, threading damp malarious glens, or crawling along dizzy precipices where snow hid the pathway, and one false step meant death, Eden held his way with honourable tenacity. Lawrence would have recalled him, but allowed himself to be over-persuaded by Sir Cecil Beadon, his lieutenant in Bengal. Reaching the capital on March 15th, the mission found a Council under the ostensible presidency of the Rája, but really inspired and controlled by the chief already mentioned, the Penlo of Toungso, or the eastern Province. Here, amid jeers and insults, exposed to the ridicule and horse-play of a crowd of barbarians, Eden was constrained to sign a treaty conceding all the demands of Bhutan. He then decamped by night, and returned to British territory on April 12th.

The Government of India at once sent a letter to the Durbar, in which the extorted treaty was entirely disavowed, and atonement for all offence, peremptorily demanded. Six months, however, passed without any reply or notice; and on November 12th, 1864, Lawrence issued a proclamation setting forth the misconduct of Bhutan, and annexing the Western—or Bengal—passes. A brief demonstration ensued, during which the passes were seized almost without the firing of a shot. Suddenly, when all thought of opposition appeared to have been abandoned, the Bhutanese forces fell upon the easternmost position, a fort called Diwángiri, held by 500 Sepoys. Being without supplies or support the force retired, losing its two guns. But this reverse was soon retrieved by the advance of a strong column under General Tombs; Diwángiri being reoccupied, and the enemy everywhere chased back into their hills. The Rája and his Penlo soliciting a cessation of war, the Government agreed to hold its hand on condition of a formal cession of all the conquered passes and adjacent lands —a tract about 180 miles in length by 25 in breadth—the liberation of all kidnapped British subjects, and the restoration of the two guns lost at Diwángiri. As the revenues of the State depended mainly on the territory thus annexed, the Government agreed to pay rent for it, pending good behaviour; so that the Durbar could salve its pride by saying that it had rendered India its tributary, but was not the less bound to good conduct under heavy bail. The terms were accepted, and their best justification is to be found in the unbroken tranquility which has since prevailed. The Western Dwárs —the passes leading from Bhutan into Bengal—have been formed into nine Parganas (fiscal unions) under the Government of the Lower Provinces; they are in course of conversion into tea-plantations; the Eastern Dwárs are less prominent, being subject to Assam, and chiefly productive of timber and rice.

The relations of the Government towards Native States within Indian limits gave but little trouble since the balm of the new policy had soothed the irritation set up by Dalhousie's indiscriminate escheats. The change of policy had found an echo in the breast of the present Viceroy. Originally an annexationist (and able to point with just pride to the bright side of annexation in his model Province, the loyal and prosperous Punjab), his zeal was now tempered by the shock of the great revolt which had fallen on no one with more of astonishment than on him. He had come to see the great value of the Native States, and he got a glimpse—it may be doubted if he ever attained to a full perception—of the danger of hurrying Western ideas into the moulds of antique Eastern civilisation. We should be struck with the absurdity of blaming Solomon for not establishing a penny-post from Dan to Beersheba; yet some of our Anglo-Indian reformers would think nothing of disarming a Pathán chief, and then asking him to subscribe to a dispensary.* At all his Durbars Lawrence used to harangue the chiefs, assembled out of all corners of medieval barbarism, on the evils of infanticide and the blessings of female education.

Not but what there was a difference between these things and a policy of annexation or unrestrained interference. States on the larger scale—what in Metcalfe's time might have been called "Independent"—were generally left alone, and were not the less prosperous or well-administered. Mádhava Ráo in Travancore, Sálar Jang in the Nizám's territory, Dinkar Ráo at Gwalior, were all Statesmen of genuine ability and principle; and all such received an honest support from Lawrence. But the grandson of Amir Khán—who had succeeded to the

* "The Old Pindari," Sir A. Lyall's famous ballad.

chiefdom of Tonk—felt the weight of the Viceroy's displeasure when he thought he could with impunity abet an act of treacherous murder. The young Nawáb was deposed and brought to Benares as a State-prisoner, while the State was intrusted to the charge of a Council of Regency, pending the minority of the Nawáb's infant son. Warning was taken in time by the Rájput ruler of Márwar, or Jaudhpore; whose tyranny seemed to be provoking a rebellion. These things began in 1865, and in the following year the Viceroy held a Durbar at Agra, which was attended by no less than eighty-four chiefs of Rájputána and Central India, Sindia and Holkar, the Begam of Bhopal, and the Rájas and Ránas of the oldest and proudest Houses of the Rájputs; the investiture of those selected for the new order—the Star of India—furnished reward for past merits or retaining-fee for the future; though unfortunately Takht Sinh of Jaudhpore had to receive Vice-regal censure not many months later.

In 1868 the Mysore question began—as it were—to stir in its sleep. The titular Rája died in the Spring, after thirty-seven years of retirement. Contrary to the Viceroy's wishes, the adopted son of the deceased was proclaimed Rája of Mysore; but he was only six years old, and the State was put under a Regency for the next few years, Major Malleson being appointed Chief Commissioner. It was on this occasion that Lawrence was led to issue his famous circular asking the provincial officials if they did not think the Natives were happier under the British sway than under that of their own rulers.* By this indication of his own views, the Viceroy seemed to anticipate the conclusion; at any rate it was generally favourable to him. The universal testimony of those consulted was that the people were, indeed, possessed of much more security,

* He added the saving-clause—*sua si bona norint*—which made sport among the Philistines, who asked what might be the value of a happiness of which you were unaware?

and provided with far more sources of prosperity under the just and punctual system of which His Excellency was the head.

The question, of course, remains very much where it was before. It is impossible to conceive any mode of taking a *plebiscitum* on such a matter—yet it cannot be solved by any number of foreign functionaries consulted as to their own success—which is really all that the inquiry came to. As an answer to the suggested comparison of a noble lord, who about that time assumed the Indian Ministry at Home,* the move was prudent. "But in the main," so a distinguished and well-informed writer argues, "the discussion was academic." It was, indeed, hardly even that—apart from the fact that all the persons who recorded opinions were officials of the Government whose efficiency was in question—it could hardly be a matter for even academic discussion whether the respect for the rights of individuals and for the interests of society were not a better thing in itself than a condition of stagnation varied by civil war. Yet there was, in the decried system, an element of adventure, of career open to ability, which cannot but have its charms. British India has not produced a Salár Jang. Again, the British, as Sir John allowed—almost boasted—are not bound by the views of the Natives, but by their own sense of what is right; yet the most efficient and conscientious schoolmaster will hardly believe that he always pleases his pupils, or that they do not think that they would be happier at home.

The only further diplomatic duty of this administration was in preparing the ultimate relations with Afghanistán and Russia, which were not completed till after Lawrence had left the scene. It has been already seen that Lawrence laid down

* Viscount Cranborne, Secretary of State, in the Derby Ministry, from June, 1866, to March, 1867; subsequently—as Marquess of Salisbury—Prime Minister and Foreign Secretary.

the strictest rule of non-interference—so long at least as the affairs of Afghanistán were only disturbed within the limits of that country—and the surmise has been expressed that, in leaving the Bárukzai chiefs to settle their quarrels in their own way, without active interposition, his attitude was in accordance with what he knew to be the desire of the deceased Amir. Towards Dost Muhamad, indeed, Lawrence had felt personal friendship, founded on the experiences of direct intercourse; and, when Dost Muhamad was no more, Lawrence still thought of his memory kindly, and felt sympathy for the family and a desire for the welfare and peace of their State. While, therefore, adhering firmly to his *de facto* principle—so that at one time he was prepared to regard the country of the Afghans as re-divided into its former three Provinces, each under a separate Amir—he hastened to give Sher Áli substantial proofs of his friendship when that chief finally overthrew his last opponent and ruled, from Kábul, over a united Afghán land. This happened at the end of 1868, and gave to the relations of the two countries the direction afterwards followed up by Mayo, and maintained until the unfortunate rupture of ten years later. But to Lawrence also were partly due the subsequent understanding with the Government of S. Petersburg, the policy of "the neutral zone," the delimitation of the Afghán frontier, and the restoration of rational relations between the two European powers. All these had been provided for by him.

[Trotter, as already cited; also "Life of Lord Lawrence," by R. B. Smith, 12 vols., London, 1883; and "Lord Lawrence," by Sir C. Aitchison (Rulers of India), Oxford, 1892.]

SECTION 3.—Although the people of India may not have felt the same appreciation of British rule as British officials wished them to feel, it is not to be supposed that so strong a mind as that of their then Viceroy was permanently misled by illusions. The people of India have never been historians; the traditions of the Great Anarchy were worn by the handling of three generations; they could now only see that they were in the hands of aliens, somewhat pedantic and unsympathetic, whom it was not easy to deceive; and who insisted on the performance of many things utterly at variance with popular custom, especially on the punctual payment of taxes. Two fundamental notions guided the Indian rulers of that school; one which a British nobleman declared to be "fertile of administrators but barren of statesmen."

One of those ideas was thus expressed by Lawrence: "In doing the best that we can for the people we are bound by our conscience, and not by theirs." The other may be stated in the words of his admiring disciple, Sir C. Aitchison: "A prosperous and contented peasantry he considered to be a more solid foundation of our (British) power than a landed aristocracy." These two propositions are enough to show the change that had come with conquest and annexation; both combine to indicate the spirit in which the Empire of the Queen was administered and to contrast it with that of the Company. It might be too much to say that they were unknown to Cornwallis and his school—to Tucker and Munro, Metcalfe and Elphinstone: but if these great founders of Empire recognised such principles it was only as parts of a complicated code, to be used on occasion but not otherwise. The words and deeds of the best men of that time show that they too had a "conscience," but they never let it overbear the convictions of the public: and they studied to promote the prosperity of the peasantry through the landed aristocracy without dislocating the national framework of society. Nevertheless, the extension of experience and the increased responsibilities of ever-expanding authority, could not fail to affect a mind so acute and so powerful as that of John Lawrence. Although he had once separated from his brother Henry on the landlord question, he may have subsequently thought over the the opinions of that highminded man, the true representative legatee of the good old school. The Punjab, indeed, could not test any such afterthoughts very closely: there were great nobles there as elsewhere; but sixty per cent. of the land is held by communities, or villages, of peasant-proprietors. When therefore the period for reviewing the settlement in the Punjab recurred, as it did early in Lawrence's administration as Viceroy, he felt no hesitation about introducing, and passing through the Legislative Council, an Act for the definition and protection of tenant-right in the Province. In so doing he had the complete consent and support of the Lieutenant-Governor, the experienced and excellent Sir Donald Macleod; and a successor, writing fourteen years later, bore testimony to the success of the measure in regard to the objects for which it was devised.

About the same time a similar problem presented itself in Audh, though in very dissimilar terms. The sturdy and very numerous yeomanry of the Punjab had—with aid from circumstance and goodwill from the authorities—both asserted and made good their status. In Audh, where the peasant-proprietors were neither numerous nor very sturdy—and where the good will of authority was somewhat lacking—it had appeared to Lord Elgin in 1863, that the policy of Mr. Wingfield, the Chief Commissioner, was tending to obliterate the sub-proprietary rights in spite of an injunction dating from Canning's patents. Mr. Wingfield had been struck, like all observant Anglo-Indians, with the ill-success of the policy favoured at the annexation. That policy has, it is true, been overstated by its opponents; a great many of the large landholders had established their claims. Nevertheless the fact remained that Audh was the only Province of India in which rebellion had, in 1857, been at all general. That the great Barons, the Talukdárs, should have resisted an innovation which to their minds threatened the loss of property and power was natural: but the odd thing was that they were joined in such resistance by the very peasantry for whose protection the innovation was intended. So that Mr. Wingfield and those who supported him were not entirely without some justification, always conceding their premises, for deprecating the project of asserting non-existent rights in favour of a population by whom those rights had been energetically repudiated.

But Lawrence was no ordinary civil officer to press a generous policy to a dangerous extreme. His intellect and experience combined to enforce upon him the commonplace (so often re-echoed in talk, so often neglected in practice) that the safest progress is to be made in the middle of the road. Stated concisely, the case stood thus. After the Mutiny and the issue of the famous confiscatory proclamation, new patents had been given to about 272 Audh Talukdárs, claiming to be landlords of two-thirds of the Province. A transferable and heritable title was thereby conferred; but it was subject to a condition which was intended to be as valid as the title itself, being indeed part-and-parcel of that title; the grants were declared, "subject to any measure which the Government may think proper to take for the purpose of protecting the inferior Zemindárs and village occupants from extortion and of upholding their rights in the soil."

A similar provision had formed part of the permanent settlement in Bengal, where it had been so long neglected as to have become well-nigh obsolete. But it did not appear to Lawrence that he would be doing his duty if he allowed such neglect in Audh. "Did ever anyone hear," he asked, "of the Government of India learning that a class of men were not having fair-play . . . and then failing to interfere?"

The remonstrances of Elgin had been overlooked by the Chief Commissioner; but Lawrence and Durand, who had become Secretary of the Department to which Audh was subject, did not allow their letters to be treated as waste paper; and

Wingfield had to adduce argument in defence of his position, pleading prescription, to which the Viceroy made answer that, short of breach of contract, it was never too late to repair an injustice. In the present proposal either no breach of contract was involved; or, if such there were, it was one that had already been committed by the Talukdárs themselves. So far from the conditions of the old society having been abolished by the Mutiny, they had been specifically revived by Canning; and the rights of the peasantry rested on the same title as those of the landlords. Wingfield however held his own; and the Viceroy was obliged to depute Mr. Davies, afterwards better known as Sir Henry Davies, to hold a searching enquiry into the facts as Special Commissioner. From Davies's report it was concluded that, under the Talukdárs, proprietary rights had been hopelessly submerged; but that tenancy-rights still undoubtedly survived and ought to be maintained by law. Ultimately Wingfield retired from the service, and was succeeded by Sir John Strachey; the Talukdárs were persuaded to accept a compromise; and in 1868 was passed the Audh Tenancy Act whereby about one in five of the cultivators received fixity of tenure at fair rates. Further legislation of this period protected the improvements made by this class not only in Audh but in the Punjab and North-West Province; and the actual holder of the land, as he had the chief power, had now the greatest interest, in reclaiming waste, draining marshes, and constructing minor works for the storage and distribution of water for irrigation.

In the case of Bengal, Lawrence found, or fancied, that his hands were, in some degree, tied. It was reserved for a later time to see the tenants under the Permanent Settlement fully protected by law; but, during Lawrence's administration an important step was taken to procure for them the full benefit of such legislation as had been already completed. An Act had been passed in Canning's time which had given definition and protection to many tenantries in the North-West Provinces, where seventy-five per cent. of the land was cultivated by tenants and of these nearly half held at fixed rates only alterable by judicial award. The same law applied to Bengal; but in Bengal local conditions for a long while enabled the Zemindárs to elude its action. Lawrence, however, urged Beadon to take the matter up and do all in his power to see fair-play done to the helpless multitude. By a ruling of the Chief Justice it seemed likely that the ryots would be all left in very much the position of tenants at-will; but in 1865, the case being referred to a full-bench, the other Judges unanimously set aside the ruling of their chief; and henceforth a door of escape stood open for the Bengal ryot. The full-bench judgment of 1865 is further remarkable for having elicited the doctrine that the Regulation of 1793 was quite incompatible with any notion of the Zemindár being absolute proprietor. Further enquiries were made, which cannot be charged with precipitation; but it was not till fifteen years later that the Act was drafted which now fully defines and protects the rights of cultivators in the Lower Provinces.*

That part of India was, at that moment, in a state of most extraordinary distress. Usually, whatever troubles may befal the agriculturists they are free from the famines that afflict the less fortunately-situated regions of India. But in 1865 the rainfall in the Lower Provinces had been precarious and generally short: and the rice—which is the staple crop—almost entirely failed. The worst of the calamity fell upon Orissa, which Province, by October, had wholly broken down. The symptoms failing to give sufficient warning to the Local Government, prices rose to an extent which made it impossible for the bulk of the population to obtain food. When relief-

* The subject will be resumed later on: the reasons which deprived Act x. of 1859 of its full effect under the Permanent Settlement may be conjectured, but there is no room for their discussion here.

works were, at length, opened the wages were paid in coin; and as there was nothing purchasable the relief proved illusory. The argument of those who should have provided against the calamity was that the rise of prices would attract supplies from elsewhere: but it now appeared that there was no food near enough to come by land or river, while the setting-in of the monsoon impeded the landing of supplies sent by sea. Less than 10,000 tons of rice were got into Orissa up to the end of October, barely sufficient—as was reckoned—for the saving of 250,000 lives. The famine was followed by floods which destroyed the new crop, and submerged the huts of the peasantry; what with one disaster and another, one million died out of a population of four millions.*

But out of evil came good, as is always the case where people are earnest and able. Measures were taken for the canalisation of Orissa, the regulation of the river discharge, and the improvement of the communications by land and by sea. It was also arranged that, in future, money necessary for such sorts of undertakings should be raised by loan and added to the national debt, the yearly interest being regarded as premium for famine-insurance. The establishment of this apparently obvious principle has done more for the people of India than many more showy measures. In the last two years of Lawrence's administration a sum equivalent—at the rate of exchange of that day—to one million and a half of British sterling was borrowed for "Reproductive Public Works," and almost all was spent on works of irrigation.†

Elsewhere it was a time of great, almost inconvenient, prosperity. In Central India and the West new sources of

* On February 12th, 1867, the Viceroy presided over a public meeting in Calcutta for the purpose of raising money for the relief of surviving sufferers, heading the subscription list with 10,000 rupees.

† Before the Franco-Prussian war the Rupee was commonly exchanged at the rate of ten to the pound sterling.

profit were thrown open by the increasing demand for raw cotton. In four years the price of the staple rose more than fourfold; and the volume of trade aggregated one hundred millions in a year. Consequently prices rose; wages remaining almost stationary except at Bombay and other sea-port towns. Speculation was pushed to a most dangerous degree; a share in the "Back Bay Company" of Bombay on which £500 had been paid up sold in open market for £2,650. The inflation survived, in some measure, the end of the Civil War in America to which it was originally due; for—whatever losses may have fallen on greedy speculators in Bombay or Calcutta—the exports continued to flow; and both producers and moderately-minded distributers continued to thrive, aided by wise assistance from the Supreme Government.

Two new Provinces about this time entered the lists of progress. The popular and intelligent administration of Sir A. Phayre left British Burma scope for enormous development; the population and revenue of the Province doubled themselves, while the revenue of the Province reached the substantial figure of ten millions of R.x., then equal to so many pounds sterling.* In the Central Provinces, too, signs of advance were unmistakable; due partly to the increase of the cotton-trade, but in great measure to the watchful energy of Mr.—now Sir Richard—Temple; one of the youngest and most distinguished of the Punjab school already mentioned. By the end of 1868 there were one thousand five hundred and seventy public schools in the Province; the revenue had risen nearly fourteen per cent. though many of the assessments on land had been lowered; the foreign trade of two and a half millions had expanded to the value of thirteen; the population was increasing at the rate of one per cent. in two years, which appears to be the normal rate throughout the more fortunate regions in British India.

* *See* footnote on previous page.

One consequence of all this progress was a demand for increased efficiency in the administration all over India; a demand to which Lawrence hastened to respond; the salaries of subordinate officials were, moreover, most properly and almost unavoidably increased, both in order to enable them to live comfortably and to maintain them above the levels of irresistible temptation. Many establishments were at the same time augmented or created anew; and the total expenditure of the year was thus raised by above eight per cent.

The ultimate upshot, however, of the undoubted progress which marked the administration of British India, from the death of Elgin to the retirement of Lawrence, was a net deficit of nearly three and a quarter millions. Sir C. Trevelyan, indeed, created a surplus of 2,800,491 R.x. in 1866; but he retired in that year, being succeeded as Finance Minister by Mr. W. N. Massey, in whose first year the surplus disappeared and in its place appeared a deficit of over two and a half millions. Massey reduced this deficit by more than a million in the following year; but in the year 1868-9, when Temple had taken Massey's place, the deficit rose to the alarming height of 4,144,643 millions; and an income-tax which finally exceed three per cent. on incomes above fifty R.x. a year was the only discoverable remedy. Although, therefore, there was much progress and a certain quantity of actual property to show for the money, it cannot be said that the administration of Lawrence was distinguished for financial success.

It was in administration—as might have been anticipated—that the victories of the great Civilian were won. The undertakings of Dalhousie were completed with the loyalty of a faithful follower. Education received a powerful impulse; telegraph-work an immense development. Guaranteed companies were aided and urged to finish their railway-lines, while an extensive system of cheaper lines was begun out of public funds: these State-Railways being built on the metre-gauge.

In 1868—the year before Lawrence retired—the Government resolved that in future all Indian railways should be constructed by the ruling power;* and a similar rule was laid down for works of irrigation which, in the hands of private companies, had proved a failure. In Post-office reform Lawrence bettered his example by doubling the weight allowed for the minimum rate of half-an-anna ($\frac{1}{32}$ of a rupee). In the matter of cotton-cultivation a stimulus was afforded by the appointment of a Special Commissioner, at first for Central India and Berar alone, but afterwards employed to inspect and report for Hindustan also. The Forest Department, finally organised under the Inspector-Generalship of Dr. Brandis, in 1862, embraced an area almost equal to the whole of England, Scotland, and Wales. In 1865 an Act was passed declaratory of the rights and powers of the State over this large surface; and in the following year the Inspector-General was sent to Europe to arrange for the training of Forest-officers in the State-schools of Forestry in Germany and France. Lastly should be mentioned the Minute by which Lawrence re-organised the Department of Account.

[In addition to books already cited see "Progress-Statement" for 1882-3, by Mr. James S. Cotton; printed by order of the House of Commons, 1885.]

* Nevertheless in 1891 there were some 1,200 miles of railway owned by Native States and earning about a quarter of a million annually.

CHAPTER XXII.

PEACE AND PROGRESS.

Section 1: Foreign affairs from 1869 to 1875—Section 2: Finance and Reform from 1869 to 1875—Section 3: Education and Progress from 1869 to 1875.

SECTION I.—When, in the course of 1868, it became known that Sir John Lawrence's tenure of office was not to exceed the conventional five years, Mr. Disraeli, then Prime Minister, made choice of Lord Mayo as his successor in India. Before the end of the year the Ministry had been compelled to resign by the results of the General Election; Mr. Gladstone and his followers took up the administration, and the Duke of Argyll replaced Sir S. Northcote as Secretary of State for India. No change, however, was made in the nomination of a Viceroy; the disastrous policy of 1835 was not taken as a precedent; and Mayo went out, assuming charge in Calcutta January 12th, 1869. He was a man of forty-six, genial and popular, with parliamentary and official experience: and he had the good sense to adopt the views and carry on the proceedings of his predecessor in almost every respect. The personal elements of the new administration underwent some fluctuation; but for the most part the staff consisted of Mr. Barrow Ellis in charge of the Home Department, Sir John Strachey with the newly-constituted Department of Trade; Finance continued to be managed by Sir R. Temple, the Department of War was under Sir H. Norman, that of Law under Mr.—afterwards Sir H. S.

—Maine, succeeded in 1870 by Mr. J. F. Stephen—afterwards a puisne Judge of the High Court in England—the Viceroy keeping Foreign Affairs and Public Works in his own hands. Lord Napier was Governor of Madras, and Sir S. Fitzgerald of Bombay. The Indian Foreign Office—the old "Secret-and-Political Department"—has been described as consisting of three great branches. The strictly "Foreign" relations are, of course, those which the Government of India has to maintain with border-countries, such as Afghanistán, Nepál, and occasionally Muscat or Zanzibar. But, besides these, the Foreign Office of Calcutta undertakes the supervision of the Native States within the Indian limits. Lastly, the Foreign or Political Department is the one which maintains administrative control over the local affairs of some small Divisions of the Empire—Ajmere, Berár, Koorg, etc.—which, for certain special reasons, have not been amalgamated with any Presidency or large Province. It is in regard to the first and second of these that the work of the Viceroy in charge of the Political portfolio is most anxiously responsible.

A brief mention has already been made of the views of John Lawrence in regard to Afghanistán. A long experience had led him to think that the value of this outwork of the Empire depended very much upon the confidence that the Government of India could inspire in the Afghán mind. As to invasion, he was convinced that the neighbour who first violated Afghán territory would be regarded as an enemy, while the neighbour who repelled the violation would be regarded as a friend. He knew the objections to such a policy, both from a European and a Native standpoint. The Afghán faction that was for the moment depressed would go to almost any lengths to obtain British aid: and the persons of experience at home who desired to oppose a stronger barrier against Russian advance thought that British aid should lead to British influence. But Lawrence took things as he found them, with what was called "masterly inactivity;" and he impressed his views to a great extent upon the mind of his successor.

The result of all that Lawrence did, up to his departure from India, was certainly not unsuccessful. While Sher Áli was only in possession of Herát he had recognised him as Chief of Western Afghanistán: when Sher Áli returned to Kábul he acknowledged the event by gifts of money and muskets. Sher Áli, hopeful, if not quite satisfied, proposed a visit; but had no opportunity of carrying out his design before the Viceroy retired.

Mayo renewed the negotiation; and the Amir came down in peace by the road that some of his predecessors had taken in other conditions. He had the most to gain from the interview; always supposing that he could obtain what he wanted. The Viceroy's object was a simple one: he wished to conciliate his barbarian neighbour and open the way to "friendly intercourse." But he entered on the scene with an expressed objection to "any treaty or promise of permanent subsidy . . . or meddling or interfering." The Amir looked much farther, asking for a treaty of alliance with him and his dynasty, together with a fixed annual subsidy; nothing of which however he could obtain. "Moral support" was all that was offered, with a promise of arms and money at the pleasure of the Government. In this way the weak point in the frontier was to be fortified at the least possible cost.

At the same time measures were taken, in concert with the Government of Great Britain, to establish reasonable relations with the Russian advance. Mayo himself was disposed to view the matter with considerable indifference. He had travelled in Russia, and the result of what he had seen there had been to make him think slightingly of the power of that Empire.* He believed that a policy of peace was essential to the consolidation of the Russian position in Central Asia; and

* See extracts from his letters *ap.* Hunter: I. 272.

he declared himself certain that if that Empire did not pursue a just and honest course "she will lay up for herself much trouble and danger." The ultimate result of the line taken by Mr. Gladstone and Lord Granville in hearty collaboration with their Tory Viceroy was that the Emperor expressed himself satisfied. General v. Kauffmann, the Russian Governor of Turkestan, reported to Prince Gortchakow in a similar spirit; and matters were put in train for the delimitation of Afghán territory.

Nor was Afghanistán the limit of the influence aimed at by Mayo. His endeavour was to surround British India with a rampart of friendly powers; and with this view he seems to have sought the welfare and good-will of even the smallest and weakest of these border States. The Khanate of Biluchistan, for example, which separated Afghanistán from Sindh, was another ill-cemented aggregate; such as the one had been and the other was still; where a military chief held dubious rule over a number of insubordinate barons. But, apart from domestic uneasiness, the Khán of Kelát was also troubled by the pretensions of his western neighbour, the Sháh of Persia, whose unrectified boundary ran down from the neighbourhood of Herát nearly due South to the shores of the Gulf of Oman. After much negotiation the Sháh was persuaded to accept the arbitration of British Officers; and Colonel F. Goldsmid going to the country held a local investigation and drew up a convention which was accepted by both sides. On this basis Major O. St. John made a regular survey in 1872, and laid down a boundary-line from Gwadar, on the sea-coast of Mekran, to the point where the Helmand river turns East from the swamps of Sistan. Meanwhile Goldsmid went North, to discharge a similar duty for the frontier between the Persian realm and the territory of Sher Áli. With the remaining States—Kashmir, Nepal, Bhutan, and Burma—no difficulty was for the present experienced. The curious endeavour to hold commercial and diplomatic relations with the insurgent Yákub Khán at Yarkand broke down with the re-establishment of the Chinese authority in Eastern Turkestan; and the memory of it only demands record here as a warning against premature acknowledgements, which are not likely to do much good, but not unlikely to give just offence to friendly neighbours.*

Within the Indian borders the Government of this period adopted a policy of occasion. On the North-West, looking at the Mahában and Black Mountain affairs, it was held that prevention was better than punishment; and a vigilant police was preferred to destroying crops and "killing people for the sake of prestige." Nevertheless, on the opposite border, in the difficult country between Assam and Burma, a force had to be employed for the protection of the tea plantations of Cachár against the Lushai tribe. These savages, trusting to their almost impenetrable forests and glens, were contracting a habit of foraging which it was necessary to break. "Cruel raids"—as the Viceroy called their incursions—had been going on for some years; and the ineffectual methods adopted in retaliation had done more harm than good. Even here, however, a policy of mere destruction was not adopted; but the skilful and experienced Robert (Lord) Napier (of whom we have already had glimpses) planned a short winter campaign, in which a number of small bodies of picked men were moved rapidly about the hill-country; punishing none but the guilty, and producing terror and submission in a manner more complete than could have been reasonably expected from more indiscriminate chastisement.† But, looking to the various out-

* The Musalman rising in East Turkestan was crowned with temporary success about 1865, owing to a mutiny of the Chinese garrison; the Chinese recovered the Province 1876-7.

† Napier was made a peer—by the title of Baron Napier of Magdala—for his services in Abyssinia (July 1868). He must be distinguished from Lord Napier-and-Ettrick, the contemporaneous Governor of Madras.

rages of the Daflas and Nagas, in the same neighbourhood, not many years later, it may be doubted whether this little war produced an effect properly proportioned to the cost which it is understood to have involved.

Lord Mayo's last effort for the external welfare of India took the form of a visit to Burma; on returning from which he was assassinated, at Port Blair in the Andamans, February 8th, 1872. The murderer was an Afghán convict, under sentence of transportation—but none could be more ardent to express sorrow than the Amir of the country from which he sprang. The place of the deceased Viceroy was for the moment taken by the first Member of Council, Sir J. Strachey; but ere long he was relieved by Lord Napier-and-Ettrick, who came up for the purpose from Madras, just as Denison had done on the death of Lord Elgin more than nine years before. In the following May he, in his turn, made over charge to Lord Northbrook, a distinguished English politician and member of the family of Baring, famous in finance. About the same time Lord Hobart entered on the Government of Madras, held by his ancestor in the last century. Sir Philip Wodehouse succeeded Fitzgerald at Bombay; and Mr. (since Lord) Hobhouse took Stephen's place as Law-Member of Council. Sir William Muir was selected to have charge of the Finances; Sir P. F. Haines succeeded Napier as Commander-in-Chief of the Indian Army, but this was not till 1876.

One of Lord Northbrook's first acts after assuming office was to endeavour to dissuade the Khán of Khiva from a fruitless, and indeed unjustifiable, opposition to the demands of the Russian Government. The Turkman subjects of the Khán were incorrigible slave-dealers; and the Czar was justly and seriously offended at their raids into Russian territory, for which he was preparing stern reprisals. In his alarm, the Khán bethought himself of seeking the assistance or mediation of the Government of India; but he got nothing there save friendly advice to submit; such counsel it was the duty of that Government to give, and it would have been well for the Khán to have adopted it.

The spirit of impartial benevolence displayed by the Viceroy in this affair was in strict accordance with the policy of the Home Government. Nor was the Czar at all backward in responding. The northern frontier of Afghanistán, proposed as the limit of British influence, was, after some discussion, loyally accepted by the Russian autocrat; and the concession of the line of the Oxus—which conveyed to the Afgháns the possession of Provinces over which their sway had before been doubtful—was expressly declared by Gortchakow to be a peace-offering to the British. Colonel—afterwards Sir Richard—Pollock was deputed to meet the Amir—whose mind, never very settled, had been disturbed most needlessly by these transactions—but Sher Áli preferred to send an Envoy to Simla in order to hold personal conference with the Viceroy. The Afghán made his appearance in July, 1873, when it appeared that his master was alarmed on two grounds. Sher Áli feared on the northern border the approach of Russia, brought into close contact with him by the new arrangements; and he professed that the western boundary had not only been fixed unfavourably to himself, but—such as it was—had been already infringed by the Persians. It was a delicate position: the Amir and his advisers were clinging hard to the theory of a complete alliance with the British; whereas Lord Northbrook was instructed to adhere as closely as might be to the old policy of Edwardes and Lawrence. It is easy to see how this rift must have tended to widen more and more until it eventually sent the Amir away in a direction which was as opposed to British wishes as it was to Afghán interests. For the present, however, the Amir continued loyal to past engagements, if not positively friendly; and a little sulkiness on the part of a baffled barbarian chief was not regarded with much anxiety.

In the following year, indeed, a remonstrance addressed by the Viceroy to the Amir, on an act of perfidy towards the son of the latter, produced an increase of irritation, but on the whole Afghán relations were undisturbed.

In that year the Foreign Office was much troubled by complaints against Malhár Ráo, the Gaikwar or Mahratta Chief of Baroda, who had been misconducting himself for the last three years and was now warned to amend his ways under penalty of deposition. The Resident, Colonel Phayre, was very obnoxious to the ill-conducted Mahratta, as the instrument—and, indeed, the cause also—of this unwelcome interference; and in the course of the year 1874, it was reported that an attempt had been made to take his life by poison. Sir Lewis Pelly was deputed to relieve Phayre as British Resident, and to take charge of the administration of the country, Malhár Ráo being put under arrest and committed for trial on a charge of abetting an attempt to commit murder. Six Commissioners were appointed to form the Court, three of them being Natives of distinction and three British officers. Serjeant Ballantine, of London, was retained for the defence.* The trial began on February 23rd, 1875, and lasted about five weeks, at the end of which it was found that the Rája of Jaipore was entirely convinced of the prisoner's innocence, all the Englishmen equally so of his guilt, and the remaining Commissioners—Sindia and Dinkar Ráo—for a verdict of "Not proven." The case was one of extreme delicacy, and was referred to the Home-Government for disposal. Mr. Gladstone's Ministry had by this time gone out of power, and the Marquess of Salisbury had succeeded the Duke of Argyll at the India Office. He preferred a course which avoided all scandal, deposing Malhár,

* The learned Serjeant, it is said, received a fee of twenty-thousand guineas; he was ably opposed by Mr. Scoble, Q.C., Advocate-General at Bombay, afterwards Sir A. R. Scoble, K.C.S.I. and Member of the Viceroy's Council.

not on the finding of any of the Commissioners, but on the accounts—amply verified—of his previous maladministration. He was interned in Fort St. George, and a young kinsman installed at Baroda in his stead. Sir T. Madhava Ráo became prime minister, and Mr. Philip Melvill—who had gone to Baroda as one of the Special Commission—remained as British Resident.

In October of the same year, a College for Native Nobles was opened at Ajmere, under the appropriate title of "Mayo College," the lamented Earl having planned its institution. The College is supported partly by the interest of an endowment-fund furnished by the Rájput aristocracy, for whose service it is intended, and partly by a subsidy from the State, the first principal was Major O. St. John, already noticed in connection with the Biluch boundary, and subsequently knighted for services in that country. Other institutions of a like kind were opened about the same time in other parts of India; and some success was obtained in the development of healthy minds and bodies among youths destined to exercise almost autocratic rule over millions of British subjects. In many States an imitation of European institutions was also arising, Courts-of-law, Councils-of-administration, and the like; the City of Jaipore became a model for public works and sanitation, with gas-works, a hospital, museum and botanic gardens. To us who have travelled—however hastily—over the centuries of war, anarchy, and despotism, to which India has been too generally subject, these will seem symptoms of a wholesome progress, even if we wish that they were more numerous; and the opinion will receive confirmation from further facts noticed in a later part of this chapter. The most complete rivetting of the political fabric took place in 1875-6, when H.R.H. the Prince of Wales visited the great Eastern Empire to which he was Heir-Apparent.* The chiefs and rulers

* The Prince landed in Calcutta in December, 1875, having previously visited Bombay and Madras.

flocked from near and far to meet the eldest son of the Queen, in his great encampment upon the Calcutta "Maidán." Thither came the Rája of Kashmere, Ranbir, son of the famous Guláb Sinh of the old Punjab war days; the Maharája of Patiála, head of the Cis-Sutlej States; the great Rájput chiefs; the Mahratta representatives of the Houses of Holkar and Sindia; the Begam of Bhopál and the Maharája of Travancore; with—by no means the least important—Sir Jang Bahádur, the all-powerful Premier of Nepál, who had lent all the resources of that State to aid the British cause in Audh in 1857. The Prince proceeded to Upper India and returned the visits of the Chiefs, being everywhere received with unreserved honour, homage, and hospitality. Politically speaking, the tour was a vast and unqualified success.

Among circumstances of somewhat less hopeful character may be briefly noticed the recrudescence of lawlessness alluded to above, on the North-Eastern Frontier. The Dafla tribes, carrying on a system of raids on the northern border, at last provoked some of the punishment that they had long deserved. An expedition was sent against them in the end of the summer of 1874, and they were compelled to surrender a number of British Indian subjects whom they had abducted. More serious was the provocation given by the Nágas, a hill-tribe on the eastern border of Cachár, and partly owning a sort of convenient allegiance to the Rája of Manipore. Surveying parties had been employed from time to time in verifying boundary-marks and gathering topographic knowledge in the Nága hills, which are of considerable scientific importance as containing the watershed between Bengal and Burma. Of these operations the Nágas have sometimes shown a jealousy even beyond the the usual reaction of barbarism at the contact of civilised man. But in the beginning of 1875, undeterred by the somewhat lenient treatment experienced by their Dafla neighbours, they fell suddenly upon a British surveyor, and murdered him with the whole of his followers, amounting in all to 81 persons. Later in the same year another officer, engaged in the same duty, experienced the like fate. For the present no serious steps were taken to chastise this intractable set of savages. It was not till 1881 that the proper measures were at last adopted, let us hope with success.

Of the third branch of the Foreign Department during this period there is no necessity to speak; it will be best considered as a part of the whole Empire, of whose condition we are next to take such notice as our space allows.

[See Trotter, *ub sup.* and Hunter's "Earl of Mayo," 2 vols., London, 1875.]

SECTION 2.—Indian Finance, as we have already had occasion to notice, is a difficult and delicate matter. As regards revenue, the British Government has been met by the fact that the people who are governed despotically, and by aliens, make no great distinction between taxation and robbery; so that the Governor-General who desired peace and popularity has always been closely confined to the rent of land for the chief sources of income.* In the matter of account, which is such an important part of finance, the Government had contracted all sorts of evil habits, due to its commercial origin to a great extent; and there appeared to be no means of framing estimates that would have any sort of relation to subsequent results. In the second year of Lawrence, when Sir C. Trevelyan held the purse, there had been a handsome surplus;

	* LAND.	OPIUM.	TAXES.
1842-3	13·56	2·09	5·75
1862-3	19·57	8·06	13·55

These were the principal heads of revenue from Ellenborough to Lawrence, expressed in millions of R.x. The rise of taxation proper was principally due to Lord Dalhousie's annexations, and to fiscal reforms consequent on the Mutiny. But even the higher figure represents but a light incidence per head on a population of over one hundred and seventy millions. The taxes were salt, customs, stamps, excise.

but the three succeeding years had been all marked by disappointment. Trevelyan's successor had always "budgeted for a surplus," but by some unfortunate crisis each year had ended the other way. In the financial year 1868, when Lawrence was succeeded by Mayo, another of these unforeseen catastrophes occurred; and it soon appeared that a similar unpleasant surprise was in preparation for the year that was to come. Both in England and India the Government authorities became thoroughly alarmed. The Viceroy applied himself to the matter; and, without awaiting the recurrence of another budget, remedial measures were at once brought forward. At these great dissatisfaction was expressed by the English newspapers, and it is probable that a vast number of people were really injured, alarmed, or annoyed. But those who were responsible for the administration were assured that strong and instant action was the only hope. What that action was must now be briefly told.

In their genuine anxiety to avoid new taxation the Indian authorities at first attempted to fill the gap with the sacrifice of superfluous establishments. The first to go was a portion of the amount allotted to Public Works, from which a sum reckoned as equivalent to £800,000 was saved. In other Civil expenditure a further saving, estimated at £350,000 was made. Proposals, which were only accepted in part, were sent home with the object of reducing the number of regiments and batteries in the army, while increasing the number of men in each corps, so that the actual military strength of the country should not suffer. And when all that could be done in this direction had been effected or provided for—but not till then—a temporary increase was made to the unpopular income-tax; and the salt-duty was equalised, so as to bring the rates of Madras and Bombay to a level with those current elsewhere. It was hoped that by this combination of economy and taxation the deficit would be supplied and the difficulties of the year surmounted. But it still remained to make such provision for the future as might prevent the recurrence of trouble and scandal, such as appeared inevitable under the existing system. To do this it was necessary to probe that system deeply, and when that was done a cause of financial disorder was laid bare, from the removal of which the happiest effects were reasonably anticipated.

Up to this period a centralisation of the most primitive kind had characterised Indian Finance. If a local Government husbanded the monies allotted to it the savings were forfeited at the end of the year. If such a Government were modest in its demands the presumption arose that its wants were few. On the other hand, the audacious got all that they clamoured for; or, like a certain zealous Governor of the period at Bombay, they spent the money first and applied for it afterwards.*

Mr. Samuel Laing, during the latter part of the Canning administration, made an attempt to break through the pedantic uniformity of this over-centralised routine, and to create a proper sense of responsibility on the part of the minor Governments, by transferring initiative, to some small extent, from the shoulders of the weary Titan of Culcutta to theirs; his scheme, in fact, contemplated relieving the Imperial Budget to the amount of half-a-million, and leaving the minor Governments to provide for local expenditure—to that extent—by local taxation. He here hit upon the right principle, for the main objection to direct taxation in India was, that the people thought that it was a penal exaction the proceeds of which were shipped in specie to England. By laying out the money in the regions where it was raised, publishing the local budget, and so far as might be possible, consulting the wants and wishes of each commune or city, it has since been found possible to remove

* The writer remembers Lord Canning's amused look, when told that a request for an extra sweeper in the Dispensary of Dehra Dun was before the Government of India for sanction.

this one—if no others—of the evils of direct taxation; and to combine something of local autonomy with considerable relief to the finances of the Empire. The heads of administration finally selected by Lord Mayo's Government for transfer to local management, expanded the scheme far beyond the limits contemplated by Mr. Laing; and the result was to confine the estimates and undertakings of the Imperial Departments to purely Imperial duties, and to ensure the preparation of timely returns, so as to keep the Government exactly informed of the actual state of its affairs. The services that were thus made over to the various subordinate administrations, included Jails, Registration, Police, Education, Roads and Civil Buildings, together with a variety of minor matters as to which local knowledge and local management were indispensable to efficiency and to the due insistence on local responsibility. For some of these services the Local Governments, under the new system, had to provide out of annual grants made to them unconditionally by the Supreme Government; the rest of the supplies being furnished by local rates and taxes. These were to be, in future, levied under the control of the Government of India—so far as might be needful to preserve general principles—yet entirely at the disposal of the respective administrations. The aggregate sum thus available for local service in the year 1889-90, reached a figure of nearly twenty millions, and although a cynic might object that this large sum —or a great part of it—was additional taxation, yet it was, in any case, all spent where it was raised. Moreover, as Sir H. S. Maine observed, when the plan was first projected, it represents money on which the Government of India cannot lay its hands; so that it cannot be spent on unjust war or vainglorious extent of frontier. The same judicious observer had pointed out—before the time of this great reform—that the financial system, "if it be not on the point of an inevitable collapse, is in great danger of going to pieces, unless the strain be lightened somewhere." One of the immediate dangers had been the virtual impossibility of forseeing or resisting the demands of the minor administrations, which demands—as another able member of the Government said at the time—were without limit, because there was no limit to their wants. So long as they had nothing to do but to dip into a purse for whose condition they were not answerable, it was hardly possible to draw a line beyond which their ideal of good administration should not go. But when each administration had its own purse, with the responsibility of filling it and the knowledge that when empty it would remain so, economy became at once enforced by strict necessity.

By these measures, therefore, a great deal more was secured than a solvent Budget. It was indeed contrary to Mayo's own wish, that they should be described as "decentralisation." The control and command of the central authority were not intentionally affected; nevertheless, the wholesome parts of "Home Rule" were either attained or put in course of attainment; and an approach was thus made to the ideal state of things, where the integer of common management coincides with the integer of common interest and information.

Another part of Indian finance, of which the social importance was much in excess of its apparent money-value, was the Salt Tax. The complete reform of all the evils connected with this impost did not come to be carried out till a later period than that with which we are now concerned; yet something was done towards their mitigation. To abolish the tax entirely, did not—and does not yet—enter into the mind of any practical statesman; and the reason is plain. There is no other way of making the bulk of the Indian population contribute to the expenses of the State. In a foot-note to a recent page, it was shown that the chief sources of revenue were few and indefinite. If a Native of India is not a landowner, and refrains from using dutiable products and stamped paper, then the duty on his salt is his sole contribution to the maintenance of the army, navy and police; and of the canals and forests which temper the vicissitudes of climates. and of the roads and bridges, by means of which he moves and has his being.* Under recent reforms, this tax falls at the rate of, say sixpence a head—or about one day's wage, and if the average peasant of India did not pay that, he would pay nothing, but be entirely protected at the expense of the few thousands of persons concerned in other trades, and of the holders of land assessed to fiscal-demand.

Nevertheless, however inevitable, it was held that this Indian *Gabelle* should be levied with some approach to uniformity, if not without one single remediable abuse. Under Lord Mayo, a narrow-gauge line of railway was begun, to connect the great salt-lake of Rájputána with the chief marts of Hindustan; while the rate of duty was at the same time reduced. It may therefore, be fairly contended that, the effect of the policy in its later developments, has been to produce present reforms, whereby the price of this prime article of consumption has been lowered about 65 per cent. to dwellers in Hindustan. In Mayo's time, however, the proportion which the produce of this tax bore to the total gross revenue of the couutry was nearly 25 per cent. higher than it is now.

When Mayo's labours were cut short by murder, the finances were in a state of healthy progress, in all respects but one. In the first alarm of the discovery of 1868-69, it had been—as we saw—with reluctance that taxation had been increased. The salt of the poor bore some of the burden, the rest was laid not on the rich—there are no rich in India—but upon the less

* These means of communication have almost annihilated famine for millions who never use them or pay for them directly. In ordinary times the price of food is lowered, in times of local dearth equalised, by every improvement in the means of distribution.

poor; and it took the form of an enhancement of the Income Tax; great complaint resulted, and this led to inquiries which convinced most thinking men that this kind of direct taxation—especially as a general levy for Imperial purposes—was entirely unsuited to the existing conditions of Indian Society. This accordingly became one of the earliest subjects, connected with domestic administration, that Lord Northbrook had to study. His calm and disciplined intellect soon convinced him of the soundness of the adverse opinion, which had also impressed itself latterly on his lamented predecessor. In March, 1873, the Income Tax disappeared from the budget, and the Government of India used its reserve powers to warn the subordinate administrations against any present increase of local taxation that might cause the people to think that decentralisation meant increased burdens in a new dress.

Soothing measures were indeed becoming highly desirable, especially in Bengal, where agrarian discontent was making a feeble effort, and where the very unusual phenomenon of drought was making a yet more threatening appearance. The Spring harvest of 1874 was an almost total failure; stocks were low; and the failure of the winter-rain had extended into Hindustan. Lord Northbrook associated with Sir George Campbell (Lieutenant-Governor of Bengal) the energetic Minister of Finance, Sir R. Temple; and the memory of the late disaster in the adjoining Province of Orissa gave any further stimulus that might be needed to officials all under the influence of the best precept and the best example: 480,000 tons of rice were imported—chiefly from Burma—by great exertions carriage was procured to distribute food to the afflicted districts; a railway 50 miles long was begun as a relief-work which should have a more than temporary utility; house-to-house visitors ministered to the wants of the infirm. By these and similar means the famine was kept under such command that it may be roughly but faithfully said that no deaths occurred from starvation. The operations entailed a total cost of 6⅓ millions, partly supplied by private benevolence, in England and elsewhere, partly made good out of the finances of the State, When the famine was subdued Campbell went to England where he entered Parliamentary life—in which he bore a useful part till his death nearly twenty years later. Temple succeeded him in the Government of Bengal.

In spite of the great cost of the Bengal famine and of the entire abolition of the Income-Tax the budget of 1873-74 showed as small a deficit as could have been reasonably expected; and it was converted into a small surplus by the end of the next financial year, during which almost every item of receipt evinced an upward tendency. Great changes were about this time introduced into the construction of State-railways. Up to the rule of Lord Northbrook it had been an accepted maxim that such lines ought to be built as cheaply as possible; and with that view the "metre" gauge had been almost invariably adopted. But there had all along been an earnest minority who had objected to this the various inconveniences due to break of gauge, amounting—on the main line—to the entire transfer of whole bodies of troops from one class of rolling-stock to another. In Mayo's time only two great connections awaited completion; the continuation of the line from Delhi to Peshāwar—highly essential for the protection of the North-West Frontier—and a link on the Indus Valley connecting two separate portions of the Sind, Punjab, and Delhi Railway. These being more than mere "feeders," and actually portions of the arterial system, were now excluded from the "metre" class and completed on what in India is known as the "broad" gauge; that is, a breadth of 5ft. 6in. uniform with the main lines.*

In April, 1875, Madras had the misfortune to lose Lord

* "Progress Report" for 1882-3. Printed by order of the Commons, 1885.

Hobart, one of the most earnest and well-informed of her many Governors, whose claims to the gratitude of the people for a time committed to his charge included a steady opposition to Mayo's salt-policy. He succeeded in shelving for a time a proposal favoured by the Supreme Government whereby the rate of duty on salt in his Presidency would have been raised on the ground of uniformity. In the latter part of the year a sweeping reform of the Customs Tariff was made which made the exportation of cotton, wheat and many other staples free, and greatly lowered the duty on most imports. Unhappily a protective duty on American cotton formed part of the new tariff, which was a needless restriction, bringing little to the revenue and causing general and natural discontent.

By the end of the financial year 1875-6 appeared a handsome surplus: but at the same time appeared also—for the first time—that ominous item of "loss by exchange." This may be briefly explained as due to the demonetisation and depreciation of silver in European countries, while the Indian Government was still bound to receive its revenues is that metal though paying its English debts in gold. The exchange now falling to one shilling-and-ninepence caused a difference of about two-and-sixpence on the £; or—on a remittance of, say, sixteen millions—a total apparent loss of two millions. It did not however appear that the purchasing power of the Rupee underwent any depreciation in India; and it was argued that the fall in exchange brought compensation to the people of the country by stimulating their export-trade.*

The only other reform by which Lord Northbrook can be said to have distinguished his useful but unostentatious administration was in a real extension of the employment of Natives in public service, a matter apparently more easy to talk of than

* In the ten years ending 1883-4 the aggregate volume of trade rose 55 per cent. But the rise of the export-trade was 65 per cent., while the imports only rose 47 per cent. in the same period.

to effect, but for which he did something. In the beginning of 1876 the Viceroy—supported by his Council—found himself in sharp opposition to the Government at home on the question of sending British representatives to the Court of Kábul against the wish of the Amir. They vainly begged for leave to pursue "the policy adopted by Canning, Lawrence, and Mayo" towards that State, and deprecated the change as involving danger to the peace of Afghanistán and to British interest. These remonstrances failing to command attention Lord Northbrook resigned office; and left Calcutta in April, universally respected and regretted: a Native journalist paying him the quaint tribute that he "annexed no territory, he committed no plunder, but he gave the land rest." The new Viceroy was Robert, Lord Lytton, son of the politician and man of letters once known as Edward Bulwer, who had been a friend of the Premier, Lord Beaconsfield.

[For further details on the subject of this Section see "Annual Financial Statement," for the official years 1860-61—1873-74. Calcutta, 1873.]

SECTION 2.—Before proceeding to examine the administration of Lord Northbrook's successor, Lord Lytton, we ought perhaps to take the opportunity of briefly reviewing the work of the twenty years that had followed the retirement of the last of the Company's Governors. Some readers may recollect the words of Elphinstone, quoted in the preface to this history, and our implied undertaking to do something towards the record of operative facts in connection with the progress of the people of India in "liberal ideas" and capacity for self-government. In these respects much still remained to be done in 1876; nevertheless it is hardly too much to say that since 1858 a new India had arisen. The heterogeneous collection of incoherent countries had begun to undergo the process of integration which is still going on. Under Dalhousie India had consisted of a number of communities with languages, creeds, and customs, various and mutually abhorrent; and the tendency of the Government was to regard those communities as so many scholars of a great school of which Britannia was the mistress. Under Lord Northbrook a distinct change was visible: the communities had become adolescent, and were beginning to be conscious of common claims and objects, and of a kinship, partly of blood partly of long and close proximity, rapidly drawing closer under the recent unifying operations of English law, language, and material improvement. When, for a trifling outlay, a Native man-of-business, passing from Agra to Bombay, found persons of whom he had scarcely heard transacting affairs on the same principles and by the same methods as in his own district, he could not fail to experience a sense of Indian nationality, however faint and vague it might at first appear.

All these things are part of Education in its widest sense. In the more strict official meaning also, education as mere school instruction had been doing a great work. Ever since the famous despatch of 1854 a certain organisation of the Department of Public Instruction had been established; universities (for examination and the giving of diplomas) had come into existence soon after the Mutiny; public colleges and schools soon flourished in great and increasing numbers; middle and elementary schools were systematised, inspected, and aided by grants. Under Mayo measures were taken to make public instruction more attractive and palatable to the Muslim community; no religious interference, preference, or privilege was allowed. In the six years from 1854-55 to to 1870-71 the progress of schools and attendance had answered to these reforms. In Bengal the number of pupils had risen 60 per cent.; in Hindustan 400 per cent.; the number of schools multiplying in like proportion; in the Punjab a similar development took place; the progress in the Central Provinces has been already mentioned; in Madras and Bombay the increase of institutions was considerable; in 1871 over a quarter of a million youths were receiving public or inspected education in either Presidency.

If, now, we are to inquire into the effect on the rising generation that may have been produced by all this increased training and enlarged knowledge, we shall find mixed results presenting themselves. For, while to the youths themselves a wholesale alteration of condition and mental habit must needs have been afforded, yet as a whole the population of India will perhaps appear to have been much less affected. The most advanced and accurate instruction will influence the memory more than the judgment; and of education in its higher action the effects are limited, in all times and places. What the peculiar limits were, in the India of the times under examination, may be partly realised from what has been shown in these pages; and still more, perhaps, from the testimony of Native scholars who have made the best use of the training obtainable.

The outcome of the examination of these things is to show that the pursuit of knowledge was chiefly undertaken for material ends; and that when knowledge was obtained it was of but little immediate value towards national enlightenment. The study of law and the study of medicine were followed for the openings that they might open to Government employment. The Bachelors, Masters, and Doctors of the universities became versed in all sorts of Occidental learning; but they considered themselves to have earned a right to posts in the public service, and when disappointed became disloyal if not dangerous. When they took off their hoods and gowns and went to their homes, they resumed Hindu habits and superstitious practices amongst the members of the family that they found there; leading—so to say—two lives at once.

The second of these evils could only be cured by a gradual levelling-up of other strata of society. So long as a few hundred graduates were possessed of knowledge that they could not share with their kinsfolk and their compatriots, they had but a fatal gift like King Midas in the Grecian fable. The first evil, however, it was partly within the power of the Government to remove. The path was shown and the example given by the zeal and intelligence of Sir George Campbell; though, after his retirement from office, the scheme was allowed to fall into disuetude under his predecessors. Campbell was indeed to a great degree responsible for the collapse of his system of appointments: he honourably tried to connect the University of Calcutta with the public service; but he left without putting on record any formal rules, and so his tentative efforts were allowed for a time to drop. It was not till 1888 that an enlightened Lieutenant-Governor was able not only to revive them but to organise them into a system. It would be premature to say more upon the subject here, beyond pointing out that the scheme of Sir Steuart Bayley is so obvious that one wonders it was not adopted long before: it is based on the simple principle of making the appropriate university degree an essential qualification for candidates for almost every sort of high public post.

Amongst other signs of accelerated evolution must be taken the great increase of published literature, amounting to no less than four thousand works in one year—the last of Lord Northbrook's Viceroyship. English was fast assuming the character of India's chief learned language, a fact which—however it might be regretted by Oriental scholars—is not without its importance. Out of the vast number of publications above mentioned one-eighth consisted of English books—a proportion equal to that of all the classical languages of the East put together. Now, whatever be thought of the relative merits of English as compared with those languages, it cannot be doubted that the change that was going on in India was, slowly but surely, in the direction of substituting Western science for Eastern speculation. And for this substitution there were only two means possible; either European treatises must be generally translated into Asiatic languages, or the people must learn to read the works of their instructors in their original tongue. And, since that tongue was generally used in the practice of law and commerce, while the books required for educational use were difficult to render into alien linguistic vehicles, and were often distinguished by their style almost as much as by their substance—for all these reasons the spread of English was so natural as to call for no further explanation.

Nor was original thought wanting. In northern Hindustan a reformer arose, in the person of Dáya-Nand Shástri, who attempted to revive and purify the Vishnavite form of Hinduism by precept and example. A still more effective reform was begun in Bengal by the once-famous Keshab Chandar Sen, who founded the sect or school known as "the Brahmo-Somáj," for developing the Theistic movement begun long ago by Ram-Mohan Rai. Babu Keshab visited Europe, and his eloquent discourses were admired in English congregations. Many other isolated instances of distinguished adaptability to the new influences might be given did they seem appropriate to a sketch like the present.* It must, however, be enough here to add that about two hundred Native journals were now in circulation; not always wholly commendable in their aims or conduct, yet deserving notice among symptoms of movement; while intercourse between the ancient races of India and the active peoples of Christendom was immensely stimulated by increased facilities for visits to Europe and even to America. The unwillingness to cross the sea was confined to the Hindus, who were supposed to "break their caste"—*i.e.*, become *ipso facto* excommunicate—by eating food cooked on board ship. Means now began to be contrived for meeting—or circumventing—this class of obstacle; and many Hindus, even some ladies of that class, visited London, Paris, and New York, in the search for employment or of mere knowledge.

* See Trotter, "India under Victoria," II. 341.

Among the Muslims another kind of barrier was in existence, and now began to yield. With those Puritans of Islám a worship of the Korán had engendered a tenacious conservatism and a dread of novelty in ideas and associations such as may be faintly realised by those who are acquainted with the history of Europe and North America in the 16th and 17th centuries. To hold familiar intercourse with unbelievers was dangerous, to send one's children to their schools was deadly. The Wahábis of Patna, who sent men and money to the irreconcilable colony at Malka-Sitana till their proceedings were stopped by the prosaic, but successful processes of the Penal Code in Mayo's time, were only carrying out these principles; the further stage, at which they would have gladly arrived, being insurrection and general massacre. But against such movements a counter action was now arising in the very bosom of Islám itself.

Sayid Ahmad Khán was the great practical deliverer of the Indian Muslims; all, and far more, to them that Keshab Chandar would fain have been to the Hindus. The scale of the present work forbids all attempt to sketch, however slightly, the early efforts of this remarkable man. But their great and abiding importance will reward the study of all who feel a genuine interest in Indian progress. Soon after the Mutiny, in which he both acted and suffered in the cause of law and order, the Sáyyid published his first social manifesto, in the shape of a vernacular treatise on Muhamadan loyalty. Addressing his co-religionists in tones of righteous indignation, he reminded them that it was their privilege to live under the shadow of a great and just Government, while it was their duty "to identify themselves heartily with Christians and espouse their cause." That duty, he further maintained was one that was enjoined by their own religion. In 1869 he took, what was a bold step for an Asiatic of fifty, who could not speak English: he went to England with his two sons, whose education he determined to complete in that country. The result of this journey was to fill him with disgust for the social institutions of his countrymen, and to inspire a resolution to do whatever he could to elevate them, and particularly to elevate the Muslim section of them by putting them on a footing of moral and intellectual unity with Europeans. In this most generous and admirable effort he did not hesitate to combat the prejudices of Europeans and Asiatics alike, boldly telling both classes of their faults, and spending his time and his substance in bringing them together. For the next nine years he conducted a journal on these lines: he opened his house with unstinting hospitality to Natives and English alike,and he founded, at Aligarh in the North-West Province, an Anglo-Muhamadan College, where all modern science should be taught in the languages of both classes.* About the time of Mayo's assassination the Sáyyid's zeal involved him in danger from the animosity of fanatics of his own creed, and the heads of Islám issued a decree to the effect that he was Antichrist, and that his removal, by whatever means, was both lawful and to be desired. But the reformer held on his course with heroic indifference, and lived to have his reward in seeing the beginning of a wholesome change in public opinion.

During Lord Northbrook's administration much was done to improve the status and prospects of all classes of the Native community. A Hindu judge sat on the High Court Bench, and the employment of Native lawyers as subordinate judges became common in the Provinces.

In the legislative Department many useful reforms characterised this and the preceding Viceroyalty. The great jurists who presided over the work (H. S. Maine and J. F. Stephen) worked on the same lines, one after the other, codifying, repealing, and simplifying. Evidence was so dealt with as to be

* The College was opened for work on the Queen's birthday, 1875. The laying of the foundation of the building did not take place till two years later: v. *inf.*

intelligible to the most untrained judicial officer; contract was put upon a footing at once scientific and simple: criminal procedure received a thorough revision; all these important statutes were enacted in 1872. In the following year were passed Acts for amending the Rent and Revenue law in the North-West Provinces and many useful projects on minor matters became law in that and the two succeeding years.

We have thus reviewed the principal elements of these two administrations, from 1869 to 1875-6, as forming one continuous period. Inferior in aggregate duration to the single incumbency of Dalhousie, they present a record of wise and moderate progress, scarcely interrupted, save for one sinister moment in the beginning of 1872; and, taken together, they mark the commencement of the national biography of modern India.

[In addition to books mentioned in preceding Sections of this chapter the student will do well to refer to "Liberal Education in India," by Nagendra Náth Ghose, Calcutta, 1878, and article by the same in "Calcutta Review," No. 156, p. 327; also "Life of Syed Ahmed Khan," C.S.I., by Col. Graham, Edinburgh and London, 1885. Also Appendix II. to the present volume.]

CHAPTER XXIII.

LORD LYTTON.

Section 1: Second Afghan war—Section 2: Famine and Finance—Section 3: Administration and Law.

SECTION 1.—In relating the political transactions of 1873-4, it was mentioned that Sher Áli, the Amir of Afghanistán, had taken umbrage on several accounts: he thought that the Government was unfriendly in regard to boundary-questions, and to undertaking his defence against his neighbours; while he resented as an unwarrantable intrusion a remonstrance addressed to him by Lord Northbrook on his conduct towards his son, Yákub. Had the Government continued to treat these things as they were treated at first, they might have subsided; the temper of a barbarian—however ill-conditioned—being of little cogency when opposed to his own interest and that of his advisers and subordinates. But the proposal to admit British officers into the country as permanent official Agents offended and alarmed all those warlike chiefs, full of the traditions of forty years before, and jealous of an independence, which, if not really threatened, might, in the light of the past, easily seem to them to be endangered. Nor was any commensurate advantage proffered to induce a change in the feelings of the Afghans on this matter; had there been the offer of a new treaty, with a promise of offensive and defensive alliance, that might have been a consideration for them, while it would have furnished some justification for the desire to have a complete British representation in the country. But the orders on the subject reserved "entire freedom of judgment as to the obligation of material support," while at the same time the Government would only abstain from "interference in the internal affairs of Afghanistán," so far as such interference was "unnecessary."

The Amir would not—and probably could not—give his assent to these proposals; but he sent an Envoy to Simla in September, 1876, who was received by Lord Lytton sternly and not without menaces; returning to Kábul with an offer of the terms, already notified, on the basis of which the Government of India would be prepared to confer with the Amir at Pesháwar. At the same time, the British influence in Biluchistan was strengthened by the occupation of Quetta under friendly arrangement with the Khán of Kelát, who was its leading chief. This was another blow to Afghán susceptibilities; the Government of India was not perhaps acting beyond its actual rights, but the step was naturally construed as one of aggression, or at least of menace, in existing conditions. Lord Lawrence raised the question, at home, from this point of view; but his warning voice awoke no echo in high places. He was only "an old Indian," and the politicians of the Opposition did not at first take up the question strongly. In the beginning of 1877, Sir L. Pelly was deputed to meet Nur Muhamad, the Minister of the Amir, at Pesháwar; the irreducible minimum of his instructions being "the principle that British officers should reside in Afghanistán." This was the condition, *sine quâ non*, of any possible negotiations. In vain did the Minister urge the precedents established by all the late Viceroys, Lawrence, Mayo, Northbrook; asking what new circumstances could have possibly arisen to call for such a change; and renewing the arguments, already so often shown and accepted, against a course so abhorrent to his countrymen, so fraught with certainty of mischief. Pelly had but one reply, "this was the price of the Viceroy's friendship." On March 26th, the Minister died; and, as Lord Lytton refused to recognise the officer who came down from Kábul to take his place, the conference terminated.

Meanwhile events were occurring in Europe which had a decided tendency to revive the scare of a Russian aggression and to restore, in essentials, the situation of forty years before. On April 24th, 1877, the Czar had found occasion to declare war against the Sultan of Turkey, whom he accused of violating the treaty-rights of Christians in Eastern Europe. On May 1st, the British Cabinet signified disapproval in a despatch to which the Russian Chancellor replied mildly, assuring the Foreign Secretary, Lord Derby, that British interests would be treated with scrupulous respect. On August 9th, the British Premier announced in the House of Lords that, subject to that condition, his Government intended to preserve a "strict neutrality." By the end of the year the resistance of the Turks had been overcome; and in January, 1878, the Russian army having forced the last defence, was in full march for Adria nople. On the 17th of that month, the Queen's speech, read on the opening of Parliament, expressed sympathy with the vanquished and a hope that an appeal from her Majesty would have the effect of inducing the Czar to entertain overtures for peace. In speaking to the Address, Lord Granville, objected that peace was not an exclusively "British interest"; but the Government, so far from concurring in this view, attempted to stimulate the Czar's pacific tendencies by ordering the Mediterranean squadron to the Dardanelles; and on the 31st, the House of Commons was asked to vote a credit of six millions sterling towards warlike preparations. After some debate, the vote of credit was carried, on February 8th, and several other circumstances transpired to confirm the impression that the country was drifting into war. On the 21st, indeed, Lord Derby announced the receipt of conciliatory despatches from

St. Petersburg, promising to make no further approach towards Constantinople unless a landing should be made from the British fleet; and on the 3rd of the following month, the Treaty of St. Stefano was signed by the Porte; but the British Government at once insisted on its being submitted to a Congress of the European powers. Somewhat keen discussion ensued on this, between St. Petersburg and London; and on April 17th, during the recess of Parliament, the British Ministry ordered the Government of India to send a number of regiments of all arms to Malta. This measure, being regarded as a menace by the Russian authorities, was met by an order to the Governor-General of Turkestan to depute a Mission to the Court of Kábul, where it was known that the Amir Sher Áli was in a mood of—perhaps not unnatural—ill-humour.

Upon the subject of this Mission there can be no doubt, so far as Russian feelings and intentions are concerned; it was a distinct answer to various words and deeds of the Queen's Government, and—as such—may be taken as a symptom of Muscovite policy in Asia and a clear signal for future guidance. Whenever Great Britain opposes her in Europe, Russia will make a demonstration on the northern frontier of British India. But that demonstration will probably be full of peril for the Afgháns; and it is in this aspect that the Mission of 1878 becomes so questionable. Rawlinson considers that an interchange of communications, hostile to British interests, had been maintained between Kábul and Taskkend ever since 1873, when Lord Northbrook, acting under instructions from the Duke of Argyll, had refused to make an unconditional promise of aid and protection to the Amir. On the other hand it was contended, by those who appealed to the great authority of Lawrence, that Sher Áli did not desire a visit from his dangerous neighbours; and that the reception of Kauffmann's Mission—however offensively it might have been intended on the part of Russia—gave the Government of India no sufficient cause of quarrel against the Amir.

Before that Mission could reach Kábul, the Russian Government had agreed to the principle of a Congress, and had entered into a secret agreement with the British Cabinet as to the general lines of the future.* The latter had also made a special covenant with the Porte; but these things did not materially hinder the work of the Congress, which terminated, July 13th, giving the British—as Lord Beaconsfield announced —"peace with honour."

However that may have been, all danger of Russian interference appeared to have passed away. So at least thought Sher Áli, who received the Mission with bare courtesy, and probably only thought how he could rid himself of his visitors at the earliest date.† So, however, did not think the British Ministers; and on August 14th, Lord Lytton sent a letter to the Amir informing him of the approaching visit of Major-General Sir N. Chamberlain as a special Envoy to his Court. Sher Áli replied by new protestations; he could fairly urge the difference that plainly existed between the two cases; the Russians were dangerous, if not hostile, neighbours against whom the Government had often been asked to protect him; that they should have sent a Mission was no fault of his, and he meant to send it back as soon as he could safely do so. But the Indian Government was his old friend and ally, perfectly acquainted with the difficulties of his position.‡

* Made public by the audacious enterprise of Mr. C. Marvin and an evening paper in London, June 14th. (v. "Annual Register," for 1878, p. 67-8.)

† It was said afterwards (by Yákub) that Colonel Stolieteff took leave of Sher Áli of his own accord. (Conversation reported by General Roberts, October 22nd, 1879.)

‡ Yákub told Roberts that his father had corresponded with General Kauffmann ever since 1873. But nothing material is proved to have come of the correspondence.

The arguments were fair, and seemed stated in good faith; but the British Tories of 1878 seemed bent upon a repetition of the errors of their Whig predecessors. Chamberlain left Pesháwar on September 19th, sending on Major Cavagnari to arrange for an advance with the Afghán Commandant of the Fort of Áli Masjid at the entrance of the Khaibar Pass. The Commandant, however, with all due courtesy, assured the Major that the Mission could not pass without special orders from Kábul. Notified in London by a curt telegraphic despatch, the news of this incident caused angry excitement among high and low, indifferently assuaged by letters which the veteran Lawrence addressed to the nation through the medium of "The Times" newspaper. The apparent rebuff, he urged, was really no more than might have been expected from the course of provocation long pursued. The Government of India had erred, and ought to hold out the olive-branch itself. As a mere matter of interest, there was more to lose than to gain in a new Afghán war. The Afgháns were of more use, Lord Lawrence reminded his countrymen, as friends than as foes. But the retired Viceroy's pleadings were entirely neglected, the nation had raised money for warlike objects, and was understood to be determined to have a war with someone. A letter from the Viceroy was sent to Sher Áli, by the post, and the Amir was therein warned that unless he made an ample apology and agreed to receive a permanent British Mission at Kábul, he would be treated as an enemy. The letter was dated October 31st., and the last day of grace was to be November 20th. By that day no answer had been received, although a messenger was, in fact, on the way with a letter, dated November 19th, in which the Viceroy's terms were virtually accepted. On the 21st war was declared, and three British columns were converging on the Amir's country, before his messenger had reached Pesháwar. In December Parliament met, but the majority of the Cabinet, and the temper of the people generally combined to encourage the prosecution of an expedition, for which the Natives of India would be made to pay.

The columns of attack were led by three of the best officers then in the country, and the forces were on a scale almost suggestive of a more important undertaking, than the mere imposition of a British Mission upon the Amir. The brief sketch of the country, more or less owning the sway of that chief, which was given in a former chapter should be referred to in connection with the map. From these it will be seen what were the strategic objects immediately contemplated, though, it may be suspected, that a possible reinforcement of Sher Áli by his supposed allies beyond the Oxus was at first regarded as within the bounds of possibility.

The first column was to be assembled in the Kuram valley to the South of the direct approach up the Kábul River. It was under the command of Major-General F. Roberts, afterwards Lord Roberts, and comprised, besides a force of engineers and field and mountain artillery, a few squadrons of cavalry, and six battalions of Native infantry together with the 8th Foot. It crossed the frontier on November 21st, with the evident intention of threatening Kábul by the Pewar Kotal and Shutr Gardan passes. The column of direct attack, meanwhile, was in readiness at the mouth of the Khaibar, led by Lieutenant-General Sir S. J. Browne; in engineers and artillery his force resembled that of Roberts, but he had four British battalions and eight of Native infantry, besides being somewhat stronger in cavalry. Thus constituted Browne's column captured Áli Masjid on the 21st, the same day that saw Roberts advance; but it took the troops just a month to force their way to Jalálábad, which the advance guard entered on December 20th.

The other column, commanded by Lieutenant-General (afterwards Sir Donald) Stewart, was the only division provided with siege guns; it had also a full regiment of British cavalry—the 15th Hussars—and two corps of Bengal cavalry. There were brigades of infantry, each with a British battalion, and the column was preceded by a small force under Major-General Biddulph, commanding at Quetta, and followed by a reserve division, under Major-General Maude. This powerful army in itself sufficient to conquer the whole country, remained inactive till December 7th, and Kandahár was not reached for another month, when it was entered without opposition.

Roberts was at first very successful. By a skilful night march he turned the defences of the Pewar Kotal, while the enemy was preparing for an attack in front. On the 9th December he reached the Shutr Gardan Pass, 11,200 feet above sea-level, but was unable for the moment to advance on Kábul. Nevertheless, the news of his success, and of the probable occupation of Jalálábad, by the force under General Browne, completed the despondency of the Amir, already much shaken by the death of his favourite son and destined heir. Hastily releasing the ablest of his offspring, Yákub, whom he had kept in prison for the past three years, he committed the defence of Kábul to his charge and departed northward, hoping for aid from the Russians. Falling sick at Mazar-i-Sharif, the ill-starred Sher Áli expired on February 21st, 1879, attended by the medical attaché of the Russian Mission. Whether it was that the once soldierly spirit of Yákub had been broken by his father's ill-treatment, or whether the Afghán chiefs had satisfied themselves that no help was to be expected from Russia, certain it is that negotiations soon commenced, and the column of General Browne advancing to Gandámak, was met by a letter from the new Amir, announcing his intention of a speedy visit. Accordingly he arrived on May 8th, and on the 26th of the same month the treaty was concluded. By this instrument, British control in regard to foreign relations was admitted, with the correlative obligation of defence and protection, conditional on the admission of British representatives into such parts of the country as the Government might desire. The Amir on his part undertook the protection and encouragement of commerce between Afghanistán and India, and for the commencement of a telegraph line to Kábul.

So far there was little to criticise. In defending Constantinople the British Government had given alarm and offence to Russia, and that power had retaliated by a decidedly unfriendly move in Central Asia.* The Indian Government had then made its counter-move, from which it was not perhaps easy to recede after the Russians had made peace in Europe, and loyally held their hands in Asia. The unfortunate Sher Áli had suffered, and his disappearance had cleared the situation.

So again, with respect to territorial rearrangements. Jalá'ábad and Kandahár were to be restored, and the outposts retained on Afghán territory were reduced to the minimum required for the "rectification of frontier" postulated in the correspondence.† India now held the line from Pesháwar, across the Kurram, Gomal, and Thall-Chatiáli passes, and along the border of Biluchistan to the west side of the Khojak. This was called "the scientific frontier" because it was considered right that the Government should have knowledge and power on the exterior glacis of its natural ramparts, instead of sitting, ignorant and helpless on the hither side. The future now depended upon two factors; the character and power of the Amir, and the judgment and discretion which might be used towards him by the Government of India and its agents.

To take the latter into full consideration would require an amount of knowledge which is certainly not general, and is perhaps not possessed by anyone. Many communications that pass between public officials are never recorded and are often destroyed when their immediate object has been attained; while

* So far was Sher Áli believed to be from desiring the visit, that public opinion at the time credited him with the poisoning of the official by whom Colonel Stolietcff was admitted across the border.

† v. Governor-General of India to Secretary of State, d. 7th July, 1879, par. 11.

some important events are caused, or influenced, by mere word of mouth. Thus, what may have passed between the Viceroy and the officer whom the Viceroy was resolved on sending to represent him at Kábul might largely affect the opinion formed upon the case, if only it could be known: but without such knowledge we are left to the bare records, and must be content with the amount of information that they may have been intended to impart. From the papers that have been given to the world it would appear that the Mission was acceptable to the Amir Yákub Khán, and that in Major—now Sir Louis—Cavagnari he had the especial friend and Envoy that he would desire to receive.*

As to the genuine feelings of the Amir, however, and more especially as to his capacity, there is perhaps less difficulty. There had, indeed, been a time when he seemed the greatest living Asiatic; but whether his success in the civil war had been due to a youthful energy afterwards broken by misfortune, or whether the prince had received credit for projects and deeds really proceeding from one of the skilful officers often attached to youths in such a position, Yákub was evidently no hero in 1879. The lowest estimate that can be formed from the impressions recorded in General Roberts's despatches will be confirmed by those who, like that distinguished officer, saw and conversed with Yákub Khán at this period.†

It should seem that Cavagnari must have observed what was so patent to all; and, if so, there is great probability about the rumour, common at the time, that he endeavoured to persuade the Government of India to defer the Mission until a strong rule should be established at Kábul. But in point of fact, no delay was allowed. The Envoy arrived at Kábul on July 24th,

* Telegrams in "Afghanistan Correspondence" No 1. (1880) p.p. 4-7. Also "Further Correspondence," No. 7, p. 14-15.

† The present writer is able to give personal testimony from his intercourse with the fallen chief after he arrived in India.

meeting with a splendid reception. He was accompanied by Mr. Jenkyns, as Secretary, and Dr. Kelly as Medical Officer; Lieutenant Hamilton, V.C., commanded the escort. Salutes were fired, bands played "God save the Queen," and the officers were conducted to the quarters made ready for them in the Bála Hissar. For a few weeks all seemed to go smoothly, the Envoy visiting the Amir and the Amir returning his visits. For the Native officers and men of the Mission escort, indeed, the life was not so pleasant: even the Musalmans of the party were excommunicated by the Afgháns; while those who were Hindus or Sikhs hardly dared to leave the four walls of the Residency: but false shame kept them silent, so that the British Officers were not fully aware of the hatred which their presence excited.* Up to the 19th August the Envoy's diaries continue to report current events; but none of later date appear to have been recorded, though Lord Lytton says that, "All's well" was wired on September 2nd. For the subsequent events there is only Asiatic evidence which—as indeed is usually the case—abounds in vague and contradictory statements. What can be regarded as fairly certain may be briefly summarised as follows.

Early in the month of August several regiments arrived from Herát, in a lax state of discipline and with some grievances which they expected to have redressed through the British Officers: the worst of these grievances being that their pay was in arrears. The Amir caused the men to be disarmed, or deprived of their ammunition; some of the regiments were then paid in full and many of the men departed to their homes; but all were in a state of discontent; and some corps—which remained in Kábul—had not been paid at all. On the morning of September 3rd, some of these—apparently household troops—were called up and offered one month's arrears, which they

* Blue-book, No. 1. of 1880, p. 127. The officers had an Afghán escort in their daily rides.

refused to receive: they then went in a disorderly and threatening manner to complain to the Envoy, by whom they were referred to the Amir. Meeting with no redress in the palace they broke into open mutiny, unhorsing their Commander-in-Chief, and threatening the Amir, who took refuge in the apartments of his women. They then returned to the Residency, the doors of which were closed in their faces. Stones began to fly, the officers and their men gathered on the roof, and shots were fired on both sides. The fury of the Afgháns being now thoroughly roused, a number of them broke open the adjacent armoury and provided themselves with arms and ammunition. Other corps now joined them, and the Residency was besieged. For some hours the officers and men offered a stout resistance, and some two hundred of the assailants were shot. At length the Afgháns succeeded in setting fire to the place; Cavagnari—who had already been wounded—was killed by the falling of a roof beam; the other officers rushed to the now open gate; where they were killed, fighting bravely, by the entering mob.

The Amir immediately despatched a regretful message by electric telegraph; and Roberts came up as fast as he could from his camp on the Shutr-Gardan. As the detachment under General Baker approached the city, Yákub came out and joined the British. Roberts moved on: and on October 6th was encountered by the mutineers and a medley of armed tribesmen whom he repulsed with slaughter; and on the 8th his advance-guard under General Massey* took possession of the fortified cantonment at Sherpore.

Meanwhile the luckless Amir—who had taken refuge in the British camp—announced his fixed determination to abdicate, and to proceed to reside, as a private person, in British India;

* Denham Massey of Crimean fame. "Redan-Massey" as he was called in the army. Thirty two guns were captured, many of them the gift of the Government of India. The Bála Hissar was demolished.

whither he was accordingly escorted in all courtesy; he has continued to live there ever since. These events have been detailed for the purpose of showing the difficulty which the Government of India must always expect to find in dealing with the internal affairs of the Afgháns, a people bloodthirsty, vindictive, fanatical and treacherous; brave in the defence of their independence, but ill-disciplined, insubordinate, and without confidence in their chiefs and in each other. The rest of the war may be summed-up in a few words. In the absence of a regular Government, General Roberts assumed authority in Kábul, proclaiming martial law and prohibiting the bearing of arms in and around the city.* Herát continued in the possession of Sardar Ayub Khán, the brother of the Ex-Amir: Kandahár, garrisoned by General Stewart, was under the administration of a friendly Afghán chief entitled "Wali." But the state of things was not only provisional but extremely unsatisfactory; and the drain on the Indian finances—though not at first properly realised—was felt to be growing dangerous. Roberts was twice attacked in December; and although he held his own he was unable to collect revenue. At Kandahár, Stewart got a little grain through the newly-appointed Wali; but evidently the occupation of both regions was being carried on at the expense of the Indian revenues.

Accordingly Sir D. Stewart was directed, towards the end of March, 1880, to advance on Ghazni, and communicate with Kábul. On the 21st he delivered a farewell address to the assembled notables and immediately began to move. On the 19th April he was encountered at Ahmad Khel, about 20 miles South of Ghazni, by an enormous force of resolute fanatics, 3,000 of whom charged home upon the flanks of his little force. The steady fire of the Sikhs and Gurkhas, sustained by their arms of precision, proved too much for the enthusiasm

* Eighty-seven Afghans were put to death by sentence of court-martial, most of them for sharing in the attack on the Residency.

of the Gházis, who were repulsed about 10 a.m. with a loss to the British of 17 killed and 126 wounded.

The day before this action was fought, Lord Beaconsfield had resigned office in face of an enormous Liberal majority returned at the General Election. Mr. Gladstone was sent for by the Queen on April 23rd, and on May 7th the policy of the Government in regard to Afghanistán was announced in the House of Commons. By that time Lord Ripon was already on his way to India, charged with the duty of relieving Lord Lytton. The instructions now made known to Parliament and the country included the formation of a Native Afghán Government and the withdrawal of British troops.

These pacific intentions were stimulated by events. Before June was ended, Ayub Khán marched from Herát with a large force and invaded the territories held by the Wali of Kandahár. General Primrose, who commanded the troops left there by Sir D. Stewart, believed that if not opposed, Ayub intended to turn eastward, seize Ghazni, and cut the communication with Northern Afghanistán. He therefore sent out General Burrows with all the troops that he could spare, to watch the progress of the invader, and—if requisite—bring him to an engagement. The Wali's levies deserted to the enemy, and Burrows, coming upon Ayub's force, at Maisand, without due warning, on the morning of the 27th July, was taken at a disadvantage. The British artillery and infantry fought bravely, but were overpowered. The Sind horse could not be made to charge, and Burrows was forced to retreat, with the loss of many officers, men and guns. The 66th Foot made a resolute stand, and were annihilated. But their heroism was not in vain, for it enabled the wreck of the army to retire unmolested, and even to carry off most of the horse-artillery guns.

For the next six weeks, the garrison of Kandahár, was beleaguered; but Sir D. Stewart, on hearing of their trouble, had sent off a fine force of 10,000 men, under Sir F. Roberts, who—leaving Kábul on August 9th—arrived at Kandahár on the 31st, and inflicted a crushing defeat on the enemy, next day. Meanwhile events were ripening rapidly in Kábul. In the beginning of the year it had been resolved to offer the post of Amir, to Sardar Abd-ul-Rahman, a grandson of Dost Muhamad, who had been residing at Trans-Oxiana, under Russian protection; it was at the same time determined to withdraw the army from Afghán territory as soon as possible after the establishment of a settled form of Government. For the furtherance of these projects, a political officer was sent to Kábul, in the person of Mr.— afterwards Sir—Lepel Griffin. After some negociations the Sardar consented to accept the Amirate; but the compaign in the South necessarily revived the question of the exact amount of territory to be placed in subjection to the new Amir, whilst it probably delayed the departure of the army. On the 22nd July, the new Amir was publicly and formally installed by General Stewart; and it was announced that British troops would be withdrawn from every part of the country, excepting such places in the South as might be necessary for command of the Western route. In August the evacuation began, with the entire consent of the new Amir; and the march of the troops, by Gandámak, Jalálábad, and the Khaibar, is considered by experts to have been a masterly display of military management on the part of Sir D. Stewart. A discussion ensued on the question of Kandahár, in which the experts showed much difference of opinion; but it was finally decided to add that Province, as also Herát, to the dominions of the Amir, retaining such posts on the west of the Frontier as should give easy access in time of trouble.

In fact, the basis of India's defence has been shifted from the line of the Indus to the Western slope of the Sulaiman range, and from Pesháwar to Quetta. This is the net result of the war, and it is not to be regarded lightly.

[Information in Parliamentary papers, 1877-1880.]

SECTION 2.—In addition to the strategic advantage mentioned in the last section, the Government of India gained from the experiences of these eventful years, a very useful lesson. They learned that the Frontier of the North-West was really a European question, to whose solution they could only contribute by avoiding all possible offence to the Afgháns, and by the conciliation of the Indian races. In the latter object, it cannot exactly be said that Lord Lytton's administration was altogether successful; and the determination of the Ministry at home to throw nearly all the burden of the war upon the finances of India, was almost as unfortunate as the attempts to force a British Resident upon Kábul.

Never was India in a safer position; seldom have operations in the field been less necessary for her defence, or the expenditure more heedlessly incurred so far as India was concerned. And, as if to enhance the gravity of all these blunders Nature was in one of her unkindest moods; and the country was scourged at the same time with manifold physical disasters.

On the last night of October, 1876, a storm-wave fell upon Lower Bengal, which in the space of three hours, swept away man and his work from the surface of nearly 3,000 square miles. So sudden was the calamity, that in some villages not more than one-third of the population had time to escape by climbing into trees, the rest being drowned with their helpless cattle. Sir R. Temple, the Lieutenant-Governor, with prompt energy repaired to the scene, and all was done that could be thought of. But the crops were destroyed, the fields turned into salt marshes, the water tanks filled with brine. Pestilence followed, and cholera took tithe of the miserable survivors.

The capricious monsoon, which wrought such havoc in this region, withheld all supply from the south-east Districts of the Madras Presidency, and a large part of the Deccan.* In November, it appeared that an area of over 140,000 square

* Kaládji and Sholapore appear to have suffered most on that side of India.

miles, was attacked by drought, and that twenty-six millions of human beings were in danger. The Duke of Buckingham at Madras, and Sir P. Wodehouse at Bombay, promptly applied themselves to provide against the coming trouble. Mysore and the Nizám's dominions were presently drawn into the danger: the import duty on food-grain had to be taken off; relief-works were opened; the impotent and the shame-faced were fed at home.

In the shadow of these calamities, it was resolved to celebrate the assumption of a new title by the British Sovereign. In August, 1876, in proroguing Parliament, the Queen had declared her intention of assuming the title of "Empress of India;" and the Prime Minister, Mr. Disraeli—who at the same time became an Earl—instructed Lord Lytton to make known the change of style to the princes and peoples of the new Empire. Accordingly the 1st January, 1877 was fixed for an assemblage to be held at Delhi, to which all the rulers of the East were invited, from Sher Áli at Kábul, to the Governor of "French India" at Pondicherry. And the pageant duly took place—although not in the presence of either of those potentates—while 600,000 starvelings were already employed upon the Southern relief-works, and 250,000 gratuitously fed; in Mysore, Mr. C. B. Saunders, the Resident, was hard at work on the alleviation of local distress; the Duke of Buckingham at Madras, made large purchases of grain.

Meanwhile "the princes and peoples" held their pageant at Delhi, on the very spot where, twenty years before, the forlorn hope of Britain had borne five month of heat and danger, for the sake of law and order, and for the punishment of the mutinous sepoys. Here, before a numerous and distinguished assemblage, the Viceroy delivered an address, conveying a gracious message from the Queen-Empress, and announced the creation of the "Most Eminent Order of the Indian Empire." On the same day Her Majesty's new title was proclaimed, with due ceremony, at Calcutta, Madras and Bombay; a number of persons imprisoned for trifling offences were loosed from prison, and honours were conferred upon many distinguished persons, European and Asiatic; among the latter, Sindia and the Cashmere Rája were made Generals in the British Army. The Viceroy then left for Aligarh, where he performed a duty to many people more important and interesting, in laying the foundation-stone of an Anglo-Muhamadan College. Cool observers thought that the Empress business was an attempt by Europeans to play the Asiatic game, which would never have been made by Warren Hastings or the Wellesleys. But everyone could appreciate the honour and sympathy shown to Sáyyid Ahmad Khán, the man who had spent his means and his life time in trying to reconcile sixty million Muslims to a Christian rule.

Lord Lytton then proceeded to Calcutta, and turned his attention to a terrible trouble, that was slowly but surely gaining ground. The parts of the Peninsula that had escaped the first drought, had been so depleted by the effect of the railway communications acting on greatly enhanced prices, that when, in the summer of 1877, the drought made its way northward, there were no reserve stocks on which the people could fall back. Yet it was absolutely necessary to keep alive enough of the cattle to work the wells in the neighbourhood of the villages. Within twelve months, nearly two-hundred-and-seventy thousands tons of food were known to have been carried by land to the Deccan; and now the North-West Provinces and the Punjab were afflicted in their turn, by drought and short crops. At the same time the near approach of war in Afghanistán made the Indian Government apprehensive of the consequences of a renewal of the somewhat lavish outlay by which the famine of 1873-4 had been alleviated, and almost neutralised, in Bihár. Temple was once more employed, but this time under instructions that efforts to mitigate suffering must be tempered by a strict regard for "the severest economy." Applicants for relief were made to undergo a genuine and serious labour-test; gratuitous relief was only to be given in the shape of cooked food, and in the most extreme cases. And, the better to control any tendency to sentimental sympathies in the local authorities, Temple was to visit all centres of administration and enforce the new policy.

With that able and loyal public servant to hear was to obey. As, under Northbrook, he had given his best attention to the saving of life, so now he devoted his invincible activity and his great administrative ability to the saving of money. In the middle of January he was already on the border of the Nizám's dominions, inspecting and taking notes. He expressed himself satisfied with the action of the Bombay Government, to which he was shortly to succeed; but he warned the Viceroy against too indulgent a treatment of the revenue-payers, in consequence of which warning remissions, proposed by Sir P. Wodehouse, were changed into temporary suspensions of demand. He then passed through the "Balaghat," famous in the old war-time as the starting-point of Haidar's expeditions; and here he found painful evidences of the presence of drought, dearth, and disease. An outbreak of epidemic often dispersed the labourers on the relief works, to be driven back in a few days by sheer want of means to buy bread. As he drew near the provincial capital the signs of misery became more and more pronounced. Nevertheless, in pursuit of economy, the Commissioner felt it his duty to point out that the Madras rate of relief-wage was higher than the rate adopted at Bombay, and to urge the Duke of Buckingham to reduce it to the same level. The experiment was accordingly made, but proved a failure. Dr. Cornish, the local Health-Officer, after a fair trial, reported that the people on the reduced rate were dying in a manner which would sweep them all away in a twelvemonth, while the birth-rate was steadily falling. In the two months for which the change had lasted a third of the labourers had left the works to go on the cooked-food scale of relief; and he maintained that 1½ lbs. of food a day had been proved to be the minimum on which a working man could be kept alive. After a long discussion these arguments were accepted, and the old scale of wage was resumed on the Madras relief-works.

In May the indefatigable Commissioner became Governor of Bombay, and some seasonable rain came to greet him soon after. But the supply proved precarious, and the distress grew worse in the Deccan. About 600,000 were receiving relief in Bombay and Mysore: in the Madras Presidency the number reached two and a half millions, two-thirds of whom, being unfit for labour, had to be supported without return. The Viceroy, with commendable earnestness, presently came down from Simla to the torrid desolation of the plains. General Kennedy, who had done excellent work in the Bombay territories, was now transferred to Madras, where the hands of the Government were, to some extent, strengthened by private benevolence. But the number of people to be relieved showed no tendency to decrease, rather the reverse, until the middle of October. Then a change set in, slowly enough at first, but gradually growing until the end of 1878, when the relief operations at last came to a close.

Elsewhere, though neither so severe nor so enduring, distress was serious and widely spread. In the Punjab there was scarcity, due to exportation rather than to drought. Both causes had their effect on the contiguous Province of Hindustan, where the Lieutenant-Governor, Sir George Couper, was censured for precipitate suspensions of revenue-demand. The whole revenue was ultimately realised in the North-West Provinces and Audh. In Bombay there was a loss from this source of forty lakhs*; in

* A "lakh" is one hundred thousand rupees.

Madras nearly two millions of Rx. were lost beyond recovery. The total expenditure on relief-operations had been estimated at over eleven millions, against which there was but little to show, either in the shape of permanent works effected or of lives prolonged. During the two years of greatest intensity in the Madras districts (1877-8) the deaths were nearly 300 per cent. in proportion to the births; and the whole loss of life, including starvation, epidemic, and deficient fecundity, was reckoned at about seven millions of human beings, with an increase of about 40 per cent. upon the normal death rate.

With resources thus crippled the Government of India was led into a war, which, as we have seen, lasted for exactly two years; at the end of which it was destined to entail, counting in the charge for frontier railways, the loss of a sum-total of twenty millions, and to swallow up the margin intended in the estimates to be laid out on productive public works, and act as a "Famine Insurance Fund."* Fortunately, the year ending 1879 had been, in spite of the southern famine a period of financial prosperity, and almost every head of income had exceeded expectation. The accounts showed a surplus of over two millions in spite of "loss by exchange."† In February, 1880, accordingly, a surplus appeared in the estimates, and very sanguine telegrams were sent off to the Secretary of State at Westminster. The war-charges for the year 1878-9 and 1879-80 would be under four millions, those of the current year being estimated at a little over the moiety. No loan was needed, nor any new taxation contemplated. The war estimates had proved very accurate, and were believed ample for all contingencies contemplated. Charges would be met out of current

* See explanation in "Finances and Public Works of India," Stracheys. London, 1882.

† The revenue was received in silver, the home-charges being paid in gold. The exchange had fallen to 1s. 7½d., consequently the Indian Government "lost" nearly £3,000,000 by over-payment on 16 m.

revenue. On the following day a letter was sent to the Secretary of State, undertaking to remit, by bills during the year 1880-81 a sum of £16,900,000. But before the middle of March a change was evidently indicated, and the Secretary was requested to reduce the amount of his weekly drafts, soon after which, on his remonstrance and call for explanation, the Government of India reported "Outgoing for war very alarming, far exceeding estimate."

That was on the 8th of April; on the 13th it was announced that the cash-balances had fallen in three months from thirteen krors, or million Rx., to less than nine, owing to "excessive military drain;" following on which temporary accommodation had to be got from the Bank of Bengal. On April 21st the Under Secretary at the India Office addressed a minute to the Secretary of State, Lord Cranbrook, in which attention was drawn to these announcements, and on the following day a despatch was sent out to the Viceroy, showing that there appeared a deficiency of not less than five and a quarter krors. This vast error was evidently due to an under-estimate of war liabilities, which had led to such mis-information being laid before Parliament, and to the sudden discovery of inability to "meet the usual drawings."

The day after the date of this despatch the Ministry resigned, having abstained from further action. Lord Lytton at once threw up the Viceroyship, and Lord Ripon was sent out with such speed that he landed at Bombay before May was gone. His predecessor remained at Simla till near the end of June, endeavouring to extenuate the past mishaps by eloquent minutes. A loan was sanctioned by the new Secretary, the Marquis of Hartington, and at once subscribed for; at a premium indeed, but only at the rate of 4½ per cent.

It may be enough to add that, at the end of the season Lord Hartington, in reviewing the crisis, had no difficulty in pointing out the causes of a blunder which had given rise to inconvenience and alarm, rather than to any serious or permanent damage to the position of India in the money-market. The Government of Lord Lytton had made its initial error in estimating the cost of the second year of the war on the basis of that brought to account for the first. Not only had there been much expenditure in 1879 for objects which had become more costly in 1880, still more serious was the point that the Government was only aware of what had been *audited*, not of all that had been actually *spent*. The same thing had been unavoidably going on all through the second year: the system in fact allowed of continual payments to military chests in the field which were not brought to account for many months, and in the meantime only appeared as head of "Advances." But the great negligence was evidently that of the heads of Departmental Account, who failed to notice the enormous amount to which these advances were growing and the fact that they were not really recoverable, having therefore assumed all the character of ordinary Expenditure. The necessity of comparing the outgoings from local Treasuries with the figures of the Military Accountant-General before the preparation of Sir J. Strachey's budget does not appear to have occurred to any of the responsible officials.

It only remains to add under this head that a Commission—appointed in 1878—investigated the causes and cures of Indian Famines; and produced a "Report," written by the able Secretary, subsequently (as Sir Charles Elliott) the Lieutenant-Governor of Bengal, which has formed a valuable storehouse of facts and counsels for future guidance.

[Chief authorities to be consulted on subjects of this Section are:—"Report of Famine Commission." London, 1880. "Correspondence on Estimates for War in Afghanistan." London, 1880-81.]

SECTION 3.—The remaining branches of Lord Lytton's administration need not detain us long. Affable, accomplished, and variously gifted, his Excellency was yet unable to confer upon the country so much benefit as might have been reasonably looked for: notwithstanding that he was well aided by good and loyal councillors, and the work done was often original and even brilliant. Besides Sir J. Strachey (Finance Minister from December, 1876, to the end of 1880) his principal advisers were Colonel Sir A. Clarke, R.E. (Public Works), Major-General Sir E. Johnson (War), and Mr. Whitley Stokes (Legislation), in succession to Mr.—since Lord—Hobhouse. For the greater part of the time Bengal was represented by the Hon A. Eden—once Envoy to Bhutan—and Madras by Sir A. Arbuthnot; while Mr. James Gibbs was the Bombay Member.

Yet all this combination of wit, wisdom, and experience could not hinder the occurrence of disasters, and even blunders—which are sometimes worse. Thus, in 1876, the Government made a vain attack upon one of the higher Courts of Justice, in spite of the often-proved principle that forbids all avoidable conflicts between the Executive and the Judiciary. A country-born Christian, named Fuller,* practising as a Pleader at Agra, was provoked into boxing a servant's ears. The boy went off—somewhat needlessly—to complain to the police, who had no authority to take cognisance of such a trifle: on his way he tried to climb a wall, but fell and ruptured his spleen, and, the accident proving mortal, his assailant was summoned before a magistrate, by whom he was fined for an assault. Lord Lytton hearing of the case, directed the Local Government to bring it to the notice of the provincial High Court; where it was at once found that the magistrate's decision was as consonant to law as it was to reason, frequent rulings having established the obvious principle that a man committing a trifling assault could not—under the Penal Code—be held answerable for a subsequent event which he had not intended and could not have forseen. Stimulated by generous

* Mr. Fuller had been born and brought up in India.

philanthropy, and ill-advised by those whom he consulted, the Viceroy concluded from Fuller's name that he was a European, and that the Courts had, in a spirit of pedantry, let slip a favouring opportunity to chastise the brutality of race. The provincial authorities, better acquainted with both the facts and the law, allowed the storm to go by; and the Viceregal Minute virtually flew up to the same limbo that had once received Ellenborough's discourse on the "Gates of Somnath."

The next questionable display was the "Imperial Assemblage" at Delhi, which has already been mentioned. That was an event which perhaps was not wholly in vain, and one for which, in any case, the Viceroy was not responsible. The licence-tax, to be made a special source of famine insurance, was not a very happy inspiration. In 1877 the Viceroy publicly stated that the Government was pledged "not to spend a rupee of the special resources thus created upon" anything but works of a purely protective kind. Before two years were over these resources had been cast into the Curtian pool of deficit. Another calamity—but one which no human foresight could have prevented—took place at the beautiful health-resort of Naini Tál in the Kamaon hills, where a landslip fell on the 18th September, 1880, carrying away men, women, and houses, and laying waste the scenes of social pleasure. Cricket ground, band-stand, library, assembly rooms, were all swept into the lake, while the loss of life included forty-two European visitors and over one hundred Natives of India. As the place is the summer capital of the North-West Provinces, great efforts were made to repair the damage, and—by drainage and other works—to guard against the recurrence of such a catastrophe.

The various misfortunes of the time were enhanced by a considerable increase of criminal misconduct on the part of the general population. In India the number of what may be termed professional criminals is not relatively large; on the other hand the numbers are considerable of those who, though by habit and preference they may lead a life of harmless industry, are so ill-provided with means that protracted scarcity leaves them but little option between starvation and robbery. Thus, in 1877 grain-riots and wholesale plunder broke out among the hardy races of northern India; while even the ordinarily submissive people of the Carnatic fell into lawless courses. In Mysore the stupefying of travellers for the purpose of plunder grew into an organised system such as that of the Thugs had been half a century before. The Mahráttas of the Deccan—always ready to take their own part—broke into anarchy, some attacking their creditors, others forming gangs for purposes of brigandage. In 1878 this state of things grew to be a political menace; and the Records of the Bombay Government, kept at Poona in a beautiful old palace of carved timber, were destroyed by fire, the work of incendiaries. Two regiments of infantry and one of horse were sent against the Deccan brigands, who were dispersed, their leader being taken and hanged: the persons who had caused the Poona conflagration were brought to justice.

The people became once more quiet, under the combined influence of repressive measures and a gradual return to normal prices. Nevertheless, it was evident that, ever since the time of Lord Northbrook at least, agrarian disorder existed in the Deccan, and a vigorous attempt was now made to discover and apply the cure. The legislation on this subject began, in 1879, came to an end—for the time at least—in 1880, and under the guise of a "Deccan Agriculturists' Relief Act" formed a Court of insolvency for the agriculturists of South-West India. The difficulty had arisen from the progress of society, whereby the tenants had come into possession of transferable property: this made a valid security for debt, which (owing principally to the immobility of national habits) continued to be contracted at the same high rate of interest as had prevailed in days of misrule, when there were no means of enforcing claims against a dishonest or bankrupt debtor. Under the reign of law which had now begun the tenants were liable to have decrees given against them for the amount of a usurious claim, and to be sold up in execution and evicted from ancestral holdings which formed the sole subsistence of their families. The idea of the Acts of 1879-81 was to restrict the number and extent of such transactions: when brought into Court, claims on bond debts were to be examined on their merits, usurious accretions disallowed, and the debtors to be protected against imprisonment or eviction when the decree came to be executed. The security on which debt could be contracted being thus impaired, while the high rates of interest were liable to be cut down by the Court, a serious check must be put on the contraction of money obligation; and, since the money was largely raised for unprofitable and extravagant uses, it was hoped that the apparent interference with the freedom of contract would be justified by results. The report of a Commission appointed some ten years later leads to the belief that these hopes have not been altogether disappointed. This report, however, may be expected to furnish matter for further legislation.*

In Bengal, also, though from somewhat different causes, measures were begun for the relief of the cultivating classes not sufficiently protected by Act x. of 1859. A note of warning had been sounded at Patna, so far back as 1873, when an agrarian disturbance, based on an anti-rent combination, gave intimation that distress was becoming intolerable, and that the usually submissive population of Eastern Bengal might give serious trouble. Not long after, a sign of discontent appeared in the opposite direction, the landholders of Bihár complaining of the excessive burden thrown upon them by the action of the law on which the claims of the tenants were based. It

* v. Report on working of the Deccan Agriculturists' Relief Act. Calcutta, 1892.

thus became apparent that Act x.—however well it may have worked in Hindustan—was not completely suited to any portion of the Lower Provinces; and a fresh Commission was appointed in 1879 whose report—presented in the following year—supplied matter for several years of discussion and for a change in the law, which will be related in the next chapter.

Whilst benevolent efforts were thus set going for the benefit of the toiling masses, an equally well-meant innovation was devised for a higher class of Native society. Ever since the Charter of 1833 this section of Indian mankind had been continually assured that the British Government did not desire that creed or colour should form any bar to employment in the public service; nevertheless, the "Covenant"—a kind of Civil Commission inherited from the last century—continued to produce an almost equivalent effect. This was because, whilst a certain kind of employment was set aside for covenanted officers, the covenanted service could only be entered through a competitive examination held in London. Inasmuch as that examination was, for many reasons, almost closed to Native youths, it happened that—in spite of all promises—no more than nine Indian gentlemen held posts in the Covenant Service in the year 1878. In that year Lord Lytton's Government devised a scheme by which it was contemplated to appoint Natives to a certain number of posts without requiring the diploma of the London examinations, and the scheme was sanctioned by the Secretary of State with indispensable modifications. At first appointed, on the recommendation of the Local Governments, and on probation, the young men would finally enter the ranks of "Statutory Civilians," and be entitled to promotion on rates of pay somewhat lower than what were deemed requisite for Englishmen brought from home to labour in exile. It was soon, however, perceived that some definition of the word "Native" would be requisite. It was very likely Lord Cranbrook's vague notion, in framing the rules, that all the people of India were either Muhamadans or Hindus; and, speaking generally, that is not far from the truth. Yet it was not intended—as need hardly be explained—that a religious test should be established, which would not only exclude Parsees and Jains, but would absolutely make it penal to hold the creed of the master-country. Accordingly, in the present code of Civil Service Regulations, a Native is defined to be "any person born and domiciled within the dominions of Her Majesty in India . . . of parents habitually resident in India, and not established there for temporary purposes only." In 1888, Sir S. Bayley systematised the appointments to the "Uncovenanted Service," as already explained; and it may now be fairly said that the share of the people in lucrative and dignified employment is not confined to general protestation. It is, clearly, not in any rational relation to the numbers of those who could be found if desired; but on the other hand, it may be argued that—so long as the British nation considers that it has a mission to introduce Western ideas into the administration of the country—it is unavoidable that most of the controlling posts should be held by Western officials, and that such men can only be fitted for those posts by passing an apprenticeship in posts of a similar character but lower grade. In a word, to qualify a British officer to be Lieutenant-Governor of a Province, the best training is that which he will obtain by beginning his service as an Assistant to a District-Officer, and rising gradually in the department of local administration. That is the fair and reasonable defence of the existing system, which is evidently and professedly, a special arrangement necessitated by special circumstances.

A measure of more questionable character was taken by the Government in 1878. Fortified by the previous assent of the Ministry at home, Lord Lytton carried through the Legislature in the course of one day the whole three stages of an Act for the control of vernacular publications. Inasmuch as the effect of this was to revive the Censure abolished by Metcalfe nearly half-a-century before, it would seem that so retrogressive a step ought not to have been made the occasion for suspension of the standing orders. But it was held that to invite discussion might have involved a letting loose of the flood whose control was the very object of the law. The Native Press produced journals and pamphlets for which—so it was argued—there was no real need or demand; but the absence of paying circulation was supplied by inducements to political discontent and by personal scurrility leading to blackmail. Instances of these abuses were not difficult to obtain, and were recorded in Council; but it was not shown that the existing Penal Code was insufficient for their due punishment if properly applied. The result was the short-lived Statute known—until its desuetude and repeal—as Act IX. of 1878.

Such were some features of this administration; able and well-intentioned, no doubt, but not always wise, and mostly unfortunate. Lord Lytton has been said, by a recent writer, to have "taken Antony and Verres" as his models.* Nothing can be more unjust; he neither governed as a vulgar and rapacious Propraetor, nor lost the world for love. If he resembled any ancient ruler, it was rather that Roman of whom a stern critic said that every one thought him fitted to govern until they saw him governing.

[Parliamentary papers, Annual Register, "Calcutta Review," Vols. 71-2, London, 1885.]

* "England under Gladstone," by J. H. McCarthy.

CHAPTER XXIV.

CONCLUSION.

Section 1: Policy of Lord Ripon—Section 2: Panjdeh and Burma—Section 3: Summary.

SECTION 1.—With the treatment of current events and contemporaneous controversy History, in its proper acceptation, can have no concern. For History, being by virtue of its name the report of a scientific inquiry into the origin and progress of nations, cannot concern itself with the discussion of unsettled questions; nor can it be expected to decide whether the events that are taking place in our presence are tending to progress or the reverse. If we are thus generally debarred from anticipating the verdicts of events, least of all can we judge living men.

Especially is this the case with the Marquess of Ripon, who belongs to a school of statesmen still under trial, men whose policy has evoked criticism to a degree almost unequalled in the events of the present reign. Lord Ripon was the grandson of a Yorkshire country gentleman, Sir Thomas Robinson, who had, to the surprise of men, come to be a member of the Duke of Newcastle's cabinet in the days of King George II., and had been raised to the peerage as Lord Grantham at the beginning of the next reign. His second son was President of the Board of Trade in 1818, and was made a peer in 1827, by the title of Viscount Goderich. When Canning died he was for a few months Prime Minister: in 1833 he became Earl of Ripon, and Lord Privy Seal; and died in 1859. The son and successor of this statesman had sat in the Commons as Liberal representative of several Yorkshire constituencies; and after succeeding to the peerage was made Secretary of State for India. His selection as Viceroy under the next Liberal Government was thus—if he wished it—an accomplished fact; and he began his incumbency by going on to Bombay with almost unequalled rapidity, and by delivering frank and eloquent speeches from the moment of his landing. The first duty that awaited him after taking charge was the evacuation of Afghanistán, and the handing over to the new Amir of the whole country, from Kábul to Kandahár, and from Herát to the foot of the western Pamir. He then turned, under inspiration from the Queen's Ministry, to the work of infusing a liberal spirit into Indian administration; and never, since the days of Bentinck, has there been such rapid movement in this direction, or so much alarm and indignation excited among the Anglo-Indian community. On such contentious matters we may touch lightly without expressing any judgment. But, before doing so, we may glance at a subject which admits of but one opinion—the restoration of the Wodeyar dynasty to power in Mysore.

This State, it may be remembered, had been usurped by Haidar Áli, the famous soldier-of-fortune, about the middle of the 18th centuty, but his Empire was of short duration. On the defeat and death of Haidar's son, in 1799, the territories they had filched from their neighbours were taken back, and the remainder of the country was restored to the Hindu line in the person of Rája Krishna Ráj. From that date the State was administered, during the Rája's minority, by Purnia, a Mahratta Brahman, who was both able and honest; in a few years the annual revenue rose to nearly three-quarters of a million. On Purnia's retirement the Rája tried to carry on the administration, with the result that the revenue dwindled, the treasury was depleted of its reserves, and the people suffered and fell into anarchy. The State was accordingly sequestrated in 1831. And the British methods of business, carried on by selected Natives, and directed by excellent British officers, gradually brought about the required reforms. The famine of 1877-78 fell on the country with special severity, and 280,000 of the small population were in receipt of relief; while the deaths averaged 120 per diem; including remissions of land-revenue the State lost a million of Rx. But the prosperity of Mysore only suffered temporary interruption; and in the beginning of Lord Ripon's rule the debts of the late Rája had been paid; a number of vexatious imposts had been abolished; and the yearly revenue had increased to over a million. The State, with these improvements and a handsome cash-balance under a good Native staff of officials thoroughly trained to their work, was handed over to the lawful heir, 25th March, 1881. The Native machinery is now under a Native Minister, but the system has otherwise undergone but little change, and the prosperity of the State and people shows no symptoms of deterioration. When an Englishman thinks with sorrow of the story of Audh he can have no better consolation than the memory of Mysore; and he can only wonder why the course so successfully pursued in regard to the one could not be adopted in the case of the other.

Some of the success in Mysore, with much of the prosperous tranquility of the Carnatic and its dependencies, was due to the good qualities of the local Governors. The Duke of Buckingham had been succeeded by Mr. W. P. Adam, who died at his post, to the general regret of all who knew his unselfish character, on the 24th May, 1881, just one day before the formal completion of the Mysore arrangement. He was succeeded by Sir M. E. Grant-Duff, a distinguished diplomatist and statesman, son of the Capt. Grant—or Grant-Duff—whom we have seen as the friend and colleague of Elphinstone, and the historian of the Mahrattas. Bombay was administered by Sir James Fergusson, who had succeeded Sir R. Temple in April, 1880.

The period of Lord Ripon's administration was one of uninterrupted peace, during which the Government of India enjoyed abundant leisure for internal reform, of which, in the opinion of hostile English critics, it availed itself with pernicious impulse. It is held by this school of politicians that in domestic as in foreign affairs there may be an activity that is not masterly, and what a poet has called "raw haste half-sister to delay." To bring European institutions into Asia is compared to transplanting to the banks of the Ganges a full-grown British oak.

Leaving metaphor and questionable analogy aside, it is our business to see what Lord Ripon's Government was, and what it did. At the beginning of his Viceroyalty he had for colleagues Major E. Baring—since Lord Cromer—as Finance Minister, an able and sympathetic councillor; Sir D. Stewart as Military Member, and later as Commander-in-Chief; the Law Member being Mr. Courtenay Ilbert: on the whole a Government well-prepared to carry out a Liberal policy under the inspiration of Mr. Gladstone, the Premier at home.

One of the first of the steps thus taken was the repeal of Lord Lytton's Vernacular Publications Act. The question of the Press in India was one that had divided men of the greatest distinction for more than fifty years. Sir Thomas Munro was strongly opposed to complete liberty, though forward in the advocacy of liberal principles generally. That the British in India should largely avail themselves of Native agency, and should endeavour in all legitimate ways to command Native support and sympathy, he was ever ready to maintain. But he recorded a clearly pronounced opinion against unfettered journalism, in the very maturity of his experience and responsibility. When Governor of Madras, and not long before his decease at that post, he penned a Minute for the consideration of the Governor-General, and the Court of Directors, in which he laid down two points which he considered to be essential to the welfare of the country. "The first is that our sovereignty should be prolonged to the remotest possible period; the second that, whenever we are obliged to resign it, we should leave the Natives so far improved . . . as to be capable of maintaining a free—or at least a regular—government among themselves. If these objects can ever be accomplished it can only be under a restricted Press."* But the Governor-General whom Munro desired to move was the Marquess of Hastings, who declared, about the same time, that "he was in the habit of considering the freedom of publication as the natural right of his fellow-subjects;" and further, "that it was salutary for supreme authority—even when its intentions were most pure—to look to the control of public opinion." Acting on these principles he removed almost all restrictions on the Indian Press, and the appearance of the first vernacular newspaper dates from that period.† Then came Mr. Adam—to whose goodness and wisdom Metcalfe bore warm testimony. And this *ad interim* Governor-General, who had done as a Member of Council what little he could to obstruct the proceedings of Hastings, now issued an ordinance (during his temporary tenure of the Governor-Generalship in 1823), by which the liberal arrangements of his predecessor were entirely neutralised, so that an enterprising Indian journalist who sought to benefit by them was deported to Europe. During the latter part of Lord W. Bentinck's rule the Anglo-Indian Press was abusive to the verge of scurrility, but was treated with almost contemptuous indifference. In 1835, Metcalfe—as we have seen—removed all restrictions by legislative enactment. During the Mutiny a temporary law suspended the liberty of the Press,

* Arbuthnot: "Sir Thomas Munro," London, 1889.

† "Lord Hastings" (Rulers Series), Oxford, 1893.

European and Native alike; while Lord Lytton's Act imposed new, and what were meant to be permanent, restrictions. These, according to one who was at that time a member of the Indian Government, were ample for the purpose of repression.* But the question still remained as to whether repression was desirable: and on this it was decided by Lord Ripon's Government that the only desirable form of repression was that which proceeds from a dread of undergoing the ordinary penalities of the Law, which, it was believed, would be found always adequate to correct the publication of seditious or calumnious sentiments. Lord Lytton's Act was accordingly repealed. It may, perhaps, be said that the question was rather eluded than determined: the Vernacular Press had great faults, of which the greatest was the want of circulation and of reason for existence. But this did not apply to Anglo-Indian papers, which were also conducted with real ability, and offered a channel for the unofficial expression of opinions by officials of originality. Yet it is an almost indefeasible maxim of Indian Government that the same measure of liberty and law shall be applied to all classes of the community alike.

The application of that maxim, however, could not be made without sometimes provoking opposition among the handful of white settlers in India who, even when not connected with the administration, claimed a kind of class-ascendency which was not only in the conditions of the country but also in the nature of the case. It was perhaps natural that in a land of caste the compatriots of the rulers should become—as Lord Lytton said—a kind of "white Brahmans": and it was certain that, as a matter of fact, the pride of race and the possession of Western civilisation created a sense of superiority, the display of which was ungraceful and even dangerous when not tempered by official responsibility. This feeling had been sensitive enough in the days of Lord William Bentinck, when the class referred

* Arbuthnot, *ub. sub.* p. 159.

to was small in numbers and devoid of influence. It was now both more numerous, and—by reason of its connection with the newspapers of Calcutta and of London—it was far better able to make its passion heard.

The first offence given by Lord Ripon was his attempt to extend to the Native public the power of urban and rural administration, known variously as Self-Government, Autonomy, or Home Rule. The citizens of Calcutta, Madras, Bombay, and a few other large towns where there was a large European community, had long been in possession of Municipal institutions; but in the interior of the country the principle was to make all purely local administration dependent on the European District-Officers. Yet the germs of Home Rule already existed: not only in the traditional institutions of the rural communes so often described, but in towns and cities where—in whatever leading-strings—local bodies regulated the conservancy and the watch-and-ward of the streets. All indeed was backward, and the administration was in the hands of the foreign officers on whose heads was the responsibility. Into this feeble body Lord Ripon attempted to breathe the breath of life. In the general outline European principles were observed; but the scheme was generally considered crude and hasty; and it was not confined to urban communities where its rudiments already existed, but was extended to rural populations whose notions of administration went no farther than a yearly audit of village accounts. Such people had always looked to the authorities for all other kinds of service: and were no more inclined than people would be elsewhere, to discharge offices for which, as they believed others received pay. Thus, in the beginning of 1883, when they had seen something of the scheme, the Municipal Commissioners of the City of Agra informed the Lieutenant-Governor of the North-West Provinces that they considered that the fact of the local officers serving on the Committee secured to them advantages that could "hardly be overstated." This advantage it was the main object of the scheme to remove; but the Agra Committee assured the Government that they "would regret any change in their constitution which deprived them of that assistance." Time alone could avail to frame autonomous institutions with which the popular mind should be in such harmony that the presence and aid of some of the District Staff could be forgone. If that were the case in large and intelligent centresof trade and manufacture, what are we to think of the wisdom of endeavouring to dispense with official guidance in the rural communes? Yet even here the Government declared that the trained, paid, and responsible servants of the State should not be even ordinary members of the Committees to be elected in their Districts. This ukase was enough to bewilder more practised and experienced electors than the shopkeepers and ploughmen to whom it was addressed. On the result of the elections being known it was generally found that the Chief of the District had been chosen—and that not as a member only but as Chairman. There is no occasion to go into details. The great need of such folks is not to govern but to be governed. Their ideal of freedom is freedom from trouble and taxation.

As a method of limiting and supplementing Imperial Revenue, however, the system has been successful. The elected members have not, in the ultimate arrangements, been made to wholly exclude the District officials; but the latter are in such a minority as to make it conceivable that the popular representatives can do as they like, subject to the approval of the Government, and that they do really provide for the wants of their respective localities. This may be said to be a sort of compromise between the old autocracy and Lord Ripon's innovation; and the fact that nearly three millions of R.x. are thus raised annually—to be spent on local improvements—is a sure sign that the scheme has not wholly failed.

The opposition to the Local Government Acts, in their

original form, was chiefly confined to the Civil Officers of the higher class, and was based on public grounds. But the next step taken by the Government towards the assertion of Native authority caused a storm of personal indignation among all classes of European British subjects from one end of India to the other. On February 2nd, 1883, Mr. Ilbert moved for leave to introduce into Council his Criminal Procedure Amendment Bill, being supported by a letter of the preceding March from Sir A. Eden, Lieutenant-Governor of Bengal, who had addressed the Government of India urging the necessity for doing away with race-restrictions. Under the Criminal Procedure Code of 1873 no Magistrate or Session-Judge could enquire into a charge against a European British subject unless he was himself such; except in the Presidency towns where there was no distinction of race. The proposed reform excited immediate and vehement opposition in Calcutta, although the European inhabitants of that city were not likely to experience any of its effects: it was the denizens of the "Mufasal," or interior, who feared the loss of the privilege by virtue of which persons of their race who might be charged with offences were entitled to claim trial before a Magistrate of their own blood. This privilege was—so they believed—essential to their having a fair trial; and harrowing pictures were drawn of the outrages to which themselves and their families would be exposed under the proposed law, which might possibly bring them under the jurisdiction of Native Judges. Meetings were held at various places in India; and in July a deputation appeared before the Secretary of State at the India Office, in Westminister. On the 1st of August, Mr. Bright addressed a large gathering of people at Willis's Rooms in London, and explained the Liberal view: and on the 10th of the same a mass of papers was sent home by the Government of India, containing opinions, for and against the Bill, which had been collected all over India. At length the agitation ended in another compromise; but it seemed to many that it had formed a fresh instance of unnecessary activity, or—as it was called at the time—"breathless benevolence." It was true that the intention of the Bill had been to give logical completeness to the direction that the law had been taking ever since the days of Bentinck and Macaulay; and that the number of Courts whose jurisdiction was to be extended was as small as the number of persons whose cases would be affected was insignificant. But men are not altogether ruled by logic; and the trifling effect of the change was even thought to be a reason for abstaining from action which undoubtedly raised class-passion to a degree that was not altogether seemly. One good result, however, was that in future all criminous Englishmen would be able to claim trial by jury—a right which they had not before possessed, excepting when tried before a Chartered Court.

Lord Ripon's sincere desire to do good was shown in other and less questionable reforms. Acting on the recommendations of the Famine-Commission, he created a Department of Agriculture, or rather gave new life and organisation to one that had been devised by Mayo, but allowed to absorb itself in other Departments. The benefit of distinct responsibility and division of labour was soon shown; and it is hoped that some of the cares of the Indian husbandmen have been lightened and that more will become lighter in future. The Cadastral surveys that have been pushed on in subsequent years, the exemption of improvements made by the agriculturist from assessment, the collection of statistics, and the diffusion of useful rural information, these are among the things already put in train. The indebtedness of the Deccan husbandmen led to an extension of the legal relief already mentioned; and another Act was passed impowering the local authorities to lend money for agricultural purposes. Most of all was the wisdom of the Government displayed in the persistent tenacity with which it carried out the protection of the cultivators in

Bengal, so sacrificed by Cornwallis and so inadequately guarded by later legislators. But this Act did not become law under Lord Ripon; and an account of its origin and completion will be more appropriately given hereafter.

In 1882, another important step was taken, in the appointment of a Commission—of which Mr. (afterwards Sir) W. W. Hunter was the President—for the purpose of initiating measures to make primary instruction more genuinely popular while higher grades of teaching should be linked with the strengthened system of self-government. The Commission reported in 1883; and many of its recommendations have borne good fruit. A correct classification of schools was made; the hedge-schools of the villages were brought under State-aid with inspection; while most of the high-schools and colleges for higher teaching were thrown on the Municipalities, although continuing to receive grants-in-aid from Imperial sources.

The revenues of the Empire were fully adequate to all the demands to which these benevolent exertions led. The Budget of 1881-82 showing a surplus of over two-and-a-half millions of R.x. Major Baring was enabled to abolish the customs-duties on the importation of foreign piece-goods, and indeed, to make an almost complete sweep of such duties altogether. Yet, so far were Native industries from suffering that mills for spinning and weaving increased and multiplied, both in the Deccan and in Hindustan. The abolition of the cotton-goods' duty was generally attributed to Lord Ripon and Major Baring, by whom it was finally incorporated in the Budget. The credit of the policy, however, belongs to Lord Lytton and Sir John Strachey, by whom it was devised and prepared.

The commerce of British Burma formed an exception to the universal prosperity; for the wilful despot, Thebaw, who reigned at Mandalay, granted monopolies of every kind of produce, which greatly crippled the trade of the European merchants at Rangoon. Lord Ripon, visiting the place at the end of 1881, received a deputation of mercantile residents, and on that occasion a memorial was laid before him in consequence of which the Government of India addressed the King in a firmly-worded remonstrance in January, 1882, after the Viceroy's return to Calcutta. The monopolies were immediately condemned, though not actually abolished; and in April, 1882, a Mission was sent to India which seemed likely to end in improved relations between the two countries. The Envoy and his suite—one of whom had been educated at Woolwich—visited the Viceroy at Simla; but, after three months of constant negotiations, the Mandalay Durbar refused to sanction the treaty which had been provisionally adopted in India. The Envoy left Calcutta for Rangoon on September 7th; and the relations of Burma and India become more strained daily.

The only remaining event of importance during the period was the despatch of a contingent from India to Egypt. The expedition was prepared under orders from London received in Calcutta, July 10th, 1882; the last transport left that place, August 31st; the campaign ended by the capture of Cairo, September 14th; and the troops were all back in India by the end of October. This brisk little war furnished another leaf to the laurels of Sir D. Stewart, the able Commander-in-Chief of the Indian forces; but the charge to the Indian Exchequer was estimated at over a million.

During the year 1882, many changes occurred in the subordinate Governments; Sir A. C. Lyall—formerly Foreign Secretary—becoming Lieutenant-Governor, of the North-West Provinces, while Mr. Rivers Thompson succeeded Eden in Bengal, and Sir C. U. Aitchison took the place of Sir R. Egerton in the Punjab. In August, 1883, Sir Auckland Colvin became Finance-Minister; and his first Budget showed but a small surplus; but this attracted little attention being clearly due to the cost of the Egyptian expedition. The Viceroy visited Haidárábad in the winter, for the purpose of installing the young Nizám, and the rest of his time was not marked by any important incident. Lord Ripon resigned in the autumn of 1884, being succeeded by the Earl of Dufferin, who took charge on December 13th, of that year.

["Annual Register." "Annals of our time," 1878-87. The "Calcutta Review," Vols. LXXIII. to LXXVIII.]

SECTION 2.—Lord Dufferin had, for nearly a quarter of a century, been a man of mark. Already distinguished by accomplished literary skill, he had been selected, by Lord Palmerston in 1860, to investigate the circumstances of the massacre of the Maronite Christians of the Lebanon in the summer of that year. Then, for two years, he served as Under-Secretary for India, afterwards, for six years Governor-General of Canada; then Ambassador, first at St. Petersburg, afterwards at the Porte. By a training so varied and so full of great responsibility, he was singularly prepared for the high post which he was now to fill.

Some very important matters were ripening for the new Viceroy's disposal. It was mentioned in the last Section that Lord Ripon had inherited from the preceding administration an obligation to do something for the settlement of a perennial conflict between the landholders and the tillers of the soil in the Lower Provinces, and had accordingly prepared a project of law. Having described—so far as the scale of this work allowed—the privileges that had been accorded to Zemindárs by former Governments, we can only here add that neither they nor the ryots were entirely contented with the state of affairs that had since accrued. In some parts of the territory administered by Mr. (afterwards Sir A.) Rivers Thompson a feeling existed among the Zemindárs that their tenants were two much favoured by Act x. of 1859, which had been chiefly enacted to meet the needs of Upper India. In other parts the tenants were so dissatisfied with their practical disabilities that instead of seeking legal remedies they sought refuge in violence and refusal to pay rent. Enquiries were made which led to projects of reform, till March 1883, while Lord Ripon was yet in power as Viceroy when a Bill prepared by Mr. Ilbert was made over to the charge of Sir S. C. Bayley who had come into Council the year before. Sir Steuart accordingly on March 12th explained the object and reasons of the Bill, and was followed by the Rája of Darbhanga and a very able Native Member, Bábu Kristo Das Pal. The line taken by these gentlemen was peculiar; while admitting the need for legislation they objected to most of the detailed proposals of the Bill, and each showed, before he sate down, that he was opposed to all real reform. On the 13th the Debate was resumed, when Mr. Ilbert endeavoured to give it a little historical interest by referring to 1793 and the pledges then given, both by implication and expressly, that the rights of the tenants should have protection. Major Baring took the ground of actual economic facts: in Bengal, he contended, the Zemindárs had been endowed at the expense of the community and were not entitled to any special consideration. In support of this assertion he adduced statistics which showed that while in the Punjab 54 per cent. of the net produce went into the Treasury, and as much as 88 per cent. under the modified Ryotwary of Bombay, here—in Bengal—the proportion was only 33 per cent. Other statistics were quoted to show that the prosperity of the population was as dependent on permanence of quasi-proprietary tenure as was the fiscal position of the State in a country where taxation was so difficult and unproductive. As for Act x. of 1859 (of which the Bihár Zemindárs complained) Major Baring said that he found that it had in Bengal entirely failed to protect the ryot; and he produced a list of no less than twenty-seven illegal cesses which were at that very hour collected in the district of which Calcutta was a part. In closing the Debate Sir Steuart Bayley observed that, if the Zemindár, under the Permanent Settlement, was the considerate and merciful being represented by his advocates, the proposed reform could have for him no terrors. The Bill was introduced, read twice, and committed. But it led to a discussion almost as vehement as that which had arisen round the judicial question—and it was not until the expiration of two full twelvemonths that it became law, as Act VIII. of 1885.

At the conclusion of this business Lord Dufferin proceeded to the Punjab, and had a meeting with the Amir of Kábul at Ráwal Pindi on April 2nd, 1885. Stirring intelligence reached them there, by which it was made to appear as if the collision between the Russians in Turkestan and the Afghán allies of British India, so long a subject of anxiety, had at length occurred. In order to a right understanding of these events it will be necessary to take a short retrospect.

In the north-east corner of Khorásan is an oasis which has long been known as Merv, and in modern times it had belonged to the Amirate of Bokhara, until 1856 when it was occupied by the Tekké Turkmáns. Watered by the Murgháb river, it supports a population variously estimated at from a quarter to half a million: even under Tartar cultivation it is productive, and it is an important station on the road from Khiva to Herát. In 1883 the Russian officers in those regions had shown some intention of occupying the district, but the Government of St. Petersburg had appeared to discountenance the project. The local chiefs, too, seemed anxious to preserve their independence, having in 1881 constituted a newspaper correspondent named O'Donovan their agent, and sent him to Constantinople to plead their cause with all the powers of Europe. Nothing definite, however, had ensued; and the Tashkend officials continued their operations—much as some of the early British officials had formerly done in India—without paying much attention to the wishes of their employers in Europe. At length, in February, 1884 it was announced that on the last day of the preceding month the Merv chiefs had come to Askabad and sworn allegiance to the Czar. On this General Kumaroff, the Russian Governor-General, took possession of the city of Merv and the surrounding country, bringing his outposts within 200 miles of Herát. These events naturally alarmed the Amir; and seemed to call for a final determination of the frontier between the territory under his rule and the southern region of Russian Turkestan. Without any imputation against the good faith of their Muscovite protectors, it was too probable that the Turkmans would be constantly tempted to claim such conveniences as water-courses, pasturages, or mountain-passes; and that disputes of that kind between them and their Afghán neighbours would not improbably arise calculated to compromise the good relations between the two great Empires to which, respectively, they look for protection and peace.

In accordance with these considerations a joint commission of delimitation was arranged during the year, General Sir P. Lumsden was deputed on the part of British India, accompanied by some European officers and a small escort. The disputed frontier lay between the Hari Rud on the west, and the point to the east where a small river called the Khusk runs into the Murgháb at Pul-i-Khishti, or "Brick-Bridge." All to the north was roughly known as Panjdeh, to the south as Badghis; the former belonging to Bokhara and Merv, the latter to Afghanistán; while the boundary line was so vague as to leave certain points quite open to debate. The westernmost of these points was the Zulfikar Pass, leading from Khorásan to Badghis, that on the eastern side was between the Brick-Bridge and Meruchak, at a place called Panjdeh, and commanding the entrance into the Province of that name. General Kumaroff advanced with a force of Russians and Turkmans to the north of this point, while a small Afghán column threatened the bridge.

The presence of each was as unfortunate as unnecessary; an electrical atmosphere was unavoidably created: on the 30th March—while the Viceroy was on his way to meet the Amir—a collision occurred, in which the Afgháns were driven back with loss, and both the Amir and the British authorities became greatly excited. But the Russian Government preserved its calm, declaring that the Afgháns had been the aggressors, and that the highly-coloured accounts which had reached India and England were due to misrepresentations on the part of the Afgháns.

Few things could be worse than a war between two civilised nations about a scuffle over a bridge in Central Asia. Yet if those nations were to avoid war without losing the respect of themselves and of the world, there were at least two subjects demanding a considerable employment of the resources of diplomacy. First, was the gossip of excited Afgháns to outweigh the persistent assertions of a Russian Viceroy as to his own motives and conduct? Secondly, what was to be done for the delimitation commenced under such sinister omens?

During the whole month of April the negotiations on these subjects went on. The attitude of the Czar was irreproachable, maintaining the dignity of his nation and his army, yet meeting the British proposals in a spirit of courtesy and conciliation. In India the discussion was watched with keen interest; and offers of service reached the Government from many Native States. But happily war was averted. Panjdeh, it ultimately appeared, was not a possession on which the Amir was disposed to lay stress, and the Russian Government agreed to the neutralisation of the debateable land so long as the delimitation should be pending. If any farther misunderstanding was left, or should arise, the Czar would agree to refer it to arbitration. These offers were accepted by the British on May 4th; as to General Kumaroff's conduct further discussion was courteously waived, and the language of the last despatch from St. Petersburg was adopted as the basis of the future proceedings. Sir Peter Lumsden was at once recalled; and the frontier was finally determined, by his successor acting amicably with the Russian Commissioner, so as to leave the Afghans in possession of Meruchak and the command of the Zulfikar Pass. The result was hailed, by those best qualified to judge, as a happy instance of the success of peaceful discussion, and a gratifying proof of the loyal spirit animating the princes and peoples of India.*

With a less civilised, though less powerful, neighbour the Government of India got into difficulties which admitted of no such peaceful solution.

It was stated above (v. last Section) that the Mission from Mandalay left Calcutta, after a summer of fruitless discussion, in September, 1882. Since then the commerce of Rangoon had continued to suffer; while the foolish tyrant massacred his own people and refused to give fair treatment to his neighbours. It was now understood that he was seeking an alliance with the French and meditating a joint attack, with them, upon the countries lying between the French possessions and British Burma, the chief of which was Siam, ruled by a King in alliance with Queen Victoria.

In the midst of these anxieties it was probably a relief to the Government of India, which was still trying to negotiate, to learn that the despot of Mandalay had declared war. In his proclamation, received in November, 1885, King Thebaw pronounced the British proposals "ridiculous," and promised to lead his troops to victory. He was, however, so good as to add that no injury should be done to any Europeans at a distance "only after the frontier is crossed by an invading army will their slaughter be allowed." On the 14th of the same month General Prendergast advanced as far as Thayet Myo, then the frontier town on the Irawadi; a Burmese war-ship was captured

* Parliamentary Papers: "Central Asia, 2-4." 1885.

by two boats' crews of H.M.S. Turquoise, and a proclamation was issued declaring that Thebaw had ceased to reign. On the 16th and 17th two engagements took place on the banks of the river, in the second of which the Burmese made a stand of over three hours, when their fortification was taken by assault, with a loss on the British side of thirty-two killed and wounded. On the 27th November, active operations were closed by the total collapse of the defence. When the British expeditionary force reached the old capital, Ava (on that day), Thebaw's envoy met them with a prayer for peace. The General replied that the only terms that he was authorised to offer were that the King should give himself up; that Mandalay should be surrendered; and that the Burmese army should lay down their arms and become prisoners. The envoy retired to Court that evening, but returned next day with a message from Thebaw accepting these hard conditions. The forts of Ava were at once given up, and all the Burmese troops present gave up their arms and were allowed to disperse. On the 29th, General Prendergast proceeded to Mandalay and received the submission of Thebaw himself, who was at once sent on board a steamer with his family, and conveyed down the river Irawadi, and finally interned in British India. The people of the capital offered no resistance, and arrangements were made for a temporary administration of the country pending further orders.

The only other political transaction of the year was a Durbar at Gwalior for the purpose of restoring to Sindia that famous fortress of his predecessors, which had been held by the Government of India ever since its capture by Sir Hugh Rose in June 1858. This graceful courtesy was shown to Sindia on December 2, 1885, when Lord Dufferin made an appropriate speech, and the Maharája in reply said that the deepest wish of his heart was now gratified. Jaiaji Sindia died in fact soon after, having reigned forty-two years; during which he had been actively loyal to his British allies, and the most distinguished of Native Princes, especially in matters of military administration. He held the rank of General in H.M.'s army, the Grand Cross of the Bath, and many other honours, including the right to a salute of nineteen guns as a permanent compliment, with two more personally when visiting any British station.*

The Viceroy's next journey was to Burma, where things were not going at all smoothly. The Government of that country had become almost a nullity before the fall of Thebaw who never stirred beyond the walls of his palace, and only displayed authority by putting to death his own blood-relations. Armed boats practised piracy on the upper waters, and three European agents of a Bombay trading association were massacred. It now appeared clear that nothing but a strong and systematic rule would restore order, and Lord Dufferin accordingly proceeded to Rangoon to conduct final arrangements, having previously (January 1, 1886) proclaimed that the country was annexed to the British Empire. This, with the exception of a few scraps of frontier acquired purely for strategic purposes on the North-West, was the first annexation of territory since the time of Dalhousie; and it was opposed by some politicians in England as a return to a bad old system, but was generally held to be justified by circumstances, as a special case. The utter collapse of Native power, the disorganisation surging up to the British borders, and the danger apprehended from the French in the eastern part of the Peninsula, combined to justify the action of the British Government.

It must be added that the subsequent course of events has done much to corroborate these views. The robber-gangs have doubtless given trouble, but that must always happen when a civilised system succeeds to a long anarchy. Lake crushed all opposition in the field when he turned the Franco-Mahratta armies out of Hindustan; but fifteen years elapsed

* "Imperial Gazetteer of India." Vol. V. (art. "Gwalior State.")

before order was entirely established by the capture of Háthras. These things being duly considered, the prosperity of Upper Burma since the annexation cannot be denied. Roads, railways, and works of irrigation have been set on foot; the brigand bands have at last been dispersed and driven out of the country; any trouble from the raiding of borderers will continue to be duly encountered, and will, it is hoped soon disappear.

Few other incidents marked this fortunate period, the most notable being the commencement of what has been called "The Congress Movement," set going by a few advanced politicians, one of whom had been a Secretary to Government. The movement aimed at the removal of certain alleged grievances by constitutional methods. Meeting annually at some central place—Madras, Bombay, Calcutta, Allahabad—the Congress drew up proposals for infusing an elective principal into the Legislature, for admitting Natives of India to the Volunteer ranks, and for separating the judicial branch of the Public Service from that which discharged executive functions. In some of their projects the reformers have been, perhaps, premature, but the principle of self-government seems taking root. Thus, the Indian Councils Act of 1892 has recognised that the numbers of the Native Councillors ought to be increased, and, while leaving to the Local Government the determination of details, has yet distinctly pledged it to the introduction of elected members into the Legislature, and even into the Executive it may be; though that may not come quite yet. Great care will doubtless be taken to give a due share to representatives of the Muhamadan community whose social condition is believed to be in urgent need of amelioration.

In our next and concluding section we must take a brief view of the past, with a general estimate of present social results, and a summary out-look towards the immediate future. The purely historical part of our work may well end with Her Imperial Majesty's Jubilee, in 1887, when the leading men of all classes in India exhibited their loyal feelings in a manner which will challenge fair comparison with similar celebrations in any part of the Empire.

The Finance-Minister during Lord Dufferin's rule was Sir Auckland Colvin, afterwards (21st Nov. 1887) Lieutenant-Governor of the North-West Provinces. In 1886 Lord Connemara—brother to the lamented Mayo—succeeded Sir M. E. Grant-Duff as Governor of Madras: in the preceeding year Sir J. Fergusson had given over charge of Bombay to Lord Reay. The administration of Sir Mountstuart Grant-Duff has been described in some able and sympathetic Minutes which are well worth the trouble of perusal. They throw new and unexpected lights on the land, tenures, antiquities, etc., of the territories under the Presidency of Fort S. George.

[Consult the "Annual Register," from 1884 to 1887: The "Calcutta Review" for the same period: and Parliamentary Papers on Burma. Also "Minutes by the Governor," 1884-6 Madras, 1886-7.]

SECTION 3.—The history of India, which we here close, presents certain features of resemblance with that of Italy; a country imperfectly protected by a northern wall of snowy mountains; held for a long time by a dominant race; sinking its nationality till it became a mere "geographical expression"; and then, after the lapse of many troubled ages, beginning to make progress towards unity. Indeed, such a unity was long ago an ideal of India's more earnest minds; though often interrupted by dreary spaces of discord and anarchy, and only realised at last under the slow tentative processes of an alien occupation. When the British Empire of India was first formulated by Lord Hastings* nothing could appear less like

* "Our object in India ought to be to render the British Government paramount, in effect if not declaredly so . . . and to oblige the other States to perform the great feudatory duties of supporting our rule with all their forces, and submitting their differences to our arbitration." [Private Journal already referred to.]

the *Bhart-Kand* of the ancients; no Asoka was there, issuing benevolent edicts to willing hearers, no Vikram delivering his people from barbarian invaders. Nevertheless Lord Hastings was making—perhaps unconsciously—an appeal to the same sort of instinct, the general desire for brotherly peace if not for national existence, the craving for rest which might lead eventually to prosperous advance. Once only before—during the darkness of the centuries that succeeded the Empire of Asoka--had this ideal appeared like a pillar of fire to guide the people: the great and good Akbar had during a long reign done something towards an imperial foundation. But there was no machinery to Akbar's hand by which his scheme could be matured or made durable; and the anarchy which succeeded to the collapse of his great-grandson's attempts was the worst and the longest that India had ever known.

Then appeared upon the scene a new spirit: that of maritime adventure and extension of trade, faintly touched—here and there—by the hand of political ambition. This has been clearly shown by a brilliant modern writer who has had the skill to make Indian subjects attractive and to teach in writing the lessons he had learned in a high and varied experience. Speaking of the commencement of modern Eastern commerce, Sir Alfred Lyall has shown how the rivalry of the Dutch nearly expelled the British from India in the days of the Stuarts; how the latter gradually recovered their position in the last quarter of the 17th century; and how the old Company of that period desired to found their trade upon the basis of Empire, and even ventured to try conclusions with the might of Aurangzeb. In December 1687—when Sir Josiah Child was Chairman—the Directors of what was then a merely commercial association, wrote to their factors at Fort S. George a despatch even stronger than the letter of two years later which Sir Alfred has cited in his book.* "That which we promise ourselves in a

* "Rise of British Dominion in India." (University Extension Manual) by Sir Alfred Lyall, K.C.B., D.C.L. London, 1893.

most especial manner from our new President and Council is that they will establish such a polity of civil and military power, and create and secure such a large revenue to maintain both at that place, as may be the foundation of a large, well-grounded, sure English dominion in India for all time to come."* This was, indeed, to strike the Imperial note; yet it was mainly the premature enthusiasm of one man, or at most of two. For the scheme was bound to defeat by the double difficulty of time and place; nor was Child's brother, Sir John, the wisest leader to whom the conduct of the enterprise could have been confided on the spot. The result was a complete failure: the Company's agents could not obtain more than a mere foothold in the Carnatic, for which they not only had to pay rent, but on more than one occasion to hand over a heavy ransom when threatened with attack. An attempt that they made, with truer instinct, to obtain a permanent lodgement on the Bengal coast led to their entire expulsion. It was more than half a century before they were able to secure the position in the Delta of the Ganges which was ultimately to become the basis of an Empire.

Then came the momentary triumph of the French in India; the bold and far-reaching endeavour of Dumas and Dupleix. These men, successively vested with the status of Imperial Deputies, took possession of Madras, and seemed likely to extirpate British trade and influence from the Carnatic. The turning-point, however, was attained in 1756, when Dupleix was abandoned by his employers in France and his successor, Godeheu, made peace with the British of the South. In the following year Clive was enabled to take the bulk of the Madras forces to Bengal win the battle of Plassy, and make the Calcutta Council paramount in Bengal. Then came the

* "Report on the old records of the India Office," by Sir G. Birdwood, K.C.I.E. London 1891.

series of events recorded in our CHAPTER VII. The battle of Baksar and the grant of the Diwáni, giving Clive a legitimate position, at the same time that Coote crushed the last resistance of the French, left the Company supreme in the whole vast eastern regions from Lucknow to Tanjore. But the supremacy had been won by slow degrees and almost unconsciously.

The explanation appears to be that the agents of France had made a mistake in endeavouring to establish an Empire at the wrong place and before events were ripe. The French Company grew weary of efforts which had no apparent result; and the Government of Louis XV. shrank from the continual strain upon their naval and military resources. The British on the other hand, confining themselves to the work of the present, and always looking to immediate objects of attainment, availed themselves of the day of small things until greater prospects opened naturally.

The Home-Government then stepped in. Having always a good squadron of war-ships in Indian waters, and having—ever since 1754—begun to strengthen the Company's hands by sending out battalions of the British army, they now—1773—passed an Act of Parliament for the regulation of the Company's administration whereby the nation became committed to a scheme of Empire* and a share in the grave responsibilities of dominion in Asia.

Adam Smith, the great British publicist of the day, drily remarked upon this: "To found a great Empire for the sole purpose of raising up a people of customers may at first sight appear a project only worthy a nation of shopkeepers." But it was that practical spirit that first gave them the political power; the subsequent interposition of the King's Government, by which conquest was completed, being only due to the fact that the Company had found itself unable to secure customers otherwise than by founding an Empire.

* 13 George III. c. 63.

The rest of the process was, perhaps, a foregone conclusion, but it did not seem so at the time. The great projects of Wellesley alarmed the Company and brought about his resignation and the attempts of his successors to stop the flowing tide of dominion. The Marquess of Hastings was ere long forced, by circumstances for which he was hardly at all answerable, to make his country the paramount power all over the Peninsula. Then matters again seemed to become stationary until the wars of Hardinge and the annexations of Dalhousie prepared the scene for the complete incorporation of all India in the Empire. The work had been done by statesmen unavoidably charged with almost autocratic power, acting often independently, sometimes in positive disobedience of the policy desired in London. "I suppose you will hang me for this," wrote Wellesley to Pitt after the conquest of Sindia. Lord Hastings completed the destruction of the Mahratta power almost as an episode in the suppression of the Pindaris undertaken against the expressed opinions of Canning.

The abolition of the Company in 1858 removed the fictitious government of the "Secret Committee," and left the Ministry of Great Britain in open and responsible exercise of the controlling power, which was very much strengthened by the telegraphic connection between the two countries The existing system, therefore, while preserving features of resemblance to that of earlier days, is actually something very different. The Secretary of State, like his predecessor, the President of the Board of Control, is a member of the Cabinet, and his Council, in some degree, represents the Court of Directors, departmentally divided so that each group can be consulted by the Secretary in regard to the affairs of each department; while resolutions involving the expenditure of Indian funds require the concurrence of a majority of all the members. But in political affairs the work is done in the "Secret Department," where the will of the Secretary, as a member of the Imperial Government, is supreme. Hence it has sometimes happened of late years that a Viceroy belonging to the party out of power at home has received such sudden and unpalatable orders that he has been unable to retain his office. Nevertheless it seems as if the strange elements of Indian administration renders the whole class of subjects distasteful to politicians absorbed in less remote interests; and there is thus a certain tendency to leave India a kind of Home Rule still.

Thus the Viceroy—or Governor-General-in-Council—has in ordinary times a good deal of initiative, especially if he be in cordial relations with the Ministry of the day. The nature of his Councils has been already explained, the one a Cabinet of high officials, each in charge of a department, and the Viceroy being an active member (generally in charge of foreign and political affairs); while the other is a purely legislative assembly in which elected members are now being associated. The bills are brought forward on the initiative of the Cabinet, private legislation being unknown. At the first reading they are debated, and—some of the members being Native Chiefs and others independent Europeans—it may well chance that a strenuous opposition is raised, and that the Bill undergoes serious modifications: the debates are held in public, and fully reported in the "Gazette." After the second reading it goes into committee, when the comments and objections of the Press and outside public are considered: the Bill, as amended, then passes the third reading, after which the sanction of the Viceroy is mostly a matter of course; but a strict ordeal has yet to be faced when the Act is transmitted to London. It sometimes happens that the changes it has gone through in the last stages of its progress through Council bring censure and dissent upon a law originally framed with the approval of the Secretary of State. In such a case correspondence, delay, and even further changes may be entailed. Still, on the whole, it may be said that—always subject to the Viceroy being generally in accord with the home Government—India enjoys a fair amount of legislative independence.

The law of British India may be considered in four classes:

1. The common law of the Hindus, and that of the Muslims or Muhamadans.

2. The regulations of the Governors-General and of the minor Presidencies, passed before 1833.

3. The Penal code and connected Procedure.

4. The later statutes regulating matters not covered by the common-law of either of the great religious bodies.

As to the first, something has been already observed; it need only here be added that Hindu and Muslim law are administered under a tacit compact arising from the origin of British power, which was not based—as in the case of Ireland—upon any complete subjugation of hostile races, but rather resembled (in this respect) the conquest of Canada or the Mauritius. The people made no general resistance, but passed with little or no friction from the hands of one set of alien rulers into those of another and more efficient class. The British occupation being in its very essence one that made for order, was bound either to respect existing institutions or to introduce new. And since the inhabitants were already in possession of ancient systems resting on a religious sanction, it was natural to adopt the former method.*

In regard to the second class of laws, it will be enough to say, that, with the exception of two or three bearing on revenue, the Regulations have been entirely superseded or absolutely repealed.

As to the Penal Code and Procedure, it may be claimed without fear of contradiction that they have been universally

* For a summary of the Company's original position the reader may consult the judgment of Lord Brougham in the case of the Mayor of Lyons. For further details on Law see App. II.

accepted all through India, as a reform and boon of the clearest kind. The young learn the Code as a school-book; it is adopted in Native States, and in the absence of a Law of Torts, the Code is freely used by the bulk of the population in the interior as a means of enforcing specific performance, obtaining redress or revenge, and settling the controversies of daily life. Being applicable to all parts of the country, the Penal Code, forms a bond of unity, almost an ideal of moral conduct.

The more recent enactments of the Government of India have taken the shape of small Codes on special subjects. Mortgage, Contract, Easement, the law of Evidence, the regulation of Land Revenue, Rent, and Tenure, were all subjects lying outside of what may be called the Levitical purview of the ancient Common-Law of the Hindus. The law of Islám being more modern, touches upon some of these matters and where it does so will probably be duly considered by the Courts. But strict and absolutely legal provisions are a necessity of growing communities, and there is an increasing tendency among the peoples of India, generally, to submit their disputes to the clear and impartial arbitrament of Anglo-Indian law.

In these explanations we have been looking at the results arrived at by the gradual development of British power in that part of India which has been directly incorporated in the Empire. But there are many large tracts in which Native authority has been maintained; from the Nizám's country—as large as the United Kingdom of Great Britain and exercising almost complete sovereignty—to some little fief in Western India not very distinguishable from a private estate. The total area of what is called "Feudatory Territory" is over six hundred thousand square miles. These countries have in most instances their own laws and institutions; some of them coin their own money and have courts exercising plenary powers over life and property. They mostly pay annual tribute or contribution towards local contingents, and many of them also maintain troops for Imperial service, under instruction and inspection of European officers assigned by the Government for that peculiar duty.

The legislative authority of the Government of India does not extend to the vassal-states, whose relations with that Government are carried on through the Foreign Office. Nor does the power of the Legislature extend in ordinary practice to the making of laws for the special use of the various great Provinces. In the older Provinces, or "Presidencies" there are two Councils exactly resembling those of the Governor-General, save that they are subject to his control, in virtue of the "Charter" of 1833—more properly 3 and 4 Will. IV., c. 85. Bengal obtained the power of making its own local laws in 1861: and a Legislative Council for the North-West Provinces was created in 1887. All these bodies differ from the usual British and Colonial model in essential particulars; besides their partially non-elective character they are differentiated by the want of financial and administrative controlling power; and it is to be noted that measures begun in one session, but not completed, are carried forward to the next, instead of lapsing and requiring for final enactment to be reintroduced and discussed *de novo.*

But the most un-English peculiarity of Indian Government is one that lies at the very bottom of the whole administrative fabric. The integer of management, and the concrete image of the British rule as presented to mankind in India, is the District-Officer. An Indian District is in point of area and population something corresponding to an English county or shire. But the Officer in whom the charge is vested answers to nothing known in England, Scotland, or Ireland, and resembles much more nearly the Prefect in some European countries. On him devolves the supervision of almost every branch of administration and collective life, in all India beyond the great seaport towns. In the latter, municipal authorities and stipendiary courts divide many of the duties; and, if ever the *Mufassal* becomes ripe for the introduction of Lord Ripon's policy, such may be the system there also. But at present, however he may be aided by District Councils, Local Boards, and other popular machinery, the officer variously known as Magistrate-and-Collector, or as Deputy-Commissioner, still retains great influence, and the strings of many agencies converge in his office. This idea, foreign to British conceptions, must be regarded as a survival from Mughal times, though the jealous and suspicious nature of that Government disposed it to divide between the Faujdar and the Diwan the duties which in British India are centred in the same man.* The total number of Districts in British India, of one sort or other, is now returned as 235, the larger being in the Madras territories where there is no intermediate officer between the District and the State; in the rest of India the Districts are grouped in Divisions over each of which is a supervising authority called "Commissioner," whose business it is to see that the principles and rules of the one are carried out in the administration of the other.

The items of Revenue administered by the District Officers—under the control of the Board of the Province—form the chief sources of the State's income, and this at once accounts for a great part of the importance of these posts. Taking the net Revenue to be, roughly, about 50 millions (Rx), nearly 70 per cent. of that sum comes from those sources—land, excise, provincial rates, and assessed taxes; of which the land revenue alone is over 20 millions. So far as can be learned the land-revenue does not act as a tax, being merely a portion of the

* This Mughal system extended to the administration of larger groups than Districts, and this explains Clive's "Dual Government" under which the Company's agents exercised the fiscal power in Bengal while the police etc., were still under the Nawáb. Some even of the Districts were of excessive area. That of Bellari, for example, was as large as the kingdom of Belgium, it has recently been divided.

rent—and a less portion than was ever taken by any former Government. The wise and moderate Akbar claimed a third of the *gross* produce; the system introduced under Bentinck aimed at taking between 65 and 75 per cent. of the net profits of which the modern Governments only demand 50 per cent., or one-half; and this is estimated to mean from one-eighth to one-tenth of the gross yield according to the strictness of the scrutiny. The rate per acre also varies in various parts, being six times as high in Sindh as in the adjoining Punjab. The average rate—for all India with the exception of Bengal—is less than a rupee and a half. The preponderance of the rural revenues and the agricultural population* must be taken into consideration when we find an officer of such high rank and power bearing the humble title of "Collector." The agrarian prosperity of the rural districts is the nucleus of the national welfare, as the revenue collected from the land is the sheet-anchor of Finance; and all this depends on him.

For the items received by the Collector form the irreducible minimum of the State's income: otherwise there is no obligatory or unavoidable tax in India, with the single exception of the excise on salt, which acts as a poll-tax at the rate of about two Rs. a year for a family of five. This is the contribution of the masses to the cost of administration; and there are many millions of families in the country who pay nothing else whatever. The rest of the taxation falls on the well-to-do.

The question, doubtless, may still be asked, whether a civilised administration be any benefit to such a community, whether it is even worth sixpence a head *per annum?* The happiness—it may be argued—of a people consisting mainly of ploughmen, and their wives and children, ought not to be altogether measured by the extension of railway-communication, or the increase of commerce in a few seaports. Such crude tests may be those by which it is easiest to exhibit the progress

* Estimated at 70 per cent. of the whole inhabitants of India.

of a country; and, so judged, India can be shown to have made enormous progress since—say—the accession of King William the Fourth, and the new Government of India Act of 1833, above cited. But it is still conceivable that the people at large may be affected injuriously by some of the elements of that advance. It is at times accompanied—for instance—by a rise of prices which will not benefit those who have nothing to sell but their labour; and no power to procure a commensurate rise of wages. Those who have lived up the country have seen, in periods of scarcity, the spectacle of railway-trucks carrying away the food which the people cannot afford the means of purchasing at the rate which that food will sell at other places. Here the labourer suffers alike from the rise of prices and the fall in the cost of transport. Again the interest of money does not appear to decrease in proportion to the improvement in the security on which it is borrowed. When the exorbitant rates of interest that prevail in rural India first became customary there were no cheap and impartial tribunals to enforce the payments of debts, nor any fixed ownership of land to be foreclosed on default of payment, yet the agriculturalists are still in the habit of raising money at 36 per cent. and even higher, on good mortgages, or bonds which can be taken into a small-cause court and proved; and in such a court decrees can be obtained in a few days and executed, if need be, by the whole force of a great Empire. Rapid and certain justice is a beneficial product of civilisation; but it may not be felt as such by a poor debtor, compelled to discharge a debt doubled by a rate of interest which arose out of very different conditions.

But of all the transient troubles due to the establishment of good government, the greatest is probably that caused by the removal of restraints on the fecundity of the population. No accurate census was taken till the year 1871; but, so far as can be judged from previous estimates, the population of British

India doubled itself in the sixty years ending with that of the last enumeration. The Province of Bengal alone now contains as much as nine millions in excess of the United States, whose territory is twenty-three times as large; and in many of the rural districts of Hindustan there are more human beings on a square mile of culturable land than are to be found in the most crowded parts of Belgium. So far as this increase is kept pace with, by the improvement of production and of general welfare, it affords matter of congratulation.* But it implies other things also: increased competition and anxiety for a people mainly dependent on agriculture, increased difficulty for rulers responsible for the welfare of such a rapidly increasing multitude.

It was mentioned above that Sir John Lawrence, when Viceroy of India, issued circulars to select officers, in which he called for opinions as to the relative happiness of the people under British and Native systems of administration. It was something of the nature of a leading question; and the veteran civilian prompted the reply by suggesting that the British subjects were happier, if they only knew it. The real question, however, was, or ought to have been, were the people happier on their own belief and in their own way? It may very well be that the average man prefers the ease of an uncrowded scene; while the lottery of life, the chance of a prize among a large number of certain blanks, might prove more acceptable to men of exceptional ambition than the most ably-administered dead-level. Moreover some of the more substantial advantages of British arms and British commerce extend to all alike, whether ruled by Rájas and Nawábs or by Collectors and Commissioners.

There is no branch of Indian administration more efficient

* The general rate for British India is 234 per square mile, the rate in Native States being but little over 100. The rate of increase between 1881 and 1891 has sunk to 9·5 or less than one p.c. per annum, and in some parts has begun to disappear.

for feudatory, and non-feudatory, than the machinery that keeps the peace, hinders robbery by land and sea, and protects the capitalist and the producer. But the cost is enormous, and it falls exclusively on British subjects. A quarter of the gross expenditure, at least, goes to the two heads of "Marine" and "Army." The total strength of the latter force is 218,805 officers and men, of whom nearly a third consists of Europeans, and this relatively small army involves a yearly cost of about twenty millions (Rx.) Another very heavy item of expenditure is due to what are known as "home-charges," estimated at sixteen millions (sterling); and this, having to be made good in depreciated rupees, involves a great and increasing cost in what is called "loss by exchange." The home-charges are composed, partly at least, of sums paid for services past and present, such as civil and military pensions, the charges incurred for the India-Office and the purchase of stores, interest on loans, and private remittances: all these being represented by the Secretary of State's bills, bought in London by mercantile men, who want to send money out to India, and paid for at the current exchange of the day. The rest of the value of her excess-imports India receives in treasure; a sum which averages ten krors—or millions of Rx.—part of which is hoarded, but which is, to a great extent, coined and added to the currency, in which form it goes to stimulate production.

These items* may be taken to form an aggregate of nearly forty millions of Rx., which happens to be about the equivalent of the actual taxation of British India, including the land revenue. The rest of the administration, Civil, Public Works, Education, etc., (the Post Office just paying its own outlay) is maintained out of other sources of Revenue, such as Opium, Railways, Canals, and receipts not derived from the taxpayer. But, as we see, the people of India pay, in taxes or in rent, the

* Army, etc.	Excess exports.	Loss by Exchange.
21,000,000	16,000,000	2,250,000

cost of their protection and general relations to the master-country, and are entitled to do all that they fairly can to get full value for their money. In answer to such a claim, the present Government can point to a rate of wages, which if it be still too low, has risen threefold since the days of Akbar; to a taxation which the bulk of the people can almost wholly escape; to a fixed, if inexorable, charge upon the land. And it is a distinct gain, if, in spite of some rise in prices, articles of decent comfort, such as piece-goods for wearing apparel, are still easily to be procured.

This on the whole, must be allowed to be a good record. The troubles above mentioned are a drawback which will yield to time and knowledge, being mainly due to the fact of the administration being, we need not say "too good," but inspired by ideas to which the people have not as yet quite attained. As the rate of increase in population diminishes, (which it has already shown signs of doing,) as education improves and extends, the benefits of peace and order will be more appreciated, and more reasonable ideals will take the place of much that is still unsocial and backward. If we look back at the misgovernment of the Mughals and the anarchy that followed, we shall see the justification of such hopes. An able Russian publicist has stated this in terms which it might have seemed ungraceful for an English writer to employ:—

"In reality," wrote the late Michael Katkoff in the *Moscow Gazette*, "in reality the English have been the saviours of India. During whole centuries the history of India presents one continued spectacle of murder and devastation. The bloody era terminates with the Conquest of India by the English, whose Government has been more mild, humane, and just than all the Governments under which the Hindus have ever lived." *

* Katkoff (died 1887) has been called the apostle of Russian ideas, and the representative of his country's Chauvinism. At least he was a favourer of ideas not usual amongst Englishmen, and that is just what gives his testimony the greater value. The date of the above extract has been unhappily mislaid.

[The subjects summarised in this Section are treated in detail in the reports of "Moral and Material progress" presented to Parliament yearly, and especially in Sir W. Hunter's "Indian Empire," London, 1893, an able and exhaustive review of past events and present conditions. The works of Sir G. Birdwood and Sir A. C. Lyall cited on the margin are also worth a reference, though some of the conclusions in the text are at variance with those of the last-named.

The latest financial report, dated Calcutta, March 23, shows an estimated deficit for the year 1892-93, of over one million Rx. The fall in exchange below the rate originally taken as a basis of calculation has caused an addition to the expenditure, without which there would have been a small surplus.* A similar deficit is looked for in 1893-94, and from the same cause; and it is explained that the fall in exchange has, in two years, added Rx.4,142,400 to the expenditure, or an increase of ten per cent. on the net outgoings annually. The Government declares that India is solvent, but evidently regards with anxiety the increasing home-charges and the decreasing value of the Rupee.]

* By recent regulations the Indian mints have been closed to free coinage and a governmental rate has been affixed to the rupee. But the difficulty, though thus temporarily evaded, cannot be regarded as finally solved.

END OF VOL. II.

APPENDIX I.

THE GENESIS OF THE FIRST AFGHAN WAR.

BY the courtesy of the India Office in allowing access to the despatches of the period—never before published, or only in an imperfect form—the whole facts of the case are now, for the first time, forthcoming.

The earliest symptom of the movement appears in the Secret Committee's Letter of 25th June, 1836, when the Foreign Office was under Lord Palmerston, and Sir J. C. Hobhouse was President of the Board of Control. The Secret Committee was—it must be remembered—obliged to send out to India whatever instructions might be ordered by His Majesty's Government for the time being. The year 1836 was the last year of the reign of King William the IV., and the easy going Lord Melbourne was nominally head of the Ministry. These things being premised, it will hardly be too much to assume if we attribute the origin of the instructions to the Foreign Secretary.

In the letter above cited there is clear evidence that the information from Persia was beginning to cause apprehension in Palmerston's mind, that the new Sháh of that country was being pushed forward to the line of the Indus by Russian instigation, which it was desirable to counteract, yet not to directly oppose. It states that from information, supplied by Mr. Ellis—who was about to resign his mission in Persia—it appeared that, so early in the year as the month of February, overtures had been received by the Persian Court from Dost Muhamad, relative to a conquest and partition of the territories on the border then held by Kamran, the head of the Popalzai clan.* The Khan of Khiva was also understood to be entering into engagements with the Government of the

* This most improbable story—resting on mere gossip—was completely at variance with all that subsequently came out.

Czar. The Governor-General was therefore enjoined to watch affairs in those quarters, and to counteract the progress of Russian influence, either by a political or commerical mission, as in his discretion might seem best. He would also hear from the new British Minister at Teheran—Mr. McNeill, to whom the Government in London would communicate their instructions.*

Doubtless, this was the original ground of Auckland's frigid letter to the Dost when, on assuming charge of the Government, in India, he received that potentate's application for advice and assistance in his controversy with Ranjit Sinh, the Maharája of Lahore. Failing to obtain satisfaction from the Governor-General, Dost Muhamad turned to the Sháh of Persia for aid against the Sikhs. In July, 1837, the Sháh advanced upon Herát; but by that time Burnes was well on his way to Cabul, and had received letters of welcome from the Dost, informing him of the arrival at Cabul of a Russian envoy, and promising to "pay no attention," to him until Burnes should make his appearance. Burnes also heard from McNeill that he had intercepted correspondence between the Russian Minister at Teheran and the Dost's rebellious brethren at Candahar.

The next important stage in the instructions sent to India through the Secret Committee is a letter dated 10th May, 1838; in which the Governor-General is informed that, in consequence of the receipt by the Dost of a letter from the Emperor Nicholas, Burnes is to be ordered to withdraw from Cabul unless the Dost will give up all comunication with Russia. At the same time he is warned against doing anything calculated to lead to controversy with the Court of St. Petersburg. [This despatch was one of the two London letters included in the Blue-Book of 1859.]

On the 22nd of the same month, Auckland reported the withdrawal of Burnes from Cabul, and enclosed his Minute of the 12th, with copy of his instructions to Macnaghten for the negotiation with Ranjit and Sháh Shuja, which resulted in the Tripartite Treaty. The Governor-General admitted that the "emergency" and the "rapid march of events," might compel him to act without awaiting instructions from London.

* This letter is cited in the Governor-General's despatch of 13th August, 1838 as the foundation of his subsequent action.

On the 13th of August Auckland reported the fullest details of Macnaghten's negotiations, and assumed the entire responsibility of the projected restoration of the Saduzai monarchy, as stated in the text, and he refers to the Government Committee's letters of June, 1836, and May, 1838, as justification. But before that letter had reached the British Government a despatch had been by them dictated to the Secret Committee in which the policy had been sanctioned by anticipation. This, by far the most important of the papers in question, bears date October 24th, 1838, and is deserving of textual quotation :—

"We have heard," the Committee are made to say, "with the utmost regret that the mission of Capt. Burnes has failed, and that a Russian agent has been openly received at Cabul."

"We have hitherto declined to take part in the intestine dissensions of the Afghán State . . . But as our efforts to cultivate a closer acquaintance with Dost Muhamad have failed, and his brothers at Candahar have thrown themselves into the arms of a power whose approach to the Indus is incompatible with the safety of her Majesty's Indian possessions,* it becomes our imperative duty to adopt a policy by which Cabul and Candahar may be united under a sovereign bound . . . to become and remain the faithful ally of Great Britain." Such a prince, they add, is Sháh Shuja ; and they are disposed to concur in the opinion offered by Wade on January 1st. "A comparatively insignificant effort," they think, would suffice, but the Governor-General must take "means to prevent almost all possibility of failure."

This letter was forwarded by the Malta mail of October 27th, *one day after the arrival of Auckland's despatch of May 22nd ;* and in a subsequent letter, dated November 9th, the Committee, referring to their last, observe :—

"You will have seen . . . that, previous to the receipt of your advices . . . we had determined on recommending the course which you had, without any knowledge of our wishes, determined to pursue."

So far, then, one seems to perceive a sort of competition between

* This phrase is remarkable : India was then supposed to be in the possession of the Company ; but here the Company is utterly ignored. The passage teems with assumptions.

London and Simla for the discredit of initiating the ill-starred project. But in less than a month there comes a note of wise but tardy caution. On December 4th, the Committee hopes that His Excellency has made every effort to conciliate the Dost, and that he has full persuasion of the Sháh's popularity and ability to maintain himself in power without "continued and manifest interference of the British Government."*

By that time the Bengal column had assembled at Firozpore; and, before the letter could have been received, was well on its way to join the Bombay column in Sind. Yet the warning might well have been born in mind, and had it been acted upon when Sháh Shuja was enthroned in the Bala Hissar of Cabul, much disaster might have been averted by discontinuing the manifest interference.

Finally, on December 21st, a last despatch was sent out, acknowledging the declaration of August 13th, in which Auckland announced his determination "to give the direct and powerful assistance of the British Government to the enterprise of Sháh Shuja in a degree which was not in the first instance contemplated." This was not contravened, or even noticed.

From the papers it can only be concluded that the mind of Lord Auckland had been gradually influenced, until he became impressed with the necessity of substituting the Saduzai dynasty—the "Duranic Empire" as it was called—for the Amirate of the Dost, led thereto by fear of Persia and Russia. But it appears almost equally certain that the British Ministry made that policy their own; not merely by adoption but by prior suggestion and subsequent encouragement, so that they would even have enjoined it on the Governor-General if he had not originated it himself. Without seeing private correspondence, long since beyond reach, no more can be known; but Palmerston did much of his work, it is understood, by that channel, in India known as "semi-official."

* The tone of this letter almost suggests another hand. The "chairs" of the period were Sir J. R. Carnac, Sir Jas. Lushington, Sir R. Jenkins, and Mr. B Bayley, all experienced Indian statesmen.

APPENDIX II.

NOTE ON INDIAN LAW.

IN a brief work, such as is here undertaken, details of the Law and Administration will not be expected. The general principles have been stated from time to time, as occasion arose; so that the student may be able to judge of the progressive course of Britain's work in India. The labours of the civil reformer have never been long in arrear of the work of the soldier or politician; and a congeries of Eastern communities has been—or is being—welded into an organic whole. In order, however, to aid the appreciation of this task and of the degree to which it has been performed, it may be useful to take a rapid view of the progress of British Indian legislation from the passing of the Statute 13, Geo. III., c. 63, when the Royal—or "Supreme"—Court for Bengal was established by Act of Parliament. Instances have been shown, in preceding pages, of unseemly conflicts of jurisdiction between the Court and the local authorities: scandals which were reproduced in subsequent years at Bombay. Nevertheless, the intention and effect of the measure were fully determined ultimately. The Court was to have authority in the Presidency-town where it was placed; and all European British subjects, resident in the dependent territory, were liable to its applications of English Law. A further interpretation established the doctrine that the English Law so applied meant all non-repealed Statutes in force up to 1726, the date of the first introduction of English jurisprudence by the foundation of the so-called "Mayor's Courts" at Calcutta, Madras, and Bombay. And this included, of course, all Statutes that might be passed by Parliament with special advertence to British India. The Hindu and Muhamadan populations beyond the urban limits of the three Factories remained subject to the special systems of their respective religions: but the Governor-General exercised the power of framing Regulations, with the aid and assent of his

Council. That power was expressly conferred by the Act of Parliament above cited; and was also exercised by the minor Governments, of Madras and Bombay, before the end of the eighteenth century. These ordinances had all the force of law, but with an understanding that they were not to alter the privileges of Hindus and Muslims in regard to civil causes. Their chief scope was in introducing some degree of humanity and logic into criminal justice, and in giving order and permanence to fiscal administration, especially in regard to land; and the Regulations have now, for the most part, become obsolete, even when not positively repealed. The Bengal Code of Cornwallis, in 1793, and the Code of Elphinstone at Bombay, are the most conspicuous examples of this almost extinct Regulation-law. Both have been mentioned in this work.*

It has also been related in the proper place how, when the Company's Charter was renewed in 1833, the making of laws for all India was vested in a special Legislative Chamber (v. Vol. II., p. 145), and a Ministry of Law was constituted and intrusted to Macaulay, who was also appointed Member of an Indian Law Commission. This Commission prepared the Indian Penal Code —which was not finally enacted till 1860—and also drafted a variety of valuable reports. The Indian laws henceforth ceased to be called "Regulations," and became known by the more formal name of "Acts": such a number of such a year with a general title, *e.g.*, "Act XIX. of 1873, Land-Revenue, North-West Provinces." The constitution of the Chamber—or Legislative Council —has undergone changes, from time to time; and H.M. Judges of the Chartered Courts are not now allowed seats. Lastly, an attempt has been lately made to introduce something of the representative element; but this is too recent to admit of any record of its operation. These Councils are now to be found in all the main divisions of the Indian Empire; but the Council of the Viceroy is supreme over those of Madras, Bombay, Bengal, and the North-West Provinces, whilst it still legislates directly for the Punjab, Central Provinces, Burma, and Asam.† The subjects as to which

* Vol. I., 284-91. Vol. II., 106. For Madras Regulations, Vol. II., 72.

† The Viceroy can still issue Regulations for certain backward tracts, scheduled in a special Act.

the supremacy of the Council is reserved include taxation, currency, postal administration, the Penal Code, and such-like matters with which the Local Legislators are expressly debarred from treating; and these subjects symbolise the unity of the Empire of which they are organic and universal elements.

It would be impossible within the limits of a work like this to describe all the subjects of even the Viceroy's legislation. The local laws are, of course, exclusively local; but the laws of Imperial character are in themselves too numerous, and often too technical, to be set forth in a brief chronicle. Regarded broadly, they will be found to fall into three classes:—

1st. The most important class—so far as the daily lives of the inhabitants of Indian countries are concerned—is that which deals with crimes and misdemeanours, and with the means by which they are to be prevented or punished. The grounds of this appreciation of Penal enactments, and Laws of Police and Procedure, will be briefly stated presently.

2nd. Almost equally vital in the affairs of a population chiefly occupied in agriculture are Laws connected with Rent, Revenue, and the tenure of land.

3rd. The last main group of enactments includes those which regulate Civil Procedure, Evidence, and all those relations of life and property which lie beyond the religious codes of the great religious denominations.

A few words must suffice to explain the nature of each class and to characterise some of the Statutes by which each subject is regulated. Those who are without personal experience of simple states of society may not find it easy to realise the degree to which the welfare of the people may become dependent on penal law and the officials by whom it is administered. When these latter are corrupt and unscrupulous persons capriciously applying an uncertain system, there are only two alternatives open to the people. The more submissive are reduced to a servitude which forbids all welfare or progress; the less submissive adopt a sort of outlawry, and seek in anarchy an escape from an almost intolerable oppression. As soon as British power became at all consolidated attention was necessarily drawn to these evils. The penal system —such as it was—belonged to the dead or dying rule of Islám;

and some notice of its peculiar character has been already recorded in connection with the reign of the orthodox Emperor Aurangzeb, or Álamgir I. (v. *sup.*, Vol. 1, p. 174). So early as the first administration of Cornwallis, Courts were established to administer what—though nominally the Muhamadan penal code—was already subjected to Western ideals. The rules of evidence were modified, the punishment of death was put under regulating limits, barbarous punishments were disallowed, principles of juridical reform were enunciated in the preambles to the laws. Some years later a further step was taken, when a Regulation was issued containing a schedule of miscellaneous offences punishable at the Magistrate's discretion within defined limitations. Finally, in 1840, an Act was passed giving the Magistracy a summary jurisdiction in regard to trespasses on land or houses which might be thought to threaten a breach of the peace. The combined result of all these measures was to gradually raise criminal law to a standard somewhat resembling that of civilisation; while at the same time, the habits of the people were weaned from club-law to litigation, and some remedy was provided for everyday wrongs in the absence of a formal Law of Torts. Parallel legislation attempted the reform of the Police, the facilitation of appeals, and the creation of popular confidence in the Courts of First-instance. The Law Commission of 1834 found in the Regulations a quantity of evidence as to the wants of the country; and it was ultimately found possible to draft a common code for the whole land from Pesháwar to Cape Comorin. This was the famous "Indian Penal Code" which, after twenty-six years of discussion, was finally shaped by Sir Barnes Peacock and became the law for all India soon after the abolition of the Company's rule. From whatever point we regard it the measure will appear equally useful. By accurate definitions and moderate limitations of sentence it guides the Courts without binding their discretion. By skilful adaptation to Eastern habits it wins the confidence of the people, while its scientific method recommends it as an instrument of popular instruction. Nor are these uses confined to British Provinces; for the Code is not only adopted in the tribunals of Native States but is also a class-book in many of their schools. Finally, the Indian Penal Code has the great merit of permanence: it is above all things desirable that the regulator of popular life should be certain and free from needless variation; and this merit the Code possesses in perfection, having been now in force for more than thirty years without requiring any organic change and hardly any serious interpretation. The Procedure by which this body of law is enforced has been somewhat less durable; yet here also organic change has been, to a great extent, avoided. Some changes of detail and some rulings from local Benches apart, the conduct of police-enquiries, and of criminal trials alike, has continued since 1862 to be guided by the same principles.

If this great and almost unqualified applause is due to criminal jurisprudence in modern India the like can hardly be postulated for the land-laws which have been passed for various parts of the Empire by the supreme legislature. The systems of the minor Provinces have been subject to control by the local legislatures; and the principles which have already been mentioned as prevalent in the administration of land and its revenues in the wide territories of Bengal, Bombay and Madras, have not admitted of very much legislative change. But there are still wider tracts, the North-West Provinces, the Central Province, Audh, and the Punjab —about 500,000 square miles, inhabited by over one hundred millions of people—for which legislative plans have been formed and reformed many times during the half century that succeeded the establishment of the Supreme Legislative Council. Such change is to be regretted, even though it can be accounted for. The provisions affecting the land were stereotyped in the original "Presidencies" with a heroic confidence engendered of benevolence and want of knowledge. When British administration began to spread northwards the minds of the rulers were becoming more cautious; they gained a sense of the difficulties inherent in the subject and were "sicklied o'er with the pale cast of thought." Some of these embarrassments have been noticed above (Vol. I., 413 ff., and II., 139 ff.); they involved cases and situations where the welfare of great communities was dependent on the decision of rulers who, however well-meaning, were not always well-informed; the best, probably, that could be then done was to make tentative arrangements and avoid all that could compromise the future. As knowledge extended and the tendency of measures was revealed by experience, mistakes could be corrected, the public aspirations satisfied, the confidence and concurrence of the people gradually gained. If these things are at last in a way of attainment, we need not too deeply deplore the blunders of the past. It should be added that the reservation of powers to the Legislative Council of India has not precluded that body from occasional interference with the local affairs of the minor Presidencies when large questions affecting the rural communities have been thought to call for such action. Instances where the Council of India has legislated for Bombay, Madras or Bengal, on other than reserved subjects, are infrequent; but enough of such cases have occurred to show that the principle is well established. Thus, between 1879 and 1888 there have been several Acts passed for the relief of indebted agriculturists in territories subject to the Government of Bombay, although the local council had power to deal with the matter, so far as statutory non-reservation went.* Again, in Bengal, the "Tenancy Act" of 1885—briefly described in the account of Lord Ripon's rule—was passed by the Governor-General in council, after discussion extending over three years, without any objection or action from the Government of Bengal.† Examples of this sort should be noted as indicating that the general delegation of non-reserved subjects has by no means extinguished the powers of the supreme legislature.

The last of our classes includes the question of Civil Codification such as was carried out in France under ordinances begun by Louis XIV., and terminating in the Code issued in 1810 by Napoleon I. To determine how far such a task could be profitably undertaken by the Government of British India much inquiry and discussion would be requisite. An attempt in this direction was made by Lord Lytton, and the result may be seen in the report of the Commission appointed by that nobleman.‡ The general effect was that—given certain conditions—a general Civil Code for all India would be a good thing; but that, until the conditions were fully ripe, the existing laws and precedents could only be part digested so far as certain specific matters were concerned. The reply of the

* v. Acts of the Legislative Council, XVII. of 1879, to XXIII of 1886.

† Act VIII. of 1885.

‡ The members of the Commission were Mr. Whitley Stokes, Sir Chas. Turner, and Mr. Justice West; and the Report was sent to the Secretary of State on December 5, 1879.

Secretary of State to the letter forwarding this report was received within the following year; and it conveyed sanction to the latter part of the proposal, while reserving opinion upon the general question of Codification. This question, indeed, is still far from finality. A common body of law for a vast geographical area supposes a social body with common interests and common ideals: if absolute unity does not exist there must at least be an evident tendency to unite; and then a common Code may accelerate the process of union. In the old French monarchy a traveller—according to Voltaire—had to change his laws as often as he changed his post-horses. Nevertheless, a strong federal tie had begun, ever since the days of Richelieu, to connect the various Provinces of France; and there was already a general readiness to respect and follow the Roman law; yet even so the work lasted more than a hundred years. Codification will be desirable and useful for British India when two processes have been clearly observed in active operation: There must be a fusion of races and a fusion of creeds. When British power was first established by the grant of the *Diwani* in 1765, the area of administration was almost confined to Bengal and Bihár; and, even there, three great legal systems competed for acceptance in regard to civil jurisprudence. The impossibility of reconciling the native laws with English principles was not, perhaps, at first accepted. "The British legislature," according to a competent contemporary, "instead of extending the laws of England into these remote, populous, and long-civilised countries, resolved to limit the administration of English law." Several statutes empowered the rulers of Bengal to make laws on this principle; and by 37, Geo. III., cap. 142, it was laid down as "essential to the future prosperity of the [country] that all regulations passed by the Government affecting the rights, properties or persons of the subjects should be formed into a regular Code." This projected Code was to "preserve—as much as can possibly be done—their institutions and laws to the people of Hindustan, and attemper them with the mild spirit of the British Government." * These aspirations naturally came to nothing; and fifteen years later

* "Hindustan" was only the Court idiom for India, and had no local meaning.

Harrington agreed with Sir James Mackintosh that "there was but one way of forming a Civil Code—namely, that of gradually building up the law in proportion as the facts arise which it is to regulate." In the meantime the Hindus and Muslims continue to live under their respective systems, founded on the archaic view of religion as a divine and supreme authority for the administration of man's relations and affairs. Nothing more alien to Western conceptions of law can be conceived. In European systems the proprietary possession, whether of land or of chattels, is usually regarded as absolute and individual, chattel only differing from land by certain accidental attributes. As a lawyer equally experienced in both systems has observed, "ownership in England may be joint, but the presumption will be to the contrary: it may be restricted, but only in special circumstances and under special provisions. In India, on the contrary, joint-ownership is the rule, and will be presumed until the contrary is proved." Such views of property throw great obstacles in the way of transfer; indeed, sales made without the consent of a number of co-sharers are often voided: akin to this is the hindrance of private contract arising out of Pre-emptive right. If contract be thus impeded by Hindu and Muhamadan ideas, much more is Codification opposed in the direction of succession, marriage, adoption, and many of the more familiar aspects and relations of human life. Yet all these, in addition to limitation, mortgage, and easement, have been made the subject of special statutes of the Indian legislature, avowedly intended to form so many chapters of a future Civil Code; but in all of them the necessities of the case have involved limitations of operation which make them (for the present) of no wider application than would attach to a British statute declared to be only binding on Socinians, Atheists and gipsies. More promising, perhaps, are the attempts that have been made to digest the local laws applicable to particular Provinces. The Punjab Laws Act—IV. of 1872—may be taken as a fair illustration of this class of law: though here, too, exception has had to be made of twelve main branches of domestic affairs.

We must therefore conclude with the Commissioners that "in the sense of a general assemblage of all the laws of a community no attempt has yet been made, in India, to satisfy the conception of a Code. The time for its realisation has evidently not arrived.' When the present social effervescence shall have subsided and the newly-constituted Councils have had time to grow into a national representation, use may be made of all the inquiries, discussions and experiments which alone have been hitherto possible. To cite once more the able and eloquent language of the report :—

"The experience of the world, the decay of superstitions, enable us now to go back with comparative intellectual freedom to really first principles. In pursuing this course we come upon springs of thought and action common alike to Hindu, Musalman, and Christian. At these we should pause and appropriate all that they can yield to us ; employ the results with frugal skill ; and having thus established the base-line and some of the principal points of our system, leave the developments of details to time, to the sure germination of sound thoughts, and to the action of the Courts continually checked in any tendency to aberration by the constraining influence of great and conspicuous landmarks."

When rulers and people shall be united a Code will be born on Indian soil, as if by natural process. Meanwhile we cannot do better than meditate upon those fine words of Edmund Burke :—

"Government is a practical thing, made for the happiness of mankind, and not to furnish a spectacle of uniformity for the gratification of visionary politicians."

[See Report of Commission, 1879. Also Chap. on Law, by Sir J. F. Stephen, in Hunter's "Life of Mayo." The author is much indebted to the kindness of Mr. S. Harvey James, Secretary in Leg. Dep., for other materials.]

APPENDIX III.

RECENT BOOKS ON INDIA.

SINCE the present work was undertaken a number of more or less important publications have appeared, showing the increased interest taken in the subject, and throwing upon it a variety of fresh lights.

Mr. Romesh Chunder Dutt's "Ancient India" is the first of what promises to be a useful series.* As explained by the Editor, Mr. John Adam, it will be the object of these monographs to correct the tendency of specialists to confine their attention, in working the field of Indian history, to "special periods or particular areas." In all such works he finds "a universal want of balance; the writer insensibly, but inevitably, brings to the front the epoch [which] he has studied in detail, or the district where his experience has been gained," The avowed object therefore of this series will be "to correct this tendency by assigning each epoch to a writer who has made it a subject of special research." The subjects already announced are: "Ancient India" (the volume now under notice); "The Muhammadans," or the History of Hindustan (including Bengal), by J. D. Rees, C.I.E.; "The Mahrattas," or the History of the Deccan, by the Hon K. T. Telang, C.I.E.; "The Dravidians," or the History of the Peninsula Proper, by the Editor; and, finally, "The British Power in India" from 1800 to the present time, by J. S. Cotton, the accomplished Editor of "The Academy," and biographer of Mountstuart Elphinstone. Mr. Dutt's work treats of the history of the country—or rather of the northern regions—from the uncertain date of the first Aryan invasions (here assumed at 2,000 B.C.) down to the approach of the Muslim Conquest. Dividing this long, but obscure, subject into five epochs. the

* "Epochs of Indian History," London, 1893.

author treats of each epoch respectively in four separate chapters; and his study will be found to embrace much interesting information on manners, belief, and practices, from the standpoint of a patriotic Hindu.

Mr. Adam's complaint against the specialists is hardly applicable to Sir W. Hunter's encyclopædic work which, after some tentative appearances, has now taken a definite form.* Originally an article n the "Britannica," then expanded into Vol. VI. of the "Imperial Gazetteer," it has had the benefit of frequent revision and of collaboration by many experts of various kinds, whose assistance is duly acknowledged. The present edition has but one serious blemish: has become too vast and heavy in bulk to be used with convenience, consisting of more than 850 pages, presenting a complete panorama of the entire dependency from every point of view, and brought down to the very latest date. The story and the statistics have been alike modernised; the history of religion in India has been re-written; the revenues of the Muslim Emperors have been re-examined under the light thrown on them by recent studies of the coins and metric standards of their times. There is also a general history, commencing with the earliest authentic records—which receive more critical treatment here than in Mr. Dutt's volume—and ending with the administration of Lord Lansdowne. A book so full of instruction deserves respectful attention, and will repay continual reference, both of which, however, might have been more fully commanded if it could have been cut in two. The student of history might then have found occupation in the first fifteen chapters, while a second volume would have furnished all requisite information to the journalist and to the member of Parliament.

The numismatic and metric records of the past have received fuller consideration from Mr. S. L. Poole in separate works.† The result is to lead to a higher estimate than that taken by the present

* "The Indian Empire: its Peoples, History, and Products," By Sir William Wilson Hunter, K.C.S.I., etc., etc. 1893.

† "Catalogue of Indian Coins in the British Museum," 1892. Aurangzeb. "Rulers of India," by S. L. Poole. etc., 1893.

[Mr. Poole has also contributed, on the subject of Mughal Revenues, to Sir W. Hunter's work.]

writer, so far as the revenues of the Mughal Empire are concerned. In regard to what has been sometimes termed the "casual" revenue, that derived from customs, fines, escheats, benevolences, etc., Mr. Poole admits uncertainty. Even in regard to land-revenue he appears to shrink from endorsing the extreme calculations of the late Edward Thomas. No "Turkish Ruler of India" could ever have had the financial skill to extort a permanent land-revenue of eighty millions of pounds sterling from the parts of the country included in the Mughal Empire in the period of its widest extent. The misconception arises, apparently, from the readiness of European visitors of those days to believe in the riches of a country which produced Peacock-thrones and Taj-Mahals. They were thus disposed to accept estimated maximum rent-rolls as if they were budgeted accounts based on actual averages of receipt. Moreover Mr. Poole gets some of these extravagant estimates by rendering French statements as if the writers used the *livre parisis*, whereas they referred to the *livre tournois*, which was only about three-fourths of the former. It is of the deepest importance to remember that India is, and always has been, an extremely poor country, and that the constant difficulty of its governors—one by no means destroyed by modern developments—is to introduce and maintain Occidental administration out of the resources supplied by an Oriental income.

The commencement of these modern developments receives important and interesting record from the labours of Sir George Birdwood.* Assisted by Mr. William Foster, the able and accomplished statistician of the India Office has put together two most valuable collections of early official papers bearing upon the establishment of the East India Company, with that of its trade, out of which such mighty consequences were to spring.

That the East India Company contemplated a territorial Empire from the first is the thesis of a remarkable book that has been already cited, the work of an author whose originality of thought is as undoubted as his clearness of exposition is attractive.† Sir Alfred

* Report on the "Old Records of the India Office," 1891. "The Register of Letters, etc., 1600-1619," 1893.

† Sir A. C. Lyall, "The Rise of British Dominion in India" (Murray's "University Extension Manuals"), 1893.

Lyall shows how the unflinching rivalry of the Dutch almost expelled the old British Company of Sir G. Birdwood's records; how the latter gradually regained their position in the last quarter of the 17th century; and how the gradual collapse of the Mughal Empire left the country, without a valid Central Government, as a hunting-ground for adventurers. The decay of the Dutch and the colonising ambition of the French are then shown; while the masterly treatise of Captain Mahan, U.S.N., is cited for its illustration of the difficulties which beset the French in competing for India with the maritime superiority of Great Britain.* In all this there is much that the student ought to ponder. Whether the gradual acquisition of political sway in Bengal and the Carnatic was the result of a deliberate purpose entertained by the founders of the British Company is a different question. The view taken in the present work is the more usual one, that political sway came, almost accidentally, as to the son of Kish. It is true that the Company had written out strongly on the subject of subordinating trade to Empire towards the close of the reign of James II. Sir G. Birdwood is well aware of this, and was the first to draw attention to the letters. But the movement was premature, and was probably due to the enthusiasm of one man—Sir Josiah Child—misplaced and disastrous in immediate consequences. For more than half a century after the failure of Child's effort the English Company maintained an inoffensive attitude and minded their immediate business. As Sir George distinctly, and indeed emphatically, points out, "the East India Company never suffered itself to be deluded with the idea that 'Trade follows the flag'; while the French have over and over again demonstrated for our edification [that] it does not." It was only when trade could not otherwise take root that the flag was raised to protect it; that the Factories grew into Presidencies, and that the Market became an Empire. Sir Alfred's bright and very pleasant volume ends with an expression of earnest but moderate expectation. "Whatever," he observes, "may be the eventual advantage to England from her possession of India, it seems already plain that the effect upon the general progress of the human family must be very great."

The volumes of the "Rulers of India" series which have

* "The Influence of Sea-power upon History." N.D.

appeared lately* are all of the nature of careful and instructive monographs. A sort of supplemental volume has been added which admits, if it does not demand, a more detailed mention.† As has been shown in the text, Thomason was not the originator of the "joint responsibility," or village, settlements in Upper India; but that system owed both good and evil to the determination and conviction with which he carried it into effect. There was great good in the policy which turned vague communal rights into definite and valuable property; but there was a germ of evil in an assessment of State-dues on that property which was not to vary for thirty years, whatever deterioration the assets might undergo, and which was likely to be increased at the end of that period. Rather than lose their place upon the land, the peasant-proprietors would make use of the newly-acquired value of their estates to borrow money in bad years on that security whenever they might be at a loss for the means of paying the Government demand. Crushed by heavy interest and too often bad economists, they seldom cleared off these encumbrances; and they as often lost their rights by foreclosure as they might if they had been sold up as defaulters by the State officials. The old landholders — often usurpers, perhaps—were, in any case, men of more substance; and it was a serious question, though not within the scope of Sir R. Temple's Memoir, whether the making of the settlement direct with the peasants was not as bad for the communities as it was certainly hard upon the Talukdár.

Such, then, are the principal contributions to the history of India which there was not opportunity to describe in the body of the present work; and they may, one and all, be commended to the notice of students anxious for a more than superficial acquaintance with a branch of history which is full of romance and which ought to have a peculiar interest for citizens of the British Empire.

* "Hardinge," by Lord Hardinge; "Aurangzeb," by S. L. Poole; "Marquess of Hastings," by Major Ross, of Bladensburg. By the courtesy of the University Press I have been enabled to see advance sheets of Trotter's "Auckland."

† "James Thomason," by Sir Richard Temple, M.P. 1893.

INDEX VOL. II.